D1609431

THE KING'S BODY

SACRED RITUALS OF POWER
IN MEDIEVAL AND
EARLY MODERN EUROPE

THE KING'S BODY

SERGIO BERTELLI

TRANSLATED BY R. BURR LITCHFIELD

THE PENNSYLVANIA STATE UNIVERSITY PRESS
UNIVERSITY PARK, PENNSYLVANIA

Library of Congress Cataloging-in-Publication Data

Bertelli, Sergio.
    [Corpo del re. English]
    The King's body : sacred rituals of power in medieval
and early modern Europe / Sergio Bertelli ; translated by
R. Burr Litchfield.—New rev. & enl. ed.
        p.   cm.
    Includes bibliographical references and index.
    ISBN 0-271-02102-0 (alk. paper)
        1. Europe—Kings and rulers—Religious aspects.
2. Divine right of kings. 3. Kings and rulers—Religious
aspects—Christianity. 4. Kings and rulers, Medieval.
5. Power (Christian theology).   I. Title.

JC375 .B4613 2001
321'.6—dc21
                                            00-057142

First published in Italy as *Il corpo del re: Sacralità del potere
nell'Europa medievale e moderna.* © 1990 Gruppo Editoriale
Fiorentino. Second edition © 1995 Ponte alle Grazie.

FOR LUIGIA, CATERINA, AND OLIVIA,
THREE YOUNG LADIES WHO HAVE GIVEN
MY LIFE MEANING.

TO MARIA GRAZIA, WHO RECENTLY
ERUPTED INTO MY WORLD.

Contents

Illustrations

Preface to the First Edition

Anticipations of parts of this book have appeared on five different occasions: the third and fifth chapters were read, in abbreviated form, at the conference "Fürstliche Politik, Patronage und adelige Gesellschaft," organized by the London Deutsches Historisches Institut (Madingley Hall, Cambridge, 10–12 December 1987); the third chapter again, along with the fourth chapter, were read at the Annmary Brown Memorial Library at Brown University, Providence, Rhode Island, in May of 1988; the second chapter was read at the memorial conference for Eric Cochrane organized by the Newberry Library, Chicago, Illinois, in May of 1988; the fourth chapter was presented as a lecture at Rutgers University, New Brunswick, New Jersey, in June 1988; the thirteenth chapter was read at the UCLA conference "Violence in Europe" in June of 1988; and an anticipation of the seventh chapter was published by the *Archivio Storico Italiano* in 1987.

My research in the libraries of Rome, London, Paris, and Providence were supported by the Italian Consiglio Nazionale delle Ricerche and by the Ministero della Pubblica Istruzione (now Ministero dell'Università e della Ricerca Scientifica). The Chicago Istituto Italiano di Cultura supported my research at the Newberry Library with a travel grant.

I wish to thank those who have supported, advised, and assisted me, particularly Professor J. B. Trapp and Dr. C. R. Ligota of the Warburg Institute, Mr. Richard Harrington, Curator in the John Hay Library in Providence, and Professor Vittorio Peri of the Biblioteca Apostolica Vaticana. I thank Natalie Z. Davis, Felix Gilbert, Nicolai Rubinstein, Burr Litchfield, and Anthony Molho both for their support and for their long friendship. Finally I thank all my friends who participated in the Florentine seminar of the "Laboratorio di Storia" on the sacred rituals of the body (Bertelli and Grottanelli 1990), who consistently challenged my ideas.

Preface to the English Edition

We live in an age of republics, of heads of state, presidents, and prime ministers. The few constitutional monarchs that still survive have merely representative functions. Thus, since its subject is the rituals of power of medieval and early modern Europe, this book plunges deeply into the past, into an age that extended, roughly, from the early Middle Ages to the executions of Charles I of England and Louis XVI of France in the seventeenth and eighteenth centuries.

This may seem to be a lengthy period, and I want to ward off any suspicion that I am advancing an etiological view of human behavior. But the more I advanced in my research, the more I discovered in the past the deep roots of rituals that at first seemed innovative. "The invention of tradition" is an oxymoron to the extent that all rituals pretend to be ancient.

Nonetheless, a deep hiatus separates us from our ancestors. The first years of the century that has just ended saw the waning of great centralized empires (Austria-Hungary, Germany, Russia, and even the Ottoman Empire). This transition produced an entirely new dimensioning of power. We have entered into what, to borrow the image of Serge Moscovici, we could call the "age of crowds."[1] The names of scholars who concerned themselves with this phenomenon—Gabriel Tarde, Scipio Sighele, and Gustav Le Bon— became more numerous in the nineties of the nineteenth century, and the *meneur des foules* ("leader of crowds"—a term used by Gustav Le Bon) also appeared as the standard-bearer for Max Weber's "charismatic leader." Freud's essay *Massenpsychologie und Ich-Analyse* appeared soon thereafter, in 1921. But it was, above all, the appearance of the mass political party at the end of the nineteenth century, particularly socialist parties, that raised concern about the new organization of politics in the transition from limited to universal suffrage. Gaetano Mosca's *Elementi di scienza politica* appeared in 1896, preceded in 1884 by his essay on parliamentary systems: "Sulla teorica dei governi e sul governo parlamentare." Roberto Michels's sociological analysis of political parties in modern democracy appeared in 1912, and he appended a significant subtitle to his work: "Studi sulle tendenze oligarchiche degli aggregati politici" (A study of oligarchic tendencies in political groupings). These were the first steps of a new science of politics. We might imagine that Marc Bloch's *Les rois thaumaturges,* published in 1923, was a counterpart to these studies in the field of European political history.[2] The contrast between the *religio regis* (cult of the king) and the charisma of a modern political leader could not have been made clearer. Bloch's book soon became a classic of modern historiography. It contrasted the figure of the medieval king, to whom was attributed supernatural powers derived from his *Christomimèsis* (imitation of Christ), to the political leader, who derived his authority from popular investiture by his party and / or electoral base.

But are we so sure that the scientific and industrial revolutions of the sixteenth to nineteenth centuries completely overthrew the ancient beliefs on which the societies of the Old Regime were based, and are we so sure that the old rituals of power have disappeared?

---

1. Moscovici 1981.
2. Bloch [1923] 1961, 21.

Here is an aspect of our recent history that has completely escaped Eric Hobsbawm, who entitled his history *The Short Twentieth Century*, implying a break, a gap between the century now passed and previous ages. For her part, Natalie Zemon Davis, following the guidance of George Rudé's *Faces of the Crowd*, speaks of a "pre-industrial crowd violence."[3] But where should we draw the line between the pre- and postindustrial worlds? And then, how can one ignore the need for rituals that survived the revolutionary tempests of 1789? What relationship should we make between the heart of François I in the basilica of Saint-Denis and the heart of Marat exposed in the hall of the Cordeliers in Paris? Or how should we interpret the liberty trees, the Cult of the Supreme Being, and so many other revolutionary rituals that, a few years later, gave place to "The Distribution of Eagles" (1808), which was made eternal by the painter Jean Louis David? Napoleon had to wrap himself in rituals so as to externalize his own power. It is enough to look at the great Ingres portrait of the Corsican enthroned (1805) to be aware of how much historical and archaeological erudition lay behind this Roman and Carolingian apparition.[4] To be sure, the immediate message reached a restricted circle of persons (as many soldiers, bureaucrats, or courtiers who were present at the ceremonies and took part), but printed images of these events were diffused in innumerable copies to popularize awareness of them and to make the people into participants. This was close to what happened in the ancient world when citizens pressed to the gate of their city to welcome the *imago* (image) of their sovereign or when after a triumph soldiers were given inscribed tablets with a pictorial representation (*picta*) of his battles.

This continual need to reinvent tradition (to the extent that ritual appears to be repetitive)[5] confirms the extent to which ritual is based on communication and to which it has an active and constructive function in a given society.[6] From this perspective we can recognize that rituals are historical events. Reconstruction and analysis of the symbolic forms in which power was wrapped at different times are an aspect—and certainly not the least important one—of the very exercise of power at that given historical moment.

This book studies a world that is lost. Nonetheless, events since 1815 have continued to demonstrate that the recourse to ritual is a constant of power. Even after the Napoleonic orgy of Roman eagles and Carolingian insignia there was no hesitation in adopting such symbols. They followed the triumph of the German emperor William I in Berlin (1870), the funeral of Victor Emanuel II in Rome (1878), and the diamond jubilee of Queen Victoria in London (1897). If the triumph in Berlin gave the central place to the figure of William I, and the funeral in Rome to the body of a sovereign who had unexpectedly died in the prime of life, the diamond jubilee was organized around a corporeal evocation of the "Great Mother."[7] May we speak, for all these events, of "Theatre of power"?[8]

In strongly autocratic societies, leadership requires the visibility and physical presence of a prophet. In order to appear clearly, his charisma requires particular signs typical of himself that make him immediately and physically identifiable. Large posters bearing his portrait are carried high by demonstrators and cover the whole façade of buildings. Specific symbols accompany, and are obsessively repeated in, the mass public spectacles

3. Davis 1973, 53.
4. Bertelli 1998.
5. Boyer 1963; Gluckmann 1972; Bloch 1989, 42; Diaz Cruz 1998.
6. Rothenbuhler 1998.
7. Aldobrandini 1990.
8. Geertz 1980; Bertelli 2000.

arranged to venerate him: the lictor's fasces, the swastika, the bundle of arrows tied with a bow, the hammer and sickle.[9] Such symbols are placed at the center of flags, at the end of flagpoles, even on the chests and arms of demonstrators. As for the leader, often a particular feature characterizes him in the eyes of the masses. Picasso seized on Stalin's large mustache. More often it is a military uniform, from Francisco Franco to Fidel Castro, a sign that the society he controls is an armed society and that its revolutionary origins persist and are not forgotten. Even when President Bill Clinton, in May of 1999, went to review the American troops stationed in Germany, on their way to Kosovo, he put on a military uniform to remind people of his function as supreme commander.

In a different sense, the plain uniforms, without military stripes, of Stalin, Mao, and Ho Chi Minh attempt to show that these leaders had been simple soldiers among soldiers and that they too had not forgotten the permanent state of war in their respective regimes. Symbols of these types have dominated, and still dominate, the "mechanized masses," to use the term of P. Reiwald.[10] Such masses have always needed a physical body to venerate (or destroy). The Soviet regime identified itself physically with the body of Lenin, a body that since 1924 had been exhibited in Red Square and continually cared for by a medical team to keep it fresh and prevent its corruption.[11] Numerous dictatorial regimes have appealed to this laboratory (at least between 1949 and 1995) to preserve the cadavers of their founders: Georgi Dimitrov, secretary of the Comintern and founder of the Bulgarian Communist Party; Choybalsan, Mongolian dictator; Klement Gottwald, head of the Czech Communist Party; Ho Chi Minh, leader of the Vietcong; Agostino Neto, president of the Republic of Angola; Kim Il Sung, dictator of North Korea.

The fear of an interregnum, which is given a specific treatment in the pages that follow, has also been a widespread cultural constant. The Spanish dictator Francisco Franco, when his body was infected with gangrene, was operated on several times and given life-support tubes to delay as long as possible the end of his rule. The Algerian leader Boumedienne was kept alive for a long time through dialysis. In China, a whole medical team, the "group for emergency assistance," was organized in 1995 to prolong the life of Deng Xiaoping.

On the other hand, the cadaver of the Italian dictator Mussolini underwent the shame of a dethroning, by crowds otherwise reputed to be "civil." His body was first exposed on a sidewalk, with the chest bare, just as the crowd had admired it in life, in the tabloids as in the movies, at the time of the "battle for grain," when he was shown helping grain harvesters. The flagstaff of a Fascist labarum was put in his hand as a scepter. Many fired at the body with their guns. He was then hung by his feet on a gasoline pump, and following a culturally received procedure, the crowd accosted him with ritual insults. Fearing the possibility of a similar outcome for his own cadaver, Hitler had his body burned, but the Russians and Americans made long efforts to find the remains, thus showing the importance they attributed to them. When, on 18 November 1978, 912 Americans committed suicide in the jungles of Guyana, the United States government took pains to find the body of Jim Jones, the "prophet" of the People's Temple, cremated his remains, and scattered the ashes in the ocean.[12]

9. For the Soviet Union, see Lanec 1981; for Hitler's Germany, Mosse 1980.
10. Reiwald 1949.
11. Zbarski and Hutchinson 1997.
12. Pozzi 1992 (with an ample bibliography).

This book traces the history of sacred rituals that some might think have disappeared. But power in the contemporary world is still wrapped in them. The difference with the past is in the mode of procedure. Before the time of the executions of kings in the seventeenth and eighteenth centuries, the sacred was closely tied to the religious sphere, and one can speak truly of a *religio regis*. Now these rituals are tied closely to the subconscious of the modern crowd. While they have lost their ties to religion, they have returned to be a kind of magic. Thus, reversing the title of the volume by Keith Thomas, we could say "magic and the decline of religion," rather than *Religion and the Decline of Magic*.

Having been unable to revise the second Italian edition of this work (published in 1995) completely, I have made some further modifications in the text for the English edition, so as to provide readers with some further results of my research. An entire chapter has been added to Part I, to re-elaborate my essay "Lex animata in terris."[13] The chapter on "the lord's dinner" has been partly rewritten to incorporate a paper presented at a conference organized by the University of Verona in May 1991.[14] The chapter on "rituals of violence" has been enlarged on the basis of the English version of a paper I read at a seminar at the Institut für Geschichte of the University of Salzburg, "Der Tod des Mächtigen," in November 1993.[15] The section on papal coronations has been revised to take account of the paper "Ostentatio genitalium," which I read at Villa I Tatti for the opening of the academic year at the Harvard Center of Italian Renaissance Studies in 1995–96.

The bibliography published at the end of the first edition has been enlarged, not only to document the sources, as any good scholar should do, but also to provide readers with their own point of departure for proceeding beyond the present work.

Bellosguardo (Florence, Italy), July 2000

13. Now in Cardini 1994.
14. Now in Profeti 1992.
15. Now in Kolmer 1997.

Introduction

IN THE MONTH OF NOVEMBER 1441, at Dijon, the duke of Burgundy received a visit from the duke of Brunswick. "And he was honorably treated," Olivier de la Marche, *maître d'hôtel* and captain of the guard of Charles the Bold remembers, since the duke of Burgundy spoke German "and knew how to behave toward nobles of the Empire; for each nation has its own way of proceeding." Every nation has its own customs, etiquette, and rituals.[1]

Nature, Claude Villette wrote later, at the beginning of the seventeenth century, "leads us to observe ceremonies," and he defined ceremonies as "the external act of religion, the witness of a cult, and the private service that a man renders to God."[2] Only to God? Or was there another divine (or deified) being to which Europeans of the late Roman period, the Middle Ages, and the early modern age addressed their "witness" of a cult?

We live today in a world where ritual and religion are two distinct concepts, separated from one another by the secular experience and the political thought of the seventeenth and eighteenth centuries. But if we attempt to transcend the hiatus produced by the scientific revolution (the basis and foundation of the succeeding industrial revolution), then a world is revealed that was completely different from our own, a world that did not make our distinctions. This world was deeply immersed in the ritual that pervaded the collective imagination of medieval and early modern Europe and that descended indirectly from the late Roman Empire.

In a study of the cult of kingship, it might seem strange to use methodologies more closely linked to anthropology than to social history. Roland Mousnier has done so recently, although we might question the legitimacy of a work so strongly based on a comparative and diachronic approach, with no consideration of geopolitical boundaries or the specificity of chronology. Even limiting our attention to western Europe and, temporally, to the Middle Ages and early modern period, it is not easy to generalize the different reactions to similar stimuli produced by different "cultures." As D. Sperber has justly observed, "interpretive generalizations are not the awkward expressions of a scientific anthropology still in its infancy; they are the antiquated tools of an ethnography which, when mature, should be able to do without them."[3]

Undoubtedly, the rejection of a comparative approach is something difficult to accept,

1. Marche 1883–88, 1:272.
2. Villette 1611, 1.
3. Sperber 1984, 45.

after the work of generations of ethnographers following comparative methods. On one hand, it is true that "the very repetition of the same rituals—despite their infinite variations—permits the study of society; roles that otherwise might only exist in thought become actions, and therefore more explicit and observable."[4] But on the other hand, it is also true that a particular ritual or symbol is never fixed or fossilized; instead, it changes and develops along with the society that expresses but may not entirely comprehend it. Its very obscurity may assure its effectiveness.[5] A single comportment or gesture can assume different meanings depending on the "culture" using it; but it can also change its message within this culture. We must thus distinguish formal acts, intentions, and stylization from what we could call "behavioral gestures," and remain attentive to their nature and function.[6]

A rite can take on different meanings as its use changes.[7] But it can also be repeated without any surviving understanding of its original message; other meanings are found for it, which become impenetrable barriers. A rite never wants to be enclosed in a logical system.[8] The case of the legend of the female pope Joan, examined in Chapter 11 of this book, is an excellent example. With the passage of time, rules of etiquette can change their meaning, just as similar questions can produce different answers. Sometimes one is confronted with what Desmond Morris has called "residual gestures" because they are used outside of their original context.[9] As M. F. Facinger has written insightfully, "in the institutions of a given society changes are slow and subtle; transformations are mostly the result of an adaptation to exigencies of the moment, rather than of conscious innovations."[10]

But also "culture" (understood as a system of symbols) "is public because it is meaning"; it is the "forest of symbols" externalized in the complexity of ritual.[11] This ritualized behavior "generates in some way the conviction that religious conceptions are true and religious directives are valid."[12] One means here by "religion," in its broadest definition, the worldview of a particular society, including also the cult of the leader.

In field research conditioned by the "culture" of anthropology ("Down with them!" cries Bronislaw Malinowski, who was influenced by the theories of Lombroso),[13] we must admit that "one cannot speak of ritual unless one takes into account that ritual is an expression of deeply felt faith, which goes beyond rationality or a scientific attempt to explain it."[14] We must consequently conclude that our own culture, the culture of our own time, is a barrier that prevents us from entering into civilizations of the past, which we want to describe as historians and no longer as ethnographers.

Nonetheless, at least within the vast area contained by the Roman Empire—or rather Christendom, from Byzantium through that part of Europe that later recognized the sole supremacy of the Roman pontiff—we must, although remaining alert to identify the de-

4. Forster and Ranum 1982, vii.
5. See Izard and Smith 1979.
6. See Bertelli and Centanni 1995, 9–28.
7. Bourdieu 1980, 27.
8. Bloch 1989, 41.
9. Morris 1982.
10. Facinger 1968, 31.
11. Geertz 1987, 49. For the relationship between ritual and religion, see Goody 1961.
12. Geertz 1987, 167; Turner 1967.
13. "I went to the village with the intention of taking pictures of types," Malinowski 1989, 65.
14. Bourdieu 1980, 36.

velopment of specific rites, still concede that Constantinople was the inexhaustible font, the great model, that through Rome inspired successive courts.[15] Of the twenty-four pontiffs between John IV and Adrian I (640–772), fourteen came from parts of the Greek world.[16] This helps to explain why the cult of kingship grew to such an extent in the West after Charlemagne's coronation in Rome on Christmas night 800,[17] to reach its apex in the fourteenth and fifteenth centuries.

This was something that infected the whole regal tradition of the West and that was imitated, followed, and re-elaborated by all other courts, both royal and princely.[18] Other moments to emphasize in the relationship between Byzantium and the West were the education given to the young Otto III (who died in 991) by his mother, Theophano (he was a nephew of the emperor of the East, John I Tzimisces), and the accession to the marquisate of Montferrat (in 1306) of the porphyrogenite younger son of Emperor Andronicus II, Theodore Paleologus.[19] To point to Venice as the head of the bridge that led to Byzantium would be rhetorically redundant.

This continual osmosis created the milieu, as I have already indicated, that provided for a unitary development.

But already before that Christmas at the beginning of the ninth century, France was in contact both with the Lombard world and with Celtic culture. About 737 Charles Martel sent his young son Pepin to Pavia, to Liutprand (a Lombard ruler), for adoption.[20] The pilgrimage of Virgil of Salzburg through the continent, and his arrival at the court of Pepin at Querzy in 743, permit us to see him as a bridge between France and the Celtic world, which was the model for the ceremony of anointing in the Frankish realm in 754 (as opposed to the thesis of its Visigothic derivation).[21] When Count Alvaro Vaz d'Almada, Knight of the Garter and duke of Avranches, attended a British ceremony under Henry IV, he asked the deacon of the royal chapel in 1448, William Say, to provide him with a description of the chapel and the offices celebrated there to please his own sovereign, the young Alfonso V (the Magnanimous, king of Naples and Sicily).[22] To satisfy this request, the deacon wrote the *Liber regalis,* following the *Ordo consecrationis regis* in the missal of Abbot Lyllington of Westminster, which was written before 1386. But perhaps this monk was unaware that even the missal he copied was based on the *Ordo coronationis* of King Charles V of France (1364),[23] the first link of a chain that confirms the *imitatio* followed by medieval courts in their elaboration of etiquette, rituals, and ceremonies. As C. A. Bouman noted, in studying the formulas for royal anointing, "accession prayers and Ordines, written in different parts of Western Europe, turn out to be related much more intimately than was formerly supposed."[24]

The court, the imperial court or the court of a great king, was a veritable school of

15. See Fishwick 1987.

16. For the formation of Roman ceremonial, see Nabuco 1966.

17. See Llewellyn 1990.

18. See *Sacral Kingship* 1959.

19. On him, see Knowles 1983.

20. Jarnut 1982, 112–13.

21. Poupardin 1905; Nelson 1977 and 1986; Ellard 1933; Enright 1985, 94ff.; Devisse 1985; Bautier 1989; Jackson 1995, 23. For the Leofric Missal analyzed by Schramm, see Nelson 1980. For the Visigoths, see Orlandis Rovira 1962; Sot 1988; for the Anglo-Normans and the Angevins, Foreville 1978–79; for Byzantium, Nicol 1976.

22. Ullmann 1961, 10.

23. *Liber regalis* 1870; *Coronation Book* 1899; Ullmann 1961, 22–26; Hedeman 1990.

24. Bouman 1957, 50.

comportment. On the request of his uncle, the emperor Frederick II, the son of the king of Castile was sent to him to be educated, and two orphan sons of John, king of Jerusalem, also lived at the Hohenstaufen court.[25] As well, when Alfonso the Magnanimous conquered the kingdom of Naples (1443),[26] the splendor of his court became a model, which inspired the duke of Urbino in 1458 to send there two of his illegitimate sons, Buonconte and Bernardino, as pages to learn etiquette (the unfortunate youths got the plague instead, but that was a tragic twist of fate).[27] When Isabella d'Este married Francesco Gonzaga, marquis of Mantua (1490), and Elisabetta Gonzaga married Guidobaldo, duke of Urbino (1477), the customs and etiquette of three Italian courts fused (Mantua, Ferrara, and Urbino), permitting Messer Baldasar Castiglione to use them as a model in *The Courtier*. As well, when the young Federico Gonzaga was held hostage by Pope Julius II,[28] he was attracted by his captor's passion for antiquities, and he dreamed of a *renovatio* of the classics in his native Mantua, but he also learned etiquette and ceremonials that he grafted onto the culture of the Po valley.

In short, marriages and wars, pilgrimages of monks, exchanges of minstrels and musicians, of actors and painters, contributed to the great "acculturation" that unified the forms of life, rituals, and etiquette of European courts through the Middle Ages, well before the publication of *The Courtier* (1526) or the adoption of Burgundian ceremonial by the imperial courts of Austria and Spain under Charles V.[29]

All this helps to justify a synthetic treatment of the cult of kingship in the whole of western Europe, always keeping in mind the debt this cult owed to Byzantium. But the study of the ceremonial and rituals of the past is not limited to court behavior. After years of debate about "popular culture," the study of the cult of kingship allows us to penetrate into that *troisième niveau* discussed by Lucien Febvre: the history of mentalities, which is perhaps the only way to bridge the gap that separates us from the culture of the past.

A page at the court of Louis XVI wrote: "Ceremonies are the most important support of royal authority. If one takes away the splendor that surrounds him, he will be only an ordinary man in the eyes of the multitude, because the populace respects his sovereignty less for his virtue and rank than for the gold that covers him and the pomp that surrounds him."[30]

Count Hezecques, in a certain sense, anticipated at the court of Louis XVI what Meyer Fortes has affirmed in our own time regarding inaugural rites: "The mysterious quality of continuity through time in its organization and values, which is basic to the self-image of every society, modern, archaic, or primitive, is in some way congealed in these installation ceremonies. . . . Politics and law, rank and kingship, religious and philosophical concepts and values, the economics of display and hospitality, the aesthetics and symbolism of institutional representation, and last but not least the social psychology of popular participation, are all concentrated in them."[31]

Forgetting our own culture for a moment, let us ask what veneration of the sovereign meant for people of the late Roman Empire, the Middle Ages, and early modern Europe.

25. Kantorowicz 1988, 287 and 367.
26. On the city, see Foucard 1877; on the king, Ubeda 1950 and Ryder 1976.
27. Dennistoun 1851, I:113–14.
28. Luzio 1887.
29. See Petrie 1958; Pfandl 1958; Valgona y Diaz-Varela 1958.
30. Hezecques n.d., 189.
31. Fortes 1968.

Kenneth Scott has stated that "the true religious belief in the divinity of the king or emperor must be sought among the lowest and most ignorant classes."[32] Could there be a culture limited to the lowest classes? Should we deduce from this that Eusebius of Caesarea and all the panegyrists before and after him were conscious liars? And what should we say of Dante Alighieri, who in *De monarchia* speaks of the "necessity" of the institution of monarchy, in a sense that is deeply religious? Should we call the father of French historiography, André Duchesne, a mere servile courtier because he dedicated himself to the study of French coronation ritual? And what should we say of Goethe? In his autobiography, recalling the election of Joseph II at Frankfort, he wrote: "A politico-religious ceremony possesses an infinite charm. We behold earthly majesty before our eyes, surrounded by all the symbols of its power; but while it bends before that of heaven, it brings to our minds the communion of both. For even the individual can only prove his relationship with the Deity by subjecting himself and adoring."[33] Would it not be better to recognize that men of different social and cultural extraction, literate and illiterate, were all sincere in their veneration of the sovereign? In this way was not the cult of the king, the *religio regis,* a unifying factor for medieval and early modern European society? In this case we would have to admit "there was no shortage of credulity in the educated upper class."[34] The Neapolitan chronicler who witnessed the entry of Charles V into Naples in 1535 provides an example. The emperor wore against the skin of his chest a purse into which were stitched pieces of the claws "of the great beast" as a guard against apoplexy, as I discuss further in Chapter 3 below.[35]

I would say even further: great monarchs were sincerely convinced of their role, without any Machiavellian reservations. Frederick II's persecutions for heresy occurred within the sacerdotal concept of the state, which required that each subject remain anchored in his own religion. The crime of heresy closely touched the state, God, and the wounded majesty of the emperor.[36]

G. B. Ladner has written that "the symbolic world view of the Middle Ages cannot be understood without reference to a sacred history which was conceived as a coherent sequence of divinely planned happenings from creation through the events of the Old and New Testaments and the salvation-oriented progression of mankind."[37] But this observation requires correction: "sacredness" was not based only on biblical faith tied to the sphere of the church. Even if it had been, we would have to understand it in the broader sense given by Lucien Febvre when he attempted to delineate a world, deeply permeated by religion, in which there were no distinctions or separations between sacred and religious, between king and priest.[38]

Even the sphere of sexuality was immersed in these religious cultural parameters. If Rustico the hermit in Boccaccio's *Decameron* wanted to put "the devil into hell," and "the resurrection of the flesh" occurred with Alibech's nakedness, the priest in the first of the Aretino's *Giornate,* who was preparing to sodomize a nun in a convent, opened with his hands "the pages of the missal of the arse."

32. Scott 1932, 328.
33. Goethe 1864, 1:168.
34. Bowersock 1972, 179.
35. "Racconti di storia napoletana" 1908–9, 116.
36. Kantorowicz 1988, 222–33 and 245.
37. Ladner 1979, 230–31.
38. Febvre 1968, bk. 2, 307ff.

To understand our cultural distance from the past in this area, it is worth mentioning the example, cited by Leo Steinberg, of how the diaries of John Evelyn were abridged. The editor carefully cut out all the sermons heard and annotated by the diarist between 1660 and 1705. "We have here a type of retrospective secularizing imposed as well on the modern perception, for example, of Newton, Kepler, Leonardo da Vinci, or, indeed, the whole of Renaissance culture. It takes some effort of historical imagination to replace the institution of public preaching where that culture maintained it—near the center of its intellectual, moral, and social life."[39]

The cult of kingship too, with the continual recourse of the monarch to a *Christomimèsis* (imitation of Christ), an autonomous Christlike sacerdotal function, shows us to what extent the world of the past was immersed in the sacred and how closely that sacredness was associated with religion. The representation of Otto III enthroned in the Aix-la-Chapelle Gospels is famous. The emperor is portrayed in the position of the *Maiestas Domini* used for the representation of Christ. Surrounded by symbols of the evangelists, he is placed within a nimbus (a sign of ascension to heaven) and supported from below by a representation of the earth, while the hand of Christ descends to infuse him with wisdom. In the same way, in other representations, wisdom is infused by God into the Son.[40] Under the nimbus are placed two scepters, and still lower two warriors and two prelates, to indicate the vassalage of both. This is both a political and a religious scheme of representation, in an indissoluble unity. And this symbolism can also be traced in the multiplicity of functions assigned to the *cappella regis*. This was a structure at the top of the court's administrative hierarchy that dissolved into and united with it. It was a place used as a meeting hall, where the monarch met with his bishops, but it served above all as the place where all the religious ceremonies connected with the life of the court were carried out.[41]

As for Frederick II, he went so far as to call Jesi, the city where he had been born, "where our divine mother gave us birth," "our Bethlehem," and he celebrated his own *dies natalis* (birthday).[42]

We must try to rid ourselves here of a certain Marxist-Plekhanovian dialectic that mechanically counterposes dominant to dominated and continually searches for a "class culture" in the lower orders. This attitude imagines that it is possible to find in ex-votos—to give one example—evidence "of the silent world of those who have never seen the written word,"[43] as if the nobleman, the noblewoman, the patrician, or the merchant did not also present their patrons *in celestibus* (in heaven) with propitiatory offerings and ex-votos, immersed as they were in a culture that did observe such neat class distinctions. Was there a difference between the vow of Louis XIII[44] and so many other promises made to the divinity by kings on battlefields or at times of natural calamity?

What people of the Renaissance were acutely aware of was that their ties with the past were loosening. They sought ancestors in classical antiquity, but in reality the scientific revolution was changing all of their cultural parameters. *Crise de la conscience européenne* was the title of a famous book by Paul Hazard on the development of the intellectual his-

39. Steinberg 1986, 162.
40. On the divine hand, see Kirigin 1976.
41. Ullmann 1961, 1 and 7–8.
42. Kantorowicz 1989, 504–5.
43. Vovelle 1989, 15.
44. Laurentin 1988.

tory of seventeenth-century Europe, but we could better say "crisis of European religious consciousness." When crowds of believers transformed themselves into an "audience," we may presume that some deep change occurred, and a break was perceived between the way in which people once related to the mystery plays, or to the sacredness of music, and the modern approach to them. At the beginning of the eighteenth century, Domenico Scorpione lamented: "Our century is so corrupted that many rush into the churches only to enjoy music, and if this is not embellished with theatrical arias, as their taste requires, [they] go away muttering."[45]

In all his work Ernst Kantorowicz insisted on the continuity between the ancient and medieval worlds. Traveling further in this direction, we should perhaps extend the Middle Ages through the early modern period, not excluding the Renaissance, as Delio Cantimori proposed in a well-known lecture of 1955.[46] This was echoed by Hugh Trevor Roper in his concept of the court of the "Renaissance"[47]—a period that included the fifteenth and sixteenth centuries and that did not know of "cultural" gaps.

I think that such considerations will help to clarify the distance of this book from other works that have appeared in recent years, when my research was already quite advanced, if not yet completed. I remember, for instance, an essay by Richard Jackson that focused on the French *sacre* (coronation), but had little awareness of what was happening concurrently outside of France, and also lacked any socioanthropological perspective. I remember also the volume by Alain Boreau that reconstructed the legend of the female pope Joan on the basis of the earlier work of D'Onofrio, authors who both offered much information but missed the deeper origin of the ritual of the *ostentatio genitalium*.[48] I remember, finally, the recent essay by Ralph Giesey, who has extended his own interpretive model drawn from the deaths of kings of France to the dukes of Burgundy and the grand dukes of Tuscany.[49] In his first essay on oath-taking in Aragon, and then above all in his study of French funeral rituals that appeared in 1960, Giesey, a student of Kantorowicz, had the great merit of following the route already opened by his master.[50] Giesey noted that a constant of the French royal funeral ceremony was the absence of the succeeding king. If the king were not dead until his coffin was lowered into the tomb, it would be a contradiction to show the new sovereign in public. This is confirmed by Jennifer Woodward: "The absence of the succeeding monarch at the funeral ceremony was traditional. None of the Tudor monarchs mourned at the funeral of their predecessors."[51] There seem to have been exceptions, however, as Giesey has revealed in his most recent book on the funerals of the emperor Charles V and the grand duke of Tuscany Cosimo I. But Giesey has not taken into account the exceptional situation in which Philip II of Spain and Francesco I of Tuscany, the successors, found themselves. Both inherited the government of states when their fathers were still alive, and then ascended to thrones after abdications. The funerals represented for both a legitimization of power and an end of tutelage. From this, and not from a lack of anointing, came the difference of the Spanish and Italian funeral ceremonies from Giesey's model of French funerals in effigy.

45. Scorpione 1702, 108.
46. Cantimori 1955.
47. Trevor Roper 1967.
48. See also Ingersoll 1993.
49. See Giesey 1987.
50. Giesey 1968 and 1960.
51. Woodward 1997, 62. On Iberian funeral ceremonies, see Varela 1990.

PART I | Triumph and Death

1   His Majesty

> Let there be one ruler, / one king, to whom the
> son of devious-devising Kronos / gives the scepter
> and right of judgment, to watch over his people.
> —ILIAD, II:204–6

IN HIS *SIETES PARTIDAS* KING ALFONSO the Wise said that "emperadores et reyes son como comenzamiento et cabeza de los otros," "alma e cabeza, et ellos los membros" (emperors and kings are the birth and brain of humankind, soul and brain, and the others are the limbs).[1] The state was like a human body, in which the king was the soul and brain; the subjects the limbs. In England, during the last agonizing days of sickness of King George V, a psychoanalyst observed the reaction of three of his patients. All exhibited worsening symptoms of physical and mental conditions. The night after the death of the sovereign, one dreamed he had shot at a man who resembled his father; another had depressing memories of the death of his own father; the third patient dreamed that his father was dead.[2] In 1978, in New Guinea, 912 Americans testified to their attachment to the charismatic leader Jim Jones by committing collective suicide.[3]

Since the world began, no community has failed to recognize a leader, a mediator between the community itself and heaven. Whether this leader was a priest or a warrior is a secondary matter. A. M. Hocart has justly observed that kings and bishops are but two branches of the same tree,[4] and Géza Roheim, studying the divinity of kingship, wrote that this "is either an earth-born power projected into heaven, or the shadow of heaven upon earth."[5] The idea of the divinity of kingship began in Egypt and developed into a complex political and religious system. "The main purpose of this cosmological speculation was to show that Egypt was primitively ruled by gods and that the unification of the two parts of Egypt was the realization of a divine plan."[6] Egyptian influence on the evolution of kingship in classical times can be dated from the conquests of Alexander the Great, even though it developed much further in the Roman world.[7] Hellenistic political thought elaborated the idea that the sovereign was the compassionate manifestation of God to humanity, the shepherd of his flock, father and benefactor, font of law, or better still the very personification of law. Since the sovereign was *pater*, any regicide was judged a parricide, in fact the greatest parricide. After the discovery of a conspiracy against Emperor Frederick II in March 1246, the guilty were judged on the basis of the Roman

---

1. *Las Sietes Partidas* 1807, pt. 1, intr., and *ley* v, II, p. 3.
2. Fairbairn 1936, 278–84. Cf. De Grazia 1948, 114.
3. Pozzi 1990.
4. Hocart [1927] 1969.
5. Roheim [1930] 1972, 204.
6. Dvornik 1966, 1:5.
7. Taylor 1931.

law *Lex pompcia* and trcatcd as parricidcs, closcd up in a leather sack (*culleus*), and cast into the sea.[8]

"This sublime conception of kingship was destined to offset the danger that always besets the concentration of absolute power in the hands of a single man, while the king's divinization made such concentration bearable and acceptable to his subjects."[9] Thus the very image of the sovereign stamped on the obverse of coins—in place of images of divinities, who were the celestial patrons shown on coins issued by the Greek cities—served to guarantee the purity of the metal.

The inheritance of Greek political thought was not, however, transmitted directly to the Roman republic. A cultural shift was accomplished at the end of the first century B.C., in the time of Julius Caesar, the patron of Cleopatra; Pompey, the conqueror of Jerusalem; and Anthony, the lover of the same Cleopatra in Alexandria.[10] The deification of Caesar was a fundamental step in the development of the Roman cult of kingship. The divine immortality of Octavius, as *divi filius* (son of god), was recognized on his death, and in life he received the honors reserved for a *divus*.[11] Asiatic cults entered the political life of the West through a Roman filter, leaving their mark as much on regional traditions as they did on the church liturgy of the High Middle Ages. The church fathers identified government with *patria potestas* and considered the emperor to be the guardian of the world. Fritz Kern writes that governments were thought of as miniature images of divine government.[12] I would say, rather, that divine government was imagined through the model of the earthly one. Elements of the imperial cult were integrated into the Byzantine Empire in a religious syncretism that developed basically two features: the Stoic doctrine of providence (*Providentia augusta*)[13] and the association of the ruler with the sun, a theme that appeared in Rome after the accession of Heliogabalus in 219. This was when the circle of solar rays was adopted, a Hellenistic symbol. After the conversion of Constantine, the diadem lost its rays, but it was still not abandoned. The solar heritage was not the only regal trait received from the past, however, since the West, well before the coronation of Louis the Pius (816), took from Israel a conception of kingship based chiefly on anointing. Thus Christian monarchy overlay and fused together different regal cults. "Christian thought of the Eastern Roman Empire was based upon Hellenistic political thought . . . what appealed most forcibly to the imagination of Christian writers was the notion of divine monarchy."[14] Eusebius of Caesarea, in *De laudibus Constantini*,[15] gave these theories their Christian meaning, the monarch being Christ on earth. In *De monarchia*, Dante, referring to the king, spoke of his "necessity." Even the emperor's apotheosis (his deification on his death) was replicated. In 337, after Constantine's conversion to Christianity, the Roman mint struck a coin with the legend DIVUS CONSTANTINUS PATER AUGUSTORUM (divine Constantine, father of emperors), showing the emperor ascending the heavens riding in a solar chariot.[16]

8. Kantorowicz 1988, 638–40; Nardi 1980.

9. Dvornik 1966, I:278.

10. Blumenthal 1913.

11. Dvornik 1966, II:491. But see also Pippidi 1945.

12. Kern [1914] 1939, 7.

13. Brehier and Battifol 1920; Charlesworth 1936 and 1939; Fears 1977, 221ff.

14. Dvornik 1966, II:611.

15. PG, xx.

16. Cohen 1888, VII, n. 760; Bickermann 1929 and 1972; Boer 1972; Settis and Frugoni 1973, 51ff.; Halsberghe 1972, 167ff.; Cameron 1976, 19–20.

Fig. 1   Christos Helios in the celestial chariot of fire, Giulii mausoleum, arcosolium, Rome, Grotte Vaticane.

Even the idea of the king as animate law was introduced in the new religion. The iconography of the *traditio legis* (e.g., in the Ambrosian ciborium)[17] refers frequently to this kind of royal worship. In Bertand de la Tour's sermon in memory of Charles of Calabria (the son of King Robert of Naples) we can read that "iste dominus Karolus fuit fedelissimus deo, dei etiam vicarius" (this lord Charles was most faithful to God, whose vicar he was).[18] It was not until English constitutional thought of the fourteenth century that a different concept of the king appeared, as subordinate to natural law: "the king is under God and the law, for it is the law which makes the king." In his political treatises, Sir John Fortescue (1394–ca. 1476) quoted Saint Thomas Aquinas: "Rex datur propter regnum, et non regnum propter regem" (the king is given to the realm, not the realm to the king), to affirm the distinction between a "dominium regale" (royal dominion) and a "dominium politicum et regale" (political and royal dominion), the second only applicable to England.[19]

Dante's image of pope and emperor as "two suns" is well known,[20] and the solar cult always remained tied to kingship. In fact, one of the appellations of the Roman emperor was *Sol invictus* (unconquered sun).[21] Reflecting the same meaning, the coronation mantle

17. Bertelli, Brambilla Barcilon, and Gallone 1981, 20–31.
18. Quoted in D'Avray 1994, 152.
19. Baumer 1940, 10–11.
20. Kantorowicz 1963, and here, Part II, Chapter 8.
21. See L'Orange 1935; Halsberghe 1972.

Fig. 2   Saint Francis in the celestial chariot of fire, Giotto, Assisi, Basilica superiore.

of the emperor Henry II was spangled with stars.[22] We could add that a solar chariot transported Alexander the Great to heaven,[23] that one of the versions of the death of Romulus repeated the same legend, and that the *Christos-Helios* was presented with the same chariot in the mosaic of the Giulii mausoleum (Fig. 1; it is now located under the Confessional of St. Peter in the Vatican).[24] The solar chariot was also used for Christ by Bishop Rabbula.[25] Saint Francis of Assisi made his ascent to heaven in a similar chariot, at least as depicted in the images left to us by Giotto (Fig. 2) and by Taddeo Gaddi, based on the tale of Bartolomeo de Rinonico in *De conformitate vitae beati Francisci ad vitam Domini Jesu*. Even if western Christendom did not accept the solar cult for its own kings,[26] one must admit that a hundred years before Louis XIV, who called himself the "Sun King," Cosimo I de' Medici as grand duke of Tuscany played with the assonance of his own name with "cosmos."[27] The duke also thought the battle of Montemurlo (where his adversaries were defeated) was a personal "resurrection," which allowed him to assume the zodiacal sign of Capricorn, the same sign used by Caesar Augustus.

Even without resorting to deification, Byzantium knew Caesaro-papism.[28] What distinguished the Christian Byzantine emperors from their Hellenistic and Roman predecessors, who had already recognized the sacredness of kingship, were the priestly characteristics inherited from the tradition of divination.[29] The kings of western Christianity, who were weaker with regard to the papacy, tended to adopt the binomial *rex sacerdos,*

22. Schramm 1963, 26; Paul 1983; but see also Poelnitz 1973; *Le soleil* 1983.
23. Settis and Frugoni 1973.
24. Testini 1966, 76.
25. See here, Chapter 4, page 65.
26. Brown 1982b.
27. See Forster 1977.
28. See Dagron 1996. For the imperial image, see Grabar 1936.
29. Dagron 1996, 21.

focusing on the assimilation of sacred and profane, when they did not aspire directly to sainthood, for themselves or their ancestors,[30] as with Saint Louis (Fig. 3).[31] It seems unlikely that the Carolingians had to seek further for the supernatural powers attributed to them—which the Frankish *reges criniti* (long-haired kings)[32] had possessed earlier—than the unction they received from the church, to which they had submitted. "The ecclesiastical revolution under the early Carolingians had created a theoretical structure of kingship."[33] It was precisely to attenuate this submission that they developed the idea of the "Regnum Davidicum."[34] In the Holy Roman Empire, Otto III wanted to call himself *Servus apostolorum,* with reference to Saints Peter and Paul: "The emperor associated his government with that of the pope, the successor precisely of Peter and Paul."[35] As a tenth-century *Ordo* for the imperial coronation prescribed: "The prayer finished, the elect proceeds to the choir of Saint Gregory with the cardinals, arch-presbyters, and archdeacons who have assisted him during the office of anointing, and after having clothed him with the amice, alb, and girdle, they bring him to the sacristy before the pope, who makes him a priest and gives him the tunic and dalmatic."[36] For France, Villette emphasized approvingly that "Charles the Bald never entered a church without his dalmatic, to show that in church he was a member of the clergy, and outside of church he struck with his sword as a king."[37] A page noted with regard to Louis XVI that "every day the king attended Mass. . . . When the king was in the lower part of the chapel, he was presented with the *corpse* to kiss it," and, he added, "it was one of the prerogatives of royalty, since the king was considered to be a subdeacon."[38]

As well, under Emperor Frederick II the royal court itself was presented as a twin of the church. The body of imperial functionaries was considered in the same way as a religious order: the order of justice.[39]

At Bologna, in the coronation ceremony for Charles V, the young emperor took off his royal clothing to put on the almice and *mozzetta* of a canon of St. Peter's ("recipitur a Canonicis in Canonicum S. Petri"). He sang with the clergy; then, taking off the vestments of a canon, he put on the sandals and tunic of a deacon and over this a sumptuous cope; then he put on royal clothing again to receive anointing. He served as a deacon in the pontifical Mass offered by Clement VII, and then returned to sit on his own throne, where he sat with his own imperial garments ("Quo facto redit ad suum sugestum, ubi riassumit insignia sua imperialia, et sedet").[40] When, in Florence, Grand Duke Cosimo III de' Medici was admitted among the Lateran canons (1700), he had Carlo Maratta paint his portrait wearing a surplus and their three-cornered hat, and twenty years later he was pictured again wearing the vestments of Saint Joseph.[41] In the Palazzo Pitti there were numerous small chapels and devotional altars, which the Hapsburg-Lorraine and the

30. See Gorski 1969; Vauchez 1977; Graus 1981; Folz 1984.
31. Le Goff 1996, 298–310.
32. Wallace-Hadrill [1962] 1982.
33. Ullmann 1969; Peters 1970, 71; Sot 1988, 712ff.
34. Kantorowicz 1946, 57.
35. Ladner 1988, 35.
36. Kern 1956, 38ff.; Boisserée 1842.
37. Villette 1611, 226–27.
38. Hezecques n.d., 177 and 181–82.
39. Kantorowicz 1988, 249.
40. Giordani 1842, 33ff.
41. Langedijk 1981–87.

Fig. 3   *Rex sacerdos* (Saint Louis), Vivaldus, *Opus regale,* Saluzzo, 1507, frontispiece.

Savoy dynasties gradually dismantled. Much the same was true of the Alcázar in Madrid.[42]

Another imperial appellation was *pius*.[43] Romans in the republican period continued to call the priest celebrating certain rites that had been among the duties of their kings *Rex sacrorum*. In the imperial period Augustus became *Pontifex maximus,* at the same time supreme head of the state and of its religion, and was deified on his death. In 310 Constantine embraced Christianity, which became the new religion of state. From that moment on, the emperor was a *Christomimètes,* assuming, by this means, new priestly characteristics. A large coin minted at Aix-la-Chapelle under Charlemagne had as a motto "XC:VINCIT:XC:REGNAT—KAROLUS MAGNUS IMPERAT" (Christ triumphs, Christ reigns, Charles the Great rules).[44] For King Alfonso X the Wise, the kings of Castile were "Vicars of God, each one in his own kingdom, placed over the people to keep them in justice and truth."[45] But I think no king appeared in the guise of the Father omnipotent so much as John II of Castile presumed to do during the feast celebrated in his honor at Valladolid in May of 1428.[46]

In Byzantium the emperor of the East sat under a ciborium whose vault was frescoed with a sky studded with stars (curiously, Claude Villette saw in the similar ciborium above the high altar where the Corpus Domini was kept "the sacred womb of the Virgin mother of our Savior").[47] The throne resembled a chariot or at least had legs representing lions to symbolize cosmic movement.[48] When he left the imperial palace for a procession, the emperor walked under an umbrella, another reference to the vault of heaven, and he was surrounded by torches, which referred to solar flames.[49]

In one of those "logical instabilities" that Saussure speaks of, if the throne referred to the movement of the stars, the king instead was immobile. In this case the emphasis was placed on his resemblance to an idol. I will speak further of the immobility of the central figures in the Roman triumph, and of the sovereign's face painted red like the statue of Jove, but he also presented himself as a marble image of divinity. He was distant and mute, and silence had to be strictly observed around him.[50] At the Byzantine court, on the appearance of the emperor in the audience chamber, the basilica, or the consistory, appropriate officials (the *silentiarii*) imposed silence. J. G. Frazer, in *The Golden Bough,* says that in ancient Japan the Mikado was obliged to sit on his throne every morning for several hours with a crown on his head. He was supposed to remain immobile like a statue for the whole time, without moving hands or feet. Only in this way could he assure the tranquillity of the empire over which he reigned. Not only this, "such a holiness was ascribed to all parts of his body, that he dared to cut off neither his hair, nor his beard, nor his nails."[51]

The long hair of the Frankish kings (*reges criniti,* as Gregory of Tours referred to it)[52] was related to the same need.

42. See Gerard 1983.
43. Weinstock 1971, 248ff.
44. Kantorowicz 1946, 3.
45. *Las Sietes Partidas* 1807, II, pt. I, ley v, II:7.
46. Fernandez 1975, 101–79.
47. Villette 1611, 53; see also Smith 1936, 107ff.
48. L'Orange 1953, 82ff., 124ff.
49. Dvornik 1966, 1:523.
50. Alföldi 1970, 36ff.
51. Frazer 1911, 3.
52. Wallace-Hadrill 1962 [1982], 148ff.

Fig. 4   Priam kissing Achilles' knee, Etruscan amphora, Munich, Museum für antike
Kleinkunst 3171 (J 890).

When, in 1822, Mr. Crawford was admitted to the presence of the king of Siam, having been sent on mission to him, the king on his throne "had more the appearance of a
statue in a niche, than of a living being."[53] A few official portraits of European rulers suggest the same immobility. They were even made to be placed on the throne when the sovereign was absent. Sometimes they refer directly to *proskynesis* (servility: it was thought
that clemency resided in the knee). An exposed leg in a portrait was a clear allusion to this
(just as an exposed breast indicated virginity).[54] The figure of the king with a leg, or more
often a knee, exposed was an ancient cliché (Fig. 4). It can be found, for instance, in an in-
cunabulum of Johannes Thurocz's *Chronica Hungarorum* (Augsburg, 1488; Fig. 5), in the
Libro della ventura by Lorenzo Spiriti (printed by Gotardo da Ponte in Milan, 1501), in a
print of Charles V and his enemies by Martin van Heemskerck (1556), in a portrait of King
Charles I of England by Van Dyck, in the figure of the sovereign in the frontispiece of the
Leiden edition of Machiavelli's *Prince* of 1643 (Fig. 6).[55] It appears in Hyacinthe Rigaud's
well-known portrait of Louis XIV (cf. Fig. 7), as well as in two portraits of Louis XV
painted some years later.[56] As for immobility, one can look at portraits of Elizabeth I of
England, the Ditchley portrait, for example. The queen wears a costume so rigid that it
prevents any movement. She is represented immobile, like an idol.[57] A ceremonial was
observed at her court quite similar to that of the Mikado. We have the testimony of a Venetian ambassador: "In the royal antechamber stands a chair covered with brocade, and
this antechamber they call the presence chamber, and they have such reverence for their
king that they always uncover themselves in this chamber, because the chair represents

53. Cited in Jones 1883, 486.
54. See Bertelli 1995.
55. Bertelli and Innocenti 1979, sec. XVII, 41.
56. Reichler 1985, 55–77; Bertelli 1995. For official portraiture, see Bardon 1974; Polleross 1988; Ellenius 1966 (limited
to Sweden).
57. O'Donoghue 1894; Strong 1977.

Fig. 5   Johannes Thurocz, *Chronica Hungarorum*, Augsburg, 1488, fol. 52v.

the king, before whom you cannot pass without showing reverence, whoever you are in England."[58] This leads one to imagine a remarkable continuity with the custom attested by Dio Cassius for the Roman Empire. The *sella curulis* of Caligula was placed in the temple of Jove on the Capitoline hill, and the senators did homage to it when the emperor was absent. Thus also the throne of Commodus was covered with a lion's skin and a club placed across it, symbolizing the Roman Hercules, in the absence of the sovereign.[59] During the first church councils, the book of the Gospels was placed on a throne to symbolize the physical presence of God in the work of the council.[60] A page of the court

58. Alberi 1839–63, ser. I, II (1840): 395.
59. Dio Cassius 1970, 59, 24.4, and 72, 17.4; Weinstock 1971, 283–84.
60. Calore 1995.

Fig. 6   Nic. Machiavelli Florentini, *Princeps,* Leiden (Lugduni
Batavorum), de Vogel, 1643. Frontispiece.

Fig. 7   The knee of the young king Louis XIV (by Henri Testelin), Château de Versailles,
         M.v. 3475.

Fig. 8   The empty throne flanked with foxes and lions, *De Prins van N. Machiavel,* frontispiece, Dutch translation of *The Prince,* The Hague ('s Gravenhage), Engelbreg Boucquet, 1704.

of Louis XVI, Count Felix d'Hezecques, wrote with regret that in his time only elderly courtiers, such as the duc de Penthièvre, the prince de Soubise, and the maréchal de Biron, bowed in salute when they passed before the state bed of the king "when he was not present."[61] One wonders if the frontispiece of a Dutch edition of Machiavelli's *Prince* (1704; Fig. 8) does not refer to the same ceremonial.[62] It is even possible that the bailiff H. Gessler was echoing the same custom when he wanted to make the inhabitants of the canton of Uri bow before Emperor Albert's hat.

The theory that power descended by divine right was already present at the time of the Roman Empire. But it had a particular development in the Christian era, at Byzantium, where the emperor was seen to be like Christ enthroned, a Christ reincarnated. (And, in this respect, why did the kings of France have the entire genealogy of the kings of Judea sculpted on the façade of the cathedrals of Paris and Reims [Fig. 9], alluding to Christ as if to their own ancestor?) One must keep in mind that a royal coronation, with the Hebraic symbolism of anointing at its apex, was, in many aspects, an embalming. Thanks to this rite the king became *Christos kuriou,* the Messiah Yahweh, the "Son of God" ("this day have I begotten thee"; Psalm 2:7). To underscore his new status, his

61. Hezecques n.d., 170.
62. Bertelli and Innocenti 1979, pt. XVIII, no. 5; Bertelli 1990b.

transformation into a sacred person, the king even changed his name (or added a numeral to it). Once anointed, he became a sacred person: "Nolite tangere christos meos!" (Do not touch my anointed ones). Access to the sacrament of anointing also made him similar to a priest. Referring to the Frankish kings, Pope Paul I called them "gens sancta, regale sacerdotium, populus adquisitionis" (holy dynasty, royal priesthood, gift to the people),[63] and Pope Stephen II referred to Pepin as a "novus Moyses" (new Moses) and as a "perfulgidus David" (shining David).[64]

For the pope this "rebirth" was imitated physically. A broadside of 1555, *L'ordine che si tiene nel creare il sommo pontefice, con le cerimonie che si fanno della coronazione in S. Giovanni Laterano,* says that the newly elected pope, "dressed in black, enters on a tumbrel of the dead; the office of the dead is sung, and then he is dressed with the vestments of a bishop."

Like a priest, the king was both the advocate of his people before heaven and the sacrificial hostage of heaven among his people. He assumed the traits of a scapegoat for the sins of his subjects. In the *XII Abusivis Saeculi* of the Pseudo-Cyprian it is written that the king must "attend to prayer at the times fixed" (certis horis orationibus insistere),[65] as Vivaldus showed in his *Opus regale* (Saluzzo, 1507) with the image of Saint Louis in prayer. In his portrait of Alfonso V the Magnanimous, king of Naples, Vespasiano da Bisticci wrote that the king

> delighted much in holy writings and particularly in the Bible, which he had almost completely memorized . . . he was most pious toward the poor, most religious in hearing three masses a day, which he never missed, two low and one sung. . . . He was most diligent in what related to the divine cult. On Holy Thursday he washed the feet of as many of the poor as the years of his age; and he washed them properly, and dried them, and humbly made a cross on the right foot and then kissed it. . . . Every day he continuously recited the office of the Lord . . . and at night he did not fail to rise to say the office . . . he fasted for all the vigils of the feasts of Christ and the most glorious Virgin Mary, and every Friday he fasted with bread and water.[66]

The duc de Saint-Simon says that Louis XIV only once in his life (when he was on a campaign) failed to go to Mass. "The king never in his life missed going to Mass, except once with the army when there was a long march." He never failed to fast on fast days; instead, "some days before Lent, he announced publicly at his *Lever* that he would take it very badly if anyone were given fat to eat." He never missed sermons during Advent and Lent "or any devotion of Holy Week, great feasts, processions of the Holy Sacrament, or days observed by the Order of the Holy Spirit, or Assumption." He took Communion five times a year, "always wearing the collar of the Order [of the Holy Spirit], with its vestment and mantle." On Holy Thursday he served a dinner to the poor.[67]

This was all behavior more suited to a deacon than to a layman, which was part of the conception of the *Christomimèsis* of kingship that transformed the monarch into a *rex*

63. *Codex Carolinus* 1892, XXXIX:552; Enright 1985, 130.
64. *Codex Carolinus* 1892, XI:505; Enright 1985, 130.
65. Enright 1985, 54.
66. Vespasiano da Bisticci 1970, 86–87.
67. Saint-Simon 1983–88, V:183–85.

Fig. 9   The kings of Judea, on the façade of the cathedral of Reims (from H. E. Leblan, *La catedrale de Reims,* Reims, C. Coulon, 1882).

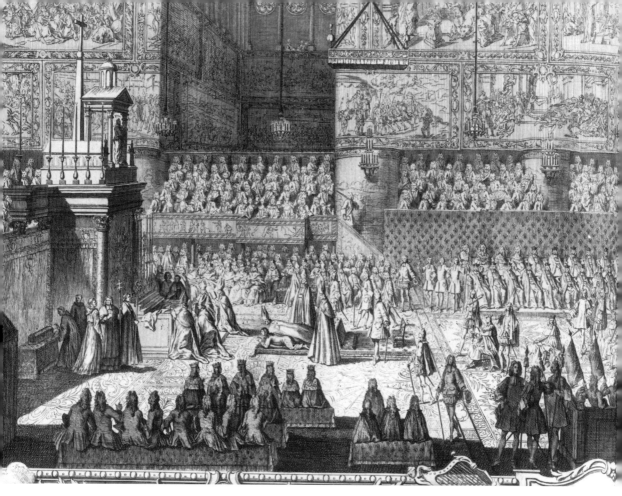

Fig. 10   The anointing in the cathedral of Reims (engraving from A. Banchet, *Le sacre de Louis XV roy de France et de Navarre dans l'Eglise de Reims le Dimanche XXV Octobre MDCCXXII*).

sacerdos, thanks to anointing (Fig. 10). It was not by chance that the archbishop of Mainz, when consecrating German kings, uttered the formula: "In this day the grace of the Lord has changed you into another man, and thanks to the sacred rite of anointing he makes you participate in his divinity."[68] In the French *sacre,* the twelve peers of the realm, in all together holding the crown above the sovereign's head, remind one explicitly of the twelve apostles.[69]

We do not know when the biblical model of Saul and David was taken up again in the early Middle Ages. The oldest dated coronations on record are those of the Visigothic kings Wamba (672), Ervig (680), Eghica (687), and Witiza (700).[70] A ceremony is described by the bishop of Toledo in the *Historia Wambae.*[71] About the same time, another coronation ceremony can be traced to Irish kings. The *Vita Columbae,* written at Iona between 668 and 704, includes a story of an angel that descended from heaven, bringing for King Aidan a codex written onto crystal: "Once, while the memorable man was living on the island of Hinba, he saw one night, in an ecstasy, an angel of the Lord, who had in his hand

68. Kern 1956, 37 and 52ff.

69. See Villette 1611, 238–39; Menin 1723; [Alletz] 1775. Cf. Millon 1931; Schramm [1929] 1960b, 163ff.; Baynes 1984; Valensise 1986; Bautier 1989; Hedeman 1990.

70. Julian of Toledo 1910, 503–4; PL, XCVI:766; Bouman 1957; Collins 1977, 41–42; Enright 1985.

71. MGHSSRMer., V, 1910; Collins 1977.

a glass book of the ordination of kings."[72] Since the text of this *Ordo* has not survived, we cannot say whether the ceremony preceded the anointing. It may be that this ordination never took place and that the reference served only to exalt the supremacy of the *paruchia Columbae*. However, another celestial mission (perhaps inspired by this one, perhaps independent) occurred on the Continent, on the other shore of the English Channel. A French poet of the thirteenth century sang that if the kings of western Europe had to resort to apothecaries for the oil necessary for their anointing,[73] the kings of France received theirs directly from heaven:

> Et molt li doit bien souvenir
> Qu'en toutes autres regions
> Convient les rois lor ontions
> Acheter en la mercerie.

> And they remember well
> That everywhere else
> Kings need to seek ointments
> For sale, in shops.

In the ninth century the archbishop of Reims, Hincmar (845–82),[74] asserted (*Vita Remigii,* 21) that his predecessor in his episcopal see, Saint Rémi, having to baptize Clovis, the king of the Franks (496 is the conventional date), did not receive in time the chrism that a priest was to bring, since a large crowd at the door of the church prevented his passage. He asked the help of the Lord, and a dove descended, carrying an ampoule with inexhaustible balm. Hincmar, who in all likelihood was the inspiration for the *Ordo* of 866 for Queen Ermentrude at Soissons, crowned Charles the Bald in 869 ("iniunxit eum Hincmarus archiepiscopus de chrismate ad dextram auriculam, et in fronte ad sinistram auriculam, et in capite" [Archbishop Hincmar anointed him with the chrism, on the right ear, the forehead, the left ear, and on the head]) and Louis the Pius in 877.[75] The motives that inspired creation of such a legend could not have been much different from the one that made an angel with a crystal book descend over the island of Iona. As the custodian of the ritual of coronation, Hincmar had to defend himself from the growing presence of the Abbey of Saint-Denis, which, as the necropolis of kings, became the custodian of another not-less-important ceremony—funerals.[76] Pope Innocent II appealed to the legend of the Holy Oil for the *sacre* of Louis VI (1131).[77] For this, even the pope used the oil of the Holy Ampoule.[78] A hundred years later its use had definitively become a part of the ceremony. It was codified by the *Ordo* of Reims of 1230[79] and by the one that followed it in

---

72. "Alio in tempore, cum vir praedicabilis in Himba commoraretur insula, quadam nocte in extasi mentis angelum domini ad se misum vidit, qui in manu vitreum ordinationis regum habebat librum." Jones 1883, 519–21; Wallace-Hadrill 1971, 55ff.; Enright 1985, 7. For the question mark, see Nelson 1986, 285–86.

73. Richier 1912, vv. 8140ff.; Schramm 1960a, 150; Bloch [1923] 1961, 220.

74. Devisse 1976.

75. Schramm 1960a, 146–50; Bautier 1989, 11–12; Nelson 1990; Jackson 1995, 25. The text for Ermentrude is in Jackson 1995, *Ordo* VI; for Charles the Bald, *Ordo* VII.

76. *Histoire de l'Abbaye Royale* 1606.

77. Schramm [1929] 1960b, 112–20.

78. Schramm [1929] 1960b, 147; Oppenheimer 1954. On Hincmar, see Nelson 1986, 133ff.; Jackson 1994.

79. Bruhl 1950; Schramm 1960a, 145–48; Jackson 1984, 190–91.

1250.[80] The kings of France based their right to be called "Most Christian" on the possession of this oil. As the *Ordo* of Reims explained: "inter universos reges terre hoc glorioso
prefulget privilegio, ut oleo celitus misso singulariter inungatur" (he outshines all the
kings of the earth by the glorious privilege of being anointed with an oil sent from
heaven).[81] Charles V of France wore a cap throughout his life to preserve the oil received
in his coronation from any external contact,[82] and he specified in his own *Ordo* that the
anointed shirt be burned.[83] The veneration was so great that Louis XI, feeling himself
close to death on 14 July 1483, wanted to receive a new anointing (so much did it give a
new life!). He was told this was impossible, anointing being a sacrament that could not
be repeated. He contented himself with summoning the miraculous flask "so as to observe the devotion we have to it."[84] On the other hand, when Edward III wanted his
anointing to be repeated, requesting this dispensation from the pope, John XXII granted
it, arguing that royal anointing "in anima quicquid non imprimit!" (makes no mark upon
the soul).[85]

As Shakespeare wrote: "Not all the water in the rough rude sea / Can wash the balm
off from an anointed king" (*Richard II*, III, 2). Could it have been less for English kings?
Saint Thomas à Becket, in exile at Sens in France, had a vision: the Virgin (more than an
angel!) had consigned a flask to him, saying that the oil contained in it should anoint future kings of England. Becket consigned the miraculous flask to a monk of Poitiers, and
this monk hid it under a stone in the Church of St. Grégoire. There it remained until a
holy man at the time of King Edward III revealed its existence, consigned the flask to the
duke of Lancaster, who gave it to the Black Prince, who locked it in the Tower of London. It was found there by his son, Richard II, who wanted to be anointed. He was told
that coronation could not be repeated. Thus the Virgin's oil was first used in the succeeding coronation, that of Henry IV.[86]

All these legends show one thing essentially, the supernatural importance of royal
anointing. In France a long discussion occurred about whether descent from the Capetian
dynasty or anointing was what gave thaumaturgic powers to the king.[87] The formula repeated when touching those sick with scrofula—"Le roi te touche, Dieu te guerisse" (The
king touches you, God cures you)—recalled the sacrament of anointing (Fig. 11). But it is
worth mentioning that other monarchies also claimed thaumaturgic powers, which were
implicitly associated with anointing. The kings of England, for instance, specialized in
curing epilepsy by distributing coins with their image, which were later reduced to rings
(cramp rings), and like their fellow monarchs across the Channel, they also touched
people sick with scrofula (glandular tuberculosis—thus called "the king's evil").[88] Even
the Angevin kings of Naples claimed thaumaturgic powers. Tolomeo da Lucca affirmed
this explicitly in speaking of Charles of Anjou, brother of Saint Louis and imperial vicar
of Tuscany. He said that the king's gift to cure the sick derived from "divina influentia super eos, ex ampliori partecipatione entis" (a divine influence over kings, their greater par-

80. Flodoardus 1854–55; Le Goff 1990a; Bonne 1990.
81. Villette 1611, 206ff.; Chevalier 1900, 224.
82. Sherman 1969, 26; 1971.
83. *Coronation Book* 1899, 32–33.
84. Marlot 1846, IV:240–45 and 669–72; Basin 1963.
85. *Three Coronation Orders* 1900, no. x:72.
86. Taylor 1820, 60; Legg 1896; Ullmann 1957. For the repetition of this fable, see Bettelheim 1976.
87. Bloch [1923] 1961, particularly chap. IV.
88. Bloch [1923] 1961; Thomas [1971] 1973.

Fig. 11   The royal touch: Francis I in Bologna, touching the sick at the time of his meeting with the pope Leo X in 1515. Bologna, Palazzo d'Accursio.

ticipation in God), specifying that this privilege belonged to kings of France, to "dominus noster rex Karolus" (our king Charles), and, it was said ("fertur"), even to English kings.[89] It is quite possible that later, when the Aragonese replaced the Angevins, the new Neapolitan monarchy did the same, especially considering the care Alfonso the Magnanimous took to present himself as a *sacerdos*. That this dynasty also had thaumaturgic powers is based on the observation that Don Carlos de Viane, the heir of Aragon and Navarre, who died on 23 September 1461, was the font of a cult, although it was not recognized by the church. A reliquary containing his hand, it was said, cured people of scrofula.[90] The further history of the Aragonese dynasty, following the expedition of Charles VIII of France to Italy and then the submission of the kingdom of Naples to Ferdinand the Catholic, interrupted this development. We know that the Aragonese of Naples had the ceremony of anointing in their coronations.[91] But it does not seem that Iberian kings, from Sancho IV onward, ever tried to heal the sick.[92]

In the Eastern Empire, as well, there is no trace of anointing until the tenth century, even if Theòdoros Balsamòn, a canonist of the twelfth century from Byzantium, in his commentary on the canons of the Twelfth Council of Ancyra,[93] said that the chrism of

89. Tolomeo da Lucca 1909, 39. See Bloch [1923] 1961, 133.
90. Bloch [1923] 1961, 133 and 152–53. For Aragonese coronation, see Blancas 1641.
91. On the Aragonese of Iberia, see the works of Palacios Martin.
92. Schramm 1960a, 61.
93. PG, CXXXVII:1156.

anointing canceled out the sin with which John I Tzimisces was marked through the murder of Nicephorus II Phocas (969), since this sacred unguent had the same power as baptism.[94] It is possible that the example on which the introduction of anointing into the Byzantine coronation rite was based came from Jerusalem, from the coronation of the Latin kings there (from 1108), this latter based in turn on French ritual.[95] The Byzantines, however, had the term *Christòs Theou* (the anointed one of God) in their liturgical formula, even before the eighth century, still without having physically introduced the specific sacrament of anointing. Perhaps they held "that the emperor, already for the very fact of being 'chosen' by God, was *ipso facto* also 'anointed by God.'"[96]

Giorgio Pachymere describes how the ceremony was eventually enacted.[97] The *Ottonian Pontificale* dictated that the "episcopus Ostiensis ungat ei [the emperor] de oleo exorcizato brachium dextrum et inter scapulas" (the bishop of Ostia should anoint the emperor with the blessed oil on the right arm and between the shoulder blades).[98] A minute description for Italy was left by Johann Burchard, who was sent by Pope Alexander VI to Naples in 1494 to direct the coronation ceremony of Alfonso II of Aragon (the son of Ferrante), in his *Diarium, sive rerum urbanarum commentarii*. At the moment of unction the sovereign lay on the ground, on four cushions: one under his knees, two under his arms, the fourth under his stomach. Thus prostrated, the apostolic legate anointed him with his right thumb, tracing the sign of the cross first on the right arm at the wrist, then, opening the special shirt put on for the ceremony, between the shoulder blades.[99] One can see how similar this ceremony was to the ordination of a priest,[100] and medieval kings always wanted also to be recognized as priests, as *rex et sacerdos* in their role as vicars of God.[101] The chrism was always perceived as a potent assurance of the immortality of the sovereign. When King Henry III, son of Henry II of England, died at Martel (11 June 1183), the body was dressed with the vestments anointed at the time of his coronation.[102]

An anointed body was a sacred body that could only show itself rarely. The *parousia* was an event limited to particular ceremonies.[103] Nonetheless, all the actions of the sovereign were "public" in the sense that his body was "public" (any community of subjects would recognize his "mystical" body). Pliny the Younger said in his *Panegyricus Traiani* that the prince should even open his private chamber. "Great fortune requires that nothing be covered, hidden; it opens up not only the houses of princes but even their bedchambers and their intimate recesses; all their secrets are exposed by Fama."[104]

An enormous importance was thus attributed to the body of the king. The whole court gravitated around his *cubiculum* (bedchamber), and the hierarchy of courtiers was assessed in relation to their distance from that body. In Byzantium the *kiuboukleion* repre-

94. See Pertusi 1976, 548.
95. Mayer 1967.
96. Pertusi 1976, 555.
97. Pachymere 1669, II:106.
98. Elze 1960, 1–2, *Der Römische Ordo in Ottonischen Pontifikale*. For the insignia, see also Eichmann 1942, 43ff.; Pertusi 1965 and 1976.
99. Burchard 1883–85, II:138–39.
100. See Wickham Legg, introduction to the *Coronation Order* 1902, xxxviii ff.
101. Maccarrone 1959.
102. Hope 1907, 520.
103. See here, Part II, Chapter 8.
104. Pliny the Younger 1975, 319ff.

sented the ideal nucleus of the sacred city,[105] just as in the papal Lateran Palace the complex of rooms gravitated around the *cubiculum*.[106] A decree at Mantua in 1470 weighed the gravity of punishments, for any discovered in the court armed, by the distance from the ruler's apartment.[107] The bishop Antonio de Guevara, in his *Aviso de privados y doctrina de cortisanos* (1539), lamented that courtiers competed to obtain rooms close to the royal bedchamber, and not to the chapel.[108]

A series of rules of etiquette arose with regard to the king's body. When a subject turned to the sovereign, he could not look him in the eye. Patrizi Piccolomini recommended keeping the eyes lowered when one addressed the pope, explaining this through the need to express modesty when talking with someone superior to oneself.[109] In the Bamum's ceremony, a different explanation is given—to look a sovereign in the eye might make him think his words had not been understood. "When you speak to the king or the king speaks to you, do not look at him directly. You should not look him in the face unless he himself has ceased to look at you. If he still has his eye on you, look at him furtively. If he asks you to speak, give him only quick imperceptible glances. Should he notice, while you speak, that you are looking at him intensely, he might think you didn't understand what he was saying to you."[110] In reality, neither of these explanations approached the truth. The norm—even in such distant places and times—was dominated by a single preoccupation, to avoid the danger of evil eye. As the English proverb said: "A cat can look at a king; curiosity killed the cat."

In the same way, the king never responded directly, but rather through an intermediary. At the Byzantine court an official, the *logoteta,* spoke for the emperor. Pier delle Vigne was *logoteta* for the Holy Roman Emperor Frederick II. When the king of France entered Rouen in 1449, the citizens offered him their assistance to further the war against the English: "The king heard them with benevolence, he responded by way of his chancellor, and thanked them for their good will."[111]

Since the king had a mortal body, the problems relating to his death were enormous. In his study *Social Origins* (1954) A. M. Hocart affirmed that "the first kings had to have been dead kings," since funerals had an important integrating function for members of any community.[112]

However, one could add that there were also dormant kings. In A.D. 350, when the Arian heresy was at its height, the death of Constantine was a severe blow to his subjects, giving rise to a prophecy of the Tibertine sibyl: the emperor was not dead, but closed in a deep sleep. In his absence, Rome would be conquered and the poor oppressed by tyranny. But the emperor would awake, bringing an age of gold. Then the Jews would be converted, and the twenty-two nations of Gog and Magog defeated. Finally, the emperor would raise his insignia on Golgotha, bringing the age of gold to an end. This would be followed by the reign of the Antichrist, who would in turn be defeated by the appearance

---

105. See Ebersolt 1910.

106. On the Lateran, see Herklotz 1985 and Scrinari 1991; also Rasponi 1656; Rohan de Fleury 1877; Lauer 1911.

107. Mazzoldi 1961.

108. On the organization of the court of Burgundy, see Cartellieri 1970; on that of France, see Boucher 1982; Le Roy Ladurie 1982; on England, Starkey 1987; on Spain, Brown and Elliott 1985; Lison Tolosana 1992; Soria 1993.

109. Dykmans 1980–82, II:451ff.

110. Tardits 1985, 194.

111. Mathieu d'Escouchy 1863, I:243.

112. Quoted in Huntington-Metcalf 1985; see also Adler 1992.

of Jesus for the Day of Judgment. Another prophecy with the same apocalyptic tone was that of the Pseudo-Methodius, which spread at the end of the seventh century among the Christian populations of Syria subjected to Muslim domination.[113]

Paul the Deacon (1, 4) relates that in Germany, in "a cave under a cliff, no one knows for how long, seven men lay in a deep sleep, so well preserved both in body and clothing, and for so long, that they had become objects of veneration for those ignorant barbarous people. From the fashion of their clothing one would say they were Romans . . . perhaps some day, since they seem to be Christians, their preaching will bring the inhabitants of that place to salvation."[114]

Denying the death of their sovereigns, communities denied their own dissolution. At the time of the siege of Constantinople by the Bulgars, in 812, the crowd broke down the gates that led to the imperial tombs and dragged the body of Constantine V from its sarcophagus, crying: "Arise! Save your endangered people!" These people even arrived at the point of believing they had seen the emperor fight to defeat the barbarians.[115] If we consider a holy patron to be the head of a particular community (*patronus in celestibus*), we could add the Roman example of Saint Peter, who, according to Procopius, in his *Bellum gothicum,* defended a breech in the walls against besieging Goths; or another, of Saint Ambrose, *dux* of the Milanese in the *Historia mediolanensis* of Landolfo, who, according to Galvano Fiamma, was seen on horseback with his *scutica,* or *flagellum,* in hand, fighting at the head of the army of Luchino Visconti during the battle of Parabiago of 1339.[116]

In the Carolingian period, the legend of *Carolus redivivus* developed along these same lines.[117]

Another similar reaction was that of the peoples of Flanders at the time of the fourth Crusade. Their sovereign, Count Baldwin, recently made king of Constantinople, was captured by the Bulgars and killed. When, in 1224, a stranger rode through the country announcing the return of Baldwin, no one doubted that the king had awakened from his long sleep. A few decades later, some Joachimites spread the word that the emperor Frederick II was not dead, but was sleeping. In Sicily, where the emperor had passed a large part of his life, people continually repeated a phrase of the sibyl: "Imperator vivit et non vivit" (The emperor lives and does not live). But also whole generations of Germans waited for his return—exactly like the whole generations of Franks who awaited Charlemagne's return to life.[118]

That the relationship between sovereign and subject was an osmotic one is well expressed figuratively in a frontispiece of Thomas Hobbes's *Leviathan* published in London by Crooke in 1651. The king was projected over his territory, composed of cities and countrysides; his arms were spread and held the double symbols of kingship: sword and crozier (alluding to the English particularity of the king at the same time ruler of the kingdom and of the church). Even his body was composed of an infinite number of small bodies, who were his subjects.

In a world where care of the body was based on the Galenic principle *homo homini salus*

---

113. Cohn 1976.
114. Paolo Diacono 1988, 7–9.
115. McCormick 1986, 137.
116. Bertelli 1978, 151–52.
117. Folz 1973a, 134–42.
118. Cohn 1976, 71ff., 113; Jackson 1969; Bercé 1990, 244–47.

("man is the cure of himself"; thus on use, in pharmacy, of the human body and its secretions),[119] the most important body was certainly the royal one. Plutarch recounts a version of the death of Romulus different from the one usually recounted (*Romulus* 27.6). He was perhaps killed by senators, who, dissecting him, each carried a piece to his own dwelling.[120] Plutarch wrote in the first century of the Christian era and thought that the senators, by doing this, wanted to conceal their crime. This shows that in his time the deeper meaning of a rite had been lost, though the memory of it remained, which contrasted with the certainly more celebrated meaning of apotheosis. In reality, this was the distribution of the body of the leader among his followers (in the terminology of Max Weber: *Vertrauensmänner*). It was a distribution not dissimilar to the Eucharistic one of the Last Supper, with the breaking of bread by Christ and its distribution among the Apostles. Was this also the trace of an ancient custom?

If not the same rite, we can trace something not so different in the monarchies of the early Middle Ages. In 877 Charles the Bald died at Brios while he was crossing the Alps. In order to transport the king to Saint-Denis, his followers tried to embalm the body. It was eviscerated and treated with spices and wine. "They took out the viscera, put them into an infusion of wine perfumed with the herbs they could find, and sealed it; and they started out toward the monastery of St. Diogène, where they intended to bury it. But the smell was so great that they were unable to carry it. Thus they put it into a chest lined inside and out with leather."[121] When the emperor Otto I died, in 973, the body was eviscerated, the intestines were buried at Memblen, and the body was transported to Magdeburg. The custom of a double burial, while not limited to the region of Germany, was eventually called "mos teutonicus."[122]

This division of the body (heart, viscera, and remains) became so common from the twelfth century on that Pope Boniface VIII felt obliged to intervene with the bull of 27 September 1299, *Detestande feritatis* (Hateful ferocity).[123] In this the pontiff speaks of a horrible custom ("mos horribilis"), which consisted in cutting up the body and boiling the pieces to separate flesh from bone ("aquis immersa exponunt ignibus decoquenda"); finally the bones, liberated from the flesh ("et tandem, ab ossibus tegumento carnis excusso") were taken to the selected place of burial ("ad partes predictas mittunt seu deferunt tumulanda"). Can we find here a trace of the belief, common to many ethnic groups, that the deceased were not completely dead or received in the hereafter if they were not freed from the flesh? This is what Elisabeth Brown suggests, referring to the essays of Hertz and of Levy-Bruhl on the collective representation of death.[124] But some further examples show that in reality there is no single explanation; we are confronted with an act that had multiple meanings.

If the custom of dissecting the body was born essentially from the need to confront long voyages to reach the locality originally destined for burial (the place of birth, the family chapel, the royal necropolis), then these macabre means were adopted so as not to

119. Manara 1668; Scarlatini 1683; Camporesi 1983.
120. See Dionysius of Halicarnassus 1968, II:56.
121. "Ablatis intraneis, et infusum vinum ac aromatibus quibus poterat et impositum locello coeperunt ferre versus monasterium sancti Dyonisii, ubi sepeliri se postulaverat." *Annales Bertiniani* 1883, 137; Erlande Brandenburg 1975, 28.
122. Schaefer 1920; Bradford 1933.
123. Digard 1890, *Registre* 3409.
124. Brown 1981, 223; Hertz 1978; Levy-Bruhl 1927.

leave the sovereign's body in a foreign land. When Henry VII of Luxemburg died unexpectedly at Buonconvento (August 1313), his body was boiled in wine and aromatics and taken to Pisa for burial. But sometimes there was the pious wish to be buried in a particular holy place: Frederick Barbarossa was on a crusade when he died (1190). His body was boiled, and the bones were removed and sent to Tyre (the midpoint of his pilgrimage) for burial.[125] In the same way, Robert the Bruce, king of Scotland, when he died in 1329, asked that his heart be buried in Jerusalem: "Emportés mon coeur avech vous, pour presenter au Saint Sepulcre, là où Nostres Sires fu ensepelis, puis que li corps n'i poet aler" (Take my heart with you to give to the Holy Sepulchre, where Our Lord was buried, since my body can no longer go there).[126] On the other hand, Richard the Lion-Hearted asked that his heart be buried at Rouen, out of filial piety, beside the tomb of his father; his brain, blood, and viscera at Charroux; and the rest of his body at Fontevrault, where his mother, sister, and part of the remains of his father were buried.[127] In the sixteenth century, the heart of Francis I was also buried separately (see Fig. 12).

For our purposes, however, another, different example has a greater interest. When Prince Charles of England was wounded in the siege of the castle of Chaluz (1189) and knew he was going to die, he wanted his body to be buried "apud Fontem Ebraudi," beside his father "cujus proditorem se confitetur." But the heart was to go to the "ecclesiae Rothomagnsi"; the viscera to the rebel "barones Pictaviae." He gave his body to his father, who had sired him, his heart to the church at Rouen for the fidelity its people had shown him, and his viscera to the barons of Poitiers, who had betrayed him; they were not worthy of a better part.[128]

At least with regard to royal burials, one must recognize that the practice condemned by Boniface VIII was still observed in the sixteenth century. On the tomb of Louis XII of France an epitaph states: "Cy gist le corps avec le coeur de très-haut, très-excellent, très-puissant Prince Louis XII, Roy de France, lequel trepassa à Paris à l'Hostelles de Tournelles le premier jour de Janvier l'an 1514. Ses entrailles sont avec son père aux Celestins dudit Paris." (Here lies the body and heart of the high, excellent, and powerful Prince Louis XII, King of France, who died in Paris at the Hospital of Tournelles the first day of January 1514. His entrails are with his father in the Celestine monastery in Paris.)[129] His wife, Anna, "since she was the daughter of the last duke of Brittany, . . . left her heart to the Bretons to be buried in the Charterhouse of Nantes, in the tomb of her ancestors."[130] On the death of Louis XIII, his heart was given to the Jesuits "for the Church of Saint-Louis in Paris"; the viscera "were carried to Saint-Denis, but the canons of Notre-Dame de Paris obtained them from the queen that very day, and Monsieur de Ventadour, one of the canons, took them to Notre-Dame the day after."[131]

Thus, one would not say that the practice of dissecting a cadaver and burying the parts in several different places was dictated only by the need to transport the most important remains (the skeleton) to the place earlier chosen for burial. We are rather in the presence of a spatial distribution of the noblest parts of a sacred body: the heart, the head (in a

125. Schaefer 1920, 478–79, 483–85.
126. Froissart 1869, 1:79.
127. Schaefer 1920, 496.
128. Roger de Wendover 1886, 283.
129. Félibien 1706, 563.
130. Félibien 1706, 374.
131. Félibien 1706, 469.

Fig. 12   The heart of Francis I in the cathedral of Saint-Denis.

Carolingian abbey in Dauphiné a relic of the head of Saint Theobald came to be known as "Saint Chef"—the Holy Head!),[132] the viscera, the skeleton. Besides the tentative interpretation of Elisabeth Brown, Alain Boureau has suggested that this might reflect a desire to multiply prayers for the dying person. "One could obtain three times the prayers, and from three different religious communities."[133] In fact, this was the thesis advanced (to be disputed) by the medieval jurist and theologian Godefroi de Fontaines at the time of a dispute over the division of the remains of King Philip II Augustus of France. Money, it was thought, should be distributed to obtain prayers from many holy places, not the body.[134] It is difficult to accept this explanation for nobles and prelates, and still more so for the sovereign. We have seen how the viscera of Louis XIII were thought to be relics, and the debate over the remains of Philip II had the same presupposition. But not even the transformation of mortal remains of sovereigns into relics of saints is entirely satisfactory. I have noted that Prince Charles of England distinguished between the faithful subjects of Rouen and the rebellious barons of Poitiers, who were only worthy to receive his excrement, but that other illustrious viscera became relics, worthy of presentation to the canons of Notre-Dame de Paris. Moreover, the legend of Romulus narrated by Plutarch tells us that the division of a sacred body facilitated the diffusion of the sovereignty associated with it through an entire ruled territory. In many medieval cases we are confronted with this distribution of the body over territory, a multiplication of the presence of the sovereign after death. In short, the point of view expressed by Alain Boureau needs to be reversed. By distributing their bodies, kings anticipated requests from below; they gave rather than asked. Another form of distribution of the kingly body was the feudal kiss on the mouth, with a light emission of saliva into the mouth of the vassal. With this, vassals would take with them a part of the royal body that would serve, wholly and for all, as a representation of the king in a peripheral and distant territory.

In revolutionary France, that is, far from religious "superstition," a heart was nonetheless publicly exhibited at the Cordeliers hall: the heart of Marat.[135]

132. Martene and Durand 1717.

133. Boureau 1988, 36. There is a long list of bodies in Bradford 1933.

134. "Pecunia est res distribuenda et dividenda diversis pro suffragiis impetrandis; corpus autem non est res dividenda vel distribuenda pro talibus." Godefroi de Fontaines 1924, 92.

135. Clark 1994.

2

AT THE END OF THE *NOVELLAE* (105.2.4) the emperor Justinian wrote: "The *tyché* of the emperor will be exempt from all we have decreed, because God has put the laws under him and has sent him to men as the living law." Latanzio, also, in his *Divinae institutiones* (IV.25.1ff.), said that God "sent his ambassador and messenger to teach mortals the precepts of his jurisdiction. . . . Since, in fact, there was no justice on earth, he sent a master, *quasi vivam legem, ut templum novum conderet*" (as a living Law, to found the new Temple). The idea of an animate or "incarnate law" (*nomos empsychos*) originated in the monarchies of the Orient and was developed by rhetoricians and philosophers of the Hellenistic period. Through Plato, the Neoplatonists, and the Neo-Pythagoreans it survived through the whole period of the Roman republic, to appear in the new Rome, on the banks of the Bosporus. The Christian church made it its own, and Christian writers elaborated the theory of the reign of the Word of Christ and of *Christomimèsis*.[1] When Leo IV proclaimed his son Constantine VI co-emperor, in 776, at the moment of coronation he presented him to his subjects with these words: "I give you my son as emperor, but remember that you receive him from the Church and the hands of Christ himself."[2]

In his *Book of Ceremonies,* Constantine Porphyrogenitus transcribed one of the *laudes regiae* that the *demos* sang, with additions, for the anniversary of the coronation of the emperor of the East:

> In your hands today in giving power
> God has confirmed you absolute sovereign,
> and [Christ] the intermediary, descended from heaven,
> has opened before you the doors of the Empire.
> Thus the world is prostrate before the scepter in your right hand,
> giving thanks to the Lord, who is pleased with this;
> He truly wanted you as a pious emperor,
> despot and shepherd, and autocrat![3]

---

1. Beskow 1962.
2. Theophanes 1883, 449–50.
3. Constantin Porphirogénète 1967, II:102. On him, see Bury 1907 and 1920; Toynbee 1973. See also Maas 1912, 28–51; Kantorowicz 1946; Pertusi 1976.

The iconography of the *traditio legis,* as it appears in the Ambrosian ciborium, focuses precisely on this important aspect of the *religio regis.*[4] Justinian expressed it definitively in his law code and transmitted it to Byzantium. From this began a new progress of the concept, through medieval jurists, who in their turn consigned it to those of the Renaissance.[5] Roffroy of Benevento wrote that the emperor Frederick II received the inspiration for his acts (*motus*) from a judgment inspired directly from heaven.[6]

Since the law was inside the monarch, it followed that with every dynastic succession it was necessary to renew the cosmic order that the death of the previous monarch had broken. Thus, the imperial *adventus* (arrival) assumed the characteristics of a renewal of the law. In the old Roman provinces, absent the physical presence of the emperor, priests and people appealed to his *simulacrum,* to his image, as if it were the person himself or his *numen.*[7] To lead the faithful away from iconoclastic doubts, Saint John of Damascus, citing Severinus of Gabala, appealed directly to the example of the *adventus.* "If, in the absence of the emperor, his image replaces him, which the leaders of the community adore and to which they dedicate festivities, inspiring magistrates and adoring notables, they are not looking at a picture, but at the very person of the emperor, presented to them not physically real but painted. Moreover, the image of the immortal king dominates not only stone but also the heavens and the terrestrial universe."[8] (In May of 1597, when the Spanish governor of the Philippines, Francisco Tello, sent as a gift to Taicosama a portrait of himself in which he was depicted with the armor and baton of command, the Japanese king was enraged, maintaining that this was a direct threat.)[9]

In the Hellenistic period, the arrival of the sovereign was celebrated like the arrival of a divinity.[10] This tradition continued under the Roman Empire with the celebration of the *adventus* into Rome and provincial cities: "The opening of the gate, the entrance through the gate is throughout expressly reported. The arrival of the king, or *soter* [savior], was seen as the beginning of a new period of prosperity, peace, and welfare."[11]

This ceremonial tradition did not cease with the fall of the empire. Medieval monarchy was monarchy ceaselessly in motion: "Itinerant kingship refers to government in which a king carries out all the functions and symbolic representations of governing by periodically or constantly traveling throughout the areas of his dominion."[12] This addressed a double fundamental need: to administer justice and to bring the law, which, since it resided in the ruler, had to be distributed through the land. But the entrance of a king, like the "descent" of an emperor into Italy, was not lacking in burdens on his subjects. Not only were they obliged to support the expense, but the visit of a sovereign often brought with it imposition of new taxes that otherwise would have been difficult to collect.[13]

Still other problems affected the mobility of the court. Keeping hundreds of people living in one domicile created hygienic problems that would have been insurmountable

4. Bertelli, Brambilla Barcilon, and Gallone 1981, 20–31.
5. Dvornik 1966, II:723.
6. Kantorowicz 1988, 214ff.
7. Tenfelde 1982.
8. See Setton 1941, 200.
9. Gill 1991, 75.
10. See Rice 1983.
11. Versnel 1970, 386–87.
12. Labarge 1982, 33ff.
13. See Berlier 1929.

had the court not periodically moved to another residence, thus permitting a thorough cleaning of the site or castle that had been vacated. This was the principal reason for movement of the court in the more modern period, when local courts had been established to administer justice in the name of the king. But earlier royal entrances, particularly frequent during the first years of a reign, and starting with the entrance into the capital just after coronation,[14] always had the characteristic of an imposition of the law, as well as of a taking possession. It was for this reason that the procession of a newly crowned pope was called the *Possessio.* These visits were accompanied by a symbolic reciprocity. The city admitted its own submission; the king renewed the privilege granted by his predecessors (and substituted new ones if the old ones had expired with the previous sovereign). At a particularly difficult moment for the French monarchy (between 1564 and 1566) Charles IX and his mother, Catherine de' Medici, found no better recourse than to undertake a long voyage to reaffirm laws and royal authority, following an itinerary along the confines of the realm, reminiscent of a kind of *lustratio.*[15] At Troyes the king was received as a new Charlemagne, a new Hector (playing on the assonance of the city's name with Troy); everywhere, in cities that were seats of Parlements, "to take his place in his palace and in the Court of the Parlement," he administered justice.[16] At Toulouse, in the midst of Lent, mummers, performing in his presence, called to mind "La pieté, et justice que porte / Toy jeune Roy" (The piety, and justice brought / By you, Young King).[17] At Bayonne they announced: "Here the people are placed under your laws."[18]

It would be fascinating to imagine that a derelict fossil of this archaic tradition might be traceable beyond the Strait of Gibraltar, in a region that had also, once, known Roman domination. Before the last century and the French colonization, in the Maghreb the sovereign twice a year organized an expedition into the interior of the country (the *hehalla,* or *harka*—field of victories) to receive tribute. The fact that the cost of the expedition was greater than the tribute collected suggests that this, in reality, was yet a further "representation" of power. J. Dakhlia, studying the symbolism of itinerant power in the Maghreb, speaks of "an archaic polity" and excludes any connection with the entries of medieval and early modern Europe. "These expeditions were interpreted as so many efforts to further the centralization and unification of the realm, efforts that became perpetual repetitions through the violence and greed that characterized the governors of these districts."[19] But still there are numerous points of contact. The itinerant courts of medieval Europe were an integral part of the grand theater of state[20] and also functioned as courts of appeal. The royal progress was followed by numerous carts of merchants, as well as prostitutes and vagabonds, constituting a "traveling fair." The royal visit occasioned markets; it brought plenty, and not only metaphorically. If, at the passage of the sultan, women rushed up with pots filled with milk, so that he could dip his finger in them to assure future wealth,[21] rather similar beliefs drifted around European sovereigns. They

---

14. See Cancellieri 1802; Gattico 1753; Bevy 1766; Lunadoro 1774, 165ff.; Bryant 1990, 89–90; Desplat and Mironneau 1997. A bibliography for the Low Countries is in Landwehr 1971.
15. Bouquet 1572 in Graham and McAllister Johnson 1974; Boutier, Dewerpe, and Nordman 1984.
16. Graham and McAllister Johnson 1974, 85.
17. Graham and McAllister Johnson 1974, 106.
18. Graham and McAllister Johnson 1974, 113.
19. Dakhlia 1988, 736.
20. See, for example, Chartrou 1928; Guenée and Lehoux 1968; Boutier, Dewerpe, and Nordman 1984.
21. Dakhlia 1988, 736.

could be accompanied by magical rites. In Russia, on 6 January, the czar would leave the Hermitage accompanied by the court and Orthodox priests. With his head bared, he proceeded onto the ice of the Neva River. Immediately after, his subjects made a hole in the ice to draw up the blessed water and drink it like a medicine.

As for violence and greed, even in Europe subjects might rebel against the onerous impositions of hospitality that accompanied royal visits (from forced housing of the court to the expense of ceremonial). When, in 1402, Martin I asked the inhabitants of Valencia to prepare not only one but three entrances, for himself, for the queen, and finally for his daughter-in-law Blanche de Navarre, the city tried to resist, and in the end it had to pay out the highest sum of money paid that whole century (6,193 *libras*).[22] Five years later the city of Carmona refused to open its gates to the people of Ferdinand de Antequera.[23]

The idea that the prince was the unique *fons juris* and that the *lex* was in *pectore ejus* was taken up by jurists at the University of Bologna, called by the Emperor Frederick II to the Diet of Roncaglia. "Tu," they answered him, "lex viva, potest dare, solvere, condere leges" (You, living law, can give, cancel, establish the laws), and still more explicitly Andreas de Isernia (died 1353), in the *Peregrina lectura super constitutionibus et glossis Regni Siciliae,* explained (D.1.3.22.V): "lex, id est imperator qui est lex animata in terris" (law, that is, the emperor, who is the living law on earth). The same concept was expressed by Johannes a Deo: "[F]or the prince is not subject to laws. He himself is the living Law on earth."[24] And Giovanni d'Andrea (died 1348), referring to the sovereignty of the pope, affirmed (C.II.VI.I–14) that if arbiters wanted to appeal to the same law as that which gave them power, they had all the more reason to appeal to the pope, "qui est lex animata in terris" (who is the living law on earth).[25]

One has to wait for English jurists of the fourteenth century to find an opinion that was diametrically opposed. "The king is subordinate to God and the law, because the law creates the king," Sir John Fortescue (1394–ca. 1476) wrote in a political treatise that referred to Saint Thomas Aquinas.[26] This idea was subversive of the *religio regis,* but it was not shared by all, even in England, since it arguably led to a *reductio ad hominem* of the divinity of the king.

If the king was the very personification of the laws, it followed that after his death the bond that kept the community of subjects united and in order might also fail. This loss created the sense of a "gap": a crisis.

Remembering the studies of van Gennep (1873–1957), we can recognize here one of the central moments of those "rites of passage" that help to define, emphasize, or conjure the peril implicit at all moments of crisis. Pierre Bourdieu has called them more recently "acts of social magic," moving the emphasis from a "passage" to a "limit," to the creation of an "arbitrary limit."[27] But none of the cases he points to (marriage, circumcision, the conferring of titles or honors) can be extended to our case. The *justitium* in an interregnum was more than a "limit," it was a "gap," a point of suspension and a moment of social anguish. It was above all a loss of identity. To the nature of this loss we will now turn.

22. Maxwell 1994; but see also Maxwell 1992.
23. Maxwell 1994.
24. Cited in Kantorowicz [1957] 1981, 131.
25. See Kantorowicz 1988, 204ff.
26. Baumer 1940, 10–11.
27. Bourdieu 1982.

3

Rituals of Violence

FOLLOWING THE INFLUENCE OF THE WORK on Rabelais by the Russian structuralist Michail Bachtin,[1] many historians have confined rituals of violence in premodern societies to the types of festivities that accompanied carnival. One should consider that it was not so much carnival that contained the seeds of rebellion, but rather that by bringing together large crowds, carnival presented the occasion for violent outbursts that had their origins elsewhere.[2]

A constant and recurrent type of violence that went beyond the specific occasion presented by a festival was what occurred on the death of a prince. This always opened a fissure in the fabric of society. Van Gennep distinguished three moments of crisis—the separation (preliminal rites), the margin (liminal rites), and the aggregation (postliminal rites)—with regard to the period of time extending between death and burial.[3] But we will consider the "margin" to be the period of time (not always the same for all societies) extending between physical death and the entry of the defunct into the hereafter. For a Roman emperor, the margin lasted a week. For a pope it was extended to nine days (the *novemdiali*), as the *Liber pontificalis* noted on the death of Nicholas V and the election of Calixtus III: "celebratis de more novem dierum exequiis, cardinal Valentinus, natione Hispanus, eligitur pontifex" (after nine days of mourning, the Spanish cardinal Valentinus was elected pope).[4] This was confirmed for a later period by Cavalier Girolamo Lunadoro: "The obsequies for a deceased pope last for nine days."[5] Twenty-four hours after death, the body of the pope was opened for embalming, and the viscera were placed in an urn to be deposited by the Cappellani Secreti in the parish church of SS. Vincenzo e Anastasio, near the Quirinal. The body was exhibited in the Vatican for nine days for different reasons. If the body was that of a supposed saint, its incorruptibility needed to be verified. As well, the exhibition of the body confirmed the legitimacy of the empty see and the convocation of a conclave.

Chroniclers emphasized the rapid putrefaction of the body of the hated pope Alexander VI (Roderigo Borgia). The recorder of ceremonies Johann Burchard wrote that

---

1. Bachtin 1965.
2. See above all Le Roy Ladurie 1979; Muir 1997.
3. Van Gennep 1909. For a further development of this concept, and on the "social function" of the rite, see Bourdieu 1982.
4. *Liber pontificalis* 1886–92, II:559.
5. Lunadoro 1774, 62. For the relation between the papal *novena* and the Roman *novemdiale sacrum*, see Freistedt 1928, 127–45.

after the corpse was placed on the bier, "corruption advanced apace, and the face became black, so that on the thirty-third hour, when I saw it, it was reduced to a black mask, or rather seemed that of a Negro, wet everywhere, the nose swollen, the mouth enormous, the tongue swollen and protruding from the open lips, so horrible that everyone said it was hard to believe. That night it was carried . . . to the Cappella delle Febbri . . . by six porters, who joked among themselves about the pope."[6] The scorn of the porters had a ritual aspect, emphasizing that the dead man was not welcomed among the saints. The same horror was echoed in the dispatch of the Venetian ambassador Giustinian: "at midnight he was carried *de more* to the Church of St. Peter and shown to the people; *tamen* it was the most ugly, monstrous, and horrendous corpse ever seen, without the form or figure of a man. Out of shame they kept him partly covered, and then before sundown they buried him."[7] It was enough to arouse the suspicion of poison, a suspicion that underlay the prudent words of the ambassador from Mantua, Giovanni Lucido Cataneo, when he reported from Rome on 19 August 1503: "his face was all black and swollen, and no suspicion of poison, although father and son had been sick at the same time."[8]

During the period of the vigil, van Gennep writes, "social life is suspended. . . . If the dead man is a chief, this suspension leads to complete immobility. From this arises the 'periods of license' that follow the death of some small African chiefs, public mourning, leave-takings."[9] In Rwanda, death of the king threw the land into such a deep crisis that fecundity itself was affected; sexual contact was prohibited. Men and women, flocks and herds, were separated for the whole four months of mourning. Even further, the enthronement that followed was linked to primordial incest,[10] a myth that suggests to me the concept of *rex a legibus solutus* (the king freed from the law). A different example that could be cited is that of Madagascar, where the funeral rites lasted several weeks, allowing the decomposition of the king's body. As the rites developed, sexual orgies and intercourse were permitted between any members of the opposite sex, irrespective of the usual social norms.[11] In other African states, even the capital was moved. The old one was destroyed on the death of the sovereign. Among the Swazi, his death threw the land into night, and the "margin" period was extended for two whole years. Only in the winter of the third year was the new capital built.[12] "The mechanism that determined the periodic suspension of the state, in the case of precolonial African kingdoms, can be seen in the personal link established between he who held power, on one hand, and the structure (places and institutions) of power, on the other. With the death of the king, the structures of the state also fell. This tie prevented the successor from reoccupying the old capital, or from installing himself on the same site where his predecessor had reigned."[13] In this continual destruction of the past, Remotti sees a temporal cycle, and he says that there was a need for regeneration in archaic societies.[14] In reality, we know that the bond between the monarch and the state structures resulted from the concept of *lex in pectore ejus* (the law within his breast).

6. Burchard 1883–85, III:243.
7. Giustinian 1876, II:124–25.
8. Pastor [1906–33] 1950–63, III (1950): 873.
9. Van Gennep 1909, 212.
10. See Heusch 1982, 132ff.; Balandier 1982.
11. Bloch 1998, 72.
12. Heusch 1982, 245ff. But see also Remotti 1986, 71–90.
13. Remotti 1993, 53. For the kingdom of Bamum, see Tardits 1980, 572ff.
14. Remotti 1993, 55.

A "marginal" period linked to the interregnum can be documented in the Muslim world as well. In Egypt, as the diaries of Marin Sanudo tell us, at the death of the sultan "Caithbei" (Qā'it Bāy), on 7 August 1496, "all the streets of Cairo were blocked and the bazaars closed, and Arabs flocked in everywhere, robbing and devastating the place."[15] The Roman noble Pietro della Valle, in a letter sent from Esfahān on 8 August 1620, recorded a similar custom in Persia. The king had fallen gravely ill, "and there was great danger to his life, so that the Chizilbascì, which are the majority and most noble part of the militia, having not seen him for some days, began to riot. Thus the Begùm . . . , hearing the dangerous tumult of the Chizilbascì, said to the king that there was no time to be lost if they didn't want to be killed in the palace, as often happens in these cases when a new king is raised up. And finally, gravely ill though he was, and very weak, he had them put him on a litter . . . and take him out to be seen by the court and soldiers."[16]

But the suspension of all law was not limited to Egypt or Persia, or to African tribal chiefs, as van Gennep and Robert Hertz believed, although they were pioneers in this field of study. The report of Pietro della Valle can be related to an episode in Rome during the fatal illness of Pope Honorius III (1227), who showed himself "exhausted and half dead" to the Roman people from a window in the Lateran Palace in an effort to end the violence that had already broken out in the city.[17]

A death that could not be hidden, because there was no immediate successor, was in fact that of a bishop, a cardinal, or, above all, a pope. Not only did the period of mourning for popes last three days longer than that for kings, the breaking of the fisherman's ring and seal clearly indicated a suspension of the law. Moreover, the empty see and the convocation of the College of Cardinals and conclave signaled the beginning of an interregnum that would not end until the election of a successor. This interregnum and suspension of the law was always marked among the papal "family" and the Roman people by disorder and looting.[18] No chronicle of a conclave fails to call this a period of turbulence and riot, which made Rome a no-man's-land, "where criminals roamed at will at the expense of the peaceful inhabitants."[19] Already in 633 the Fourth Council of Toledo condemned the violence of the interregnum.[20] A decree of the Council of Rome in 898 spoke of the illicit custom of assaulting the Lateran Palace on the death of a pope.[21] The decree threatened not only "ecclesiastical censure" but also imperial punishment (*indignatio*). In 1051, Pope Leo IX protested against the townspeople of Osimo, who had sacked the bishop's palace on the death of their prelate. They had cut down the vineyard and set fire to the houses of the bishop's peasants. What seems significant was the pontiff's condemnation of the "perverse and execrable habits of some townspeople,"[22] thus suggesting the existence of a tradition.

Exhortations and threats do not seem to have had the effect of restraining the violence. The diarist Stefano Infessura has left a detailed description of the disorders that broke out in Rome in 1484, on the death of the Genoese pope Sixtus IV. Most notably, a

15. Sanudo 1879–1915, I:321.
16. Della Valle 1650, *La Persia*, II:175.
17. Matthaeus Parisiensis [1874] 1964, II:294.
18. See Nussdorfer 1987.
19. Jones 1883, 401.
20. Barbero de Aguilera 1970, 272 n.
21. In *Conciliorum oecumenicorum: Decreta* 1962.
22. Baronio [1588–1607] 1738–45, XVII (*Annales, ad annum 1051*): 59–60.

group of youths went to the palace of Count Girolamo Riario, nephew of the pope, and sacked it ("disrobaverunt atque dextruxerunt"), leaving no door or window intact. Others went to Castel Giubileo, to an estate of Countess Caterina Sforza-Riario, "where they made off with a hundred cows and many pigs, asses, geese, and chickens belonging to the countess, and as well a great quantity of salted meat and wheels of Parmesan cheese [already!], along with a large quantity of Greek wine, and divided all this among themselves."[23] On return to Rome, they broke into the grain storehouses of San Teodoro and Santa Maria Nova. At Sant'Andrea delle Fratte, meanwhile, Battista Collerosso and his sons assaulted the shop of a baker, killing him. The Ponte Nuovo was barricaded against the inhabitants of Trastevere, who were assaulted by Bernardo della Valle and his soldiers, while bands of youths in the streets attacked any seeking shelter with their belongings, as well as the storehouses of Giovanni Battista Palavicini (cousin of Count Girolamo) and of another merchant and the *hospitium* (inn) of a Genoese. They even attacked and looted the cargo and navigation instruments of two Genoese ships anchored in the Tiber.[24]

Throughout this account at least three things stand out: the suspension of all legality, even to the point that a cohort of soldiers were involved in the tumult; the existence of bands of youths; and the fact that attacks were directed, beyond kinsmen and associates of the pope, against a minority of foreigners (in this case Genoese, to whose ethnic group the pope belonged).

Similarly dramatic were the events that followed the earlier-mentioned death of Pope Alexander VI Borgia. Again they can be followed from the diary of Johann Burchard:

He died at the hour of vespers, having received extreme unction from Bishop "Calmensis" [of Carinola, vicar of Rome, Pedro Gamboa], with the diarist, the bishop, and attendants present. The duke [Cesare Borgia], who was ill, sent Don Micheletto [da Corella] with a lot of people to close all the doors of the papal palace, but one of these drew a dagger and threatened Cardinal [Jacopo] Casanova, saying that, if he did not give over the pope's keys and money, they would cut his throat and throw him from a window. Terrified, the cardinal gave up the keys, and they went into a room behind the pope's chamber and took all the plate and two chests with about a hundred thousand ducats. About the twenty-third hour the doors were opened and the pope's death was announced. The servants immediately took away what remained in the storerooms, and they left nothing with the papal arms except the papal throne and some cushions and hangings on the walls.[25]

Washed and dressed, the body of Alexander VI was placed on a bier in the Camera del Pappagallo and then taken to the Cappella Maggiore, and thence to the basilica, "ad locum solitum." While the funeral ceremonies began and the clergy intoned the funeral chants, some soldiers who were supposed to be guarding the Vatican Palace broke into the church and tried to loot the lighted candlesticks. "The clergy defended themselves; the soldiers drew their arms against the priests, who fled to the sacristy, leaving the pope

23. "ubi centum vaccas et totidem capras et multos porcos, asinos, anseres et gallinas, quae erant Comitissae abstulerunt; intra quae maxima copia carnium salatarum, casci rotundi parmensis et ulterius casei, suppellectilia et magnum copiam vini graeci; et suppellectila inter eos divisa extiterunt."

24. Infessura 1890, 161ff.

25. Burchard 1883–85, III:238.

abandoned in a corner." Burchard said that he ran himself to save the pope's bier, along with three others, "and we carried it between the high altar and the papal throne, with his head toward the altar, and when the funeral ceremony ended, we locked up the choir." But then the bishop of Sessa, Martin Zapata, fearing that harm might be done to the body ("which would be a scandal, if someone he had offended took vengeance"), had the bier carried into the Cappella delle Febbri, "where it remained all day, with the grille well locked."[26]

Soldiers, servants, porters—all thus conformed to an accustomed ritual of violence. The conclave was convened in the Church of Santa Maria sopra Minerva, and the streets of Rome were blocked with chains to impede the passage of men-at-arms on horseback. This did not prevent the Spanish from assaulting and setting fire to the Palazzo Orsini on Monte Giordano. On the evening of 22 July a hundred of Prospero Colonna's horsemen entered the city, and all night fires were kept burning and there were cries of "Colonna! Colonna!" The following night Lodovico da Pitigliano and Fabio Orsini entered the city with two hundred horsemen and a thousand men on foot; they took possession of Porta San Pancrazio. "They killed three innocent Spaniards . . . and sacked about a hundred houses near the palace of the vice chancellor and Pozzo Albo," resisting two successive assaults, on 24 and 25 July, by soldiers of Don Miguel de Corella.[27]

Anyone who might try to give a political/ideological explanation in a modern key for such disorder (revolt against a tyrant, explosion of political and/or social discontent) would be wrong. A similar tumult, on the surface contradictory, happened at the Palace of the Inquisition on the evening of 18 August 1559, as soon as the death of Pope Paul IV was announced. The notary Roberto di Paoli tells us that many prisoners were freed "furore populi" but that the same people also threw into the flames many Protestant books "sectae luteranae" that were found in the palace, which the crowd then demolished.[28] In this case, an explanation focusing on the particular nature of the prisoners (heretics or accused as such) would entirely miss the point.

Often the recourse to looting was initiated even by the relatives and the "family" of the defunct. Amion, in his *Tableau,* writes: "[W]hen the pontiff was in his death agony, his nephews and servants carried off from the palace whatever they could. Immediately after death, the officials of the Camera Apostolica robbed the body of anything of value. But in general those closest to the pontiff assaulted him, with impunity, leaving only the bare walls of the room and the body lying on a poor mattress with an old wooden candlestick and a burned-out candle end."[29] Indeed, Jacques de Vitry, cardinal of Tuscolo (1198–1216), reported that the body of Innocent III, who died at Perugia on 16 July 1216, was denuded by the faithful: "The body was abandoned in church almost naked."[30] In his own chronicle, Salimbene de Adam (1284) said that Innocent IV, who died in Naples on 7 December 1254, "lay naked on the straw, abandoned by all, following the custom of Roman pontiffs when they die."[31] Johann Burchard, as we have seen, said much the same about the death of Alexander VI. He wrote in his *Liber notarum,* "Die veneris 4 Februarii" [1503],

---

26. Burchard 1883–85, III:240–41.
27. Burchard 1883–85, III:244–50.
28. Bromato 1753, II:577–82; Pastor [1906–33] 1950–63, VI:585.
29. Amion cited in Jones 1883, 401.
30. Vitry 1960, 73.
31. Salimbene de Adam 1966, 608.

that the pope, asking him to approach the bed where he lay sick, said "that he remembered having seen many pontiffs, newly expired, abandoned by their relatives and familiars, left in such an indecent state that they were lying naked, their private parts exposed."[32] Paris de' Grassi remembers that Pope Julius II told of his dreaded fear that, on his death, his body would be abandoned on the bare earth, while the papal apartments were given over, as usual, to looting.[33] This was the fate that William the Conqueror suffered in medieval England. Ordericus Vitalis tells that on William's death (9 September 1087) the knights and royal officials who were to keep vigil over the body abandoned it to its destiny. "The lesser attendants, seeing that their superiors had absconded, seized the arms, vessels, clothing, linen, and all the royal furnishings, and hurried away, leaving the king's body almost naked on the floor of the house. . . . Each one of them, like a bird of prey, seized what he could of the royal trappings and made off at once with the booty. So when the just ruler fell, lawlessness [*iusticario labente*] broke loose, and first showed itself in the plunder of him who had been the avenger of plunder."[34] Even the transit of French kings seems to show this cruel custom, at least through the twelfth century.[35]

We shall see shortly what possible explanations there are for such violent behavior initiated by the very familiars of the defunct. Certainly we would be misled by the theme of the fleeting nature of life in the words pronounced before the pontifex after he was crowned, during the ceremony (passed on from Byzantium) of the burning of bundles of linen straw: "sic transit gloria mundi."[36] I think we have to search in two different directions, although they are complementary: on one hand, toward the concept of the suspension of the law; on the other, toward the belief in thaumaturgic powers present, even after terrestrial life, in the body of the sovereign.

Consider the following, on the death of Henry II (1136):

> When King Henry, the peace of his country and father of his people, came to his last moments and paid his debt to death, the grievous calamity made the entire aspect of the kingdom troubled and utterly disordered. For where, during his reign, had been the font of righteous judgment and the abode of law, there, on his decease, grew up abundance of iniquity and a seed-plot of all manner of wickedness; inasmuch as England, formerly the seat of justice, the habitation of peace, the height of piety, the mirror of religion, became thereafter a home of perversity, a haunt of strife, a training-ground of disorder, and a teacher of every kind of rebellion. The sacred obligations of hallowed friendship were at once broken among the people; the closest bonds of relationship were loosened. . . . For every man, seized by a strange passion for violence, raged cruelly against his neighbor and reckoned himself the more glorious the more glibly he attacked the innocent.[37]

The danger of urban disorder associated with the death of the monarch and the interregnum was strong enough in England to oblige successors, on the eve of their coronations, to close themselves in the Tower of London. Sir George Buck, in his *History of King*

---

32. Burchard 1906, I:428.
33. Döllinger 1862–82, III:428–29.
34. Ordericus Vitalis 1969–80, IV:100–103; Hope 1907, 520.
35. Erlande Brandenburg 1975, 17.
36. See Paravicini Bagliani 1994, 190.
37. *Gesta Stephani* 1976, 3–4. See also Richard of Hexam 1861, 39–41.

Richard the Third (1619), explained that the coronation procession departed from the tower, "being not only the chief house of the king, but also the castle of the greatest strength and of the most safety in this kingdom. And he was to keep his court there until such time as the more weighty affairs of the kingdom were well ordered and settled and the troubles and seditions, if any happened (and which often happen at the alteration of reigns and at the death of princes), were composed and appeased."[38]

One form of violence that most often accompanied an interregnum was a pogrom. At the time of the coronation of Richard I (1189) Londoners abandoned themselves to two days of atrocities against the Jews, giving an example to other inhabitants of the realm. We can follow the testimony of Richard of Devizes:

> Now in the year of our Lord's incarnation 1189, Richard, the son of King Henry the Second, by Eleanor, and brother of Henry the Third, was consecrated king of the English by Baldwin, archbishop of Canterbury, at Westminster, in the nones of the third of September. On the very day of the coronation, about that solemn hour in which the Son was immolated to the Father, a sacrifice of the Jews to their father, the Devil, was commenced in the city of London, and so long was the duration of this famous mystery that the holocaust could scarcely be accomplished the ensuing day. The other cities and towns of the kingdom emulated the faith of the Londoners, and with a like devotion dispatched their bloodsuckers with blood to hell.[39]

The justification for this act given by Roger of Wendover is partial and incomplete. The king had prohibited Jews from presenting themselves at the coronation ceremony "propter magicas incantationes, quae fieri solent in coronationibus regum" (because of the magical incantations usual in times of coronation). When some were discovered, they were assaulted by soldiers and the royal guard: "the courtiers, although the Jews had appeared dressed as women, took them in hand and undressed them and frightened them with strong abuse, and while they fled from the church, some killed them, others left them barely living."[40] The task of completing the lynching was left to the crowd. In this case the pogrom did not come before but happened at the same time as the coronation. And this was not much different from incidents, more closely tied to the interregnum, that had appeared in England on other occasions.

There were similar incidents in Italy. In 1590, on the news of the death of Pope Sixtus V, inhabitants of Bologna sacked the synagogue and property of the Jews. They succeeded where the Romans had failed a few days previously. A report from Rome from 11 July tells us that when a false rumor spread that the pope had expired, the Jews, who had their market on Wednesdays in the Piazza Navona, hastened to collect their merchandise and flee, out of fear of a riot.[41]

It appears that similar acts of violence occurred in the lands of the Holy Roman Empire. On the death of Emperor Henry II (1024) the imperial castle at Pavia was sacked by his subjects.[42] The *Gesta Chuonradi* documents the preoccupation of the new emperor,

38. Buck [1619] 1982, 24.
39. Richard of Devizes 1848, III:383.
40. Roger de Wendover 1886, 166.
41. Nores 1847, 452–53, doc. XLI; Pastor [1906–33] 1950–63, X:409–10.
42. Solmi 1924.

Conrad II (1027–39), with avoiding the perpetuation of such a custom that tended to suggest a suspension of legality in the interregnum. The kingdom—the emperor said, referring to the inhabitants of Pavia—does not perish with the death of its sovereign. "Si rex periit, regnum remansit, sicut navis remanet, cuis gubernator cadit" (When the king dies, the kingdom remains, just as a ship remains after its captain has fallen).[43] These words were difficult for the subjects in question to comprehend, given that the imperial chancellery had advised them in another direction. When later, under Frederick Barbarossa (1152–90), the chancellery under the Hohenstaufen Reinald von Dassel began to call the emperor *sacrum* or *sanctissimus,* implying that the emperor had acquired his own *numen,* it seemed to follow that the place where he lived, that is, the imperial *palatium,* acquired the same appellation. How could one not see in this a still stronger link between the physical place and the *numen?*

A custom shared by many ethnic groups was not to proclaim the successor of a leader until after the final ceremony of burial. There was still, however, a "marginal" period that corresponded to the period of mourning. This period of time contained perils but could not be avoided. The belief shared by many, that an individual was not fully admitted to the kingdom of the dead until his skeleton was freed from the flesh, caused a prolongation of the period of mourning, beyond the usually fixed one of seven to nine days. In some cases seven or eight months, perhaps even a year, were required between the moment of death and the final burial.[44] For the Roman Church, a saint or canonized person was not received into heaven until his remains underwent a *translatio,* which is, strictly speaking, a second burial. The problem, in the case of the death of a leader, was assuring the government of the community and avoiding the dissolution of continuity. In the Fiji Islands, the subject tribes invaded the capital and committed every kind of excess and violence with impunity. Among the Maori, the family of the leader was robbed of its reserve of foodstuffs and mobile property. A traveler of the early eighteenth century, Bosman, witnessed a similar suspension of the law in Guinea: "[A]s soon as the death of the king becomes public knowledge, everyone hastens to rob his neighbor without there being any means of punishment, as if with the death of the king justice also died." But the violence stopped as soon as the successor was proclaimed.[45]

In his *Death and the Right Hand,* Hertz writes:

> [T]he death of a chief causes a deep disturbance in the social body which, especially if it is prolonged, has weighty consequences. It often seems that the blow which strikes the head of the community in the sacred person of the chief has the effect of suspending temporarily the moral and political laws, of setting free the passions which are normally kept in check by the social order. In Fiji, the secret is kept for a period varying between four and ten days; then, when the subjects, who begin to suspect something and who are impatient to be able legitimately to pillage and destroy, come to ask whether the chief has died, they are told that "his body is decomposed by now." It only remains for the disappointed visitors to go away, they have come too late and have missed their opportunity. The idea at work here is that so long as the decomposition is not sufficiently advanced, one is not really finished with the deceased, and his authority cannot be trans-

43. Wipo 1915, 30.
44. Hertz 1978, 43.
45. Hertz 1978, 106.

mitted to his successor: the hand of the deceased can no longer hold the scepter, but it has not yet let go. One must wait for the king to be entirely dead before one can cry: Long Live the King![46]

All this helps us to understand why, at the moment of the death of a sovereign, it was so important to avoid a suspension of the civil, moral, and political laws that held the community together and prevented an explosion of the passions that waited under their cover. "The interval [between death and burial] may be reduced to such an extent that both ceremonies form a single continuous whole."[47] What interests us is the masking of the period of mourning/interregnum, as if it were a prolonged illness.

We do not need to look far to find examples of funeral ceremonies designed to fill the void of power during the interregnum. There are not only anthropological but also historical examples of how the agony of the disappearance of a sovereign was presented in past European civilization. In ancient Rome, the death of the emperor was followed by a period of interregnum called the *justitium,* which lasted until the end of the funeral ceremonies and the cremation, the end of the "marginal" period. All judicial functions were suspended for the duration of the *justitium.* But there was also a funeral rite: the apotheosis, that is, the cremation of the body in effigy (*funus imaginarium*).[48] The custom of burning an effigy is certainly very old. Herodotus says that the Scythians, when one of their kings was killed in battle, made an image of his body "and carried it on a ceremonial bier to the tomb." Then, after the funeral, they held no assemblies for ten days and gathered for no elections, since these days were considered to be a period of mourning.[49] This also appears to have been a kind of *justitium,* arranged after, rather than before, the funeral ceremony. Another Greek, Herodian, who wrote a history of the Roman Empire after Marcus Aurelius, describes the death of Septimius Severus (A.D. 211) (the text is a sixteenth-century translation):

The Romans are accustomed to consecrate with immortality such Emperors as at their death leave either children or successors in their place behind them, and those which are endowed with that honor they canonize among the Gods. There is throughout the city a certain doleful lamentation, mixed with festive joy. And they used to intere the dead corpse very sumptuously, after the common sort of men. But then they have an image made as like the dead Emperor as may be. The same, within the porche of the Imperial palace, they lay in a great high bed of ivory covered with cloths-of-gold. And truly the same image looketh very pale, like unto a diseased patient. About the bed on either side, a great part of the day, do certain persons sit. That is, to wit, on the left side, the Senate, clothed in black garments; and on the right side many matrons, whom either their husbands' or parents' dignities do beautify . . . ; they show the continence of mourners. And thus they continue the space of VII days, during which every day the Emperor's physicians do repair unto the bed, and as though they had felt the patient's pulse, declare that he be more sick than before. Finally, when it seemed that he was deceased, certain of the most noble and worthy young men, of the orders of knights or senators, do take up

46. Hertz 1978, 49.
47. Hertz 1978, 43.
48. See Strong 1915.
49. Herodotus 1969–70, VI:59. For the funerals of Sulla and Caesar, see Weinstock 1971, 346ff., 360–61.

the bed on their shoulders and carry it through the street called the Sacra Via unto the old market place, where the Roman magistrates are accustomed to render up their offices. There, on both sides, are certain stages made with steps, upon which on the one side is a choir of boys, being noble men's sons, and on the other side are many beautiful women singing hymns and ballads in praise of the dead Emperor, measured with diverse lamentable verses. When those are finished the young men do take up the bed again, and bear it out of the city into the field called Campus Martius, in the broadest part whereof there is erected a tower, four square sides of equal height, builded of great timbers, like unto a tabernacle. . . . When they have couched a great heap of spices together and stuffed the building therewith, all the Roman knights do ride about the tower with a just course and order, to and fro, called by them Pirrichius. Chariots are also drawn about, wherein many do sit clothed in purple representing the persons of all noble men, being magistrates and capitains of Rome.[50]

Dio Cassius has a similar description for the funeral of the emperor Pertinax: "The magistrates and the equestrian order, arrayed in a manner befitting their station, and likewise the cavalry and the infantry, passed in and out around the pyre, performing intricate evolutions, both those of peace and those of war."[51]

There is no doubt that this was a prolongation of the reign, or rather a masking of the interregnum. The death was not considered such until the seven days of mourning and the cremation of the image of the emperor were accomplished. The very scene of the cremation site, with the carousel of knights revolving to military music, makes one think of the ritualization of a riot. On the other hand, the procession with chariots and images seemed to signify that the living need no longer fear the dead; he had been welcomed in Hades by his predecessors as soon as his skeleton was freed from the flesh that kept it in the realm of the living.

At the end of the reign of Constantine, when the passage from paganism to Christianity had begun, there was no less preoccupation with preserving imperial power beyond the physical death of the ruler. Eusebius writes in his *Vita Beatissimi imperatori Constantini* that at the moment of death of the first Christian emperor, his sons and successors, the Augusti Constantinus II, Constantius II, and Constans, were far away. The soldiers and courtiers decided to await their arrival in Constantinople to celebrate the funeral, but they also wanted to avoid the problems of an interregnum. Thus the body was put on a raised bier and placed

in a golden coffin, which they enveloped in a covering of purple, and removed it to the city which was called by his own name. Here it was placed in an elevated position in the principal chamber of the imperial palace, and surrounded by candles burning in candlesticks of gold, presenting a marvelous spectacle, and such as no mortal had exhibited on earth since the world itself began. For in the central apartment of the imperial palace, the body of the emperor lay in its elevated resting-place, arrayed in the symbols of sovereignty, the diadem and purple robe, and encircled by a numerous retinue of attendants, who kept watch around it incessantly day and night. The military officers too, of

50. Herodian [ca. 1550], fols. xlvi–xlvii. For the double burial, see Dupont 1986, 231ff.
51. Dio Cassius 1970, LXXV:4:2.

the highest rank, the counts, and the whole order of magistrates, who had been accustomed to do obeisance to their emperor before his death, continued to fulfill this duty without any change, entering the chamber at the appointed times, and saluting their coffined sovereign with bended knee, as though he were still alive. . . . These honors continued to be rendered for a considerable time, the soldiers having resolved thus to guard the body until his sons should arrive, and take themselves the conduct of their father's funeral. No mortal had ever, like this blessed prince, continued to reign even after death, and to receive the same homage as during his life: he only, of all who ever lived, obtained this reward from God: a suitable reward, since he alone of all sovereigns had in all his action honored the Supreme God and His Christ, and God Himself accordingly was pleased that even his mortal remains should still retain imperial authority among men; thus indicating to all who were not utterly devoid of understanding the immortal and endless empire which his soul was destined to enjoy.[52]

In this way—and the comment is extremely significant—the emperor was able to continue to govern his empire, without a dissolution of continuity. "Thus, too, he continued to possess imperial power even after death, controlling, as though with renovated life, a universal dominion and retaining in his own name, as Victor, Maximus, Augustus, the sovereignty of the Roman world."[53] A *de facto* interregnum of about three months was observed after the emperor's death, during which the laws and edicts continued to be issued in his name.[54]

The same preoccupation was present under the Holy Roman Empire. We do not know how the emperor Charlemagne was buried; even the site of his tomb has been lost to memory, although the chapel at Aix has been called the "sepulchrum sancti Karoli." But Otto III searched for it, and according to the bishop Thietmar of Merseburg, on the day of Pentecost in the year 1000 the tomb was found and opened: "[M]agni imperatoris Karoli ossa contra divinae religionis ecclesiastica effodere praecepit, quae tunc in abdito sepulturae mirificae varietates invenit" (Against the holy Christian laws, the emperor ordered that the bones of the great emperor Charles be unearthed, which were discovered in a hidden part of a wondrous tomb).[55] Thietmar added that Otto found his predecessor "in solio regio," and it has been debated whether that meant "on a faldstool" or "in a regal sarcophagus."[56] We should keep in mind that from the second half of the fifth century the *festa cathedrae domni Petri apostoli* (feast of the throne of Peter the Apostle) was established in Rome, that it involved a throne, and that it began to be observed in Gaul in the following century.[57] The count of Lomello, a courtier of Otto, also left an account of the event, which was included in the Chronicle of Novalesa (ca. 1027). The Carolingian emperor was not found lying down, like common mortals, but seated on a throne, dressed in imperial robes, a golden cross at his neck, a globe and scepter in his hand, the Bible at his feet. This was the burial custom for Byzantine emperors, and it remained, nearly to our time, the one observed for patriarchs of Constantinople.[58] It is probable that the *inventio* (discovery)

52. Eusebius of Cesarea, PG, xx:1221ff. (English trans., 1845, 228ff.).
53. Eusebius of Cesarea, PG, xx:1221b; see also Franchi de' Cavalieri 1916–17, 265ff.
54. Giesey 1960, 153.
55. Thietmar 1935, III:92.
56. Folz 1973a, 91.
57. Klauser 1971, 157.
58. See Giesey 1960, 154–55.

of the tomb was only an "invention" of Otto III.[59] What is interesting is not so much the philological reconstruction of the event—whether the remains were really those of the emperor, or whether the most illustrious of the Carolingians was really buried sitting on a throne—as the fact that Otto wanted to find him in that position. "Non enim iacebat, ut mos est aliorum defunctorum corpora, sed in quandam cathedram ceu vivus residebat" (He was not lying, as is the custom for the corpses of other dead people, but he was sitting on a kind of throne, as if he were alive).[60] The words of the Novalesa chronicle reveal the significance of a burial of this type. Did Otto III arrange it? Certainly in the biography of Conrad II written by his chaplain Wipo between 1040 and 1046, the stone throne at Aix-la-Chapelle was identified as that of Charlemagne and called "totius regni archisolium" (the throne of the whole empire).[61] Conrad, the living incarnation of the Frankish emperor, sat on it to promulgate his own laws.[62] The cult of Saint Charlemagne appeared at this time, which had such good fortune in the Germanic world.[63] Promotion of the sanctity of Charlemagne was carried forward by Frederick Barbarossa as an integral part of his own imperial program. Already in 1164 Reinald von Dassel organized a grandiose ceremony at Cologne for the *translatio* of the bodies of the three Magi kings. The imperial decree of 29 December 1165 (then the feast of the king/confessor Saint David) claimed a direct connection between the Carolingian empire and the empire of the Hohenstaufen.[64] The need to "translate" the relics was proclaimed during a ceremony presided over by Frederick himself, who had the supposed tomb reopened and the relics placed in the center of the octagon at Aix: "[T]he body of Lord Charles, taken from his marble sarcophagus, was placed in a wooden vessel at the center of the basilica."[65]

Certainly the idea of burial on a throne, which had also been linked to the prophecies of the Tibertine sibyl and of the Pseudo-Methodius,[66] emerged again in the fifteenth century, in the Po valley, at a moment of dramatic loss of identity for the subjects of the Rossi state, a vast feudal territory adjacent to the commune of Parma. Pier Maria Rossi, the lord, died while he was fighting off an attack on him by Lodovico il Moro, at that time regent of the duchy of Milan, in support of the Pallavicini, eternal rivals of the Rossi. At the moment of his death (in 1482), the war was at its height. His son and his subjects transformed the "Camera d'Oro" (the *cubiculum* of the Lord) in the castle of Torchiara into a tomb. The embalmed body of Pier Maria, dressed in cloth of gold, was placed "on a large chair," and the *nume* of its owner remained there for thirteen years. It was possible for his subjects to look at him through a hole opened in the door.[67]

Vincenzo Gonzaga, in his will dated 3 February 1612, asked expressly to be buried "in the collegial church of Sant'Andrea in Mantua . . . , not lying like the dead, but sitting on the marble throne located there, with his sword at his side."[68] Even in the early eighteenth century, after the death of Cosimo III de' Medici, grand duke of Tuscany, a "room of con-

59. Folz 1973a, 87ff.
60. *Cronaca della Novalesa* 1983, III:32; Jones 1883, 341.
61. Schramm [1929] 1960b, 26.
62. Folz [1950] 1973b, 98ff.
63. Folz 1973a.
64. Folz [1950] 1973b, 208ff.
65. Sigebertus Gemblacensis 1848, VI:411.
66. Cohn 1976, 31ff., 71–72.
67. Giovanni da Cornazzano 1738, *Additamenta*, 752–53, ad annum 1479; Klauser 1971.
68. AS, Mantua, Archivio Gonzaga, b. 330, fols. 350v–351r. Cf. Signorini 1981.

dolence" was arranged for his exhibition in a chair. "The morning of 2 November 1723 he was dressed in ducal robes and placed in a chair in the form of a throne on a bier in the great room of the ducal apartments, where he could be seen continually for three days by a great crowd of people, who came not only to weep tears on viewing this most pious prince, but also to view the apparatus."[69]

The need to respect the interval between natural death and the separation of the flesh from the bones brought with it a series of notable inconveniences. How could one exhibit the body and at the same time avoid showing the horrors of its decomposition? Above all, how could one avoid, during the exhibition of the body, the long and dangerous interval of an interregnum, with its implied suspension of the law? Perhaps precisely for these reasons the use of an effigy made of wood or wax was adopted in England, beginning with the death of Edward II (1327), if not earlier. The Romans, as we have seen, also used this fiction to resolve the problem of the marginal period (*justitium*) between the emperor's death and the celebration of his apotheosis, the *funus imaginarium*. Westminster Abbey still preserves the mannequins of kings and queens used for funeral ceremonies (the "Ragged Regiment"). The patent rolls document the payment to the artisan who did the work: "Item per trecentis libris cere ad faciendum unam imaginem. . . . Item magistro Roberto de Beverlaco pro factura dicte ymaginis sexaginta ses solidorum, et octo dinarios sterlingiorum" (Item, three hundred pounds of wax to make an image. . . . Item to master Roberto de Beverlaco for making said image, sixty-six shillings and eight pence sterling).[70] Unfortunately, full descriptions of the funerals where these images were employed have not survived, although they must have involved some element of theater, since, on the death of James I (1625), a jointed mannequin was commissioned, which could take different positions according to the needs of the ceremony. The entry in the register of the *Great Wardrobe* notes: "Payed to Maximilian Coult for making the body of the representation with several joynts in the armes leggs and body to be moved to several postures and for setting up the same in Westminster Abbey."[71] The English mannequins substituted for the corpse, which could not be preserved for the long period of mourning. At the funeral ceremony for Elizabeth I, attention was focused on her effigy. As Henry Chettle related: "The lively picture of her Highnesse whole body, crowned in her Parliament robes, lying on the corpse balmed and leaded, covered with velvet, borne on a chariot, drawn by four horses draped in black velvet."[72]

The use of life-sized wax images was not a novelty, nor was it limited to England. In a famous essay of 1902, Aby Warburg wrote about the life-sized wax votive statues that existed in medieval Florentine churches,[73] and we know that, also in Florence, in the early fourteenth century, statues of the patrons of the most important confraternities were carried in procession through churches during the offertory.[74]

The English custom of using images in royal funerals may have been reintroduced in France when the problems of an interregnum were being anxiously averted. In 1461 the Parlement of Toulouse, informed of the king's decease, resolved to suspend its audiences

69. *Relazione* 1723.
70. Hope 1907, 527; cf. Hallam 1982.
71. Hope 1907, 557; see also Woodward 1997, 171–72 (for the funeral of Ann of Denmark) and 175ff.
72. Cited in Woodward 1997, 87; see also [Camden] 1600.
73. Warburg 1932.
74. Henderson 1994, 90.

and pronounce no further sentences until it heard "news of permission from the prince ascending the throne."[75] The jurists of Toulouse seem to have been strictly applying the Roman *justitium,* just as it had been interpreted by Bolognese commentators. Accursio, in the *Glossa ordinaria,* had held "that a privilege granted before the coronation" is not valid.[76] But there was a more general problem, the functioning of officials of state. "The common law in this kingdom, to all memory, is that when the king is deceased, all holding offices or estates from him are obliged to make new provision; and by this law one could say that when the king has died, officers and magistrates are no longer what they had been, and can no longer do what they did before."[77] If a charge or benefice came directly from the person of the king, it was evident that the functions and benefits involved should temporarily cease until they were renewed by the new sovereign. In ecclesiastical law, as well, all anticipated benefices expired on the death of the pontiff who had made them.

How could one reconcile these underlying norms with the specific need to keep current affairs and the entire judicial and administrative life of the state in operation? How could one prevent a paralysis of administration and permit a continuity of functions? The answer was found not so much in the separation of the two bodies of the king—as English jurists attempted to do—as through a ceremonial arrangement that changed the funeral into a triumphant entrance: "le roy ne meurt jamais" (the king never dies). The example most often cited is that of the funeral of the English king Henry V, who died in France, at Bois-de-Vincennes, in August of 1422, during the Hundred Years War. The body was treated *more teutonico,* separating the bones from the flesh. In the obsequies, celebrated at Saint-Denis, a mannequin was undoubtedly used.[78] The funeral cortege progressed from Saint-Denis toward Rouen and Calais, and arrived in London on 5 October. Ten days later what remained of the body of the king was buried at Westminster. The mannequin of his wife, Catherine of Valois, remains to this day in Westminster Abbey. Many of the French nobility attended this royal funeral, which was organized by the English with great pomp, and the French gathered together again shortly after to give homage to the remains of their own king, "le bon roi" Charles VI, who died on 21 October. His body remained in the Palace of Saint-Pol until 11 November, and the lament of the anonymous chronicler of the *Journal d'un bourgeois de Paris* expresses the sense of collective loss felt by his subjects:

> Ah! très cher prince, jamais n'aurons si bon prince, jamais ne te verrons. Maudite soit la sort! jamais n'aurons que guerre, puisque tu nous as laissés. Tu va en repos, nous demeurons en toute tribulation et en toute douleur, car nous sommes bien raillés que nous ne soyons en la manière de la chétivasion des enfans d'Israel, quand ils furent menés en Babylonie.[79]

> (Oh dearest prince! We will never have such a good prince again, we will never find one. Cursed fate! We will have only war because you have left us. You go to your rest; we

75. Papon 1568, 91.
76. Accursio 1939, C.7.37.3.
77. Papon 1568.
78. *Journal d'un bourgeois* [1881] 1990, 103.
79. *Journal d'un bourgeois* [1881] 1990, 191 and 192–96.

remain in tribulation and sadness, for we know that we are in a state of captivity like the
children of Israel when they were taken to Babylon.)

Was an English model followed for this funeral? The account of an anonymous
chronicler seems to suggest that it was. While he says that the body was exhibited to the
people for three days, he also adds that it remained at Saint-Pol until 11 November,
Martinmas, when the funeral was finally celebrated with a procession through the streets
of Paris to Notre-Dame. This would be too long a time to exhibit a dead body. The
chronicler says that the bier was carried on the shoulders of thirty followers, "the face uncovered, or its resemblance" (thus, a mask!), with the crown on his head, "in one hand a
royal scepter, while the other hand signed a blessing with two fingers." The hand was
gilded and so long "qu'il advenaient à sa couronne" (that it extended to his crown).[80] Thus
we are almost certainly confronted with a mannequin. When, in the mid–fifteenth century, the great Jean Fouquet was commissioned to model the death mask of Charles VII
(the king had died at Mehun-sur-Yèvre on 22 July 1461), it was not for a funeral but for a
marche triomphale of the dead sovereign into Paris. This was the triumph then repeated for
all French sovereigns up to the most elaborate triumph of all, the one for Francis I, who
died in the castle of St. Cloud in 1547.[81] Jean Du Tillet, writing of these ceremonies, said
that they were copied from Roman triumphs[82] and that, as with the Romans, an effigy
was venerated.[83] But since the text of Herodian was not translated into Latin, by
Poliziano, until 1493, it seems doubtful that his was truly the source of the French ceremony. Instead, it was probably elaborated on the basis of English royal funerals, although it was possibly enriched and further elaborated after the text of Herodian became
known.

Having arrived in Paris, the royal effigy was placed in the salle d'honneur (or de deuil)—
the cubiculum funereum, as the Jesuit François Pomey writes in his Libitina[84]—on a lit
d'honneur covered with a baldacchino.[85] The "family" of the defunct sovereign arranged a
table at the center, for the king's meals, which were served with the same ceremony that
was usually observed, beginning with the blessing of the table (the food was later distributed to the poor). The entire ceremony for the funeral of Francis I is described by Pierre
Du Chastel:

> [T]he effigy remained for eleven days. And it is to be understood that during the time
> that the body was in the chamber next to the great hall, as well as while the effigy was in
> that hall, the fashions of service were observed and kept just as was customary during
> the lifetime of the king: the table being set by the officers of the commissary; the ser-
> vice carried by the gentlemen servants, the bread-carrier, the cupbearer, and the carver,
> with the usher marching before them and followed by the officers of the cupboard, who
> spread the table with the reverences and samplings that were customarily made. After
> the bread was broken and prepared, the meat and other courses were brought in by an

---

80. *Journal d'un bourgeois* [1881] 1990, 191 and 192–96.
81. Du Chastel in Godefroy 1649, 277–308.
82. On him, see Picard 1957 and Bonfante Warren 1970.
83. Du Tillet 1580 cited in Giesey 1960, 146–47.
84. Pomey 1659.
85. Godefroy 1649, 413 (funeral of Henry II).

usher, steward, bread-carrier, pages of the chamber, squire of the cuisine, and *gard-vaisselle*. The napkin was presented by the said steward to the most dignified person present, to wipe the hands of the Seigneur. The table was blessed by a Cardinal; the basins of water for washing the hands were presented at the chair of the Seigneur, as if he had been living and seated in it. The three courses of the meal were carried out with the same forms, ceremonies, and samplings as they were wont to be during the life of the Seigneur, without forgetting those of the wine, with the presentation of the cup at the places and hours that the Seigneur had been accustomed to drink, two times at each of his meals. At the end of the meal, water to wash with was offered and grace said by a Cardinal in the usual manner, except that the *De profundis* and the orison *Inclina Domine aurem tuam* were added. Assisting at the repast were the same people who had been accustomed to speak or respond to the Seigneur during his life, and also others accustomed to be present.[86]

When the moment came to transport the body to the necropolis at Saint-Denis, the four presidents of the Parlement of Paris marched beside the coffin in their purple robes (and not in mourning) to indicate that justice was not dead (Fig. 13). The funeral procession did not proceed without incident, however. Quarrels about precedence broke out around the bier until it was consigned to the monks of the abbey, who were waiting within their territorial boundaries. But the continual preoccupation with avoiding a *justitium* was contradicted in the very structure of the funeral procession: the coffin of the prince was preceded (as in a coronation procession) by the regalia, the symbols of his power. As they had preceded him when he took possession of the realm, they also preceded him to the tomb (Figs. 14–15). In the French ceremony at Saint-Denis, the banners were first lowered into the open tomb with the cry "The king is dead!" and then raised up again: "Long live the king!"

All this makes one think of a similar situation described by L. V. Helms for Bali. On 20 December 1847 Helms had the occasion to observe the funeral of Rjah di Gianjar, a festive spectacle celebrated "with an odor of sanctity." His account was analyzed by Clifford Geertz in his *Negara*. Our attention is drawn to the train that followed the procession, four thrones on four towers: the first with the body of the sovereign, the other three with his widows, who were to be immolated on the same pyre. At the very end of the procession came an unruly crowd of Sudras, members of the fourth and lowest caste, who dragged along the bodies of their own dead, exhumed to be cremated along with the sovereign. Geertz observes that "the scene was a bit like a playful riot—a deliberated, even studied, violence designed to set off a no less deliberated and even more studied silliness, which the variously imperturbable priests, agnates, widows, and tributary dead contributed to gather around the central tower."[87] With a feigned struggle, the Sudras tried to take possession of the body of the rajah, lying at the top of his tower. This struggle was repeated at the moment when the ashes were collected from the pyre. The ceremony ended with a looting of the towers. The whole ceremony was accompanied by military music; it was a "choreographed mob scene."[88]

86. Du Chastel in Godefroy 1649, 280–81, quoted in Giesey 1960, 5.
87. Geertz 1980, 119.
88. Geertz 1980, 119.

Fig. 13   The presidents of the Parlement, dressed in their red robes, flanking the royal coffin in the funeral procession of King Henry IV (18 May 1618), Paris, Bibliothèque Nationale, Cabinet des étampes, Collection Hannin, 1584.

Fig. 14   The regalia exhibited in the coronation procession of James II, from *The History of the Coronation of the Most High, Most Mighty, and Most Excellent Monarch James II,* London, 1695.

Fig. 15   The regalia exhibited in the funeral procession of the archduke Albert of Habsburg (with the pope's sword), from *Pompe funèbre du très puissant prince Albert Archiduc d'Autriche,* Brussels, J. Leonard, 1729.

One might notice that purple was also the color English sovereigns wore when they attended funerals of their subjects, not because it seemed "inappropriate for a reigning sovereign to don the color of mourning and death,"[89] but because, since the law resided *in pectore ejus* (in his breast), showing a color closely related to the concept of sovereignty emphasized the continuity of the law.

A violent funeral was certainly that of Ferdinando II, king of Naples, who died on 5 October 1496: "The body of the dead king was carried to the Castle Capuano, and there showed to the people; many came up and they all went to kiss his foot," the Venetian diarist Marin Sanudo recalled. But at the moment of the funeral ceremony, the crowd broke into the church, knocked over and took possession of the candles that were burning around the bier, making the whole court, cardinals, and ambassadors seek refuge in a chapel. "[A]ll the candlesticks in the church were knocked over with cries and insults. The princes locked themselves in a chapel, with the cardinals and ambassadors, until the tumult ended. All seemed to me in confusion, rather than in any order," the Venetian ambassador wrote, in a letter recorded also by Sanudo.[90]

If one accepts the thesis of Hertz, that funeral ceremonies have a triple scope ("one must give the remains of the dead a final funeral, assure his soul rest and access to the land of the dead, and in the end, free the living from the obligation of mourning"),[91] one can understand how the funeral of a leader might assume a greater importance than a coronation, and how, in fact, one ceremony often accompanied the other. In any event, the coronation itself often paralleled the funeral rite, as van Gennep noted in studying the ancient Egyptians. For his part, Clifford Geertz has convincingly shown that in Bali the ceremony of cremation surpassed in importance the ceremony of coronation. In early modern European history we have two examples where funerals and coronations were mixed: the emperors Charles V and Philip II, and the grand dukes Cosimo I and Francesco I de' Medici.[92] In both cases, the old sovereign had abdicated, and the son had exercised his power, to a certain extent, in tutelage. The funerals were thus at the same time an emancipation and a coronation. In both cases there was a funeral in effigy, with the successor present at the ceremony, unlike what happened in the French ritual. But missing was the interregnum, which the fiction of effigies obscured in the attempt to perpetuate the power of the dead ruler.[93]

Finally there were cases where the physical death of the lord was unnecessary. It was enough for him to be dead politically. On 2 May 1507 Pope Julius II excommunicated Bentivoglio and those of his vassals who were lords of Bologna. Their subjects were released from obedience. The following day the papal governor banned the Bentivoglio clan from the city. Ercole Marescotti and Camillo Gozzadini, patricians who had suffered under their rule, put themselves at the head of the crowd that sacked and literally destroyed the grandiose Bentivoglio palace, a masterpiece of Renaissance architecture:

> At two o'clock an order arrived from the pope, who, under penalty of excommunication, prohibited any lords or people of any state or condition, either men or women,

89. Woodward 1997, 19.
90. Sanudo 1879–1915, 1:347, 351, and 366.
91. Hertz 1978, 63.
92. See Pietrosanti 1990 and 1991; Borsook 1965–66.
93. Giesey 1987; for a critique, see Pietrosanti 1991.

from giving assistance, favor, or counsel to the Bentivogli and their followers ... at three ... the legate of Bologna forbade the Bentivogli to flee. .... That same day, the feast of the Holy Cross, at eighteen hours, Ercole Marescotti, having the consent of the legate, took to horse, along with Camillo Gozzadini. They had two hundred men on foot armed with axes and other hand weapons, and before them a standard with the arms of the Marescotti. They headed to the street of San Donato to tear down the beautiful palace of Giovanni Bentivoglio. And on their way they called for everyone to witness this destruction ... and the first fires were set around the building. .... Then, excited by the news, the plebes quickly began to loot anything they could find, even the doors, windows, and so on. The wine casks were opened, and most of the wine ended up on the ground, despite the intent of looting the casks. Some climbed up on the roof (oh wicked hands!) and began to throw down tiles to get at the beams; others, in the gardens, dug up the trees and looted the basins and statues of the lovely fountains; some were intent on ruining the strong handsome tower, and others on wrecking the beautiful pictures painted by such skillful hands. In short, none stood by idle; rather all were ready to tear down whatever they could.[94]

It is difficult to provide a single explanation for such ritual looting that was tied to the body of the lord, because such violence was not associated only with physical or political death. It also occurred at the moment when a new lord came to power. Both situations emphasized a moment of crisis, passage, and "margin." Following the classification of van Gennep, we could speak of rituals "of departure" and rituals "of entry." It is difficult to insert the case of Richard I of England into this simplified scheme, but what happened in Florence in 1537 is clear, although certainly more complex. The historian Benedetto Varchi was a witness. As soon as word spread of the election of Cosimo de' Medici as signore, by the Senate of 48, the soldiers of Alessandro Vitelli—an imperial condottiere sent to Florence to maintain order (!)—"by a secret order of Alessandro hastened to the palace of Signor Cosimo, followed by some plebeians, who shouted the usual cry 'Palle! Palle!' and 'Duca! Duca!' (a cry favoring the Medici), put it to sack along with the one of Lorenzo" (who had assassinated the previous duke, Alessandro), "carrying away even the nails, without his mother, relatives, and friends being able to restrain them in any way, with good or bad, prayers or threats."[95]

The witness of another Florentine historian, Bernardo Segni, is a bit different: "Cosimo immediately came up and was hailed by the 48 and by Alessandro Vitelli, who was in the street with five hundred infantry crying out *Palle! Palle!* To honor the new signore, and in vendetta against the dead duke, and to satisfy his greed for gold, Vitelli sacked Cosimo's house—saying that he [the new duke] had acquired a palace and an empire in exchange for a house and [his] private estate—and also the [house] of Lorenzo close by and subsequently his country house. .... He also demolished to the ground the part of Lorenzo's house with the chamber where he had killed the [former] duke."[96]

These descriptions address two rites: one, Cosimo's entry into a new life; the other, the physical demolition of "Lorenzaccio." The place of the assassination was also destroyed. The partial demolition of the house of Lorenzo and the sack of his villa outside the walls

94. Ghirardacci, RIS² XXXIII, 3:370–72.
95. Varchi 1858–59, 1:417–18.
96. Segni 1857, 329.

signified the canceling out, even from memory, of tyrannicide and its perpetrator. If this destruction can be associated with the death of a tyrant, about which I will have more to say later, the sack of the house of Cosimo, one notices, was carried out to honor his passage in status from a private citizen to a lord (a "death" and "regeneration"). It was even carried out in the presence of Maria Salviati (the mother of Cosimo) and other relatives of the new duke. Segni and Varchi were contemporary with the events they related, and with their disapproval of the sack, they indicate a moment of conflict: they disapproved of the tradition represented by Vitelli, but sympathized with the victims of the sack, which they present as an excess, and thus as an anomaly. But it was an excess that all knew would go unpunished, precisely because it was linked to a deep tradition.

A similar aversion to such excesses was shown, nearly eighty years earlier, by another illustrious victim. In his own *Commentarii* Enea Silvio Piccolomini (Pope Pius II) remembers—and what more direct witness could we have?—the tumultuous days of the conclave of 1458, from which he emerged pope: "Then the cardinal's servants sacked the cell of Enea and, following a shameful tradition, carried away his money, what little there was of it, books, and vestments. At the same time, the vile and infamous plebes not only sacked but tore to pieces his house in Rome, carrying away even the stones. Similar damage was suffered by a few other cardinals, and this because, while the people were anxiously waiting, the rumor spread from time to time that one or another of them had been elected; then the crowd ran to his house and did its work."[97]

In the broadsheet of 1555 that we have already mentioned, *L'ordine che si tiene nel creare il sommo pontefice,* it says: "When the messengers announce [the election of] the pope . . . they leave St. Peter's immediately and go through the Borgo with the crowd behind them, crying *Papam habemus,* and they go to sack his palace."

Another testimony comes to us about the conclave that followed the death of Pope Marcellus II Cervini. As Giovanni Carga wrote from Rome to the bishop of Feltre in Venice, on 8 May 1555: "The people went to sack the palaces of the Farnesi," since the rumor had spread of the election as pontiff of Cardinal Alessandro Farnese, "and the Caporione [municipal authority of the quarter] had difficulty resisting them."[98]

Repercussions from the death of a pontiff spread to the periphery of the Papal States, and similar behavior accompanied elections. Cardinal Ercole Farnese was the patron of the abbey of Follonica, in the suburbs of Mantua. When, in October of 1559, the (false) rumor spread that the cardinal was elected pope, the abbey was raised to the ground, and the orchard and gardens were dug up by neighbors and monks, with the consent of the abbot himself.[99]

Three centuries earlier, the English jurist Henry Bracton (1210–68) had felt obliged to explain that "though abbot or prior, monks or canons, successively die, the house [*domus*] will remain in eternity."[100] Here the word *domus* might stand figuratively for the *universitas,* the *collegium,* or the *capitulus,* or also for the physical edifice where that *corpus* was located.

The violence that occurred at the time of a papal election requires closer examination. When Cardinal Enea Silvio Piccolomini was the victim, we notice that he said the inci-

97. Piccolomini 1984, II:223.
98. BAV, Chigi R.II.54, fol. 233v.
99. Ginzburg et al. 1987.
100. Cited in Kantorowicz [1957] 1981, 309. Cf. Bracton 1915, IV:175, fol. 374b.

dent followed "a shameful tradition." He thought of this as an ancient practice. In 1417 the Council of Constance had published a decree, *De non spoliando eligendum in papam*.[101] To judge from the experience of Pius II, it had little effect. Even a hundred years later, Leo X was obliged to reiterate the prohibition, with the bull *Temerariorum quorundam,* on 16 March 1516. The prohibition was again repeated the following year at the Lateran Council, with the decree *Contra invadentes domos cardinalium*. Not by chance, in 1511, a member of the papal Curia, Paolo Cortesi, in his *De cardinalatu,* reserved a special section for how to build cardinals' palaces that would be safe against looting. He recommended putting a guardhouse at the entrance, "since, if some danger or tumult should occur in some circumstances, arms would be ready and the palace would be better equipped to resist a siege or fight off an assault."[102]

This ritual violence had, in reality, different aspects. On the news of the positive outcome of a conclave, the cell of the successful candidate was sacked by the servants of all the other members of the Sacred College, and even by members of the conclave itself. But this was only the beginning of the violence that swept the whole city and led to the destruction of the palace of the elected cardinal (with the same aims as the sack of the palace of Cosimo de' Medici in Florence). But other kinds of violence were related to a death (departure) rather than to an entry, as I have indicated above. They extended from the assault on the Lateran Palace condemned at the end of the ninth century by the Council of Rome, to the destruction of the residence of Girolamo Riario in 1484, the palace of the Bentivogli in 1507, the palace of Lorenzo de' Medici in 1537, and the Palace of the Inquisition in 1559. They were acts of destruction like the sack of the residence of Emperor Henry II at Pavia, which was lamented by his successor Conrad II. But it should be emphasized that the crowd did not limit itself to looting ("robbing," says Infessura), it also destroyed (trees were torn up, fountains, doors, and provisions broken up, and buildings torn down stone by stone). We must recognize that in situations such as these, ancient crowds intended to cancel out completely, in a permanent and definitive way, any trace, any memory, of a condition that had passed. Specifically, in the case of Rome, it might seem that a permanent state of revolt pervaded the city during the entire period of the empty see, but one would be mistaken to lump together violent acts that meant quite different things.

We are confronted with two distinct rituals: the first, which followed the death of the sovereign, emphasized the interregnum and the temporary suspension of the law (the *lex animata*); the other aimed instead at canceling out the previous state and signified a regeneration. But still, if one accepts the fact that "the ascent to the throne is the death of the king,"[103] then both rites had something in common.

We have noted that the signal for the beginning of the sack came from within the lordly household, from the "family" of the lord. Even today, at Cambridge University, when a professor dies while he holds the position of dean, his colleagues loot his private library.[104] Reinhardt Elze has spoken—mistakenly, in my mind—of a widespread *jus spolii* (the right to pillage).[105] He deduces the source of the ritual act from its outcome. It is true

101. See Hardt 1699.
102. Cortesi 1511, *De domo*.
103. Roheim [1930] 1972, 238.
104. I thank Professor Anthony Grafton for referring me this fact.
105. Elze 1982.

that in the Middle Ages and early modern period porters who carried away the dead followed the universal custom of robbing their clothing. No scene of the Crucifixion fails to show soldiers throwing dice for the clothes of Jesus and the thieves. In Genoa, during the plague of 1656, a compromise was reached between the servants and the porters of the dead: the clothes of the deceased went to the servants if he died naked, and to the porters if he died clothed. A similar right belonged to the executioner. Marcantonio Savelli, a judge of the Ruota Criminale in Florence, wrote at the end of the seventeenth century that "the executioner . . . shall have as a gratuity the clothes, rings, and other things the condemned man was wearing, so long as they do not exceed the value of 5 scudi."[106] This was probably a custom that transformed itself into a right. (In many states of the United States undertakers have the legal right of first claim on a dead man's estate to satisfy their bill—an ancient custom?)[107] The rights perceived as abuses by Enea Silvio Piccolomini and Maria Salviati, and that had been the object of the decrees of popes and councils, were nonetheless still observed in the seventeenth century. I think we are mistaken to look at these customs with modern eyes in terms of economic gain. We should look again for a moment at what Malinowski wrote about the Argonauts and the economy of Trobriand: "Gain, such as is often the stimulus for work in more civilized communities, never acts as an impulse to work under the original native conditions. . . . The real force which binds all people and ties them down in their tasks is obedience to custom, to tradition."[108] Medieval men lived in relation to their own lords in a total involvement, based essentially on two principles: hierarchy and honor. The man of his lord was entirely dependent on him, *perinde ac cadaver* (like a corpse), to use Saint Ignatius Loyola's famous words when defining obedience. This relationship changed slowly into a kind of professional pride that was strictly related to a position occupied within a recognized hierarchy. Between the sixteenth and seventeenth centuries, the sack, from its old sacred and thaumaturgic meaning, assumed a new meaning. It became the recognition of a servile and subordinate position, which was still linked to the physical body of the lord. It became a just recompense. If it can be compared with the *jus spolii* of the warrior, this is only because the ancient right of looting was still observed.

In his manual *Il perfetto maestro di casa* (1658) Francesco Liberati condemns, while forgetting its ancient roots, looting the palaces of cardinals: "They are worthy of contempt who, seeing with their lord's death the end of their hopes for the personal profit from the office they had exercised, carry away after [his] death the instruments and things they had used to serve him in that office."[109] From this text we learn that the train-bearer had the right to take away the two copes the cardinal had worn in the chapel; the master of horse, a horse of his choosing; the master of the wardrobe, the bed on which the cardinal died. The attendants of his chamber had a right to his clothes and to the bed in the antechamber, the barber to the washbasin and pitcher "and all the barber tools," the steward to "all the linen he possessed at the time of the death of the lord," the wine steward to the "decanters and corks," the lamp lighter to oil and wicks "and other things employed in his work."[110]

106. Savelli 1697, 153.
107. Parkes 1972, 173.
108. Malinowski 1922, 156, 158.
109. Liberati [1658], 223ff.
110. Liberati [1658], 226.

With the lessening of violence, which had signified the interregnum and thus a suspension of legality, the sack was transformed into an acquisitive right, and thus was linked, with a change of meaning, to the different functions carried out by the "family." One was no longer the man of the lord, but had been singled out for one's professional capacity; stewardship passed from being an honor to being a profession. From being the "refuge of an impoverished gentleman," as Giovan Francesco da Colle entitled his treatise,[111] it became an employment. By this time the ritual sack had begun to be thought of in the way Antonio Adami wrote about it in *Il novitiato del maestro di casa* (1636): "I knew a cook who took a little bit from all the goods that passed through his hands, and his assistants did too, taking a little bit of meat from the dishes of the gentlemen."[112] This was something still tied to personal professionalism; that meat was also theirs, from the time they had cut and cooked it. In the same way, Vincenzo Cervio, in *Il Trinciante* (1593), claimed a professional right to have a portion of the meat that was cut for the lord's plate. The carver "worthy of this name has the right, in serving his lord, to set aside for himself a plate of the food he carves, when there is more than enough for the table of the lord."[113] The innate symbolism connected with food could not be better illustrated, or the living sense of the *jus spolii,* which is incomprehensible if not inserted in the greater sphere of honor, custom, and tradition.

A way out of the perils implicit in an interregnum was found by jurists in Tudor England. The same concept expressed by Emperor Conrad II in his separation of the ship from its captain was developed in the mid–sixteenth century by Anglo-Saxon jurists. They held that

> the king has in him two Bodies, viz., a Body natural and a Body politic. His Body natural (if it be considered in itself) is a Body mortal, subject to all infirmities that come by Nature or Accident to the Imbecility of Infancy or old Age, and to the like Defects that happen to the natural Bodies of other People. But his Body politic is a Body that cannot be seen or handled, consisting of Policy and Government, and constituted for the Direction of the People, and the management of the Public weal, and this Body is utterly void of infancy, and old Age, and other natural Defects and Imbecilities, which the Body natural is subject to, and for this Cause, what the King does in his Body politic, cannot be invalidated or frustrated by any Disability in his natural Body.[114]

Separating the "Body natural" from the state's "Body politic" definitively resolved, at a juridical level, the existential agony caused by the loss of the leader. But we will see in what follows what (tragic) consequences derived from following further logical implications of this distinction, although these were necessary for the formation of the modern state.

111. Colle 1520.
112. Adami 1636, 132.
113. Cervio 1593, 5.
114. Kantorowicz [1957] 1981, 7.

Q
Qui Venit in Nomine Domini

IT WAS THE END OF NOVEMBER 1237. Cremona and Italy had never witnessed such a grandiose triumph, so enthusiastically received, as that of the victor of the battle of Cortenuova. The Roman Empire lived again in this entrance, with Pietro Tiepolo, son of the doge of Venice and podestà of Milan, marching in chains before the victor, with the war chariot (*carroccio*)[1] of the Milanese as a *spoglia* (trophy), and with the gonfalon of the commune dragging in the dust. *Miles Roma! Miles Imperator!* It was not the emperor Frederick II's first triumph; he had celebrated another on his entry into Jerusalem on 28 March 1229. Dressed in imperial purple, the *puer Apuliae* (child of Apulia) had advanced to the altar of the Holy Sepulcher to place the royal crown of Jerusalem on his own head.[2] But it was not until the *adventus* of the *Felix victor* into Cremona that Italy and the empire breathed again the air of ancient Rome.

In his *Civilisation of the Renaissance in Italy,* Jacob Burckhardt cited the apparition of Beatrice to Dante in the thirtieth canto of his *Purgatorio* as the first return of classical Roman triumphs. Beatrice was seated on "a two-wheeled triumphal chariot," adored by pious souls, "in a way which almost forces us to conclude that such processions actually occurred before his time."[3] We do not know when Dante wrote the second book of the *Divina commedia,* but we know that the poem was begun in 1307 (precisely seventy years after Cremona) and that the first and third parts were circulated before the author's death in 1321. Within another five years Italians witnessed another great event. With the memory of Cremona, Castruccio Castracani had his own triumph as lord of Lucca. He entered the city seated on a throne that was placed on a chariot. This triumph celebrated his victory over the Florentines at the battle of Altopascio on 23 September 1325, but it was postponed until 11 November, the feast of Saint Martin, patron of Lucca. The chariot was drawn by four horses (like the chariot of Apollo). A golden crown circled the head of the warrior, and he appeared on the chariot as *imperator,* immobile. "Castruccio, in a seat on a chariot, open on all sides, drawn by four white horses, dressed richly in purple and gold, with a garland of laurel on his head, showed with a serene expression, in Caesarean majesty, the dignity of a king."[4]

---

1. About this war chariot, see Voltmer 1994.
2. Kantorowicz 1989, 187. On Roman triumphs, see Payne 1962.
3. Burckhardt 1951, 254.
4. "Castruccius curru residens aperto, quatuor albis invectus equis, insignis auro et ostro, redimitus tempora lauro, in Majestate Caesarea gravitatem Regiam sereno vultu prae se ferens statim aderat." Tegrimi 1742.

Progressing from Altopascio toward Lucca, prisoners marched before the chariot "inermes et cervices denudati" (that is, with necks and shoulders bare, as if offering themselves for decapitation), and these were followed by the people of Lucca, who dragged along the spoils of war, including the Florentine war chariot (*carroccio*) and a great bell whose peals had summoned its army.[5] Like Pietro Tiepolo, the commander in chief of the enemy army, the Spaniard Ramón de Cardona walked before the victor, with his son and the Florentine commissioners. Lucca awaited Castruccio, decked with flowers. Fine cloths hung from the windows of houses, pageantries were performed in the streets, and children dressed in white, carrying olive boughs, came out of the gates to meet the victor. Having arrived at the gates, Castruccio marched all around the city before entering, thus carrying out the *circumambulatio murorum* (circuit of the city walls) of classical Rome, which Tegrimi describes using a suggestive verb: "universam urbem lustravit" (he cleansed the whole city).[6] This was thus a purification, something that was thought of as sacred. The sacredness of the ritual was all the more emphasized by the arrival at the cathedral and the chants of the clergy. According to an ancient Germanic rite, recorded by Tacitus (*Historiae,* IV:15) and taken up by Rome, lifting the king up on a great shield was an aspect of the ceremony of coronation. It symbolized the rising of the sun (in Greek: *anàtellon*).[7] This rite was also observed by Castruccio's officers, who raised the *sedia gestatoria* on which he was seated, to carry it into the church, high above the crowd ("in sella eburnea humeris ducum sublatus" [carried high on the shoulders of his followers in an ivory chair]).[8]

If we deconstruct this description, we can discern a series of themes that help us to understand the religious/sacred structure of the ceremony, aspects that also appeared in later triumphs and entries of Renaissance Europe.

Classical Rome observed three forms of the triumph: the *ovatio,* with the victor on horseback; the *triumphus,* with the general standing in a two-wheeled chariot (a *biga* if it was drawn by two horses, a *quadriga* if it was drawn by four); and finally the *progressio,* with the general seated on a throne that was loaded onto a cart with four wheels (*carpentum*). The monk Zonaras left a good description of the Roman triumph in his summary of the history of Dio Cassius: "[T]his chariot did not resemble one used in games or in war, but was fashioned in the shape of a round tower. . . . A public slave, however, rode with the victor in the chariot itself, holding over him the crown of precious stones set in gold and repeating to him, 'Look beyond!' that is, 'Look at what comes after, in the ensuing years of life, and do not be elated or puffed up by your present fortune.'"[9]

The models that Dante might have had before him were a bas-relief of Marcus Aurelius, perhaps a relic of a destroyed triumphal arch, then located in the Church of Santa Martina al Foro (Fig. 16; Leo X transported it to the Campidoglio in 1515, the year of his triumphal entry into Florence on 30 November!),[10] and the *progressio* of Constantine

---

5. "Currum ducebant boves bubalique, super quo (vetere illius aetatis instituto) ad quorundam fastus inanem ostentationem, campana magnae amplitudinis ante Ducis tentorium ponenda deferabatur, qua exercitum convocarent, et ad iter faciendum vel sistendum moneretur agmina. Caorocium ei nomen erat. . ."

6. Tegrimi 1742, 143–45.

7. Jones 1883, 184 n.

8. On the history of this period, see Beverini 1829; a brief notice of this triumph is in Green 1986, 180. On the *anàtellon,* see Kantorowicz 1944 and 1963.

9. Zonaras 1868–75, II:148–50 (VII, 21); but see also Helbig 1903; Brelich 1938.

10. Ryber 1976; Bober and Rubinstein 1986, 163.

Fig. 16   Triumph of Marcus Aurelius (in the background the temple of the Bona Dea), Rome,
Musei Capitolini.

on the north side of his triumphal arch (Fig. 17). Awareness of the Aurelian bas-relief is demonstrated in a thirteenth-century miniature appearing in the *Liber Historiarum Romanorum* (Fig. 18). It was a recurrent point of reference for artists of the early Renaissance. Another famous medieval triumph was the one of Saint Francis that was depicted by Giotto in the upper church at Assisi (see Fig. 2). The chariot is a *biga* (although a roughly depicted one—one could say that Taddeo Gaddi interpreted the chariot of the sun better than Giotto, with Saint Francis appearing to his disciples in a chariot surrounded by solar flames), drawn by two horses (while we know that "the chariot of the sun had four horses").[11] Like a Roman general, the saint stands on his feet, erect. But was there truly a classical example for this fresco? Or should we perhaps refer to the "chariot of fire and horses of fire" of the translation of the prophet Elijah (2 Kings 2:11)? Or to Ezekiel's vision of the throne of Yahweh, as described in the Book of Daniel: "His throne was like the fiery flame, and his wheels as burning fire" (Daniel 7:9)? If we remember Fra Bartolomeo di Rinonico's *De conformitate vitae beati Francisci ad vitam Domini Jesu,* the doubt would seem legitimate in this case. But let us return to the solar chariot, the one represented in the mosaic in the Julian mausoleum (see Fig. 1): *Christos-Helios* as the divine dawn, a symbol of the Resurrection.[12] This was the same chariot illustrated in the codex of the Syrian bishop Rabbula (A.D. 586), in a miniature of Christ appearing on a cosmic shield raised up to heaven by angels on the chariot/throne of Ezekiel.[13]

Less than fifty years after the events at Lucca, Altichiero returned to the Aurelian bas-relief for his Petrarchesque *Trionfo della Gloria,* in *De viris illustrubus* (1379). The difference

Fig. 17   The *progressio,* Rome, Arch of Constantine.

11. Dante, *Convivio,* IV, xxxii, 14.
12. Kantorowicz 1963, 144.
13. L'Orange 1953, 125.

Fig. 18   Triumph of Marcus Aurelius as represented in the *Liber Historiarum Romanorum* (Rome, thirteenth century), Hamburg, Stadtbibliothek.

is that the scene was now viewed from the front rather than in profile, and the chariot was depicted within a mandorla, like Apollonio di Giovanni's miniature for the *Trionfo della Fama* (1446–63). In both of these illustrations the sacredness of the scene is emphasized by its insertion into a mandorla (just as in the codex of Rabbula), making it a symbol of the ascension of souls into Paradise and making the chariot something transcendental. From the fact that the codex of Rabbula arrived in the Laurentian library in 1497 and was thus a source known only to the late Renaissance, we must deduce that both Altichiero and Apollonio must have referred to a more ancient model.

Only Stefano da Verona, illustrating the Petrarchesque *Trionfo della Morte* in 1414, low-ered the chariot to an infamous level. He imagined a group of six persons, seated in a two-wheeled chariot and guarded by an *Angelus infernalis,* as prisoners might have been taken through the streets of a medieval city on the tumbrel of those condemned to death. This is a right interpretation, if we consider that the condemned man's trip to the scaffold was a *triumphus imfamantis.*[14]

The ceremony of a triumph (or rather an entry) was well known in Europe of the early Middle Ages. In the Western world it happened on horseback; in the Byzantine world, on a two-wheeled chariot. But what counts most is that the triumph/entry be seen in a greater context, as one of the most important aspects of the adoration of the sover-eign. Otherwise, we are left with the ample bibliography put together by Bonner Mitchell,[15] which tends to reduce these ceremonies to the level of Renaissance festivals,[16] giving chief emphasis to the scenes ("pageantries") that accompanied them as primitive forms of representation. *Feasts of the Renaissance, Scene of the Prince,* "Theater and City," and *Spectacle au service de la propagande monarchique* are different, but similar, titles that show how the ceremony has been interpreted. There is only the exception of R. Eisler to affirm the deep sacred meaning.[17] Even an anthropologist of the stature of Clifford Geertz ended up by talking about a "theatre state" for similar ceremonies (although in a cultural context quite remote from the European one),[18] thus emphasizing the spectacu-lar aspects rather than the religious ones.

In the idea of a "spectacle" is implicit something received passively by the spectators. The "representation" enacted from on "high" is directed to the public ("below"), which is the recipient. On the contrary, in these ceremonies, which were among the most impor-tant in the cult of the leader, all were "actors": participants, not spectators. In a religious society the faithful are closely united with their pastor; they know the rules of the rite, speak the same language; each one has assigned to him a specific role. In early medieval Europe and during the early modern period no accounting was made of separation in a ritual between "high" and "low." Just as in a religious procession the faithful place them-selves behind the priest and the images of saints and relics, so subjects welcome their sov-ereign by joining his train and by carrying in procession loot, flags, and heraldic coats of arms. A triumphal entry requires the whole city to be involved, even if this involvement follows rigid rules of hierarchy and precedence. As Mervyn James has observed, a proces-sion is a "synchronic form of static hierarchical structure" and a "visible means of relat-ing individuals to the social structure."[19]

No one has ever taken the trouble to measure the width of two streets in Rome that trace the ancient route of the *via papalis:* Via de' Coronari and Via del Pellegrino. Well, the first was 6.20 meters wide (20 feet, 4 inches), and the second 4.50 (14 feet, 9 inches). In 1529, for the entrance of Charles V into Genoa, triumphal arches were erected along the route from the port to the Church of San Lorenzo. A sketch reconstructing this (made on the occasion of an exhibition on Perin del Vaga) and superimposed on the triumphal arch

---

14. McCormick 1986, 48–50.
15. Mitchell 1979 and 1986.
16. Jacquot 1956 60.
17. Eisler 1910.
18. Geertz 1980.
19. James 1986, 30.

erected at Porta del Molo does not leave any space for the rows of spectators.[20] Also, at Avignon in 1759, the inhabitants of the Rue du Prince complained because processions did not pass along their street. They were told that their street was "too narrow." But they replied that the street chosen, La Bencasse, was "dix pans et un tiers" wide (3 meters, or 9 feet, 11 inches), while theirs was "treize pans et deux tiers" (3.40 meters, or 11 feet, 2 inches).[21] Was this enough room for the passage of a procession and also for spectators on both sides? If spectators, women particularly, were there, they were at windows and on balconies, dressed in festive dresses (and they too were participating in the ceremony, as "attendants"). The *Journal d'un bourgeois de Paris* relates that in 1420, when Charles VI and Henry V made their entry into the city, accompanied by their queens, the duke of Burgundy, and Louis VII of Bavaria, the Elector Palatine, "the whole great Rue Saint-Denis where they entered, from the second gate up to Notre-Dame de Paris, was draped nobly, and the nearby streets too, and the greater part of the people of Paris who had standing were dressed in red [red, in heraldic language, indicated England]. And in Rue de la Kalende, in front of the palace, a pious mystery of the passion of Our Lord was acted out . . . and no one saw this mystery whose heart was not touched."[22] Mathieu d'Escouchy writes of the entry into Rouen of the king of France in 1449: "At the windows, and in many other places, there was a great abundance of ladies, young ladies, and bourgeoises, all well dressed and adorned with rich clothing."[23] Precisely a hundred years later a description of the entry into Paris of Henry II and Catherine de' Medici evoked nearly the same words as the older description: "Rich tapestries were spread on the streets; large rich rugs hung from the windows of the houses"; there was "an incredible crowd of women, young women, bourgeois women, gentlemen, officials, persons of rank, and inhabitants of the city."[24] A specific function was given particularly to women on these occasions. They were to appear, dressed in rich clothing, on balconies and in window openings, places where it was appropriate to see women's faces, along streets that were eminently the places of men. "All the streets and the windows were full of fashionable people," Le Héraut Berry wrote in his chronicle.[25] We must presume, therefore, that the crowd in the street was performing precise functions and was directly involved in the procession, whether they were going to meet the lord or joining the end of his procession or lining up on balconies and showing themselves at windows in festive clothing. Children carried palm or olive boughs; clergy, relics; members of confraternities and guilds marched behind their standards—all observed precise norms of precedence. "Processions from each parish left the city with their banners and crosses, with the four mendicant orders bearing honored relics, and they marched before the king, our sire, and did him honor and reverence as best they could," reads a print of the entry of Louis XII into Paris in 1498.[26] Heath, in his chronicle, speaking of the procession for the coronation of Charles II of England on 23 April 1661, has an account of the deployment of the citizen companies: "The streets

20. For Charles V, see Albicante 1541; for the entry into Rome in 1536, Biagio da Cesena 1877.

21. Venard 1977, 60.

22. *Journal d'un bourgeois* [1881] 1990, 162–63.

23. "Estoient aux fenestres, en plusieurs lieux et en grand abondance, les dames, mademoiselles et bourgeoises, moult bien parées et ornées de riches habillemens." Mathieu d'Escouchy 1863, 1:229. See also Chartrou 1928.

24. Godefroy 1649, 379; McGowman 1968.

25. Quoted in Guenée and Lehoux 1968, 74.

26. "Se partirent de ladite ville less processions de chascune parroisse, a toutes leurs baniers et croix, avecques les quattre Ordres mendians atout plusierus dignes reliquiaires, et cheminerent hors ladite ville audevant du roy nostre sire, et lui firent honneur et reverence aux mieulx qu'ilz peurent." Guenée and Lehoux 1968, 126.

were, as usual, lined with the different companies of the city in their liveries, attended with their banners and music."[27] If, at a crossroads, in the space before some sanctuary, in a town square, allegorical scenes were acted out, these were looked upon with the same spirit with which sacred rites were observed. "There were several representations of the histories of saints, both male and female, in many places, and these were played out very authentically," Mathieu d'Escouchy says.[28] That "very authentically" tells us how little the spectators thought they were viewing a theatrical representation. Sansovino writes about one of these representations in Venice: "David dressed royally, his harp in his hand, on which he sweetly played. . . . Shepherds on a bank, playing happily for joy. . . . Then one saw the Last Judgment. . . . Below, the dead were leaving their tombs, and one heard (but without seeing) the sounds of trumpets and drums, which much frightened the people standing near."[29] The candid people enjoying sacred representations stood before them in a manner quite different from that of people in the theaters of later periods. (In a famous movie by Pierpaolo Pasolini, *Le nuvole,* located in a puppets' theater, Iago and Othello are "killed" by the enraged audience to vindicate the murder of Desdemona.)

In studying medieval kingship, we often forget what Marc Bloch wrote:

> We only partly understand the idolatry of which royalty and kings used to be the ob-ject. . . . The difficulty we have in penetrating, on such an important point, the mental-ity of an age that literary tradition nonetheless makes familiar, comes perhaps from the fact that we often study only great theorists' conceptions about government. Absolut-ism was a kind of religion; and does not knowing a religion only through its theologians perhaps leave us ignorant of its vital sources? . . . To better understand the most illustri-ous doctors of monarchies, we must know the collective representations, the legacy of past ages, that were still alive in their time with singular strength.[30]

To speak of medieval and Renaissance triumphs means to reconstruct forms of collec-tive representation connected directly to the cult of the leader. What Burckhardt missed was that the little crowd of souls around Dante welcomed Beatrice's chariot with the for-mula *"Benedictus qui venis"*:

> Tutti dicean *Benedictus qui venis*
> e fior gittando e di sopra e ditorno
> *Manibus, oh, date lila plenis!*[31]

> (They all cried, "Blessed art thou who comest,"
> throwing flowers up and around.
> "Oh give lilies with full hands!")

This is actually the formula of a religious ceremony. When Charlemagne arrived in Rome in December 800, the pontiff sent out to meet him a mile from the gate "all the

27. Cited in Jones 1883, 171, 233ff.
28. "Y avoit plusieurs histoires de saints et de saintes en moult de lieux, qui juoient des personnages moult autentiquement." Mathieu d'Escouchy 1863, 1:233–34.
29. Sansovino 1604, 310.
30. Bloch [1923] 1961, 263.
31. *Purgatorio,* xxx, 19–21.

companies of militia with their leaders, and youths . . . singing the verses of welcome, all carrying palm fronds and singing praises."[32] And when the same pope Adrian I and Charlemagne made their entry "in venerandam aulam beati Petri" (into the venerable hall of St. Peter's), all the clergy and the other religious, "extensa voce," cried out, "Benedictus qui venis in nomine Domine" (Blessed art thou who comest in the name of the Lord).[33] Later, when the Romans begged Pope Alexander III (1159–81) to return from Anagni, and the papal procession coming from Tusculum came in sight of the city, the clergy, with crosses and relics; senators, judges, patricians, and soldiers "in apparatu decoro" (in decent clothing); the people, "cum ramis olivarum" (with olive branches), went out to meet the pope, "laudes pontificis consuetas vociferans . . . tunc videns oculos omnium vultum eius intuentes tamquam vultum Jesu Christi" (singing pontifical hymns . . . their eyes fixed on his face as if seeing the face of Jesus Christ).[34]

Vitricius of Rouen tells us the order of the procession that went to meet some relics in 396: priests, deacons, the lower clergy, youths, virgins, widows, *continentes* (women who had taken vows of chastity), elders, mothers, then all the rest of the population.[35] The same typology can be traced centuries later, but in a not-much-different context, in the *Ordo intrandi aliquam urbem in pontificalibus,* as one can read in the *Caeremonialis romanum,* printed in 1516. On one hand, it is true that "purity and renunciation, authority and devotion, detached an elite from the greater crowd of the faithful,"[36] but on the other hand, one must remember that the greater crowd took an active part in the religious ceremony and was completely involved in it. Jorge Traeger has observed that "the triumph was also an entry of Christ into Jerusalem, and this was even the concept of it in the Middle Ages: Dominica palmarum ideo dicitur, quia hae die turbae Domino receperunt" (Palm Sunday is called that because on this day people welcome the Lord).[37]

Bernard Guenée adds, in the introduction to his French *Entrées:* "At the end of the fourteenth century, everything induced Frenchmen to see a holy day or a Corpus Christi in a royal entry."[38] In fact, in the Gospels, the episode of the entry into Jerusalem—and others mentioned in the Holy Scriptures—served to confirm the fulfillment of the biblical prophecy of the *animal messianum:* "O daughter of Jerusalem: behold, thy King cometh unto thee: he is just, and having salvation; lowly, and riding upon an ass, and upon a colt, the foal of an ass" (Zechariah 9:9; see also Isaiah 62:10–11 and Matthew 21:5). "And a very great multitude spread their garments in the way; others cut down branches from the trees, and strewed them in the way" (Matthew 21:8). But people in Hellenistic-Roman society, accustomed to welcoming the *numen* of an emperor, must have reacted to such biblical texts differently. Within this context they might assume a more universal meaning: the King of Kings brought down the laws of the Heavenly City. This was probably the way the *Dominica in palmis* was perceived in the non-Jewish world. The *apàntesis* (encounter) between the new king and his subjects was configured, to use the term of Mircea

32. "Universas scolas militae una cum patronis simulque et pueri qui ad didicendas litteras pergebant deportantes omnes ramis palmarum, laudes illi omnes canentes." *Liber pontificalis* [1886–92] 1955–57, I:497.
33. *Liber pontificalis* [1886–92] 1955–57, I:497.
34. *Liber pontificalis* [1886–92] 1955–57, II:446.
35. PL, xx:445.
36. Gaudemet 1958, 186.
37. Traeger 1970, 89.
38. Guenée and Lehoux 1968, 16.

Eliade, as a *hierofania;*[39] the sacred showed itself as a force, a power, and thus transformed itself into a *kratofania:* "une manifestation de force" (a manifestation of force). One could say that it was not merely by chance that royal entrances were accompanied by the reconfirmation of the privileges of cities granted by earlier sovereigns. This was necessary to reestablish laws that had been temporarily suspended.

It is important to emphasize that Frederick II, French kings, and popes made their entries on horseback, thus observing the form of an *ovatio* rather than that of a true and proper triumph. On the other hand, Dante imagined a Roman ceremony, with chariot, but rather than describe Beatrice standing, as in the bas-relief of Marcus Aurelius, he had her sitting. It was an important difference. Was Dante embellishing an *adventus* with an echo of classicism? Was he modifying, to a considerable extent, the example of Cremona that was still alive in the memory of his contemporaries? This echo does not seem to have influenced Botticelli, a century later, when he illustrated the scene from Dante, even making one imagine that he truly had present in his mind carnival chariots, as Burckhardt thought. We see Beatrice in a two-wheeled chariot, as Dante described it, and sitting. The chariot could not be anything other than a *biga.*

One could say that the chariot thought up by Boccaccio in *L'amorosa visione* (1342) was derived from the *Commedia:*

> Ardita sopra un carro tra costoro
> grande e trionfal, lieta sedea
> ornato tutto di fronde d'alloro.

> (Venturing forth on a chariot,
> grand and triumphal, she lightly sat,
> decked around with branches of laurel.)

But certainly this was not the posture of a Roman triumph. Should we go back to thinking that it was a scene taken from something seen in a carnival? But if we did, we would be misled in our inquiry.

Let us turn for a moment to the description of Castruccio's triumph and compare it with the literary and iconographic sources for the classical Roman ceremony. We can reduce the procession's structure to the following elements:

Structure of the Triumph
1. The entry (*parousia*):
    a) through a portal
    b) through a breach in the walls
2. The route of the procession (*lustratio*)
3. The dress of the person in triumph
4. The encounter at the gate (*apàntesis*)
5. The children with crowns or olive branches
6. The offer of the keys (in the case of 1b)

---

39. "l'acte de la manifestation du sacré": Eliade 1957, 155ff.

7. The chariot:
    a) without throne (*triumphus*)
    b) with throne (*progressio*)
    c) on horseback (*ovatio*)
8. The baldacchino
9. The acts of sovereignty (creation of knights, honors, acts of grace)
10. The soldiers around the chariot
    a) singing apotropaic songs (against evil spirits)
    b) simulating a riot
11. The immobility of the person in triumph
12. The loot (*spolia*)
13. The arrival in the cathedral: elevation (*anàtellon*)
14. The sack of the baldacchino and the horse
15. The scattering of money (*jactum missilium*)
16. The distribution of food (*congiarium*)

Weisbach thought that Tegrimi's narrative was a humanistic fantasy.[40] The best that can be said is that Tegrimi was not a firsthand witness, since he was born in 1448, more than a hundred years after the event (his biography of Castruccio appeared in 1496). But he was only embellishing an event witnessed by a chronicler, Giovanni Villani, who was contemporary with it.

> In that year Castruccio ruined and burned over the *contado* of Florence and that of Prato . . . and on 10 November he returned to Lucca for the feast of San Martino with great triumph and glory. A great procession of the whole city, men and women, came to welcome him like a new king, and to do dishonor to the Florentines, he made their *carroccio* go ahead with the bell the Florentines had with their army, loaded oxen with Florentine arms, and had the bell sounded. Behind the war chariot came the best Florentine prisoners, and Messir Ramondo with lighted candles in his hand to offer to San Martino . . . , and the royal and communal banners of Florence were placed upside down on the war chariot.[41]

This is the description of a royal *adventus* done up with communal ritual (the homage of lighted candles from defeated communes offered to the patron saint of the victorious city).[42] From our point of view, Weisbach's doubts are not well taken. Even if Tegrimi mixed reality with classical memories, the problem is different. What did Tegrimi base his reconstruction of Castruccio's triumph on? We can also ask another question: Was Castruccio himself influenced by the *Commedia,* so as to use a type of chariot not generally used in classical triumphs? But also, are we sure we are not wrong to follow Burckhardt and put a hiatus (the medieval parenthesis) between the classical and Renaissance worlds?

40. Weisbach 1919.
41. Villani 1823, IX, CCCXXIII.
42. Bertelli 1978, 149ff.

The episode at Cremona in 1237 must have been recounted from father to son up to the men of 1325. Even medieval France was accustomed to royal entries.[43] Villani's chronicle itself records the entry of Queen Joanna I of Naples into Avignon in 1348, and Jean Le Fèvre, the chancellor of Kings Louis I and Louis II, refers to no less than seven royal entries in the short period between 1385 and 1387.[44] In all the French entries the king rode under a baldacchino ("the syndics, the justice, and other notables carried a canopy of cloth of gold, they being on foot, the king mounted," in the entry into Arles on 4 December 1385).[45] The ceremony, though, was even older and derived from the need of French kings to travel continually through the territory of their kingdom so as to administer justice and collect taxes. They traveled with their nomad court and were followed by a crowd of clients, merchants, the poor, and even prostitutes.

For the Catalan-Aragonese monarchy we can refer to many examples. When Alfonso V of Aragon, the Magnanimous, entered the city of Naples, twice, in 1423 and again in 1443, he created his own model.[46] The first time, the chroniclers tell us that he wore four flags on his helmet: "This Vice Roy of Aragon progressed with great honor and triumph, dressed in cloth of gold and on his head four banners, one with the arms of Pope Colonna, one with the arms of the Church, one quartered with the arms of the queen and king of Aragon, and the other with those of the Kingdom."[47] After that came an elephant carrying on its back a tower with angels, who pretended to be in combat with a group of soldiers dressed as devils. Better known—we will return to it later—was his later triumph depicted on the triumphal arch of the fortress of Castelnuovo. It follows that Tegrimi had a large variety of possible sources for describing the triumph at Lucca.

But the tradition went back even further chronologically. By way of Byzantium, the Merovingians had learned a ceremony for triumphal entries. They modified it, emphasizing the religious themes in the procession and combining themes of royal and priestly sacred rites (there is an interesting treatment of the symbolism of the procession in Villette).[48] A good example of this double use of ceremony was the triumph for royal relics (of Saint Louis of Anjou, the king of Aragon and Majorca, King Robert of Provence, and the king of France) carried to Marseilles in 1318.[49] It is thus difficult to continue to believe Burckhardt (who did not know about any of these triumphs, beginning with that of Frederick II) or the theory that there was a gradual breaking of continuity between the classical and Renaissance worlds. It is also difficult to reduce these ceremonies to spectacles, or festivals, even if we can consider them in the wider sense of a "theatre state."

When we now examine the structure of royal entries, I think the reader will have no further doubts.

1a. The portal. The portal assumed a particular importance in entry / triumph ceremonies; it clearly involved a double rite (of recognizing a boundary and of crossing). It is still

43. Bryant 1986a.

44. Coulet 1977, 78.

45. "Les sindics et le viguier, et autres notables porterent le paile de drap d'or sur le Roy, eus estans de pié, le Roy de cheval."

46. See Maxwell 1992 and Di Marzo 1864.

47. "Cavalcò questo Vice Re di Rahona con gran honore et triunpho, et lui vestito di drappe d'oro et sopra la testa quattro bandere l'una all'arma de Papa Colonna, l'altra della Chiesa, l'altra per tutto all'arma de la Regina con quella de Re de Rahona quartata et l'altra de lo Reame." *Diurnali,* 104.

48. Villette 1611, 523ff.

49. Coulet 1977, 63.

sub judice where the Roman *porta triumphalis* was located.[50] Anyway, it is clear that the triumph was thought of as a kind of expiation, a restoration of the *mana,* bought by the person in triumph. In this way the whole ceremony assumed the significance of a rite of cleansing, of purification, of which the portal was the pivot. The series of successive arches—permanent or ephemeral—reiterated this passage and multiplied and amplified the initial cleansing entry. The person in triumph was considered to be both Jupiter and king.[51] In Capua, Frederick II had the image of Iustitia Caesaris sculpted on the gate overlooking the Volturno River, in a central position below the throne of the emperor and directly above the entrance of the gate, giving it the sacred character of a *porta triumphalis.*[52] It is symptomatic that the compiler of the *Gesta Romanorum* says about this gate that the intention was to identify the emperor with the Christian equivalent of Jupiter: "The emperor at the gate is our Lord Jesus Christ."[53]

1b. The breach. For the triumph of Alfonso the Magnanimous in 1443 we have firsthand witnesses, who help to interpret it. We know that the Neapolitans had broken down a piece of the walls.[54] Before mounting into the chariot, the king had changed his clothing and performed some acts of sovereignty (the creation of knights). The Catalan soldiers of his guard marched around the chariot, wearing masks and seeming to simulate a riot.[55] The itinerary, as we have already observed, followed the route of a cleansing procession.

The classical world observed the rite of a *hieronica,* that is, the passage of a poet laureate through a breach in the walls, as a manifestation of the futility of a city with such an illustrious citizen to surround itself with walls.[56] But I think that our case was different. Alfonso of Aragon was a conqueror, just like Francesco Sforza ten years later, who entered Milan through a breach; Ferdinando of Aragon, who disembarked at Naples in 1507 to find part of the wall around the port dismantled; and Leo X, who entered Florence in 1515 through Porta Romana, part of its perimeter having been taken down and the wooden doors taken off their hinges. Thus, also, the entry of the army of Charles V into Siena (1536) was "not through the outer portal used by the signoria, but through a breach in the walls made during the war."[57] This undoing of defenses, which was substituted for or accompanied the offering of keys to the city, also had an ethological meaning: the inhabitants took down the walls (part symbolizing the whole), indicating that they were giving themselves up to their conqueror disarmed. The defeated wolf offers its throat to the adversary; the stag offers its stomach to the new leader of the herd. All these were symbols meant to deflect the aggressiveness of the rival. How could one act violently against the disarmed?[58]

This interpretation is confirmed by the entry of Leo X into Florence at the end of November 1515. He was the illustrious son who had ascended to the papacy, but also the

50. Versnel 1970, 151ff.

51. Versnel 1970, 56ff. On the triumph and the *porta triumphalis,* see also Champeau 1982 and Coarelli 1988.

52. Kantorowicz [1957] 1981, 111 and fig. 17; 1989, 479; Ungaro 1995, 559–80.

53. Battisti 1960, 16–29.

54. "Rex sese cum principibus ostendit ad portam Carmelitanum, juxta quam non modica murorum pars a civibus diruta erat, et in honorem victoris introenutis patefacta." Beccadelli ["il Panormita"] 1646, 202–16.

55. "facies velatae, simul rissantes": see Pinelli in Settis 1985, II:324.

56. Plutarch, *Symposinea,* II, 2.5.2; RE, VIII:1535–36 (J. Oehler); Makin 1921, 32; Versnel 1970, 155.

57. *Descrittione delle cerimonie* [1884] 1968, 22.

58. The breach contradicts the supposition of Versnel 1970, 132ff., that the *porta triumphalis* was supposed to be closed after the entry of the person in triumph to prevent the *manu* from escaping. This book is reviewed by Smith (1973, 244), but see also Smith 1971.

conqueror of the city after its rebellion against the Medici. As the pontifical recorder of ceremonies, Paris de' Grassi writes: the Signoria "ordered that the gonfalonier not give the keys of the city to the pope, as other magistrates had the habit of doing, because the Florentines themselves had torn down the portal and entirely dismantled it."[59] They did not offer the keys, because they had already done something more dramatic.

2. The entry and route. The Middle Ages observed two different kinds of entries: (1) the "penetration," that is, a procession that entered through a gate and went directly to the city hall or palace, with a straight-as-an-arrow typology; and (2) the *circuitus murorum* (circuit of the walls), that is, a cavalcade that proceeded around an ideal perimeter (usually the circuit of the earliest walls of the city, as we shall see, or around the cathedral), with a ring or crescent typology. The entries of kings of France into Paris seem to have observed the first typology (the arrow): from Porte St. Denis by way of the Châtelet, Pont-au-change, Notre-Dame, to the Palais de Justice.[60] The same type of route was followed in all the entries of Charles V at the time of his progress through the Italian peninsula, from Sicily to the Alps.

The *adventus novi episcopi* (entry of new bishops) is the first and most obvious example that comes to mind of the second typology (the ring or crescent). The new bishop truly "universam urbem lustravit" (cleansed the whole city). One can reconstruct a late example, the entry of Archbishop Antonio Altoviti into Florence in 1567 (Fig. 19). He made his entry through the southern gate, crossed the Roman bridge, passed the parish church behind the Palazzo della Signoria, and proceeded to the (now destroyed) convent of San Piero Maggiore (where always occurred the rite of marriage with the church of Florence, impersonated by the abbess of that convent).[61] After this rite he proceeded along the Roman *decumanus,* toward the "stone of St. Anthony" (the site of a miracle, but also one of the hermae of the sacred city), and he proceeded to circuit the cathedral before reaching the archiepiscopal palace. Looking at a map of the route, one can easily observe that it was a half circle, along the side of the ancient city of Roman foundation, followed by a circle around the chief Florentine church.

If we compare this entry with the route taken for the funeral of Giuliano de' Medici, the similarities quickly appear. Giuliano, duc de Nemours, died in the Badia di Fiesole on 17 March 1516 and was carried into the city that same night. His obsequies were celebrated on the nineteenth, with a platform raised in front of the Medici palace,

> partly covered with a carpet, and the bier covered with cloth of gold placed on that, and his suit of armor on the body with a silken cloth over it, the ducal coronet, sword, and spurs. . . . All the magistrates and the guilds were there . . . with two men on draped horses carrying the flags of the Signoria and the Parte Guelfa. And when the magistrates were seated, Lorenzo appeared in a blazoned cloak, with the whole family of the duke and duchess, dressed in mourning hoods, who also seated themselves. Messer Marcello Adriani made the funeral oration, on completion of which all the religious and clergy [went in procession] . . . following the helmet of the duke carried on a cushion by a youth.

59. "Fecerunt insuper ordinari, quod Vexilifer nullus claves civitatis offerret Papae, sicut alii Magistratus consueverunt, et hoc quia ipsi Florentini portam ad terram dejecerunt, et patefecerunt in totum." De' Grassi 1805–6. See Shearman 1975; Ciseri 1990, 21ff.

60. Bryant 1986b, fig. 4.

61. The bishop lay on a bed with the abbess and put one leg over hers to indicate the intercourse.

Fig. 19   Map of the triumphal entry of Archbishop Antonio Altoviti, Florence, 1567.

... They progressed along Via dei Fondamenti [that is, they circuited the cathedral] to the Palazzo del Podestà, to the [main] square, by the Mercato Nuovo, by Santa Trinita, by Piazza degli Antinori, by Santa Maria Maggiore, along Borgo San Lorenzo, and finally into S. Lorenzo.[62]

Those acquainted with Florence and looking at a map can easily observe that this was a quadrangular route that followed the ancient first circuit of walls (that of the Roman foundation).

62. "mezzo coperto d'un tappeto, e sopravi il fretro con una comperta di broccato d'oro, et sopra il corpo suo vesito armis bellicis con un sajone di broccato di sopra, et la berretta ducale, la spada, e sproni.... Comparsero poi tutti I Magistrati, le Arti ... furonvi due a cavallo copertati, che portavano le bandiere della Signoria e della parte, e postisi a sedere i prefati Magistrati, uscì fuori Lorenzo con il capperruccione imbastito con tutta la famiglia del Duca et di Madonna, vestiti a bruno con cappuccioni ancor loro e posti a sedere. M. Marcello Adriani fece l'oratione funerale in laude del defunto, la quale fornita seguirno tutte le religioni e clero ... seguiva l'elmetto del duca portato in su una mazza da un ragazzo.... Feciono la via de' fondamenti al palagio del podestà, di piazza, di mercatonuovo, da S. Trinita, dalla piazza degli Antinori, da S. Maria Maggiore et borgo San Lorenzo e finalmente in S. Lorenzo." Moreni 1813, 63–65.

The circuit around the walls of a city was well known by the early Middle Ages and by Byzantium, whose legacy passed to the Merovingians. Gregory of Tours tells us that when the Franks laid siege to Saragossa in A.D. 541, they saw women dressed in black, their heads covered with ashes, walking around the perimeter of the walls,[63] and it was said that the capital of the Vasates, Bazas, was saved from an Arian attack because the relics of Saint John the Baptist were carried in procession around its walls.[64] The same thing happened at the beginning of the sixth century at Orleans, with the relics of Saint Anianus.[65] In the seventh century the bishop Leodegarius hastened to Autun to support a siege with a procession around the battlements, during the course of which all the gates were sanctified with prostration and special prayers.[66]

Although these are rather early examples, one can still say that ritual cleansing was still attentively observed in the Middle Ages and the early modern period. In Naples, the Aragonese cavalcade of 1443 for Alfonso the Magnanimous entered through the Porta di Mercato, but failed to continue along the perimeter of the Angevin walls (Fig. 20). At first sight it might seem that the ancient rite was not being observed, but in looking closely at the itinerary, one discovers that the king progressed along the ancient *decumanus* and the walled precinct of the Roman city, which no longer existed. Thus he made a circuit of the ancient precinct that marked the city's foundation, as if there remained a residual memory and tradition of a sacred route, changed but still ideally present, even when the millennial stones no longer existed. There is no description of the route of the cavalcade for the coronation of King Alfonso II on 24 April 1494, a ceremony that was arranged by the pontifical master of ceremonies Johann Burchard (Fig. 21).[67] We would probably not be far from the truth if we imagined that the processional route was the same, but in the other direction, from Castelnuovo through the Porta Reale di Santa Chiara, then along the *decumanus* to the cathedral. This was the same route, roughly, followed by another conqueror, Charles VIII, on 22 February 1495.[68] It was a true and proper recognition of the territory. The king progressed from Porta Capuana (farther north than Porta di Mercato), along the *decumanus,* passed through the Porta Reale, visited all the Seggi di Nobiltà (the places where justice was administered), and finally returned to Castel Capuano.

The *circuitus murorum* seems to me an ethological recognition of territory. As Clifford Geertz has written, when kings travel through their land, showing themselves publicly, attending festivities, conferring honors, exchanging gifts, defeating rivals, "they mark it," just as the wolf and the tiger mark their own habitat with urine, almost as if it were a physical extension of their own bodies.[69]

The fact that the circuit corresponded to the precinct of the city's ancient foundation is important. The most important procession of the commune of Florence was surely the entry of the icon of Santa Maria dell'Impruneta in moments of crisis (wars, droughts, floods). She was a black Madonna (of the kind truly painted by Saint Luke) particularly associated with water. She was a Madonna with the peculiarity of not being able to remain at night inside the city walls, although she was the protectress of Florence, precisely

63. Gregory of Tours, *Historiarum libri, 3, 29,* MGHSSRMer. 1.1.
64. Gregory of Tours, *In gloria martirum* 1, 12, MGHSSRMer. 1.2:675 11–14.
65. *Vita Aniani* 1896, 473.
66. Gregory of Tours, *Liber vitae patrum,* MGHSSRMer. 3.2:675 11–14.
67. Burchard 1906, 11–14.
68. Epifania 1902.
69. Geertz 1983, 125; and see Boutier, Dewerpe, and Nordman 1984.

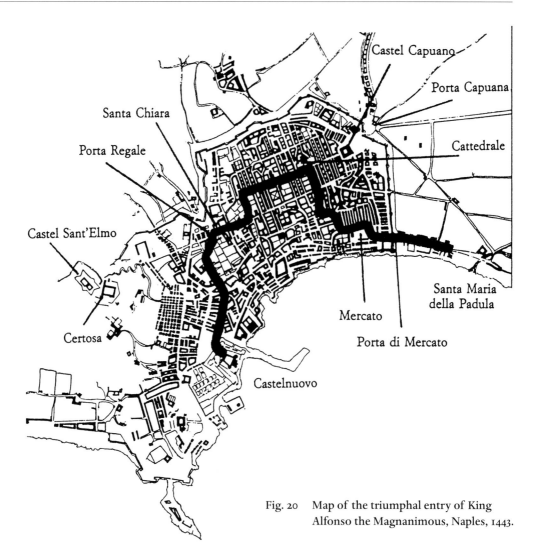

Fig. 20   Map of the triumphal entry of King
Alfonso the Magnanimous, Naples, 1443.

like another Madonna painted by Saint Luke who protected Bologna from a hill overlooking the city. Even after the construction of the larger fourteenth-century circuit of walls
around Florence, the Signoria continued to welcome the entry of the icon at the ancient
gate of San Piero Gattolini (which had been taken down),[70] rather than go on to meet it at
Porta Romana, the true entrance to the city (Fig. 22). This was the ideal point from which
the procession in the city began, although, of course, people carrying olive branches went
out to welcome the Madonna beyond the walls. Reconstruction of the route of the procession within the city indicates clearly that it was a circuit of the ancient precinct of Roman foundation (Fig. 23). In the same way, at Avignon, processions crossed the central
square twice (where the town hall stood at the heart of the city), reaching the two principal gates to the southeast and east, but never proceeded beyond the confines of the ancient commune built before the siege of 1226.[71] At a later date, in 1650, the cavalcade for
the entry of Emperor Ferdinand III into Antwerp followed a sacred circuit that was different from the more modern urban layout.[72]

70. On San Piero Gattolini (that is, Cattuario or Gatula), see Richa 1754–62, x:99ff.
71. Venard 1977, 58–59.
72. Martin 1972. For an earlier triumph of Philip II at Antwerp, see Scribonius 1549.

Fig. 21 The coronation procession of King Alfonso II of Aragon, from the Ferraiolo chronicle, New York, Pierpont Morgan Library (from R. Filangieri, *Una cronaca napoletana figurata del Quattrocento*, Naples, L'Unione tipografica, 1956).

Fig. 22   Map of the triumphal entry of the icon of Santa Maria di Impruneta into Florence
(fifteenth–seventeenth centuries).

3. The dress of the person coming in triumph: the white tunic. The ceremony of vestment
before passing through the walls emphasized the *parousìa,* and at the same time accentuated the rite of passage. Here we can refer to the Roman custom of using a *tenia,* the band
that covered the forehead of the person coming in triumph, indicating that he had been
purified. We can associate this rite with a later one. The pope,[73] after his coronation in St.
Peter's, progressed to the Lateran Palace in a solemn cavalcade, the *Processio* (later called
the *Possessio,* in the sense that the bishop of Rome was taking possession of his see; see
Fig. 43). When he arrived before the portico of the Lateran basilica, he put on a belt from
which seven seals hung, to signify that he was the lamb of the Apocalypse. In other words,
the whole ceremony was like a rite of purification in which the person in triumph was
also a hostage, a sacrificial victim, who brought his *mana* with him.[74]

73. For an analysis of papal coronations, see Guidi 1936 and Klewitz 1941.
74. See Hocart [1936] 1970, 90ff.

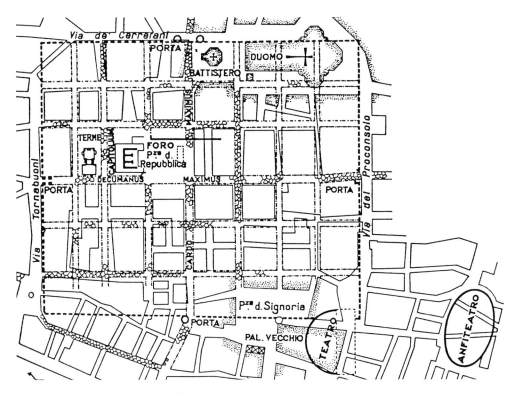

Fig. 23   The Roman precinct of the city of Florence.

For Renaissance examples of a similar rite, we may refer to the year 1453, when Francesco Sforza entered Milan (after he captured it in 1452) and Borso d'Este entered Reggio Emilia, on 25 March and 4 July respectively. After the procession on horseback, Francesco Sforza dismounted before the cathedral and ascended a platform prepared for the occasion in the cathedral close (see Fig. 26). Here the *condottiero* was welcomed with a discourse by Baldasar Castiglione. Then he changed his clothes, to be dressed in a tunic of white damask, with the assistance of Oldrado da Lampugnano, while Filippo Borromeo wrapped him in an ermine mantle, Pietro Visconti put on a hat, Gaspare da Vimercate gave him the scepter, Antonio Trivulzio held his standard, Melchiorre da Marliano gave him the ducal seal, Pietro Pusterla the sword, and twelve citizens gave him the keys to the gates.

Another kind of *anàtellon/parousìa,* similar to the one in Milan, occurred in Reggio Emilia. Borso d'Este, after the procession on horseback and the Mass in the cathedral, climbed up onto a platform: "When the Mass was finished, the lord was welcomed on the tribune by the bishop himself and the canons, and he was given a seat of honor on the bishop's chair, so that he could be seen by all, and if a crown had been put on his head, he would have been acclaimed by everybody as a royal majesty."[75]

Solemn occasions could sometimes border on the grotesque, as happened during Charles V's entry into Naples in 1535.

75. "Missa ergo celebrata et audita, dominus iterum per eundem dominum episcopum et ipsos dominos canonicos fuit associatus ad dictum tribunalem et ibi honorifice positus super dicta cathedra, ita quod ab omnibus poterat videri et merito, quia ab omnibus fuisset judicatus Maiestas regalis si coronam detulisset in capite." Ariosti 1899, 33; Levi 1889; Pardi 1906–7.

The following day, the feast of Saint Catherine, the 25th of November, in the year 1535, His Imperial Majesty Charles V, after dining at 12 hours, mounted onto a fine black horse. He was dressed in green velvet trimmed with gold fringe and embroidery, lined with richly woven cloth of gold. Besides his gilded and finely worked sword, he had a silk hat of the same color worked in the same way, and a beautiful white feather trimmed with pearls. And from the collar of his black silk shirt the insignia of the Golden Fleece hung on a gold chain. Under the silk he wore a chain with a breviary, and this was in a purse of gold brocade containing also claws of a great beast [to ward off] epilepsy that touched his skin. And the cavalcade with the lords of his court and all the barons of the realm was so numerous that it took two hours to pass. Having arrived at the Sebeto River, toward Porta Capuana, the archbishop, his vicars, and all the other bishops and prelates came out to meet him, dressed pontifically, with the cross and many relics carried piously. And His Imperial Majesty dismounted and knelt, and said a brief prayer, and the clergy returned to Naples.

A ridiculous incident befell the emperor during the cavalcade we were just describing. When the clergy had left and His Majesty had arisen, he was near Porta Capuana, where there was the gate of a garden called Guasto, and [inside was] a haystack and a gross old peasant-woman gardener. Feeling the call of nature and before returning to the cavalcade, since he was a bit distant from the horde of knights, His Majesty entered the gate in three steps and relieved himself behind the haystack. The old woman came up with a big stick in her hand, shouting, "Curses on you, shit-blood, shame on you for coming to crap here, get out," and kept shouting "Go" to get the emperor to leave. And the emperor said, "Be quiet, I am the emperor," and the old woman said, "Evil take you, you the emperor?" She had a towel over her shoulder, with one corner of it in her mouth. And one of the lords who was there took it from the woman and gave it to His Holy Imperial Majesty, since he needed to wipe his behind. And the angry woman, realizing that he really was the emperor, came to herself and answered, saying: "My lord, since you are our emperor, if you are to do us good, it is a fortunate day, do good and not ill, forgive me for not knowing you before." His Majesty remounted his great horse, which was waiting in the middle of the road, amid the cries of "Empire! Empire!" and the trumpets, horns, fifes, and singers. A sweet music sounded above the royal Porta Capuana, other trumpets on other towers, and the city walls were crowded with men and women.[76]

4. The encounter at the gate. We have seen how the Hapsburg emperor was received by the Neapolitan clergy, carrying relics. Normally, a statue of the city's patron saint was present. In Florence, along with the Signoria, the statue of Saint Zanobius (the first bishop under Constantine) received the Madonna dell'Impruneta. The statue of the patron saint personified the city, but the rite could have a double explanation. On one hand, we could connect it to the Roman imperial *adventus,* when local divinities had an important role in the reception. On the other hand, we could say that the presence of the *numen* of the patron saint, with its supernatural powers, guaranteed the community itself in some way; it was the same with relics, whose possession and exhibition was undoubtedly

76. "Racconti di storia napoletana" 1908–9, xxxiv:116–67.

a manifestation of power. But relics and the statue of the patron can also be connected with the procession of youths, an apotropaic settling of accounts with the evil spirits of anyone tinged with the blood of slain enemies.

5. The children. This was another important and recurrent aspect of all entries. The children had a specific role, referred to in the Gospels. We have already mentioned the first entry of Charlemagne into Rome in 774. An *Ordo* of the tenth century speaks of children grouped under a banner, with the clergy intoning: "Pueri Hebreorum tollentes ramos olivarum obviaverunt Domino, clamantes et dicentes: Osanna in excelsis" (The children of the Hebrews, carrying olive branches, went out to meet the Lord, singing, "Hosannah in the Highest").[77] In the frescoes of the basilica of Sant'Angelo in Formis (1072–78), in the fifteenth-century *Entrata di Cristo in Gerusalemme* by Gianfrancesco da Tolmezzo (a northern Italian painter), or in Duccio's *Maestà* (Siena) as well (Fig. 24), one can clearly distinguish the *pueri Hebraeorum:* children of five to seven years of age. An account of the entry of Charles V into Siena in 1536 makes clear that the hundred noble children who followed the banner of the city were "about ten years old, all dressed in white silk with aprons of white wool, and caps of white velvet trimmed with gold buttons and pearls, and with gold medals on their heads and necklaces, the shirts embroidered with silk and gold, and white stockings lined with cloth of the same color, with olive boughs in their hands and olive garlands about their heads."[78] Also at Siena, for the entry of Cosimo I de' Medici (1560), it is said that the clergy were followed "by a hundred noble children, between eight and twenty years of age, dressed in white cloth, with garlands of olive leaves on their caps, which were also of white cloth, and olive boughs in their right hands."[79]

It seems that these children carried out their role as an organized group. On 17 April 1127, when Charles, count of Flanders, entered Saint-Omer, "youths walked along the road carrying bows and arrows" (in this case they must have been youths, since bows and arrows would not have been well adapted to children); they, addressing him, asked for reconfirmation of their right to hunt birds, squirrels, and wolves.[80] The youths of Saint-Omer did not limit themselves to going to meet their sovereign; they also had requests (hunting as a game reserved to them). In 1449, on the entry of the king into Rouen, Mathieu d'Escouchy took care to emphasize that "as for little ones crying out 'Noël,' there were a great number."[81] We will see below how Corrado Trinci took pains to carry away four hundred children so as to deprive Spoleto of its *pueri*.

Sometimes, to emphasize their separation from the rest of the population, the children sent to receive the guest were chosen from orphans. In sixteenth-century Spain they were called *niños de la doctrina*.[82] Gabriel Millet has justly observed that the New Testament has no mention of children going to welcome Jesus; Saint Matthew speaks generically of "people" of Jerusalem welcoming the Messiah. He suggests that there was a transposition from other places in the Holy Scriptures where children are in fact

---

77. Ziegler 1931, 188–89. See also Robinson 1918.

78. *Descrittione delle cerimonie* [1884] 1968, 15–16. See Hofmeister 1938.

79. *La solenne entrata* 1560, 13.

80. "Obviam processerant pueri, arcus et sagittas ferentes, et acclamaverunt comiti quatenus feodum, quod a predessoribus suis semper pueri nostri obtinuerant: 'Haec ergo licenter egimus hactenus, et volumus eadem a te licentia ludorum nostrorum mores deinceps renovare.'" *Vita Karolis comitis Flandriae,* MGHSS, XII:597. See also Rossiaud 1976.

81. Mathieu d'Escouchy 1863, I:232.

82. Cock 1863, 36.

Fig. 24   The *pueri Hebraeorum* at the Christ's entrance into Jerusalem. Duccio di Buoninsegna,
Maestà, Siena.

mentioned ("Suffer the little children to come unto me"; Mark 10:14), and that the custom
derived from this insertion. Only in the Gospel of Nicodemus is it written that *òi paides
tòn Ebraion* (the children of the Hebrews), carrying olive branches, went to meet Jesus,
spreading their cloaks on the road.[83] This explanation was later accepted by Emile Mâle
and Noël Coulet.[84] But this is a typically erudite *qui pro quo.* The interpretation can be entirely reversed by giving more attention to the role of youths in the late Roman society
and the society of the early and late Middle Ages, which were dominated by people of
more advanced age. The presence of youths was more varied and complex than their par-

83. Millet 1916, 280–82.
84. Mâle 1922, 73; Coulet 1977, 71.

Fig. 25   The children in the funeral procession of the landgrave Maurice, from the *Monumentum Sepulcrale ad Ill.mi Celsissimique Principis ac Domini Du. Mauritii, Hassiae Landragvii . . . memoriam gloriae sempiternam erectum,* Frankfurt am Main, Amebrium, 1640.

Fig. 26   Children greeting Duke Francesco Sforza entering Milan, under a canopy (1455); medal from L. A. Muratori, *Antiquitates Italicae Medii Aevi,* Milan, Typ. Palatina, 1738–42.

ticipation in processions leads us to suppose. P. Braustein and Ch. Klapisch Zuber have emphasized the extent to which the young were considered a liminal group in a patriarchal society governed by the leaders of clans, "a fraternity of adult men, each one representing a family group subordinated to his authority. Children, youths 'under control,' female children, and members of the lower classes had no public collective identity, no place in the central representation of rituals, no political expression; they were liminal groups, kept at the margin of political society."[85] But this analysis is also only partly sustainable, because children—like virgins or the clergy (other liminal groups)—played an important central part in public rituals, and a part not limited to "entries." Medieval and ancient society assigned to children and youths (the age of maturity was usually twenty or even twenty-five years) functions with regard to acts that might produce dangers, which could reflect back on those who might otherwise be thought to have really carried them out. One might go to meet a person coming in triumph who was tainted by the *mana* of his slain enemies, or want to expel a lynched "enemy" from the social body, someone who had endangered the "common good" (a tyrant or someone convicted of particular crimes against the state). One might add that young people were often involved on these occasions and that they thus had a particular "cultural" aptitude for certain rites.

85. Braustein and Klapisch Zuber 1983, 1117; see also Klapisch Zuber 1985.

This behavior was deeply steeped in transcendent and apotropaic meaning and required the "innocence" of adolescents. The reference in the Gospel of Nicodemus to the *pueri Hebraeorum* was not the source of this ritual; the ritual was inserted into the text because the custom was already observed.[86]

Without here entering into other tasks assigned to minors, which we will examine later, it is enough for the moment to remember that the person coming in triumph was initially perceived to be an impure person, covered with the blood of his slain enemies. Only children, prepubescent and free from sin, could be the first to encounter such a warrior and receive him at the gate of the city, before he had undressed and reclothed himself—that is, before he had been purified. The exhibition of relics, on the other hand, could have a double function, both apotropaic (against evil spirits) and terrifying.

Children were assigned also to other duties, as we have already seen, such as reciting poetry when meeting the person coming in triumph ("qui ad didicendas litteras pergebant"), or serving as actors in the sacred representations arranged along the processional route within the city. This was something else. Medieval society attributed prophetic abilities to children (as to fools), the idea being that the mouths of children and fools uttered the voice of God (see Matthew 11:15–17).[87] This was a conception that remained in the Renaissance. When Queen Elizabeth progressed through the streets of London on the day of her coronation, she passed numerous "pageantries" that had been arranged: near Fanchurch, at Cornehill, at Soper-Lanes, where the queen stopped her chariot to better hear the words directed at her by a group of children: "When these wordes were spoken, all the people wished, that as the child had spoken, so God woulde strengthen her Grace against all her adversaries."[88] Who, better than a child, could express the sentiments of the city before both the queen and God?

6. The offer of the keys. See item 1b above.

7. The chariot. The model of a triumphal entry, preserved in Byzantium, passed thence on to western Europe in the celebration of the victories of Visigoths in Spain, and then into Merovingian and Carolingian France.[89] Such examples could easily have been taken up by one whose own imperial function had become a raison d'être, like Frederick II, or by an ambitious Italian condottiere, such as Castruccio at the beginning of the fourteenth century. But we can also understand why the victorious cardinal Vitelleschi, who as conqueror of Palestrina was victor over the Savelli and Colonna families in 1436, preferred to enter Rome on a she-mule, a sterile animal much more appropriate to a prelate. The patriarch thus preserved an immediate reference to the ceremony of the *adventus novi episcopi* based on the entry of Jesus into Jerusalem, while still accepting a baldacchino, a reference to a sovereignty that he had, in a certain sense, usurped.

The chariot seems to have been exclusively an imperial symbol. In solar symbolism a wheel emanating rays represented a star.[90] Thus we glimpse the great ambition of Castruccio, who was invested with the title of duke of Lucca, Pistoia, and Volterra by Emperor Ludwig of Bavaria only a year after his triumph. Plutarch, in his *Life of Camillus*, says that the Romans considered a triumphal chariot to be sacred, reserving it for kings

86. See Niccoli 1993.
87. See Grottanelli 1993.
88. Jones 1883, 157–63; Collins 1953; Bergeron 1971, 11–23; *The Quenes Maiesties . . . (1558)* 1960.
89. McCormick 1986, 297ff. See also Sawyer and Wood 1977.
90. Durand 1992, 373ff. and passim.

and the father of the gods.[91] The chariot passed to the new Christian era with the same aura: was not *Christos-Helios* the divine charioteer mentioned by Firmicus Maternus?[92] When the emperor John I Tzimisces, victor over Nasa al Kasaki in 958–59, celebrated his triumph and was received at the gates of Constantinople by the patriarch Basil I Scamandreus, he refused the two-wheeled triumphal chariot the patriarch invited him to ride in, and wanted to put in it instead the icon of the Virgin he had captured from the Bulgarians, along with other regalia.[93]

In medieval western Europe it seems that entries were celebrated using the ritual of the *ovatio,* without use of the Roman *biga* (or *quadriga*), or the Byzantine two-wheeled chariot. In this sense Castruccio's triumph might be thought to have been an innovation. That is still not to say that it might also have been influenced by the *progressio,* as this is represented on the north side of the Arch of Constantine, which refers to the emperor's return from the battle against Massentius (see Fig. 17). It shows the victor seated on a chair placed in a four-wheeled cart (*carpentum*), looking fixedly ahead. We wonder: Did Castruccio/Tegrimi refer to Dante's description of the triumph of Beatrice, or to the *progressio* of Constantine on this archaeological monument, rather than to the equally well-known bas-relief of Marcus Aurelius? Or perhaps there were other more immediate points of reference, for instance, the communal *carroccio* that appeared in the processions both at Cremona and Lucca and might be more believable in this context? We must keep in mind that the *carroccio* taken from the Milanese in the battle of Cortenuova was sent by Frederick II to Rome, with the whole baggage of sacredness that surrounded such *spolia.*[94]

Tegrimi, if he had really wanted to invent a triumph, would have had other models, but he would not have described Castruccio "curru residens aperto" (in an open chariot). He could easily have referred to the Neapolitan triumphs of Alfonso of Aragon, or the Roman triumph on 29 August 1436 of Cardinal Giovanni Vitelleschi, celebrated as an *ovatio.* The patriarch was welcomed at the major gate by the population, carrying olive branches, and his baldacchino was later sacked, like the one used by the pope.

Only two years after the triumph of Vitelleschi another *ovatio* occurred at Foligno. Corrado Trinci, lord of that city, had suffered a humiliating defeat by Pope Martin V and a significant loss of territory. On the death of Martin V (1431) Corrado reconquered his lost lands. Not only that, but with the support of Cosimo de' Medici and Francesco Sforza against the same Patriarch Vitelleschi, he pushed on to attack Spoleto, conquering and sacking it in May 1436. To assure eternal fame, he celebrated his own triumph, marching before him four hundred prisoners, along with the *spolia.* "It was a grand booty, and most of it was carried to Foligno, and they even took the chains and bells to Foligno, with trumpets [sounding] before them."[95] Dorio adds in his history of Trinci: "On 14 May, Corrado brought to Foligno four hundred youths of Spoleto, the standard of Spoleto, the chains, the locks from the city gates, the seal, and the clapper from the great bell of the commune."[96] But this, too, was an *ovatio.*

Where could Tegrimi have found his model? Did he collect accounts of the triumphs

91. Plutarch, *Camillus,* 7.2.
92. Firmicus Maternus 1907, 61.23 (*De errore . . .* , xxiv, 4); Dölger VI:51–56.
93. MacCormack 1980, 173 and fig. 10.
94. Kantorowicz 1989, 406; and see Voltmer 1994.
95. Bonaini, Fabretti, and Polidori 1850, 426.
96. Dorio 1638, 228.

of Alfonso the Magnanimous? One should note that another humanist, Porcellio, had transformed the event of 1443 in Naples into an entirely pagan ceremony, describing the Porta San Gennaro as a "porta Januo divota," calling the Church of San Antonio "sacrata Divi Antonii," and transforming Jesus (with Virgilian echoes) into "hominum rerumque sator" (the progenitor of humanity and nature).[97] We must admit that Tegrimi's account is much less imaginative and closer to plausible reality than it would have been if he had invented the account or had turned to the ceremonial of the *ovatio,* which was vaguer and less charged with sacrality, or if he had resurrected a classical *triumphus* rather than present a *progressio.*

One wonders whether to consider the text of Giovanni Boccaccio in *L'amorosa visione*— from only sixteen years after the Lucchese triumph—where a triumph is described with the central actor sitting and not standing. Even if the Neapolitan entries of Alfonso the Magnanimous were linked to an established Catalan tradition,[98] one should not undervalue the fact that the humanist Panormita and other unidentified Florentines participated directly in arrangements for the second entry. Who better than they would not remember Castruccio, the man who had defeated their fathers? And then the contemporary account of Giovanni Villani confirms Tegrimi's later account. To conclude on this point, Villani and Tegrimi provide the missing link that connects the Italian medieval and Renaissance tradition with the classical triumph, substituting, however, the *carpentum* for the *biga.*

As we have seen, the Neapolitan triumph of Alfonso the Magnanimous in 1443 was based partly on a Byzantine model. One wonders if there were other such cases in Renaissance Italy. One thinks immediately of Piero della Francesca's Uffizi diptych showing Federico da Montefeltro (but here, in fact, a *plaustrus* [wagon] is shown, rather than the four-horsed *carpentum).*[99] However, Alfonso of Aragon really celebrated his triumph, and his chariot was later exhibited inside the portal of the Basilica of San Lorenzo as a relic, whereas the duke of Urbino's was only an imaginary triumph, and the diptych remained closed up in his study. The sacred aura derived from the anointing received by kings of Naples, the only ones in Italy who received it, was clearly lacking.

The sculptured chariot of Naples was precisely the one depicted in the codex in the National Library of Madrid by John of Scylitzes (*Scylitzes Matritensis*) to illustrate an account of the triumph of John Tzimisces. As we have seen above, in 1453 two other grand entries were celebrated in Italy: the one of Francesco Sforza in Milan, and the other of Borso d'Este in Reggio Emilia. These ceremonies had in common the fact that both of these lords (the duke and the marquis) rejected chariots because, as Sforza explained, these were "superstitions of kings and great princes."[100] This is an important confirmation of the extent to which the chariot had retained a sacred character and had been assimilated to the custom that forbade their use by sovereigns who were not anointed (and we follow Johann Burchard's assertion that the kings of Naples were anointed). Also, a bull of Pope Honorius III (1216–27) that reserved the future use of chariots to consecrated princes (*inunctae personae*) was still observed.[101]

97.   The sources for this triumph are Beccadelli 1646; Notargiacomo 1845; Di Marzo 1864; Pandoni 1539 and 1895 (there is a biography by Frittelli [1900]); Tommaso da Chaula da Chiaromonte 1904; "Racconti di storia napoletana" 1908–9; Monti 1931; *Entrada* 1932.
   98.   Maxwell 1992.
   99.   Weber 1979, 135–51.
   100.   Simonetta 1554, 297v.
   101.   *Bullarium* 6584, A.D. 1221.

The chariot presented to Borso d'Este was minutely described by Malatesta Ariosti and permits some further observations. It was "unum magnum plaustrum triumphale" (a large triumphal wagon) drawn by four horses, with white trappings, emblazoned with the ducal and communal arms. "At the center of the wagon was a chair raised to the height of three steps." On the second step sat a youth dressed as Justice, with drawn sword and the scales of justice at his feet; on the bottom step was "a youth dressed as an angel." In one corner of the wagon was another youth "who represented the figure of a jurist, nicely dressed and holding a baldacchino that covered the whole wagon and was blazoned with the ducal and communal arms of Reggio." The explanation for the symbolism was given by the youth seated at the feet of Justice. This

> donna bella . . .
> La qualle el mondo rege . . .
> Già più e più anni dice che passarono
> Dopo la morte de quei boni Romani
> Cum stenti et com affanj
> E' gita per lo mondo senza pregio
> Hora Signore siendo venuto a Regio
> Vedentote venire cum tanto honore
> Tu li ha passato il cuore
> Et dice che de ti la è innamorata. . . .

> (Lovely lady . . .
> Who rules the world . . .
> Now many years 'tis said have past
> Since the death of those good Romans.
> With dearth and affliction
> She journeys sadly through the world;
> Now, Sir, you have come to Reggio
> Welcomed with such honor.
> [She] has given you [her] heart
> And says [she] is in love with you. . . .)

After this presentation, Justice addressed the lord:

> Poi Numapompilio et il nepote
> Lucio Cincinnato et Marcho Atilio
> Cinocamilo, Catone et Marchoemilio[102]
> L'animi sum da i corpi loro remoti
> Patrono mio caro, queste sedie vote
> Sempre sonno state et io, poste in exilio,
> Né mai trovai che per mio consiglio

---

102. All these names are corrupted. We can recognize the king Numa Pompilius, the emperor Lucius Verus, the consuls Titus Quintius Cincinnatus, Marcus Attilius Regulus, and Marcus Furius Camillus, probably M. Porcius Cato Censorius, the triumvir Marcus Aemilius Lepidus, but we do not know who "the nephew" of Nume might have been.

Habia voluto ascendere queste Rote
Ma puo justo Signore acorto e sagio
Che tu se giunto a lo honorato offico
A ti ritorno perché altrove un ragio
Non vegio de virtù, fra tanto vicio.
Ascende in questo loco, unde io te adagio
Premio di buoni et de li rei supplicio.

(Then Numa Pompilius, and the nephew
Lucius Cincinnatus, and Marcus Attilius,
Cinocamillus, Cato, and Marcus Aemilius.
[Their] souls are separated from their bodies.
Dear Lord, these seats
Have always been empty, and I, in exile,
Find no one who for my counsel
Has wanted to mount this tribunal.
But, just Lord, aware and wise
Since you have come to this honored office,
I return to you, because I see no other ray
Of virtue, among such vice.
Ascend to this place where I bring you
The prize for good men, and punishment for criminals.)

As I have said, Borso refused the offer of a chariot,[103] but the full description lets one see that the ceremony was a full expression of the *lex animata* (the fact that the new lord brought the law with him). Francesco Sforza and Borso d'Este both, however, did accept a *pallium,* which was another sacred symbol associated with the cult of the sun.[104] Both observed the rite of undressing/redressing (for Sforza, this involved a white tunic); both were welcomed by children carrying olive branches; both mounted a platform in front of a cathedral.

One might also ask why the Neapolitans did not offer a chariot to the king of France, Louis XII, in 1497, but instead only a baldacchino. Perhaps they did not think him a sovereign with full powers, since the pope had refused him investiture.

That the chariot retained intact its scared value at the beginning of the sixteenth century is confirmed by yet another example, that of the French king Louis XII's entry into Cremona, preceded by "the city's youths dressed in blue satin sewn with fleurs-de-lys," under a *pallium* carried by four noble citizens.[105] The king replied to a patrician, who invited him to mount into a chariot, that this was reserved to God:

Ung veillart, personne tres famée
Dire luy vint: "Ta victoire estimée
Par hault loyer requiert estre embasmée

---

103. "domino nolente pro nunc ascendere currum, duo homines ornati cum uno magno pro eorum utroque vexillo in manibus ad armam ducalem et communis Regij, ceperunt antecedere." Ariosti 1901, 28–30.
104. Gagé 1933; Kantorowicz 1963.
105. Champier 1977, 50–51.

De tell gloire

Portant, o Roy d'eternelle mémoire,

Monte lassus, au siege de victoire,

Qui conquis as par oeuvre meritoire

Et haulx labeurs."

Lors, tout honteux leur a dit: "Beaulx Seigneurs,

Au Roy du ciel en sont deuz les honneurs,

Non pas à moy, le moindres des mineurs,

Comme jadis,

Dist Godeffroy de Billion, le hardis,

Quant refusa triomphes beneditz,

Lors qu'il conquista contre payens maulditz,

La terre Saincte."[106]

(An elderly and eminent person

Said to him: "Your esteemed victory

Deserves the high reward of being marked

By such glory. Thus, oh King of everlasting fame,

Mount up, into the chariot of victory,

That you have won by meritorious acts

And great labor."

Then modestly he answered them: "Fair Lords,

The King of Heaven deserves the honor,

Not I, the least of the lowly,

As once,

Godeffroy de Bullion, the fearless,

Said on refusing blessed triumphs,

When he had conquered the Holy Land

From cursed pagans.")

King Louis, in fact, had another example of modesty to inspire him among the kings of France. When, in 1457, the king of Hungary, Ladislas V, gave to Charles VII a triumphal chariot, "a moveable and very richly appointed chariot," the French king never dared to use it, although he rode in it after his death, in effigy, for his funeral "triumph" in Paris in 1461.[107]

A similar chariot with the seat empty was apparently offered by the Romans to Pope Julius II on his return from an expedition against Bologna in 1507;[108] and still another chariot, also with the seat empty, reserved for the personification of justice, was presented by the Florentines to Leo X in 1515.[109]

Contrarily, the chariot representing the "victoria Iulii Caesaris," paraded along with ten others in Rome's Piazza Navona to celebrate the taking of Forlì (in 1503), appears to have been a carnivalesque spectacle, since Duke Valentino had already made his entrance into Rome some days earlier.[110]

106. Marot de Caen 1977, 142–43.
107. Straus 1912, 64.
108. Greenhalgh 1985, 186.
109. Pinelli 1985, 324–28; Ciseri 1990, doc. IV.
110. Ademollo 1886; Clementi 1899, 103.

In the central and northern parts of Italy, the lack of royal dynasties created a number of problems with ceremony that were difficult to resolve, particularly for the smaller signorie. In 1454, a year after the triumphs of Francesco Sforza and Borso d'Este, Basinio da Parma illustrated a copy of the *Argonauti,* depicting the triumph of Sigismondo Pandolfo Malatesta. The lord of Rimini is shown ascending a platform in front of the cathedral, but there is no trace of a triumphal chariot. If Malatesta truly wanted to mount into a chariot, he had to do it allusively by having a chariot sculptured in the Arca degli Antenati in the temple designed by Alberti. Although Weisbach—following Carandente— says that Federico da Montefeltro celebrated at least three triumphs (in Florence after the conquest of Volterra, the one described by the court poet Giovanni Santi, and the one attributed to him in effigy by his son Guidobaldo),[111] it is doubtful that these were truly triumphs. The honors given to him by Florence in 1472 were an entry on horseback and an oration in his honor pronounced in the Piazza della Signoria. There were no triumphal arches or allegorical representations along the route (which was probably of the "arrow" type rather than a "crescent"). Thus Federico only mounted a chariot in effigy, in his portrait by Piero della Francesca, and in a supposed memorial ceremony celebrated at Casteldurante six years after his death. And this resembled a French funeral/triumph of the type studied by Ralph Giesey.[112]

Cosimo de' Medici the Elder was another lord (if one wants to call him that) who celebrated his triumph allusively. The courtly poet Bastiano Foresi praised his triumph over vice in the style of Petrarch,[113] but Cosimo was careful not to make much of this.

All this leads one to believe, in short, that the possibilities of mounting a triumphal chariot were quite limited, restricted to those who could claim royal anointing.

It remains, in Italy, to discuss the *carpentum* equipped with a rich baldacchino, as is shown in a Hans Schäuffelein engraving of the entry of Charles V into Pavia. The emperor is seated at the center of a wagon, surrounded by his ancestors, while Fame, at his shoulders, holds a crown over his head (just as in Piero della Francesca's diptych showing Federico da Montefeltro). But it is uncertain whether the Hapsburg monarch really rode in this way or whether the print is imaginary. Certainly, on his entry into Siena on 24 April 1536, Charles rode under a baldacchino, while observing the *ovatio* as the form of entry. Duke Cosimo I de' Medici did the same on his entry into Siena on 28 October 1560, even if the later post mortem representation of this event on the base of the equestrian statue of the duke by Giambologna (1603) in the Piazza della Signoria in Florence shows him riding in a triumphal chariot.

8. The baldacchino. See Part I, Chapter 5.

9. The acts of sovereignty. At Milan, after the ceremony of investment of Francesco Sforza, the crowd shouted for the duke to make his son a knight, along with some of the other courtiers, "as a sign, in memory, and for the perpetual fame of so much celebration, feasting, and joy."[114] The request was for the immediate exhibition of an act of sovereignty. Leo X did this when, before setting out on the cavalcade of the *Possessio,* he covered Alfonso d'Este with a ducal mantle.[115] The detailed chronicle of the coronation of

---

111. Weisbach 1919, 66–67; Carandente 1963, 75. See also Santi 1985.

112. Giesey 1960.

113. Foresi 1885; Weisbach 1919, 68.

114. "In signum memoriam et perpetuam famam tante celebritatis, festivitatis et gloria." *Cronichetta di Lodi* 1884; Cagnola 1842, 126ff.; Simonetta 1554, 297v; Colombo 1905.

115. Penni 1513 in Cancellieri 1802, 67–84, and also in Cruciani 1983, 390–405.

the emperor Matthias (1612) says that after the Te Deum "the celebrant and his assistant and the other clergy descended and went into the choir to take off their pontifical robes. But His Majesty remained on the throne, together with the other princely electors, who remained standing. Then His Majesty proceeded to the investiture of several counts, lords, and nobles with the sword of Charlemagne."[116] Even the emperor William of Prussia, in 1872, after his triumphal procession, distributed honors to his soldiers under the Berlin linden trees, with the same meaning.

We come to the amnesties usually granted to prisoners at the time of entries (and we are lumping together entries with coronations, whose processions were similar). Jean Bodin, in *De republica* (1:10), thought the right to give grace was the fifth attribute of sovereignty. Following the *sacre* of 1611, kings of France always associated this rite with their ceremonies. In Pichon's account of the coronation of Louis XVI (1775), at the moment the shout "Vivat rex" went up in the cathedral of Rheims, "bird keepers let loose a great number of little birds to signify the distribution of grace by the king for the benefit of his people."[117] According to Jackson,[118] before the *sacre* of Louis XII (1498) there was no custom of granting amnesty to prisoners or of releasing birds. In Correggio's *Adorazione dei pastori* (commissioned in October 1522) a shepherd carries the gift of a cage of little birds, and since it was the occasion of the birth of the King of Kings, we may assume that these must have been successively freed as an act of sovereignty.[119] One wonders whether the French ceremony was introduced on more ancient models. That this was initially closely connected with the *adventus* and with triumphal processions is suggested by the concession to the duc d'Angoulême, by Louis XI, to grant amnesty to some prisoners on the occasion of his entry (1477).[120] Since this was an act of sovereignty, it could only be delegated from the lord, but it is also significant that the duc d'Angoulême thought he could exercise an act of clemency on entering his own fief. In October 1552, the criminal court of the Parlement of Paris (la Tournelle) gave out norms for the treatment of habitual criminals who voluntarily presented themselves to prisons in cities where a royal entry was imminently expected, precisely to take advantage of royal grace.[121] This was a custom that must have been tied to ancient beliefs about the glance of the king, and thus to his body. Suetonius writes, in his *Life of Titus,* that no one should leave the emperor unhappy after having been in his presence. When Jean d'Ibelin, because he had lost a brother, presented himself in mourning clothes before the emperor Frederick II, the emperor ordered that he be given scarlet clothing immediately, because the joy of seeing the emperor should surpass the grief of losing a brother.[122] According to a story in *Life of Saint Leonard* (*Vitae sanctorum*), Clovis promised Saint Rémi that every time he entered Rouen, or even passed in the sight of its walls, the gates of the prisons would be opened.[123] Even in the eighteenth century "people in France believed that the king's heart could not perceive suffering without commiseration."[124] But was it that the king could not bear to see the suffering of his subjects, or rather that his glance alleviated the suffering? The Count of

116. *Wahl und Crönungshandlung* 1612, n.p.
117. Pichon 1775, 49. See also Gobet 1775.
118. Jackson 1984, 90.
119. Chirat 1945.
120. Jackson 1984, 94.
121. Papon 1568, 530v.
122. Kantorowicz 1989, 172.
123. Marlot 1846, II:58–59.
124. Hezecques n.d., 174.

Hezecques tells that one day Louis XVI, while returning to Versailles on the road at Saint-Cyr after hunting, encountered a brigade taking a deserter back to his regiment. "The soldier, whether he knew or not that the meeting might be fortunate for him, threw himself at the feet of the king, held up his arms, and begged for royal clemency," which was immediately given him. Hezecques adds that when prisoners were being taken to prison, the guards had to make detours so as not to pass near the palace, precisely so as not to run the risk of encountering the king.[125]

In Portugal, a condemned criminal was branded an *amorado,* a word with a double semantic meaning. It indicated that anyone who had lost his *morada* (his address, or rather his dwelling) also lost the love of the king. Petitions for grace, thus, requested readmission to the grace of the sovereign.[126]

The pardon given *in adventu* must therefore have had an anthropological origin not found in Roman law or even in the practice of the Greek cities.

Another interesting case worthy of attention is the funeral of Francesco I, grand duke of Tuscany (1587). The chronicler Lapini writes: "At [Borgo] La Croce were a hundred white candles . . . six guards on horseback . . . and forty-five men let out of prison with their clothes on backward and caps . . . with olive branches on them."[127] Here, rather than an *adventus,* we have a rite of departure.

10. The Riot. Another aspect of the ceremony of triumphs should attract our attention: the dance of masked Catalan soldiers *simul rissantes* (feigning a riot) in Naples in 1443 (an act the chronicler did not understand and thought was a means for preventing any attack on the chariot of Alfonso the Magnanimous).[128] This conduct was not recorded in the chronicle of King Pere III (Alfonso's grandfather), who recorded his own coronation at Saragossa the Sunday after Easter of 1336. The king tells us only that he rode to the cathedral that day, surrounded by his vassals, who held a long chain around his horse.[129] If the chain had the meaning of an act of submission, we still find no mention of a war dance, as is described in the triumph/coronation of Alfonso the Magnanimous. We know that the game of fighting with long canes (*juego de canas*) was a habit of Spanish soldiers, but it is surprising that they wore masks. This custom was widespread in Catalonia and Aragon at least from the fifteenth century, but it was a sort of joust: a group of horsemen running after another group of horsemen, trying to strike them on the shoulders.[130] Are we facing an archaeological remnant of the Roman triumph, suggested perhaps by one humanist in the king's retinue? I will return to discuss this "riot" in the following chapter.

11. The immobility. The person coming in triumph must not turn his head to the crowd and must not hear the shouts in his honor.[131] Ammianus Marcellinus, describing the entry into Rome of the Roman emperor Constans, writes that the emperor stood erect, keeping his gaze fixed in front of him, and that "tamquam figmentum hominis" (like the statue of a man), he did not move a muscle, arm or leg. This rigidity of behavior was all

125. Hezecques n.d., 174.
126. See Davis 1987.
127. Lapini 1900, 262–63.
128. "Trasformati in habitu et facie velati, qui simul rissantes, ad hoc ut meno curri regio se appropinquasset." Fabriczy 1899, 50–51. But see also Beccadelli 1646, 94–101; Bertaux 1902, 365–79.
129. Pere III 1980, 197. See also Rio 1988.
130. Maxwell 1992, 866ff.
131. MacCormack 1981, 44.

the more praised because after the ceremony he was relaxed and friendly.[132] Such immobility can be understood, since the face of the person coming in triumph was painted red, like a statue of Jupiter. In a certain sense Romans adored Jupiter in him, or rather Jupiter's *imago*.[133] After all, even the priest of the temple of Jupiter, the *flaminus,* was a living image of the god.[134] John Scheid writes: "We are very close to a human copy of the divine statue, and the burning red face of the general and the godlike stance he assumed could only accentuate this 'resemblance.'"[135] The extent of continuity of this behavior through the Middle Ages and Renaissance is astonishing. If Frederick II welcomed with the immobility of marble those who entered Capua through his *porta triumphalis,* Castruccio, immobile, sitting on the chariot, "showed with a serene expression, in Caesarean majesty, the dignity of a king"; and perhaps Laurana sculpted Alfonso of Aragon with his head erect, his glance fixed ahead of him, immobile, as the king showed himself along the triumphal procession. His hand holding the globe was immobile, despite anything that might have been happening around him. Federico da Montefeltro was equally immobile in the pose presented by Piero della Francesca. Queen Elizabeth of England was immobile, like an idol, in her triumph at Blackfriars.

12. The spolia *(loot).* Not infrequently the chroniclers of these entries refer to the carrying of loot at the head of the procession, as I have shown for the triumphs of Frederick II, Castruccio Castracani, and Corrado Trinci. Mantegna showed this well in his *Caesar's Triumph* (now at Hampton Court).[136] The custom continued, and at the beginning of the sixteenth century, in the tense days of the League of Cambrai, Marin Sanudo recorded a Venetian procession of 10 October 1511, where a silver barber's basin belonging to Charles VIII that had been captured at the battle of Fornovo was carried along with relics.

> Then came the friars carrying vessels to be used in the Mass, and twenty-eight parish priests carrying chalices and patens, then some silver plate from San Lorenzo . . . then a *soler* [a handbarrow to carry images] with Saint Mark and Venice, that is, a costumed woman with a banner, standing before the image of Saint Mark . . . then three other *soleri* with relics . . . the head of Saint Peter Martyr . . . some silver feet, one of Saint Vito, another of Saint Catherine of Siena, and after that the large head in silver of Saint Ursula . . . . then friars carried other pieces of plate, among them a large basin with the arms of the Pesero, and a barber's basin of dark silver that had belonged to King Charles of France and was taken by our troops at [the battle of Fornovo, near the river] Taro [where, on 5–6 July 1495, Charles VIII was defeated by the Italian League].[137]

Alongside the other relics, the barber's basin may have had merely sentimental value, but perhaps as loot, or as a talisman, it could lead to a repetition of the 1495 victory against the same enemy.

If the *spolia* recalled past victories, the regalia, carried directly in front of the king in all

132. MacCormack 1981, 42.
133. Ammianus Marcellinus 1978; Scheid 1986.
134. Plutarch, *Quaestiones Romanae,* III, 190c.
135. Scheid 1986, 223.
136. For representations of classical triumphs, see Lomazzo 1584, 393.
137. Sanudo 1879–1915, XIII:130–49.

Fig. 27   The four pope's hats, coronation procession for Emperor Charles V at Bologna (1530), engraving by Nicolas Hogenberg.

coronation processions, could be compared with relics. It visually recalled the power possessed by the monarch and the essential elements of his sovereignty: the crown, the sword (sometimes doubled and tripled in appearance to emphasize still more its importance, but also to requite the desire of several officials of the court to participate in the ceremony), the globe, the scepter, the *main de justice* (for French kings), the oriflamme, the several caps of the pope (Fig. 27) (which had the same significance as the several swords).

These were symbols of power and also military symbols. Were they also attributes of a queen? This was a problem that appeared when Isabella of Castille was crowned in 1474. Some complained about the presence of the sword, and Mosén Diego de Valera wrote:

> Before her rode a gentleman of her household, who carried in his right hand a sword drawn from its scabbard, to show all how she expected to punish and castigate criminals as queen and natural lord of this kingdom and signory. This was criticized by some, who said it was not the role of a queen, but rather of her husband, and they cited some laws that declared women excluded from giving judgment. This was true for women in general, but queens, duchesses, and ladies were exceptions when they had the hereditary right of *mero et mixto imperio*.[138]

Cardinal Domenico Giacobuzzi was on the other side of this argument, citing, among his reasons for why women were excluded from the papacy, the fact that persons of the female sex could not pass judgment.[139]

13. *The anàtellon.* See Part II, Chapter 8.

14. *The sack of the baldacchino.* See Part I, Chapter 5.

15. *The scattering of money.* See Part I, Chapter 5.

16. *The distribution of food.* See Part I, Chapter 6.

138. Valera 1927, II:10–23.

139. Boureau 1989, 44.

5

A Baldacchino,
Horse Trappings, and
a Fistful of Money

FORMS OF RITUAL VIOLENCE WERE a requirement closely connected with ceremonies of coronation (to which the parallels to funerals have been emphasized frequently, first by van Gennep and then by numerous anthropologists). In coronation processions, as in triumphs, the spectators always claimed a particular right, that is, to take away the horse and horse trappings, and the baldacchino under which the monarch had marched. There was then another violent incident, this one initiated by the sovereign himself, that is, the fight over coins that were thrown out. We will return to the multiple meanings of this second rite.

The right to take possession of the horse was quite widespread over widely separated geographical areas. Sometimes this was a peaceful gift. In 1442, at the end of the cavalcade for the entry into Besançon of the emperor Frederick III as king of Rome, "Simon d'Oursan, a gentleman of the county, was given the king's horse as his right as a hereditary marshal of the empire."[1] In medieval Italy, the *adventus novi episcopi* (arrival of new bishops) was marked by similar gifts. In the case of a new bishop, a kind of *jus spolii* for particularly honored individuals was tied to the reception. In Volterra, the Gotti clan had the honor/right to receive the bishop at the gates, to wash his feet, and then to receive his shoes in exchange. In Pisa, the Lanfranchi escorted the bishop from the gate in the wall to the cathedral, and received his spurs as a gift. In Florence the Bellagi (and later, when this family had fallen politically into disgrace, the Strozzi) had the honor of escorting the bishop to the altar of the Church of San Piero Maggiore, where the ceremony of the symbolic marriage with the Florentine church was performed. This honor was protected so jealously that in 1400, when it was contested by other participants in the ceremony, the head of the Strozzi clan took hold of the bishop's pontifical vestment and literally dragged him to the altar, without losing hold of his prey.[2]

Pope Martin V, on his entry into Florence on 25 February 1419, was confronted with an assault on his *corteo* and had to intervene in person. As a chronicler writes: after a long cleansing procession that took him to the cathedral and then to the monastery of Santa Maria Novella, he had barely dismounted from his horse when the *capitano del popolo* tried to take possession of it. "A subofficial of the signoria was quicker than he, however, and mounted it himself. It seems that the pope uttered these words to the signoria: that to

---

1. Marche 1883–88, 1:278.
2. Bizzocchi 1987, 33ff.; Zarri 2000, 251ff.

honor the Parte Guelfa, which had donated [the horse, it was] not to be taken from this man by the signoria so long as it lived."[3] The experience of Pope Eugene IV on his entry into Florence on 25 April 1434 was dramatic. "At Santa Maria Novella he entered a side door rather than the church, where people grabbed the standard of the Parte Guelfa and made off with it. Then, in the cloister, the gifts given him by the signoria met the same fate, but at the hands of the drunken attendants of the pope. The pope's horse was taken away by the signoria."[4] In this last incident one notes a double sense of the ritual: the standard was taken by force to be cut into pieces as relics, while the horse was given to the Florentine signoria.

Sometimes the conquest was bloody. At the coronation of Pope Boniface VIII and the cavalcade of the *Possessio* that followed it (1294), we know that there was "a riot among the plebes, who caused much confusion, and more than forty in the pope's train were killed."[5] The Roman diarist Stefano Infessura tells us that in 1472, for Pope Sixtus IV, "there was a riot in Piazza San Janni because the men-at-arms mixed with the Romans and were pelted with rocks."[6] At the end of August 1484 Pope Innocent VIII went in procession from the Vatican to the Lateran to take possession of the cathedral after his coronation. At the Basilica of San Clemente the pope dismounted his horse, left the baldacchino, mounted into a *sedia gestatoria,* and was carried by soldiers to the portico of San Giovanni Laterano. The papal master of ceremonies, Johann Burchard, described the route of the soldiers from San Clemente to the Lateran and explained the pope's unusual decision to leave the procession at San Clemente.

> The pope dismounted and mounted into a chair carried by appointed people up to the portal of the Lateran Palace without the baldacchino. It was decided to do this because Romans at the Lateran, in order to get the pope's horse and baldacchino, which they claim is theirs, can be so violent as to threaten the pope's very life. But this was a bad decision because the soldiers and some of their fellows carrying the pope arrived with such vehemence that the reception at the Lateran portico was made impossible. The pope was carried, in fact, right up to the high altar, to the fury of the people. The pope and cardinals were nearly mobbed. As soon as the pope reached the altar and descended from the chair, the soldiers made off with it, breaking it into pieces, since they claimed it for themselves.[7]

Pius II Piccolomini ran the same risk, as he recalled in his *Commentarii,* writing in the third person: "The same day as the coronation [19 August 1458], he went in solemn pomp to the Lateran, where he risked being killed by the people fighting over his horse, swords in their hands, and saved himself through divine grace."[8]

It seems that the horse (which was an integral part of the regalia)[9] and the baldacchino had a particular value in the eyes of the faithful. We understand why Leo X on the occasion of his own coronation, as Paris de' Grassi tells us, published a decree "that no one

---

3. Corazza 1894, 257.
4. Corazza 1894, 286.
5. Tosti 1846, 90.
6. Infessura 1890, 75.
7. Burchard 1906, 1:82–83.
8. Piccolomini 1984, 233.
9. See Cardini 1981 and Traeger 1970.

carry any kind of arms or dare to impede the procession, under the penalty of being hanged. And to avoid trouble at the Lateran, about the baldacchino and horse, the pope agreed with the Conservatori and the Roman Caporioni that he would give these over peacefully and also give them their usual donation and perhaps more, but only if a tumult was avoided."[10] The words of the papal master of ceremonies confirm that violence was an integral, almost necessary, part of the rite. The soldiers who carried Innocent VIII on the *sedia gestatoria* and took possession of it after they had dumped the pontiff before the high altar of the Lateran broke it into pieces, just as on other occasions the baldacchino and horse trappings from the procession were broken up. There was nothing venal in such violence; it was a deeply religious act.

Other soldiers were the protagonists of another episode, which shows that this kind of violence was not limited to a pontifical coronation or to Rome. After the triumphal entry of Charles VIII into Naples, on 22 February 1495, and after the following cavalcade for his coronation on 15 May, there was rioting among the crowd. "There were too many to tell of; they were killing each other."[11] The French soldiers took possession of the baldacchino under which their sovereign had passed in the procession, and it cost two hundred ducats to retrieve it. The king gave it to the cathedral (exactly as Alfonso the Magnanimous had given his chariot to the Basilica of San Lorenzo).

Naples witnessed another violent incident on the disembarkation of Ferdinand II (the Catholic) and his queen Germaine de Foix in 1506. The chronicler Giuliano Passero says that when the royal couple set foot on land, they were received by the barons and ascended a platform prepared for that purpose on the quay; the platform was covered with a rich baldacchino. After the reception, the king and queen passed through a breach opened in the city wall, while the crowd attacked and tore to pieces the platform and baldacchino.

> The first of November 1506, All Saints Day, the king entered Naples with his French queen, Germaine, and when they reached the quay, cannons were shot off from the castle and from ships in the port. . . . There was not space for a grain of millet on the quay, so great was the crowd of lords and people who had gone to receive the king. When they disembarked from the galley, they remained a little on a platform equipped with two regal armchairs covered with brocade, he and his wife the queen, and then he mounted onto a mule richly draped, and his wife onto a palfrey. And the citizens of Naples took the *pallium* [the baldacchino that had covered the platform] of rich brocade with fringes of gold, which was estimated to be worth three thousand ducats. And then, the citizens and gentlemen having taken down the walls of the gate near the port, the king entered in procession into Naples, and as soon as the king had departed, they sacked the platform.[12]

One might say that even the brief use of the platform and armchairs by the royal couple had given the spot a sacred character. As with the *sedia gestatoria* of Pope Innocent III, which was torn to pieces after the ceremony of the *Possessio*, we can assume that the platform and chairs in Naples, as well as the drapery that covered them, were torn to pieces and viewed as relics.

10. De' Grassi in Cancellieri 1802, 61ff.
11. "Racconti di storia napoletana" 1908–9, xxxiii–xxxiv:514ff.
12. Passero 1786, 146; Filangieri 1954.

There is another incident that involved Charles V's entry into Siena in 1536. "He had hardly reached the last step" up to the cathedral "when the men carrying the masts of the baldacchino threw it down to cut it to pieces, and the twenty-four of them then turned to the horse His Majesty had just dismounted, to take it away as was customary. A fight developed, and His Majesty turned and with one word separated the men involved."[13] The imperial intervention did not end the disturbance, though, for "as soon as he entered [the cathedral], the men went back to tearing up the baldacchino; but some courtiers, having heard that this displeased His Majesty, prevented them. They were not quick enough, though, to prevent some of it from being taken, and it would have been entirely torn up if some guards had not run up to protect it."[14] A riot, thus, was in full development while thanks were being offered in the cathedral.

In Florence, on 30 April 1589, young patricians were permitted to take the horse trappings and baldacchino when the entry procession for Christine of Lorraine, the bride of Grand Duke Ferdinando I, having rounded the ancient Roman perimeter of walls, reached its destination at the Palazzo Vecchio.[15]

Eleven years later a similar incident was viewed more as a sport, a trick, than as violence. When Marie de' Medici, accompanied by Cardinal Pietro Aldobrandini, made her entry into the cathedral of Florence at the beginning of the long festivities for her marriage to Henry IV of France, the same noble pages who had carried the baldacchino attempted to take hold of the cardinal's mule. The court diarist Tinghi wrote: "Having arrived at the Cathedral of Santa Maria del Fiore, Her Highness dismounted, as did the cardinal from his mule. The Florentine youths who had carried the baldacchino took the cardinal's mule and contested among themselves who would be first to ride it. Piero degli Alberti mounted it, and the grooms of the cardinal seized the baldacchino, but then, with a good gift of money to the grooms, both parties gave up their prizes and order was restored."[16] How the baldacchino was finally successfully taken is narrated by Cardinal Aldobrandini: "Some lackeys hid themselves behind the wall of an abandoned house that was about the same height as the baldacchino . . . these lackeys reached out and suddenly snatched it from behind the wall. The people carrying it, aware that it was there no longer, looked up to see where it had gone, and everybody laughed and things went on."[17] The bloody assaults of fourteenth- and fifteenth-century Rome were thus resolved as a joke by Florentines of the late Renaissance, but the custom remained.

If this custom was becoming a sport, we must add that sixty years later an incident of the same kind was severely punished in England. At the coronation of Charles II, on 23 April 1661, a fight broke out over possession of the baldacchino between soldiers of the Royal Guard and the barons of the Five Ports, who had the official task of carrying it. The fight came to the attention of the king, who ordered the imprisonment and expulsion from the guard of the men most involved.[18] This example was forgotten in a few years, since another baldacchino "of cloth of gold" was looted at the coronation of James II, on 23 April 1685.[19]

13. *Descrittione delle cerimonie* [1884] 1968, 31.
14. *Descrittione delle cerimonie* [1884] 1968, 34.
15. Saslow 1996, 147.
16. Mamone 1987, 55.
17. Mamone 1987, 55.
18. Jones 1883, 316–17.
19. Aubrey 1881, 86; see also Sandford 1687.

We might note that the inhabitants of Chesne-le-Populeux, a village six miles from Reims, had the privilege of providing an armed escort for the horse on which the prior of their monastery carried the Sainte Ampoule under a baldacchino for the *sacre* of the kings of France. They were also to remain at the portal of the cathedral to accompany the prior back to the monastery, where they were supposed to be feasted for a certain period. As well, they claimed the horse and all its trappings. The custom was discontinued by Louis XV, and Louis XVI decided that the horse should go to the prior.[20]

It is not easy to tell when the baldacchino was introduced as an essential element of triumphal processions. Bernard Guenée says that a *pallium* appeared in some European monarchies about the end of the twelfth century and the beginning of the thirteenth.[21] Certainly in the fresco commissioned by Pope Boniface VIII for the Loggia delle Benedizioni in the Lateran, to commemorate his own coronation (1294), the pope was already depicted with an imperial umbrella, and the same umbrella reappears in the thematic fresco of the Roman church of the Santi Quattro Coronati. In Catalonia the first evidence comes from the beginning of the fourteenth century, at the coronation of Pere III (1336).[22] But from the beginning it was connected with royalty and with the rite of anointing. A mobile form of the imperial ciborium, the baldacchino was connected with the representation of *Christomimèsis*. As A. M. Drabek has justly noted, the king under a baldacchino stood in place of the Corpus Christi.[23] Guenée tells us that the feast of Corpus Domini (instituted with the bull *Transiturus* of Urban IV in 1264 and institutionalized by John XIII in 1317) was the only procession that employed a baldacchino (Fig. 28). The first of these processions documented iconographically was one in Barcelona of 1319/20 that is illustrated in a miniature in the missal of the Hermits of St. Augustine (Toulouse, 1362), where the monstrance is shown under a baldacchino. "Does it not seem clear that after some years of delay the subjects of Charles VI [of France], by putting their king under a baldacchino, wanted to adapt the cult of kingship to the most recent liturgical innovations, following the ancient formula of the king as the image of God?"[24] This hypothesis might be confirmed by the debate among members of the municipal council of Marseilles of 11 November 1320, recorded by Noël Clouet. At issue were the honors to give to the queen of Majorca, and the use of a baldacchino was hotly debated, and in the end appeal was made to King Robert of Provence, an indication that the baldacchino was considered an honor reserved for sovereigns.[25] This impression is reinforced by an episode involving the entry of the king of the Romans, Emperor Frederick III, into Besançon in 1442. "On his entry into the city, the citizens brought up a baldacchino woven of cloth of gold and carried by the leading burghers," Olivier de la Marche relates, "under which *pallium* the king of Rome entered, and pains were taken to convince the duke of Burgundy also to ride under it. But the duke refused and rode on the left hand of the king, the head of his horse at the level of the king's leg."[26] Feudal hierarchy prevented a vassal from entering under a baldacchino together with his lord. But it is also clear that great value was attributed to a baldacchino, and it is understandable why medieval crowds wanted to get hold of it, tear it into shreds, and possess these as relics.

20. Leber 1825, 193–94.
21. Guenée and Lehoux 1968, 14–15; see also Smith 1936, 197, and Weinstock 1971, 362–63.
22. Pere III 1980, 197; in general, see Hillgarth 1976–78.
23. Drabek 1964, 27.
24. Guenée and Lehoux 1968, 17.
25. Coulet 1977, 76.
26. Marche 1883–88, 1:278.

XII CERAE CĀDIDAE ARDĒTES TAEDAE SANCTA EVCHARISTIA BONON PATRICIIS AC MEDICIN DOCTORIB

Fig. 28 Nicolas Hogenberg, the Corpus Christi under a canopy, in the coronation procession of Charles V.

It seems not only that the baldacchino, the horse trappings, and the mount itself were the objects of particular attention by medieval and early modern crowds, but also that the apparatus connected with any part of a ritual investment could assume supernatural value. Roemer's chronicle of the coronation of the emperor Matthias (1612) tells us that the procession went along a raised platform, covered with a red carpet, that stretched from the cathedral to the town hall of Frankfurt. "The procession had hardly passed when the people took possession of the red carpet . . . , even while the procession was passing. It was torn from under the feet of the people walking on it, cut up, and reduced to shreds."[27]

My interpretation of this point is supported by a religious ceremony still celebrated in the south of Italy, at Matera. In the feast of the Madonna Bruna (another of the many "true icons" painted by Saint Luke), the faithful, when the procession is over, attack the float richly decorated with figures made of papier-mâché, keeping the pieces taken in the scuffle until the following year (Fig. 29).

These rituals that involved the violent sack of the baldacchino, the *sedia gestatoria,* shredding the cloth of the baldacchino and horse trappings or red carpet, recall one of the

27. *Wahl und Crönungshandlung* 1612, n.p.; *Inauguratio* 1613.

Fig. 29   Matera, feast of the Madonna Bruna (2 July), before the ritual sacking.

violent rituals connected with the death of a sovereign that we discussed earlier, in Chapter 3. Here again the methodological observations of Malinowski are valid on the concept of economy in cultures different from our own: this *jus spolii*[28] does not imply an avidity for the possession of goods, even if some incidents suggest that. The baldacchino, the horse trappings, and the carpet were torn to pieces, in precisely the same way that a defunct pope's bed, sheets, and blankets were. What economic value could splinters of wood or shreds of cloth ever have?

The possession of such fragments, splinters, or shreds also was quite different in meaning from the destruction or demolition of rooms or entire palaces. The former involved taking possession of objects that when used and touched by the defunct had assumed supernatural powers (just as the baldacchino and horse trappings, having been used in a *sacre,* were impregnated with a supernatural power). The latter involved a community's loss of identity at the moment of its lord's loss of life (the Roman *justitium*), a situation the psychologists call "anomie," entailing a loss of social values. The destruction of a palace, stone by stone, represented the dismantling of the state (and how often has the state been compared to an imposing edifice?).

But before reaching a conclusion about these rituals of violence, one should recall a canon of the Roman Council of 595, which associated the sack that occurred on the death of a pontiff with the crowd's pious wish to possess his relics. We have already seen how the bodies of Innocent III and Innocent IV were left lying naked on the bare ground, and how the same fate was feared by Alexander VI and Julius II, and shared in England by William the Conqueror. The remains of some popes became objects of veneration; but not only theirs.

28. Elze 1977.

We can now compare this to the behavior of medieval and early modern crowds connected with another rite of passage, the death of a "living saint." The exhibition of the body for veneration by the faithful was a kind of wake that normally lasted for three days, even if in exceptional cases this was sometimes longer. For instance, Girolamo della Marchia, who died in Naples in 1476, was exhibited for sixteen days.[29] During the exhibition of the body, the crowd acted parasitically and violently, moved as it was by the need to get possession of some relic of the saint. There was even a hierarchy of things to take: the branches of cypress (a typical attribute of saintliness) arranged around the bier were the first things to go. But more important were fragments of clothing. Still more important were anatomical specimens, which were also valued in accordance with a macabre hierarchy that the crowd had learned from the church's official cult of relics.

On 19 May 1246, Umiliana de' Cerchi, a Florentine nun, died in the odor of sanctity. Vito da Cortona, her biographer and contemporary, tells that before dying, Umiliana asked those around her to close her body up well in the shroud. "She foresaw that through faith and devotion people would tear off the linen and her clothes," which promptly occurred, as her other biographer, Francesco Cionacci, relates. "Then arose in the people a pious contest to get hold of anything that had belonged to that blessed soul. Thus it happened, as was foreseen, that through indiscreet devotion the clothing was even torn off of her body, carried away piece by piece, for relics."[30]

Marco Fantuzzi died at Bologna in 1478. Several times he had been the provincial general of the minor observants of Saint Francis. Giovan Battista Melloni, an author who collected the *Atti degli uomini illustri in santità nati o morti in Bologna* at the end of the eighteenth century, relates his burial as follows:

> The obsequies finished and the body lowered into its tomb, the transit to the morbid aspects of death followed quickly. Since the slab was not yet lowered onto the tomb, when the friars left the church, some women who had remained there, transported by a disgusting instinct (so desirous were they of having some relic of the holy man), went down shamelessly into the tomb to cut away his habit up to the knees. The pious effrontery of these women (who would have thought it?) was not punished by the Lord; he even granted health to one of them, who had been paralyzed and sick, for touching the body.[31]

Caterina de' Ricci, a nun of Prato in the second half of the sixteenth century, was assured the fame of a "saintly life" by her gift of prophecy and continual ecstasies. After her death, on 2 February 1590, as her biographer Serafino Razzi tells us,

> her holy body was taken to a church and placed on a bier, which was well elevated from the pavement (so that no violence would be done to her body or vestments by the people coming not only from Prato but also from the surrounding countryside, and even from Florence). White candles burned inside the church all around. Thus she remained for the rest of Friday, and Saturday, visited by an innumerable crowd of people, who out of devotion had thought to bring some offering, flowers or orange leaves, or some similar greenery to adorn the bier. And some too took away little bits of her vestments, and

29. Lasi 1974, 471.
30. Cionacci 1682.
31. Melloni 1773–1818, III:81.

those who could not reach these tried to touch the body. And although the friars and other persons of the monastery, who were guarding the virgin body, tried to keep the crowd distant and avoid any damage, they were unable to prevent people from cutting little pieces from her vestments.[32]

Even worse happened to Saint Theresa of Avila. Not only were her vestments divided "inter varias personas tam religiosas quam saeculares" (among many persons, both clerical and secular), as the *Acta Sanctorum* tells us, but nine months after her burial, her follower Graziano, in an inspection of the body carried out in July 1583, took the occasion to cut off her right hand (a relic that one day much later came into the possession of Generalissimo Francisco Franco).[33] Speaking of such relics, we could add what a British traveler, Allan Butler, traveling through Italy in 1745–46, recorded while visiting Padua. In the Palazzo della Ragione a memorial tablet, on what he thought was Virgil's tomb, said "that one of his arms was given to Alphonus [Alfonso V], king of Aragon, in 1451."[34]

A similarly bloody fate awaited a friar in Prato in the middle of the eighteenth century. In 1653, when the grand duke Ferdinando II elevated Prato in status from a "place" to a "city," he was concerned with giving it a "living saint," and he transferred there a friar named Benedetto da Poggibonsi, who was old and sick, from the Franciscan monastery at San Casciano. His biographer Mario Inghirami says this was to "enrich my native city with his body." Benedetto Bacci died in Prato only two years later, surrounded by the whole community. To save his body from attack by the faithful, it was guarded by a troop of soldiers. Despite this, when the autopsy was made, by surgeons in the presence of numerous friars and faithful, his clothing was pilfered, along with strips of flesh and pieces of cloth dipped in his blood. Someone even made off with "a piece of one of his nipples, removed, as was later learned, very furtively by a surgeon who was there."[35]

On the death of San Bernardino of Siena, the body remained at Aquila, and only a sack containing his books was sent to Siena. Since it was impossible to get hold of his sacred body, the Sienese literally took the hair from the ass that had brought back his library.

Within the larger frame of the cult of kingship, and of a world so permeated with a sense of the sacred, these examples should be enough to explain the sacred meaning of the sacking and tearing up of the baldacchino and *sedia gestatoria,* as well as the claim to the horse and its trappings. This was thus not—at least initially—a *jus spolii* (which suggests a pecuniary interest), but something more directly connected to the sacredness of the king's body.

It remains to examine another violent ritual, the scuffle around the triumphal procession provoked artificially by the scattering of coins. This was an ancient tradition already present in the Roman period and institutionalized through what was called the *sparsio.* A new magistrate, before assuming office, went to the forum and threw from the rostrum some coins to the people waiting below. Persius writes (*Satirae,* v, 177): "Et omnia semina super populum spargebat, ut tellus veluti visceralibus suis placaretur" (He sowed all manner of seeds over the people, so that the earth would be placated as if from its own entrails). This was a gesture promising fecundity that was associated with a ritual of conciliation.[36]

32. Razzi [1641] 1965, 278–79.
33. AASS, 15 October.
34. Butler 1803, 368–69.
35. Inghirami n.d., I, last chap., n.p.; Coppini 1988.
36. See Starobinski 1986, 7–26; NDI and RE, s.v. *Iactum* and *Candidatus.*

In the Byzantine book of ceremonies of the Pseudo-Codinus two expansions of this ceremony can be noted: the first, when the emperor had pronounced his profession of faith but had not yet appeared in public; the second, the day after the coronation, when the emperor had returned to his palace. On the first occasion "one of the senators, who was appointed by the emperor, threw out to the people what were called *épikombia*—pieces of cloth in which were wrapped three golden *numismata* [coins] and an equal number of silver ones." This was done from the sacristy of Hagia Sophia. On the second occasion, the following day, the head of the imperial wardrobe gave the emperor other *numismata* to distribute to the court before the image of Saint George Martyr. The Pseudo-Codinus states that "the reason for this distribution of *numismata* was the wish of the emperor for all the archons, their children, soldiers, and the people to celebrate with him by eating and drinking at his expense."[37] We will return to this explanation later. Meanwhile we know that the same ritual was taken up by the Roman Church on two occasions: the throwing of coins to the crowd from the sacristy of St. Peter's and other places on the itinerary of a papal procession, and the distribution to the court, or *presbyterium*.

In Rome, in fact, the first scattering of coins occurred during the pontiff's *Processio* from the Vatican to the Lateran, immediately after the coronation in St. Peter's. The task was initially entrusted to the *camarlingus* (or *camerarius*); it later passed to a specific figure in the procession: the *soldanus*.[38] There seem to have been specific places as well for throwing out the coins, just as there were "stations" along the route of a cleansing procession. The first was in the place of coronation (the sacristy of St. Peter's) after the pope had mounted his horse. The second was in the Parione district, near the Torre del Campo,[39] when the pope had crossed the Tiber, and where a delegation of Roman Jews awaited him[40] to perform their act of submission. The third was at the Basilica of San Marco; the fourth, in front of the Church of Sant'Adriano (the ancient Curia Romana); and the fifth was from the windows of a palace next to the Church of Santa Martina.[41] Johann Burchard, the papal master of ceremonies, says about the coronation of Pope Innocent VIII (1484) that when the pope descended from the sacristy of St. Peter's, the *soldanus* made "three throws of money to the people so that the pope could pass without impediment."

Let us move from Rome to Venice. An English pilgrim, William Wey, traveling to the Holy Land, arrived in the city on the lagoon in May of 1462, in the days after the death of the doge Pasquale Malipiero. He was thus witness to the election of the new doge, Cristoforo Mauro. Describing the election, Wey tells us that the new doge, on receiving the emissary of the senate with its greeting "Bona vestra nostra sunt" (Your goods are ours), responded: "Scio bene, sed rogo accipite inter vos centum ducatus et sitis contenti" (I know that very well, but please, take a hundred ducats and be satisfied). These words seem an echo of those spoken by the pontiff when sitting on the *sedia stercoraria,* but we can also understand them to have offered a gratuity for those who brought the good news. However, William Wey added that the new doge, "going towards his dwelling[,] threw coins out along the route to make a place for him to walk."[42] This was precisely the explanation offered by Burchard.

37. Codinus 1839, 254–55.
38. The *soldo* was a unity of money, normally the pay of a warrior (*soldato*).
39. Also called "di Stefano figlio di Pietro," in the vicinity of the current Piazza dell'Orologio alla Vallicella.
40. See Coulet 1979.
41. Cancellieri 1802, 20.
42. Wey 1857.

Fig. 30   Giacomo Franco (sixteenth century), the *sparsio* of the Venetian doge
(Milan, Raccolta Civica Bertarelli). The caption says: "Il Principe eleto,
dopo l'haver fatto in Chiesa di S. M.co nel Pergolo l'oratione al Populo,
entra in un Palchetto con i suoi Parenti et l'Ammiraglio, dove portato da
gl'huomeni dell'Arsenale va gettando danari intorno a Piazza poi entra in
Palazzo et sopra le scalle de' Giganti viene incoronato dal Consiglier più
Giovane" [The elected Prince, after having made his address to the people
from the pulpit of the Church of S. Marco, enters a *Palchetto* with his
kinsmen and the admiral, in which he is carried by men from the Arsenal
throwing out coins through the Piazza. Then he enters the (Ducal) palace
up the Scala dei Giganti and is crowned by the youngest Councilor].

Fig. 31   The wine fountain and scattering of bread for the coronation of Joseph I, from *Das Hoch-beehrte Augsburg . . . ,* Augsburg, J. Koppmayer, 1690.

There are some other representations of the doge's *sparsio:* a print by Giacomo Franco, undated but from the end of the sixteenth century (Fig. 30); a painting by G. Bella;[43] and a painting by Guardi. As well, close examination of these representations shows a scuffle taking place, and *arsenalotti* ("workmen from the Arsenal") who were occupied with long wooden staves beating back the crowd that was trying to get the money. Perhaps there was no other way of making a way for the newly elected doge? But did the money not provoke the scuffle? The illustrations reverse the explanation given us by Burchard and Wey: the *sparsio* provoked the scuffle, and the soldiers opened the way for the new sovereign. A miniature in a codex in Vienna (after 1590) showing the coronation of a sultan also confirms this. The painter, illustrating a *sparsio,* emphasized the result, which was precisely the provocation of a riot.[44]

Returning to the Christian world, an account of the coronation of Queen Anne of England is easy to understand. Aldermen and constables watched over the procession, "dressed in silk and velvet, with long sticks in their hands, to make the people give way and maintain order."[45] But a riot, rather than a festival, was described on the occasion of the coronation of the emperor Matthias and his consort Helena Madeleine Theresa. The chronicle of the coronation, which I have cited above, says that at the end of the procession "came several knights and archers on horseback, and in front of them one who, from the church up to the square before the Roemer, threw to both sides new gold and silver coins from the mint. The crowd, the scuffle, and the fighting among the people for the coins can be easily imagined. Considering that the people were impatient, the knights and archers, and particularly the one who was throwing out the coins, had to stand firm before the crowd or retire."[46] A series of engraved scenes showing the progress of the coronation of the future emperor Joseph I at Augsburg as king of the Romans (1690) shows the crowd clearly fighting over bread and wine thrown from the terrace of the palace (Fig. 31).

Thus, aldermen with long sticks kept Londoners at bay along the edges of the procession, and soldiers from the Arsenal kept scuffles under control around the sedan chair of the doge. In these cases—as at Constantinople, Rome, and Augsburg—it was the *sparsio* that provoked the tumult. In the iconography of the coronation of Charles V at Bologna in 1530, the *congiarium,* which seems so tranquil and orderly on the Arch of Constantine, as in a representation of a Roman triumph (Fig. 32), became a riot provoked by the scattering (and not distribution) of loaves of bread (Fig. 33), as well as coins (Fig. 34). Was this done so that the people could celebrate with the lord and eat at his expense, as the Pseudo-Codinus said?

One remembers that another contemporary chronicler testified to a similar riot. In the triumphal procession of Alfonso of Aragon in 1443, on his entry into Naples, as we have seen above, the chronicler says that the king's chariot was surrounded by Catalan soldiers "transformati in habitu et facies velati" (that is, masked), "simul rissantes" (simulating a riot), and he gives an explanation different from that of Wey or Burchard: "ad hoc ut nemo currui regio se appropinquasset" (to keep anybody from approaching the royal

43. Venice, Galleria Querini Stampalia. The cartouche at the center of the painting reads: "The doge is carried around the square of San Marco, throwing out coins until he reaches the Scala dei Giganti." On Venetian public ritual, see Marini 1903; Casini 1996.

44. Vienna, Österreichische Nationalbibliothek, Codex 8626, fol. 81. The caption reads: "Diter ptenigmeyter Reytt zulezt Wurfst asperl aus" (The treasurer rides last, throwing out coins).

45. Jones 1883, 152.

46. *Wahl und Crönungshandlung* 1612, n.p.; *Inauguratio* 1613.

TEMPLVM IOVIS
CAPITOLINI

CONSVLES

LICTORES

ARA

CONGIARIVM POPVLO ROMANO
DATVM

CAMILLI ET FLAMINII

I

TRIVMPHI MAIORIS, IN VRBE ROMANA OB VICTORIAM CELEBRATI TYPVS.

...NIS OMNIS GENERIS PASSIM OMNIBVS DISTRIBVTVS

Fig. 32   The *congiarium* in an anonymous engraving of the sixteenth century, from a Roman
           sesterce.

Fig. 33   Nicolas Hogenberg, the scattering of bread to the crowd at the coronation of the
           emperor Charles V, Bologna, 1530.

Fig. 34   The *sparsio* at the coronation of Joseph I, from *Das Hoch-beehrte Augsburg.* . . .

chariot).[47] Thus this was not to open the way for him, but to protect the sovereign. But we suspect that we are again confronted with an explanation showing the spectator's ignorance of the rite. We know that Roman soldiers marched around the triumphal chariot singing apotropaic songs to ward off evil spirits, but here we seem not to have a classical revival (the chronicler would not have failed to mention it). Perhaps we should return again to van Gennep and Hertz and the research of Hertz on collective representations of death, particularly in the ceremonial of the Fiji Islands in times of an interregnum, or even to the Negara of Geertz. The simulation of a riot was also present in the funeral procession of the Rajah of Gianjar, around the bier of the sovereign, carried out by the fourth and lowest caste, the Sudras.[48] If we return for a moment to the Roman carousel around the pyres of the emperors Pertinax and Septimius Severus, we might ask whether these were also simulated riots, accompanied by martial music.

At Venice we observe further that the scattering of coins occurred before, rather than after, the act of coronation, a peculiarity that seems to contradict the pontifical ceremony. But, in a certain sense, one could argue that the true moment of coronation for the pope was not so much the placing of the three-tiered crown on his head in St. Peter's as it was the Mass in St. John Lateran. In both Venice and Rome we are at a "marginal" moment, a period of interregnum. This was also true of the entry of Alfonso the Magnanimous before he was crowned in the cathedral of Naples, and of the funeral of the Rajah of Gianjar at Negara. The scattering of coins might thus have had a double meaning. On one hand, it emphasized that the elected person was leaving the world (he changes even his name). On the other hand, it might have been recompense given to the people for not performing the usual rites of violence. In some sense, it was supposed to be a "controlled" riot. The *sparsio* occurred, in fact, when the interregnum was not yet finished; the riot it evoked recalled the violent precariousness of the *justitium*.

But one could advance still another explanation, which demonstrates how difficult it is to assign a single motivation to a rite that might seem similar to another. The *sparsio* was not carried out using current coins, but rather with new ones coined particularly for the occasion. Looking again at the coronation of the emperor Matthias:

> The coins thrown out were of two types, both in gold and silver. On one type, the size of a common taler, was the effigy of His Majesty on one side, with a crown of laurel on his head, and the following inscription: MATTHIAS II: D:G:H:B: REX.CORON.IN.REG.ROM. 24. IUN.1612. The other side showed a royal crown in the middle, illuminated from above by the rays of the sun and from below by moonlight, with the motto LUMINE MAIOR CONCORDI. On the other type of coin, the size of a kreuzer, had on one side only the inscription MATTHIAS II.D.G.H.B. REX.CORON.IN.REG.ROM. 24.IUN.1612, but on the other side the crown, the sun, the moon, and the inscription that was on the larger coin.[49]

Jacques de Bie, in his *France metallique*, has documented all the coins struck for the *sacre* of kings of France (even those before the coronation of Henry II!),[50] and we have an abun-

---

47. See Chapter 4 above.
48. See Geertz 1980.
49. *Wahl und Crönungshandlung* 1612, n.p.
50. Bie 1636; Blanchet 1892.

dant documentation for papal medals.[51] Well, there is not one that lacks the face or figure of the sovereign on the obverse. In all these cases we have the distribution of royal effigies, which transcended the monetary value of the coins thrown out.

Thus violence for possession of the baldacchino, violence for possession of the horse and its trappings, violence provoked by the scattering of coins. These examples all refer to rites tied to an interregnum. But another type of violence was tied to rites of entry. In Naples, in 1740, to celebrate the birth of the infanta (the royal daughter), the architect Ferdinando Sanfelice designed for the square in front of the royal palace a tower in a style that seemed to be vaguely Chinese, with ritual fountains on both sides (spouting wine?). It was loaded with foodstuffs and open to the plebes, who sacked it. This was also a type of *congiarium*,[52] of which the violence was explicitly foreseen.

---

51. Fioravante 1738 and Frati 1883.
52. Mancini 1968, illustration, n.p.

6

Stuffed Bulls and Plenty of Oats

AFTER THE CORONATION MASS (or after the triumph), there was always a distribution of food. Fountains spewed out quantities of red and white wine (the royal blood and lymph?) (Fig. 35). After the coronation of Queen Anne, a fountain set up on Cheape Hill in London spewed out "continuallie wine, both white and claret, all that afternoon."[1] Bread was thrown to the crowd. Prints depicting the coronation of Emperor Charles V at Bologna (1530) show a bull being roasted (Fig. 36). One would be tempted to explain this provision of food by referring to the Roman *congiarium,* a symbolic return of abundance to the earth. Even earlier, a large distribution of wine occurred after the triumph of Ptolemy II Philadelphus in Egypt (285 B.C.).[2] But the bull presents some peculiarities that cannot be explained by the reign of Abundance.

In Roman triumphs, oxen were led to sacrifice, adorned with wreaths of flowers.[3] However, there seems to be no link between these oxen and our bull. Let us think of the animal's attributes: "power, irresistibility, brute force, these were the bull qualities that held the greatest appeal for the people who thought of their king as a god."[4] Gilgamesh, king of Babylon, was called "the mighty wild bull," and we know that the bull was a royal symbol.[5] The throne of the Persian monarchy had legs that ended with lion paws, and a footstool with bulls' hooves.[6] In Ireland the sacrifice of a bull (*tairbfheis*) was associated with coronations. A saga of the ninth century describes the election of Conaire Mor mac Eterscelae as king: "Then the king, Eterscelae, died. A bullfest was assembled by the men of Ireland; that is to say, a bull was killed by them, and one man would eat his fill of it and would drink its broth, and a spell of truth would be sung over him as he slept. The man that he should see in his sleep, it was he that would be king."[7]

In the culture of the African peoples of Swazi and Rwanda, the sovereign was "the bull of the nation."[8] The king-bull link is evident. We could add that when the Frankish king Childeric was buried at Tournai, a crystal globe and a golden miniature bull's head were

1. James 1986, 153–54.
2. Rice 1983.
3. Burkert 1983; Grottanelli, Parise, and Solinas 1985. More generally, see Hubert and Mauss 1929.
4. Conrad 1959, 75.
5. Roheim [1930] 1972, 209.
6. James 1986, 484.
7. Enright 1985, 37.
8. Heusch 1986, 165.

AQVILA IN TER ME DIOS   LEONES VINŨ   ALBŨ ET RVBRŨ FVNDENTES

Fig. 35   Nicolas Hogenberg, the wine fountain at the coronation procession of Emperor Charles V.

set beside him.[9] With regard to the illustration of the coronation of Charles V mentioned above, one might remember that this Hapsburg, when celebrating the birth of his son Philip three years earlier, killed a bull in a bullfight at Valladolid with his own hands.[10]

A chronicler who was a witness to the coronation in 1530 wrote that there was a great feast. "A bull was roasted, stuffed with animals, whose heads were seen outside its skin."[11] Nicolas Hogenberg made a series of engravings of the imperial coronation of 1530. If we look closely, we can observe several things. The bull was roasted whole, without having been skinned, its horns gilded. From its skin protruded the heads of animals, which one

9. Wallace-Hadrill 1960, 18.
10. Conrad 1959, 75.
11. Giordani 1842, doc. XLVI.

Fig. 36 Nicolas Hogenberg, the stuffed bull at the coronation procession of Emperor Charles V.

presumes were inserted whole into the body. Should we conclude that the bull was gutted and boned, and that its skin was then stuffed with the meat of the bodies of other animals? If this was the case, it was a practice similar to a Scythian rite described by Herodotus, which he thought abhorrent.[12] But while in the rite of the Scythians the bull was filled only with its own meat, here we have a bull stuffed with the bodies of other beasts, some of them mythological. These were a raven (*corvus corax*), an eagle whose beak stuck out prominently, an unskinned fox, a boar, and a goose.

The importance of roasting the bull at the moment of coronation is emphasized by Giorgio Vasari in his fresco in the Florentine Palazzo Vecchio entitled *Clement VII Crowns Charles V in San Petronio at Bologna*. The bull is clearly visible in the foreground, its head

12. Herodotus 1969–70, IV.61. See Detienne and Vernant 1979, 170ff.

Fig. 37   The coronation procession of Emperor Matthias at Frankfurt (1612). (Providence, Hay Library, Anne S. K. Brown Military Collection.)

cut off, and a soldier is oiling it. The stuffed bull also appears in engravings of the coronation of the emperor Matthias at Frankfurt (1612; Fig. 37), of the emperor Ferdinand II at Frankfurt (1619), of the emperor Joseph I and his wife Helena Magdalene Theresa at Budapest (1705; Fig. 38), and in the ceremonies in Rome for the birth of the son of James II of England, James Francis (1688; Fig. 39).

The only similar rite traceable in antiquity was the punishment for parricide. Romans considered this the most atrocious of crimes, so that neither fire nor earth could be used to dispose of the body of the criminal. Thus the parricide was sewed up in the skin of a bull (*culleus*) and thrown into water (a stream or river that led to the sea).[13] We could note that regicide was associated with parricide; it was the most horrible case of parricide. But it seems unlikely that we will find an explanation for our coronation rite along this route; we are running the risk of jumping to a hasty conclusion.

We might ask whether the animals used to stuff the bull were also associated with royalty.

The raven was an emblem of Odin, "the raven god" (*Hrafnass*). "A bird generally identified as Odin's raven replaced the Roman winged Victory on sixth and seventh century Scandinavian gold bracelets, which were derived from Roman imperial medallions. Thus the battle-bird of the divine victory-bringer of the North is a Germanic parallel and translation of the Victory of the South."[14] The raven of northern battlefields was a parallel and translation of the Roman Victory.

The explanation for the eagle is easy. We have already seen that this represented the soul of the emperor in the ceremony of apotheosis.[15]

13. Nardi 1980.
14. Chaney 1969, 133.
15. See Chapter 3 above.

Fig. 38   The distribution of bull's meat at the coronation of Emperor Joseph I, from *Das Hoch-beehrte Augsburg. . . .*

The boar was also a royal symbol, even one of the most important ones. "Certain animals are peculiarly associated with the king, and of these one of the most important was the boar."[16] We should not forget that it was also the symbol of Adonis. It was closely associated with the cult of kingship in Germany, and from there it passed to England. "Its appearance in Anglo-Saxon England with royal graves and banners, and with boar-helmeted warriors led by warrior chiefs, leads one to conclude that knowledge of its magical, god-and-king associated roles continued into Christian times."[17]

16. Chaney 1969, 121.
17. Roheim [1930] 1972, 213–14, where the author also associates the boar with the cult of Adonis.

BVE arrostito intiero in publica piazza ripieno di diversi Pollami, et altri animali comestibili da distribuirsi al volgo in occasione dell'allegrezze celebrate in Roma dall'Emin.mo e R.mo Card. OVARD di NORFOLCIA e dall'Ill.mo Sig.r Agente di sua MAESTA' BRITANNICA per la nascita dell'Altezza Reale di GIACOM PRENCIPE DI WALLIA Primogenito di GIACOMO SECONDO Re della gran Bretagna e della Reina MARIA BEATRICE sua Consorte felicemente Regi..........

Fig. 39   The stuffed bull at the feast for the birth of the firstborn son of James II (Rome, van Westernon, 1688). The caption says: "Bue arrostito intiero in pubblica piazza ripieno di diversi pollami et altri animali comestibili da distribuirsi al volgo in occasione dell'allegrezze celebrate in Roma dall'Emin.mo e R.mo card. Ovard di Norfolcia e dall'Ill.mo Sig.r Agente di sua Maestà Britannica per la nascita dell'Altezza Real di Giacomo prencipe di Wallia Primogenito di Giacomo Secondo Re della Gran Bretagna e della Reina Maria Beatrice sua Consorte felicemente regina" [Bull roasted whole filled with poultry and other edible animals in a public square for distribution to the people on the occasion of the celebration in Rome by the Most Eminent Cardinal (Edward of Norfolk) and the illustrious agent of His Britannic Majesty for the birth of his Royal Highness James, Prince of Wales, firstborn of James II, King of Great Britain, and Queen Mary Beatrice, his happily reigning queen].

With the exception of the eagle, all these symbols of kingship came from northern Europe, and the iconographic documentation I have provided all refers to northern monarchs (including the Roman ceremony of 1688 in honor of the English pretender). This might explain why the Bolognese chronicler gave little attention to the cooking of the symbolic animals; he was distracted by the distribution of the meal (the first piece having been offered to the emperor).

This leaves two animals to examine: the goose and the fox. We could make a marginal note of another medieval witness to a group of animals sacrificed together. A canon of

St. Peter's, Benedetto, describing the Roman carnival of 1142, says that the knights on Monte Tesaccio killed a bull, a boar, and a cock; "luxuria lumborum nostrorum" (the luxury of our loins), he added, referring to the cock.[18] In our case, instead of a cock, we have another barnyard animal for which we can find no symbolic meaning, unless the head and beak shown in the engraving of Charles V were those of a swan, another inedible bird. If this were true, we would have a symbol of masculine solar light. The swan accompanied Apollo in ancient Greece and became one of the attributes of royalty in England.

We are left with the fox, a well-known symbol of astuteness. It is uncertain whether Machiavelli, when referring to the double nature of the prince, half fox and half lion, was referring more directly than is thought to royal symbols. "A prince must know how to make good use of the nature of the beast; he should choose from among the beasts the fox and the lion; for the lion cannot defend itself from traps, and the fox cannot protect itself from wolves" (Il Principe, 18). This might better explain why a later Dutch engraver, when preparing the frontispiece for an edition of De regno. Adversus Nic. Machiavellum (H. de Vogel, 1647),[19] showed a fox and a lion running in the foreground (Fig. 40); or why the frontispiece of a later edition of The Prince (The Hague, Engelbreg Boucquet, 1704) should have changed the usual iconography of the throne of King Solomon (shown flanked by twelve lions), substituting six foxes lined up in front of six lions (see Fig. 8).[20]

We have reached the point of showing that most, if not all, of the animals the bull was stuffed with were royal symbols, as was the bull itself. One might ask at this point, consequently, whether this mixture might involve a distribution of the royal body.

To resolve the question, let us turn to the engraving of the coronation of Joseph I (Fig. 38). The emperor (or one of the electors) is shown on horseback, inside a wooden framework where the bull is spitted above the burning coals. Its body is already being cut up. We do not know, however, whether the bull had previously been stuffed, as in Hogenberg's engraving and in the cases of Frankfurt and Rome. The engraver was emphasizing the distribution of the flesh. The emperor is giving a piece of bull meat to a gentleman (a courtier or a subject?). We can see that the meat was distributed personally by the emperor.

Let us look at another scene from this coronation before reaching a conclusion (Fig. 41). It shows an open space, a street or square crowded with people, who are also crowded at windows and on the roofs of shops. The elector of Saxony (in the place of the emperor) is on horseback in the midst of a heap of oats onto which he is emptying out a basket. The crowd is attacking the heap, attempting to fill baskets, sacks, and even hats. The scene recalls the other, older one of the coronation of Matthias at Frankfurt in June of 1612, where different incidents in the ceremony are shown in the same engraving. There is the procession with the sovereign walking under a baldacchino; a fountain spouting out two kinds of wine is adorned with a two-headed eagle surmounted by a naked woman with a bloody sword in her hand; we see the framework where the bull is roasting; and a dignitary is on horseback in the midst of a heap of oats. The accompanying title (long enough to cover the whole page), "A brief and true description . . . of the election and coronation of the Most High, and Powerful . . . Prince and Lord Matthias elected Roman Caesar to magnify the German Empire . . . , and Her Highness the Most High and Illustrious Princess and Lady Anne of

18. Forcella 1885 and 1896; Schneider 1921, 391–93.
19. Bertelli and Innocenti 1979, sec. XVIII, 3.
20. Bertelli 1990b.

Fig. 40   The Prince with Justice, fox, and lion, frontispiece of *De regno.*
Adversus Nic. Machiavellum, Leiden, Hieronymum de Vogel, 1647.

Hungary, Queen of Bohemia . . . ," explains the scene. As soon as the emperor and princely electors entered the banqueting hall,

> *the prince elector of Saxony must carry out a function prescribed in the Golden Bull, that is, to go on horseback—in his ceremonial dress, and accompanied by councilors and secretaries—to the square where a heap of oats was prepared that morning. He carries a silver vessel. This is first given to a servant, and then to the hereditary marshal Von Peppenheim, and it is filled with oats that are to be thrown out, while the prince elector returns to the town hall. Meanwhile trumpets sound. As soon as the prince elector has departed on his horse, the people throw themselves on the oats, attempting to fill sacks and other receptacles. They struggle among themselves so that they lose most of it, trampling it underfoot and covering the neighboring streets with oats.*

One notes that the heap of oats was prepared that morning but that the sacking of it did not happen until after the initial ritual distribution to a servant. And the people did not really take the oats away; it was thrown about and wasted. Much the same happened with the meat of the bull. Here the ritual distribution was made by the Elector Palatine onto silver plates. Then came an assault on the bull. *"This is hardly finished when the people rush to the place where the bull was roasted, everyone hoping to get a bit of it. Some in the crowd demolish the framework and the beast, which are all broken and carried away. Meanwhile the trumpets sound, and His Majesty, and then the princely electors, laypeople, and clergy, seat themselves at their respective tables, observing the order prescribed in the Golden Bull."*

We are thus in the presence of further ritual assaults, of wasting and demolition. They occurred at the beginning of the royal banquet, which was seen as a kind of agape, a semireligious ceremony. The emperor (as will be shown further below) was perceived to be not only the great distributor, from whom material nourishment came, but also, in a certain sense, the immolated victim.

The fountain also had a ritual significance.

> *What the fountain in front of the city hall looked like was indicated before. There were narrow tubes under the pavement that went to a house at the top of the square, so that when the royal meal commenced, at first white wine flowed from the black two-headed eagle, as its garland announced, and also from the globe and the lion. And after that, red wine was put into a cask located high in a house, so that it would run more quickly. Meanwhile the fountain was surrounded with a crowd of people so that it was difficult to protect the eagle, lion, and other things from being damaged. And any that could get close, drank. One used his cap, another a straw, others what they could find; there was such a crowd that more wine was spilled and lost than was drunk. At the height of the excitement, even though there was plenty of wine, and it ran out for a good period, the people knocked down the garland, the lion, and the eagle, and carried everything away. Nothing was protected during the assault; everything was abandoned. Even the lead tubes buried in the ground were not spared, but torn up and taken. At one point they even tried to demolish the stone statue of justice at the top of the fountain, and they would have succeeded had not others run up in time and prevented them forcibly.*

We are confronted again with wastage, destruction, and violence that was provoked

Fig. 41   The heap of oats at the coronation of Emperor Joseph I, from *Das Hoch-beehrte Augsburg. . . .*

(even with the sound of trumpets!). One might emphasize that the opening of the conduit of wine was concomitant with the beginning of the royal meal, almost as if the blood of the sovereign was flowing out. One could also add that the electors, of Saxony and the Palatinate, were figureheads. In reality they represented the monarch and bring us back to the central point of the ceremony—the distribution of the king's body.

The poet Goethe provides a quite similar description of the coronation of Joseph II as king of Rome in 1764. The fountain with the two-headed eagle had been rebuilt. "There, gathered into a heap lay the oats; here stood the large wooden hut, in which we had several days since seen the whole fat ox roasted and basted on a huge spit." The municipal authorities watched over all the people engaged in this. The day of the ceremony finally came. It was 3 April 1764. Goethe says: "Several days before, it had been made known by public proclamation, that neither the bridge [prepared for the procession to pass over after the religious ceremony] nor the eagle over the fountain were to be exposed to the people, and were therefore not, as at other times, to be touched." Nonetheless, after the emperor and the king of Rome had passed, "in order to sacrifice in some degree to the genius of the mob, persons expressly appointed went behind the procession, loosened the cloth from the bridge . . . and threw it into the air. This gave rise to no disaster, but to a laughable mishap; for the cloth unrolled itself in the air. Those now who took hold of the ends and drew them towards themselves, pulled all those in the middle to the ground, enveloped them and teased them till they tore or cut themselves through, and everybody, in his own way, had borne off a corner of the stuff made sacred by the footsteps of Majesty."[21]

For Goethe, this was now an "entertainment." But then,

> another strange spectacle occurred . . . the handsome slender Hereditary Marshal flung himself upon his steed; he had laid aside his sword; in his right hand he held a silver-handled vessel, and a tin spatula in his left. He rode within the barriers to the great heap of oats, sprang in, filled the vessel to overflow, smoothed it off, and carried it back again with great dignity. [By doing this it was said] [t]he imperial stable was now provided for. The Hereditary Chamberlain then rode likewise to the spot, and brought back a basin with ewer and towel. But more entertaining for the spectators was the Hereditary Carver, who came to fetch a piece of the roasted ox. . . . Now it was the turn of the Hereditary Cupbearer, who rode to the fountain and fetched wine. Thus now was the imperial table furnished, and every eye waited upon the Hereditary Treasurer, who was to throw about the money [gold, silver, and copper coins, which] glittered merrily in the air like metallic rain. A thousand hands waved instantly in the air to catch the gifts; but hardly had the coins fallen than the crowd tumbled over each other on the ground, and struggled violently for the pieces which might have reached the earth. As this agitation was constantly repeated on both sides as the giver rode forwards, it afforded the spectators a very diverting sight. It was most lively at the close, when he threw out the bags themselves, and everybody tried to catch this highest prize.

The greatest battle was over the roasted bull:

---

21. Goethe 1864, 1:168.

This could only be contested *en masse*. Two guilds, the butchers and the wine-porters, had, according to ancient custom, again stationed themselves so that the monstrous roast must fall to one of the two. The butchers believed that they had the best right to an ox which they provided entire for the kitchen; the wine-porters, on the other hand, laid claim because the kitchen was built near the abode of their guild, and because they had gained the victory the last time, the horns of the captured steer still projecting from the latticed gable-window of their guild and meeting-house as a sign of victory. Both these companies had very strong and able members; but which of them conquered this time, I no longer remember.

Goethe continued with the destruction of the temporary kitchen: "In a trice the hut was unroofed, and single individuals hung to the beams and rafters, in order to pull them also out of their joinings."[22]

With regard to the earlier narrative of the ceremonies for the emperor Matthias, Goethe provides some supplementary details that should be noted: the edicts intended to avoid disorder, reminiscent of the many similar papal ones we have encountered; the distribution of pieces of carpet, made precious by the passage of some of the greatest dignitaries of the empire; the effort to explain the heap of oats in pecuniary terms that hardly fit the wastage that occurred; the three metals of the coins (like the three offerings of the Magi, or better the *épikombia* of the Byzantine emperor); the relationship between the food and the person of the emperor and the king of Rome ("now was the imperial table furnished"); the conquest and exhibition of the gilded horns of the bull by one of the guilds, which reminds us of the struggle over the horse and horse trappings; the demolition of the structure where the bull was roasted.

But with Goethe we have emerged from the world of medieval ritual. His eyes watched with detached amusement, and the very participants in the ceremony were beginning to tire of it. The young king "in his monstrous articles of dress, with the crown-jewels of Charlemagne, dragged himself along as if he had been in a disguise, so that he himself, looking at his father from time to time, could not refrain from laughing"; the crown had to be thickly padded to stay on his head and "stood out . . . like an overhanging roof"; "the dalmatica, the stole, well as they had been fitted and taken in by sewing, presented by no means an advantageous appearance."[23]

As Goethe and his friends ate a cold luncheon while awaiting the end of the religious ceremony in the cathedral, the older people present told stories of the earlier coronation of Francis I and Maria Theresa—"beautiful beyond measure, [she] had looked on this solemnity from a balcony window of the Frauenstein house." The empress had also thought the ceremony amusing. "As her consort returned from the cathedral in his strange costume, and seemed to her, so to speak, like a ghost of Charlemagne, he had, as if in jest, raised both his hands, and shown her the imperial globe, the sceptre, and the curious gloves, at which she had broken out into immoderate laughter, which served for the great delight and edification of the crowd, which was thus honored with a sight of the good and natural matrimonial understanding between the most exalted couple in Christendom. But when the Empress, to greet her consort, waved her handkerchief, and

22. Goethe 1864, 1:170–71.
23. Goethe 1864, 1:169.

even shouted a loud *vivat* to him, the enthusiasm and exultation of the people was raised to the highest, so that there was no end to the cheers of joy."[24]

Certainly Charlemagne would have been astonished to see his descendant waving the scepter and globe as if it were a just-won tennis cup, and his consort fluttering a handkerchief and cheering, like the girlfriend of an automobile racer. Was the *religio regis* truly at its end?

24. Goethe 1864, 1:167.

PART II | The Natural Body

7

A Wax Lamb

IN 1165 NERSÈS SHNORHALI, the Armenian bishop of Hamayk in Mesopotamian Syria, wrote a letter in defense of the Matal, that is, the sacrifice of a lamb as a Christian offering. The immolation included prayers and particular rites. The prayers varied in accordance with the day and the circumstance that occasioned the offering of the Matal. The victim was brought by the faithful to the portal of the church, before the cross, covered with a scarlet cloth, its head adorned with ribbons. Another scarlet cloth was kept ready next to the cross. The priest blessed the chamber. Then four psalms were sung (Psalms 32, 34, 51, and 20), and four passages, Leviticus 1:1–13, 2 Kings 7:17–19, Isaiah 56:6–7, and Hebrews 13:10–16, were read. Finally four verses were read from the Gospel of Saint Luke (14:12–15). The priest recited a long prayer remembering the supreme sacrifice of Christ and asking God to receive the offering favorably, to forgive the sins of his people, and to look upon those making the offering with favor. The victim was made to eat blessed salt (making it by this act accept sacrifice), and its throat was cut. It was absolutely forbidden to collect or drink the blood, which was reserved to God and the apostles. A portion of the flesh was reserved for the clergy; the rest was distributed to the poor, and it could not be kept by those making the offering. If it was a Paschal lamb, however, a part was reserved for the clergy, and at variance with Hebrew practice, the rest could be eaten.[1]

Reading this description, we can easily see why other Christians accused the people making this offering of paganism, and it was precisely against this accusation that Bishop Nersès Shnorhali objected. Had not this rite been accepted by Saint Gregory Illuminator (who was certainly not inferior to the apostles in sanctity) and by the Roman Church? In fact, in the *Ordines romani* XI and XII (one written before 1143, the other about 1192) one finds the description of a pontifical rite that was rather similar. As we have seen, after the celebration of Mass in the Basilica of Santa Maria Maggiore, the pope was crowned and accompanied in a cavalcade across the Esquiline Hill, past the arch of Sant'Eusebio, the monument to Marius recalling his victory over the Cimbri, and along Via Merulana to the Lateran Palace. Entering St. John Lateran, the basilica of Pope Zacharias, the cardinals and other dignitaries of the papal court chanted lauds, while the pope dismounted his horse with the help of the *primicerius*. The *secunducerius,* one of the judges, took the tiara, which he passed to the *cubicularius* to lock up safely. Then the judges carried the pope in a *sedia gestatoria* through the basilica to the Casa Major in the Lateran Palace, where a table

---

1. Tixeront 1921, 264–65.

Fig. 42   Andrea di Bartolo (fourteenth century), the lamb on the table of the Last Supper
(Bologna, Pinacoteca nazionale).

had been prepared with nine stools and a couch (*lectus*). Five cardinals, five deacons, and
the *primicerius,* "representing the apostles at the Last Supper when they dined at Passover"
(Fig. 42), waited on the pope. The pope went to a place called the *cubitorium* (or
cubiculum), where a roasted lamb awaited his benediction before being divided among the
diners, beginning with the *prior basilicarum,* and he pronounced the following formula:
"What you do, do quickly; what he has received for damnation, you accept for pardon."[2]

Comparing this to what I have already said about papal coronations, some common
elements appear. If the place was not St. Peter's, the basilica of Constantine in the holy
city, but instead Santa Maria Maggiore on the Esquiline Hill, the placing of the crown was

2. "Finita missa, coronatur, et cum Processione redit ad Palatium per montem Esquilinum, intrans sub arco, ubi
dicitur macellum Lunanum [Eumanum], progreditur ante templum Marii, quod vocatur Cimbrum, transiens per
Merulanam, ascendens ad palatium juxta Fulloniam. Introitu basilicae Zachariae papae, acceptis laudibus a cardinalibus
et judicibus, sicut in aliis coronis, descendit de equo; suscipitur a primicerio, et secundicerius judicum deponit coronam,
et dat cubiculario, quam curiose reponit in scrinio. Judices autem dicunt eum illo die in basilicam magnam leoninam, in
cameram [the *Ordo* XII has: quae dicitur Casa Major] ubi sunt praeparata undecim scamna, et unum subsellium, circa
mensam domini pontificis, et lectus ejus bene praeparatus in figura duodecim apostolorum circa mensam Christi,
quando comederunt pascha. Ibi jacent in cubitis quinque cardinales, et quinque diaconi, et primicerius ad prandum, et
prius presbyterio in camera cum manibus, sicut in Die Natalis Domini. Surgit inde, et venit ad locum, qui dicitur
Cubitorium, ubi agnus assus benedicitur, quem benedicit, et redit ad praeparatum lectum mensae. Prior basilicarius
sedet in subsellio ante lectum. Tunc Dominus pontifex tollit parum de agno, et prius porrigit priori basilicario, dicens:
'Quod facis, fac citius; sicut ille accepit ad damnationem, te accipe ad remissionem.' Reliquum agni distribuit
discumbentibus, et aliis circumstantibus." PL, LXXVIII:1044 and 1079.

repeated nonetheless, and the cavalcade was a smaller version of the *Possessio,* including passage under a triumphal arch.

But now let us look more closely than before, when I was describing ritual violence, at the cavalcade of the *Possessio.* This procession became necessary when it was decided to carry out the papal coronation at the site of the tomb of St. Peter.[3] Pope Nicholas I was the last pope to be crowned in the cathedral of Rome, St. John Lateran, on 24 April 858. His predecessor Leo IV (847–55) had already fortified the whole zone on the other side of the Tiber, around the basilica of Constantine, which had risen on the spot where tradition held that the prince of the apostles was buried. This was done to avoid another attack by Saracen pirates, like the one in 846, when they had come far up the Tiber. Now the church and its *borgo,* Transtiberim, were sufficiently secure to permit some innovation in the coronation ceremony. To be crowned over the tomb of the apostle was to capture the *mana* enclosed within it. But then, since there were no papal palaces near the basilica (the first of the Vatican palaces was not built until the time of Pope Nicholas III Orsini 1277–88),[4] it was necessary to return to the Lateran, across the whole extent of medieval Rome that was built within the great loop of the Tiber between the Theater of Marcellus and the slopes of the Quirinal, and also to traverse the wasteland ("Disabitato") that extended from the Campidoglio to San Clemente and beyond (Fig. 43; see Fig. 47).[5] It is indicative that the procession returning to the Lateran came to be called the *Possessio*—it was a "taking possession" both of the papal court and of the Roman cathedral.[6] The rite of coronation was gradually enriched with repetitions, which we will examine further below. In taking possession of the cathedral, the new pontiff went to the Sancta Sanctorum (now the Chapel of S. Lorenzo), where he was received by the court: the cardinals, bishops, and chief functionaries of the Curia. Here another rite was observed. No longer dressed in their pontifical vestments, those present were admitted to the *proskynesis:* the cardinals kissed the pope's knee, the bishops and other functionaries his foot. The cardinals and bishops held their reversed miters out to the pope, who placed some coins in them, a rite called the *presbyterium.*[7]

When, following the period of the Great Schism and the popes in Avignon, the papacy returned to Rome after seventy years of abandonment (1306–77), it found the Lateran Palaces uninhabitable. The Curia had been housed there for four centuries, and the complex of buildings constituting the Lateran had become a small city distant from medieval Rome, which was concentrated, as I have indicated, on the left bank of the Tiber in the loop of the river across from Hadrian's Tomb. The "Holy City" of the Lateran (the "forbidden city") had been isolated in the area beyond the Caelian Hill then within sight of the *"caballus Constantini"* (the equestrian statue of Marcus Aurelius).[8] Thus two reasons lay behind moving the court: the discomfort of the old palace and its distance from the city. When it was decided in 1420 to abandon the Lateran for the Vatican, the small palace built by Pope Nicholas III was enlarged, but this did not mean abandoning the Church of St. John Lateran, Rome's cathedral. Thus the rite of a papal coronation was not complete without a return to the Lateran (since the pope was the bishop of Rome) to take posses-

---

3. See Schimmelpfennig 1974.
4. See Ehrle and Egger 1985.
5. Hermanin 1911; Krautheimer 1980.
6. Besides the bibliography already cited, see Dykmans 1968b.
7. See de' Grassi 1753, 382–85. See also *L'ordine . . .* 1555; *Ordo eligendi* 1556.
8. See Herklotz 1985.

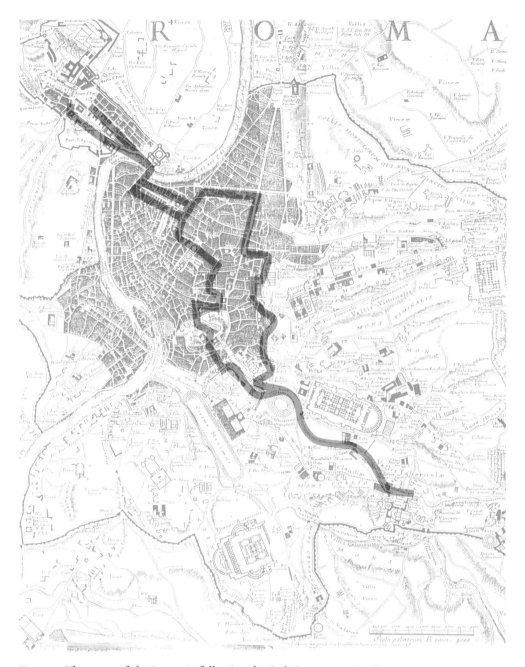

Fig. 43   The route of the *Possessio,* following the *Ordo Romanus XI* (1143).

sion of the diocese. The old procession to St. Peter's remained, but its route now went in the opposite direction.

Centuries had now passed since the institution of the ninth-century coronation ritual, and perhaps the distribution of money was even more ancient. Paul the Deacon (ca. 720–800) says that at Easter 590 Pope Gregory the Great distributed gold coins to the cardinals "et aliis axiomaticis" (that is, to the great dignitaries of the Curia, whose salary was called the *axiomaticum*).[9]

9. Moroni 1840–79, s.v. *Presbiterio.*

This distribution of money (into the reversed miters) accomplished the last act of the coronation ritual. The pontiff had taken possession of his cathedral and court by recognizing the submission of his dignitaries.

The papal master of ceremonies Paris de' Grassi tells us that, shortly after the coronation, the Curia was admitted to still another distribution. The Saturday immediately before the Dominica in Albis (the Sunday following Easter) a ceremony similar to the *proskynesis* occurred: cardinals, bishops, and other high officials, with their miters again reversed, received little, medium-sized, or large wax disks. On both sides of the disks a lamb was shown lying on the mystical book with the seven seals and holding the standard of the cross triumphant in its right hoof. Under this figure was stamped the pontifical coat of arms and the year of the pope's election. The number and size of the disks varied in accordance with the rank of the persons receiving them. The papal book of ceremonies indicates that the two rites were connected, but one wonders where the second one came from. It can be found in the first of the Roman *Ordines,* from the ninth century: "In the Lateran, on Holy Saturday, the archdeacon comes to the church to melt wax in a vessel, mixes oil with it, and blesses the wax. From this, little figures of lambs are made and set aside. During Easter season the archdeacon distributes these lambs to the people after the Mass and Communion; and they use them at home to make incense to burn at any moment of need."[10]

One has the impression that, parallel to the rite of the roasted lamb—which was restricted to twelve prelates of the church[11]—the Roman Church was carrying out another, broader distribution of Paschal lambs, as wax effigies. The ceremony must have had earlier precedents. In 417 Pope Zosimus extended the right to use the Paschal candle to all the parishes of Rome, whereas earlier this had been limited to the basilicas. All churches at Easter time were allowed to break up the wax candles remaining from the previous year, coining with the wax pieces little disks into which were mixed the ashes of martyrs, and to distribute these to the parishioners. The Easter candle symbolized—as Abate Moroni tells us—"Christ who was the light of the world." Thus this was a kind of Eucharistic distribution of the body of the Son of God. The habit of stamping the image of a lamb on the disks, which other sources confirm, connected the Paschal wax with the Agnus Dei, as if we were confronted with different steps in the development of one rite.

Amalario, bishop of Metz (775–853), tells us that Gregory the Great made a change in the ritual that is significant for our purposes: "oleum infudit, quando mysteria Paschalis agni servivit" (the pope mixed in oil when he celebrated the mystery of the Paschal lamb).[12] And what oil could this have been if not an oil used for coronation? This seems still more likely because the distribution of the Agnus was now reserved to the pope, revoking the license of Pope Zosimus. Cardinal Caetani, in the *Ordo Romanus XIV,* writes: "Saturday in the Church of St. John Lateran. Today the pope is to say a Mass. When the *schola cantorum* has sung the Agnus Dei, the pope distributes the lambs, first to bishops, then to presbyters, finally to deacons. When he throws the lambs into their miters, as with other prelates, they kiss his knee."[13]

10. PL, LXXVIII:960. See Panfili 1556 and Panvinio 1560.
11. See [Richard] 1686.
12. Amalarius, PL, CV:1033.
13. PL, LXXVIII:1222. See Raynaud 1665; Suarez [1656] 1671; Baldassarri 1714; Borgia 1775.

The ceremony ended at this point, and the pope returned to the Vatican, where a banquet was prepared in the apostolic palace. But the pope was hardly seated when an acolyte entered the hall, carrying a basket filled with still more wax lambs, and cried out: "Lord, Lord. Here are the new lambs you told of. Hallelujah! They come to the font filled with light. Hallelujah!"[14] The basket was placed before the pope, and another distribution began, this time "per familiam suam," that is, for the prelates and officials of the Curia.[15] The ancient ceremony of the roasted lamb and supper had been lost, and the fellowship enlarged. The supper now extended beyond cardinals and bishops to the whole Curia. This rite was quite similar to that of the *presbyterium,* since it was repeated in different places: in the cathedral for the cardinals and in the Vatican Palace for the Curia (later, in the fifteenth century, the Vatican distribution was moved to the Sistine Chapel).

Let us consider for a moment the material composition of these wax disks; the acolyte praised their "light." The first *Ordo Romanus* says that they were made in the Lateran. We have seen how Gregory the Great intervened to regularize and elevate the use of the previous year's Paschal candle, reserving its distribution to the pope and mixing the holy oil of coronation with the wax. About the year 1000 the ritual was again modified, elaborated, and even more closely connected with the ceremonial of pontifical coronations, and thus with the pope. Not only holy oil but also balm was now mixed with the wax: were not oil and balm the ingredients needed for an unction/embalming? Then further, the *Ordo Romanus XII,* in use at the time of Pope Honorius III (1216–27), says that the wax, before being used, had to be left by acolytes on the altar of St. Peter's for an entire night. It appears that in the fifteenth century the acolytes numbered twenty-five and that they were given a dinner appropriate to fasting ("we had bread, wine, fish, and other appropriate food"),[16] to purify the body. The day after, the white wax ("cera albissima" the *Ordo xvi* says) was mixed with holy oil and balm and presented to the pontiff to bless. The vessels used were of silver ("caldaria argentea"), as was the mixing rod ("virga argentea").

In a similarly mystical way, any objects that came into contact with the wax of the lambs had to be white. In his diary Johann Burchard provides a description of how Pope Innocent VII proceeded with the making of the disks on the Tuesday before Easter in 1486:

On the Tuesday of Easter, 28 March, seven great white baskets filled with blessed lambs were prepared for consecration, and they were lined up next to the wall *in cornu evangelii* [on the gospel side]. Then a great silver vessel in the form of a shell was prepared, filled with pure water, which the reverend bishop Tommaso Esinio, before the pope entered, blessed in a simple way with salt, as is customary to do in parish churches the day of a feast. Then the sacristan prepared one ampulla with holy oil and another with balm. The vessel with the holy water was placed on top of one of the baskets with the lambs to be blessed at the end of the Mass.

[Carried in an armchair, the pope entered.] Then he took off all his vestments down to his stole, except for his *pallium* (which was first placed on the altar and then passed to

14. "Domine, Domine, isti sunt agni novelli, qui annuntiaverunt vobis alleluja, modo veniunt ad fontes, repleti sunt claritate, alleluja."

15. PL, LXXVIII:1222.

16. Gattico 1753, 157.

the pope by the cardinal presbyter), so that he kept on only what he had underneath. While the pope turned his shoulders to the altar, a chair was placed a few steps away so that he could sit, and a footstool of the kind used by cardinals was placed before the chair, and on the footstool the great vessel with the holy water. A thurible with burning coals was also brought up, with a spoon and incense. All this ready, the pope, without his outer vestments, went to the chair, where, head uncovered, he turned to the water at his feet and said, "Dominus vobiscum. Oremus. Domine Deus Pater." Then, still without his miter, he took the ampulla with the balm from the sacristan and poured it into the water, making a cross and pronouncing the words "Consacrare etc." Then, after returning the ampulla to the sacristan and taking the other with the holy oil, he did the same with the oil, saying, "Consacrare etc." After giving the ampulla back to the sacristan, the pope turned to the basket with the lambs and said, "Dominus vobiscum. Deus omnium etc." The prayer finished, the pope was seated; and the bishop of Arles, holding the thurible, threw incense into it; the pope rose, put on the miter, and incensed the water three times. Then he sat down again, wearing the girdle and miter. At this point he was brought the wax lambs to consecrate, first the big ones, then the medium-sized, and finally the small ones. The pope baptized them by immersing them in the water, the bishops, mostly from the papal household, assisting, in their usual vestments. They lifted the lambs from the water and carried them in basins to tables covered with clean linen and spread them out to dry.[17]

Another description of the preparation of the lambs, under Pope Gregory XVI, provided by Abate Moroni (1803–83), shows that the rite had remained almost unchanged.

On the day appointed His Holiness went to the Sala Clementina in his residence at the Vatican, where public consistories are held, wearing cassock, rochet, stole, and *mozzetta,* and prayed standing before the altar. He took off the stole and *mozzetta,* received the water from the *maggiordomo* and a towel from the *maestro di camera.* Then, wearing the amice, girdle, stole, and miter, he ascended his throne and, assisted by the cardinal deacons [Agostino] Rivarola and [Domenico] de Simone, took off the miter. He said the "Dominus vobiscum" and the "Oremus Pater Omnipotens"; he blessed the water and poured the balm and holy oil into it, making the sign of a cross. Then, coming down, he took some of the blessed water with a silver spoon and divided it among the vessels prepared for the four cardinals who were to assist him. He returned to the throne and, turning toward the lambs, said, "Dominus vobiscum, Oremus Deus omnium—Domine Jesu Christe—O alme spiritus," and incensed the Agnus Dei, which, with the help of the two cardinal deacons, were immersed in the holy water, then removed with silver spoons, and carried by others to tables prepared and covered with clean cloths to dry. While the pontiff and cardinal deacons put the Agnus Dei into one vessel, the other cardinal deacons did the same with two others. . . . In the Sistine Chapel, the morning of the *sabato in Albis* [the saturday after Easter], after singing the "Agnus Dei," . . . the cardinals put on white vestments of their respective orders; . . . then Monsignor [Pietro] Silvestri, auditor of the Rota, wearing the tunic of an apostolic subdeacon, preceded by the pontifical

17. Burchard 1883–85, 1:190, 191, 196, and 199. See also Valier 1775.

cross and candle bearers, went to the Pauline Chapel to get the blessed Agnus Dei, returned to the Sistine Chapel, and chanted three times: "Pater Sancte, isti sunt Agni novelli" . . . and after this they went to the throne holding the vessels. The pontiff began to distribute the blessed Agnus Dei, wrapped in white cotton tied with purple ribbons. After receiving kisses on hand and knee from the cardinals, who also kissed the Agnus Dei, he placed them into their miters.[18]

One sees that over four hundred years the two descriptions do not differ much. But this was not a simple rite. On one hand, one notices that baptism was continually evoked, with a parallelism between the disks of wax and catechumens (so that this is often given as the explanation of the rite); but there were also frequent references to the pontiff himself. There was also the obsession with white, indicating purity. Villette said that white was "the first color of the church," a precious symbol of the nourishment of our souls, a "symbol of the body of our Savior."[19] But was this not also the color of papal vestments?[20] The whiteness was emphasized by two pronouncements of Gregory XIII (23 and 25 May 1572) that excommunicated any who dared to color the Agnus Dei or offend their whiteness.[21] For the ceremony the pontiff offered himself stripped of his outer garments: "paratus amictu, alba cingulo, stola et mitra semplici" (dressed with amice, white girdle, stole, and simple miter).[22] Remember that at the end of the coronation, when the pope entered the Sancta Sanctorum of the Lateran (or into the Lateran basilica), he removed his vestments "usque ad stolam inclusive" (including the stola) and remained dressed only in a "pluviale leve" (a long light cloak). We may assume that in both rites this undressing had a precise meaning. Would it be too far from the truth to imagine a sacrificial victim? Did not the pope appear as the lamb of the Apocalypse during the ceremony of the *Possessio,* when he reached the portico of St. John Lateran and received the belt with the seven seals? But another important detail closely connected the two rites—the ceremony of the Angus could only take place the Easter immediately following a papal coronation, and then successively every seven years thereafter (a magic number). Leaving the wax on the altar of St. Peter's the night before, and mixing in holy oil and balm, also remind one of a coronation. The wax disks, as we have seen, required the personal and material intervention of the pontiff for their production, and their distribution was reserved to him.

It is thus difficult to connect the whole ceremony of the Agnus Dei to baptism, if for no other reason, because the disks—like the broken pieces of the Easter candle—were always considered to be talismans. Vincenzo Bonardo, bishop of Gerace, said that the faithful burned them so that the smoke from the wax could free them from "diabolical illusions," and that it was also a protection against lightning.[23] Monsignor Maffeo Barberini, the special papal nuncio in France for the occasion of the birth of Louis XIII, brought the dauphin an Agnus Dei.[24] But the miraculous quality of the wax disks had been enumerated earlier and in more detail by Pope Urban VI, when he sent three Agnus Dei to the

18. Moroni 1840–79, 1:130–31; see also Clop 1913.
19. Villette 1611, 101.
20. See Paravicini Bagliani 1994, 119ff.
21. *Bullarium,* IV, Const. Omni.
22. Burchard 1883–85, II:522–25.
23. Bonardo [1586] 1621, 17. See also *Les vertus* 1662; *Virtutes* n.d.
24. Héroard 1989, 383.

Byzantine emperor John V Paleologos in 1362. Some who had possessed one, he wrote, had been cured of fevers; women had used them to ward off the dangers of childbirth; sailors had calmed tempests by throwing them into the sea. Thrown into the flames, they had extinguished fires; worn on the body, they protected against sudden death; on the battlefield, they brought victory:

> Balsamus et munda cera cum Chrismatis unda
> Conficiunt Agnum, quod munus do tibi magnum.
> Fonte volui natum, per mystica santificatum.
> Figura desursum depellit, et omne malignum.
> Praegnans servetur, simul et partus liberatur,
> Portatus munde, de fluctibus eripit unde;
> Peccatum frangit, et Christi sanguinis et angit.
> Munera fert dignis, virtutem destruit ignis;
> Morte repentina salvat, satanaeque ruina.
> Si quis honoret eum, retinet supra hostem trophaeum.
> Parsque minor tantum tota valet integra quantum,
> Agnus Dei, miserere mei, qui crimina tollis.[25]

> (Balm and pure wax with the water of chrism
> Made the Agnus, that I give you as a great gift.
> Born from a spring, mystically sanctified,
> It destroys ghosts and any malice,
> Helps pregnant women in childbirth,
> If carried with purity, it protects from the waves,
> Shatters sin and suffering with Christ's blood.
> It brings precious gifts, puts out fires,
> Protects against sudden death, and from Satan's ruin.
> If honored, it wins trophies from enemies.
> The smallest part alone is worth the whole.
> Lamb of God, who takes away sins, have mercy on me.)

The Franciscan Gabriel Sagard, in his *Grand voyage du pays des Hurons* (1632), tells that his interpreter, captured by Iroquois Indians in North America, "was miraculously saved through the potency of the Agnus Dei that he had suspended from his neck. When the Indians wanted to tear it off, it began to thunder furiously, and it flashed like lightning, so that they thought the end of the world had come [*estre à leur dernière journée*] and, terrified, released him, thinking that they were going to die for having tried to kill a Christian and for stealing his relic from him."[26] A century later, a broadsheet put out under Pope Benedict XIV explained, in about the same way, that "the figure of the adorable sign of the cross stamped on the disks stops evil spirits and puts them to flight, clears clouds away, quiets whirlwinds, lightning, and tempests. Through their divine blessing, the disks

---

25. The text, written by Andrea Frari, is in Ceresole [1845] 1887, 26. A nearly identical letter, sent by Julius III to Henry II, king of France, is in Nicolini da Sabio n.d. [1550?]. See also Grisar 1907.
26. Sagard 1632, 218–19.

Fig. 44　An Agnus Dei of Pope
Benedict XIV (1740)
(property of the author).

protect against diabolical frauds, insinuations, and temptations; pregnant women are protected and deliver their children safely; they protect against pestilential or unhealthy air,
death from epilepsy; they protect against storms at sea, floods, and fires."[27]

One can understand why the English chronicler Matthew Paris wrote that the abbot
of St. Albans, during the pontificate of Innocent IV, put an Agnus Dei "in summitate
turris nostrae" (on the top of our tower) as a kind of lightning rod,[28] and why an Agnus
Dei of Pope Gregory XI was later discovered in the foundations of the Castle of Poitiers
in France, begun by Jean de France, duc de Berry, in 1375.[29]

Other powers were added to this list when the wax disks were later modified so as to
have the Agnus Dei not on both sides but only on the obverse of the disk, and the image of
a saint—initially chosen among the apotropaic saints (who guarded against evil spirits), but
then also the thaumaturgic (healing) saints—on the reverse. It is difficult to tell when these
transformations occurred. We know that the Milanese engraver Giacomo Antonio Moro
was commissioned to make ready dies of Saint Carlo Borromeo, Saint Francis of Assisi,
and Saint Bernard for the papal coronation year 1621, and that seven years later Pope
Urban VIII commissioned dies with Saint Benedetto da Norcia, Saint Scolastica, John the

27. A facsimile of the broadsheet is in Quintana 1965.
28. *Monasticum Anglicanum* 1819–30, II:237.
29. Barbier de Montault 1886.

Baptist, Sebastian, Mary Magdalene, Catherine, Michael, Pope Marcellus, Dominick, Agnese, Chiara, and Cecilia,[30] all apotropaic saints *par excellence,* if one excepts Saint Sebastian, who was a thaumaturgic healing saint linked to the plague. An Agnus Dei produced for the coronation of Pope Benedict XIV (1740; Fig. 44) shows Saint Julian surrounded with the legend "SANCTUS JULIANUS MARTYR PODAGRA OPPRESSIS AUDITOR" (Saint Julian Martyr, the one who hears those oppressed with gout). The disk had four holes at the cardinal points through which ribbons could be passed to hang the Angus over a sick bed.

It comes to mind that a later medal of Saint Benedetto da Norcia might have originated as an Agnus Dei. As we know, it had on its obverse an image of the saint, and on its reverse a Greek cross with the inscription "Crux Sancta Sit Mihi Lux / Non Draco Sit Mihi Dux" (the Holy Cross be my light, be not the Dragon my guide) and in the intersection and all around: "Vade Retro Satana Nunquam Suade Mihi Vana Sunt Mala Quae Libas Ipse Venena Bibas" (keep back, Satan, you will never persuade me; drink the poison [yourself] that you pour out in libation). It was a medal competing with the Agnus Dei to protect against the Evil One.

Thus, during the sixteenth century (if not before) the lambs tended to lose their earlier meaning of a distribution of the body of the pope/lamb, to acquire more and more the meaning of thaumaturgic talismans. If kings of France could cure glandular tuberculosis with the royal touch, and if kings of England not only did this but also distributed "cramp rings" against apoplexy,[31] the popes could distribute talismans with even more multiple powers (against mishaps in pregnancy, apoplexy, fires, floods, and diabolical temptations). Gradually, the disks became more specialized, and then it was not enough to have just one Agnus; one of each type was needed for different maladies. In short, the Agnus was gradually transformed from a sacrificial lamb into *Sondergötter,* "gods for special occasions," with apotropaic powers against evil spirits or thaumaturgic healing powers, as the particular occasion demanded.

30. Bertolotti 1881, 185–86.
31. Thomas [1971] 1973, 235–36.

8

Oriens Augusti

THE ASSOCIATION OF THE KING'S BODY with the *Sol invictus* (unconquered sun; Fig. 45) brought on a comparison of dawn and sunset with the king's rising in the morning and retiring at night: "ortus repetit occasus" (the sunrise repeats the sunset).[1] These were the two faces of one medal. "Undaunted, the Sun with its appearance triumphantly sets evil spirits to flight, and chases away the demons of darkness."[2] Since the cosmos was thought to be a great shield (*clipeus*), the sun, with its rays, was depicted at the center. From this came the *imago clipeata* of Roman emperors. The Christian halo derived directly from this image. Christianity fully accepted the metaphor of the sun/king and transferred it to the *Christos-Helios.* Thus "Christus oriens ex alto" (Christ arising from on high), Saint Ambrose wrote, associating the sacred scarab with the *Sol salutis.*[3] "Oriens Christi figura" (The sunrise is the image of Christ), Tertullian wrote;[4] "Oriens nomen est illi" (His name is the sunrise), Origen explained.[5] Both associated dawn with the Resurrection. Thomas Aquinas, instead, imagined a birth, and explained the Christmas Mass as a "spiritual birth in which Christ rises in our hearts like the morning star."[6] But otherwise there was the often-repeated passage from Isaiah (60:2): "darkness shall cover the earth, and gross darkness the people; but the Lord shall arise upon thee, and his glory shall be seen upon thee."

When, on 14 February 1014, Emperor Henry II the Saint was crowned in Rome, he put on a purple liturgical mantle on which was embroidered the vault of heaven with stars and constellations.[7]

Based on the principle of *Christomimèsis,* two rituals assumed particular importance around the king: the *anàtellon* (rising up) and the *parousia* (showing), both closely connected with the *adventus-epiphania.* After Tacitus's account of the Germans, we find a reference to this first ritual in the panegyric that Corippus, questor of the sacred palace, wrote for the accession to the throne of the Byzantine emperor Justin II (565). He describes the *anàtellon:* four youths raised the sovereign on a great shield (Fig. 46).[8] Standing on this, the emperor made his appearance, his own epiphany, "a ceremony adopted by the

---

1. *XII panegyrici latini* 1911, VII (VI), 14.13:231.
2. Kantorowicz 1963, 124.
3. Dölger 1930 and 1932; Kantorowicz 1963, 135.
4. Tertulliano 1971, 754.
5. Origene 1916, 509, 13.
6. Thomas Aquinas 1948, 140–41.
7. Villette 1611, 226–27.
8. "quattuor ingentem clipei sublimius orbem adtollunt lecti iuvenes." Corippus 1879, 130.

Fig. 45   The sacrifice to the Sun (with halo and scepter), Naples, Museo Nazionale.

Romans, probably from Germanic tribes, as early as the fourth century."[9] But it had already been elaborated earlier by the Achaemenian kings of Persia for the celebration of the New Year (a day closely associated with the sun's rebirth). The king, seated on a throne, was raised above the heads of his men. "He rose on that day like the sun, the light beaming forth from him, as though he shone like the sun. Now the people were aston-

9. L'Orange 1953, 88–89; see also 103ff. and Kantorowicz 1963, 152.

Fig. 46   The *anàtellon* in the codex Vaticanus Graecus 752, 82r, Vatican Library.

ished at the rising of two suns."[10] The *sedia gestatoria* that Castruccio Castracani sat on when he entered the cathedral of Lucca had, certainly, the same magic value (Fig. 47).

The other rite was the *parousìa*. Usually, the *dominus* hid himself from the gaze of his subjects. Philip II of Spain attended the meetings of his council hidden behind a curtain. In a famous report from Japan sent to King Philip III of Spain in 1609 by Don Rodrigo de Vivero y Velasco, the governor of the Philippines, Rodrigo said that the Japanese "tienen por magestad que sus reyes y señores no sean vistos ni tratados" (regard it as a mark of majesty that their kings and lords are neither seen nor approached), and for this reason, at the court of Keyto, the king "està siempre encerrado" (remains always withdrawn in his palace).[11] The same could be said of the "sacred precinct" of Istanbul. In the Topkapi, Mahomet II was completely hidden:

10. L'Orange 1953, 87.
11. Gill 1991, 180.

[T]he sultan's mastering gaze, architecturally framed by windows, implied a form of domination and control that accentuated the spatial and sociopolitical distance between subject and object, ruler and ruled. The hidden ruler could not be perceived directly, but his invisible potency became known indirectly, through its effects. The power of the privileged gaze was so fully embodied in the architectural discourse of the place that to catch a glimpse of the hidden monarch became the propelling force of the ceremonial narrative.[12]

The sultan observed from a balcony over the entrance gate, or hidden behind the shutters of the Tower of Justice. "From this tower pavilion," called the "king's watchtower" in Melchior Lorich's panorama of 1559, "the sultan could observe ceremonies of the second court, political executions (for which he gave the signal by opening one of the latticed shutters), and the payment of his troops."[13]

Appearing in public was always something requiring special emphasis. When the emperor Vespasian celebrated his *adventus* in Alexandria, he was acclaimed in the hippodrome with the cry "Anàtellon!" (Arise!).[14] It is worth noting that in the circus at Constan-

Deductio Papæ in Palatium et Basilicam Lateranensem

Fig. 47   The *sedia gestatoria* in the *Possessio*, from G. Banck, *Roma triumphans*, Frankfurt am Main, Typis Arcerii, 1656.

12. Necipoglu 1991, 244.
13. Necipoglu 1991, 244.
14. Jouguet 1942.

Fig. 48   The tribune (*prokypsis*) of the Byzantine emperor with the *katapetàsmata* open. Base of
the column of the circus, Constantinople.

tinople the Green party called the victor of a chariot race "Anàtellon."[15] It seems possible,
however, that the chariot race was being likened to a chariot triumph here, and the win-
ner of the race to the person coming in triumph. The emperor Constantine Porphyrogenitus, in his *Liber de ceremoniis,* carefully recorded all the acclamations after these victories, and they seem to demonstrate that this chariot race was more a religious ceremony,
like the rigid ceremonials tied to the persons of *augustae,* than a simple sporting event.

The appearance of the emperor on the tribune was thus an event that evoked the cry
"Rise in glory."[16] Naturally, the cry went up before the emperor made his entrance and became visible (the *parousìa*). These were "cultural and ritual cries by means of which a god
was invited to make his appearance. . . . We recognize that a ritual performance had been
taking place, within which the cries of 'Rise, rise, rise' have their very specific and almost
magical function, the function of calling the not yet present *numen* of the Emperor."[17]

In the circus was a special elevated platform, on which was mounted a small wooden
tribune, the *prokypsis,*[18] from which the emperor watched the race. This small tribune was
covered with drapery, and golden curtains (*katapetàsmata*)[19] covered the front. The emperor, empress, and the *augustae* took their places inside.

The curtains were as yet closed, when the emperor, with the caesars and the *augustae,*
ascended the platform by a back stair, while the front of the stage was still veiled. In front
of the *prokypsis,* the court, the clergy, the deputations of the army, and the people assembled, waiting for the majesties to appear. Then, after the members of the imperial
family had taken their proper places on the *estrade* and had arranged themselves, the
curtains were thrown open, and the dignitaries and the clergy intoned the *polychronion.*
The emperors, now visible from the knees upward, made their epiphany [Fig. 48]. The

15. Constantin Porphirogénète 1967, II:126.
16. Constantin Porphirogénète 1967, II:29–30.
17. Kantorowicz 1963, 127.
18. Heisenberg 1920.
19. C. Schneider 1936.

Fig. 49   Lisbon, the royal chapel, with the arrangement of seats reserved for the king's
prokypsis (1), for princes (2), prelates (3), ambassadors (4), dukes (5), counts (6).
Engraving from *Colleçao de livros ineditos de historia portugueza dos reinados de D.
Josão I, D. Duarte, D. Alfonso V, e D. Josão II*, Lisbon, Academia Real das Sciencias,
III, 1793.

stage was artificially illuminated whenever the ceremony took place after sunset, as indeed it often did. In the dark of the night the *prokypsis* would give the impression of being an island of light in the brilliancy of which the *numen praesens* of the *basileus* became manifest; it was the imperial epiphany [or *parousia*].[20]

The use of a *prokypsis* was extended to other festivities, and was even used for coronations and royal weddings.[21] In the language of the church, the curtains were later alluded to as the doors of heaven,[22] and we find them up into the fifteenth century in many representations and tomb sculptures.

The connection between the ceremonies of the *anàtellon* and of the *parousìa* is now clear, as is the derivation of both from the image of the sun, the *Sol invictus*. By way of Byzantium, the solar cult reappeared in Sicily, where King William II (1166–89) was called, by the panegyrist Eugenius from Palermo, "Anàsperos forfòros" (the bearer of never-setting light).[23] Orfino da Lodi said of the emperor Frederick II that "sol novus est ortus"[24] (a new sun has risen), and Dante Alighieri compared the papacy and empire to two suns (*Purgatorio,* XVI:106–8). He also referred to Emperor Henry VII as "sol noster," "Titan exoriens."[25] In this context, one wonders whether the ceremony in the *prokypsis* also left more visible traces in Western Christendom.

Actually, traces of the ceremony can be found both in Portugal and in Italy. The *Livro Vermelho* (1462–80) of King Alfonso V prescribed a ceremony with much resemblance to the Byzantine one: the reception of foreign princes and ambassadors, which later also included audiences with his most important vassals. The ceremony took place in the royal chapel. Benches were placed horizontally, one in front of another ("da outra parte comtraria"), sideways to the altar, while the royal "curtain" was arranged on the left side of the chapel (Fig. 49). Here the king remained hidden until the curtain in front of the tribune was opened, when he appeared to the beholders.[26]

In these same years (1462–82) a not dissimilar ceremony took place in the Po valley, at the castle of Torchiara, in the feudal state of the Rossi. Here the tribune was made of inlaid wood (made in the shop of the Di Biagio; Fig. 50) and was placed in a corner of the Chapel of San Nicodemo. The wooden sides repeated themes from the Camera d'Oro: the coat of arms of the Rossi (a lion rampant) and a heart painted red and inscribed with the motto "DIGNE ET IN ETERNUM" (worthy and eternal), a reference to the love of the *dominus,* Pier Maria Rossi, for Bianca Pellegrini. On top a hexagonal cupola symbolized the vault of heaven. On the east side, a window closed by two grille doors opened toward the altar, while on another side a small door across from a door in the outside wall (now closed up) gave access to the *cubiculum*. Inside the grille windows was a love message that could only be read by the occupants: "PETRVS MA.R. NVNC ET SEMPER DE BLANCHIN" (Pietro Maria Rossi now and always for Blanche). The lord and his lady attended Mass in this tribune. The grille doors on the window were opened when the *dominus* and the *domina* had

20. Kantorowicz 1963, 159.
21. C. Schneider 1936.
22. Giovanni Crisostomo 1862, 29.
23. Eugenio di Palermo 1964; see also Sternbach 1902.
24. Orfino da Lodi 1869, 45.
25. Maccarrone 1950; Kantorowicz 1951.
26. *Livro Vermelho* 1793, 420–21.

taken their places, thus making their appearance to the attendant court and replicating the ceremonial of the Byzantine *prokypsis*.

Thus we can show that the ceremony in the *prokypsis* was known also in western Europe. Was there a link between Byzantium and the courts of the Po valley of the fifteenth century? There is not much documentation on the marquisate of Montferrat, but I think that in its transition to the Paleologus dynasty from Constantinople, we could discover a link to explain some of the diffusion of Byzantine ceremonial in northern Italy. In 1305, on the death of the last marquis of Montferrat of the Aleramics dynasty, the succession fell on Theodore, the second son of Emperor Andronicus II. The young man arrived in Genoa in 1306 and was invested with the marquisate of Montferrat by the Holy Roman Emperor Henry VII in 1310. On the death of his mother, the empress of the East Jolanda, Theodore returned to Constantinople, and he made another visit there a few years later, accompanied by some members of the court of Montferrat, and remained for four years (1326–30). He returned to the Po valley, to Casale in Montferrat, accompanied by another Byzantine dignitary, Stephan Siropolos. It is quite possible that the presence of Theodore at Montferrat, and his continual contacts with his homeland, were the link we are seeking. Otherwise, Theodore himself, in a treatise on military discipline in which he made many autobiographical references, says that he had not forgotten the court life of his youth. The presence of Siropolos at Casale probably reinforced this. Theodore died in 1338, and through successive generations his descendants tied themselves to the French monarchy, thus loosening their ties to the Empire of the East. When Federico Gonzaga, of Mantua, married Margherita Paleologus, daughter of Marquis Guglielmo I in 1530, the way was opened for succession of the Gonzaga in Montferrat. This was secured through their investment by the emperor Charles V six years later. But one wonders whether the contact between Mantua and the Paleologi had not been established earlier. Certainly, one could read the frescoes by Mantegna (1465–74) on the north wall of the Camera degli Sposi in the Castello di Corte at Mantua as a great *parousia,* a true *prokypsis.* Mantegna opens the curtain to show the whole Gonzaga family immobile. This is in striking contrast to the crowd of courtiers around them, painted along the stairway to the left. We remember that this fresco was painted in the same years that the ceremony in Portugal evolved, and that the little tribune at Torchiara was built. Should we thus read Mantegna's curtain as a true and proper *katapetàsmata?*

Around the body of the sovereign, another *parousia* was observed daily, or rather twice a day: the rising and retirement of the *dominus.* In the context of the solar cult, this could only be associated with the rising and setting of the sun. But although it happened daily, the royal sleep assumed different meanings on different occasions. On the eve of a coronation, for example, the emphasis was on the purity of his body, and the event was associated with chivalric initiations. This ceremony for King Pedro III of Aragon (1239–85) required three days of fasting, a purifying bath, confession, and a vigil the night before in the sacristy of the coronation church, which was guarded by knights-at-arms.[27] The Westminster *Ordo* (1273) also mentions a vigil and a purifying bath for kings of England.[28] A vigil was prescribed for the kings of France. The *Coronatio Ordo* of Charles V says: "the evening before, in good time, the king should come to the said church to pray, and there

---

27. *Coronación y consagración* 1849, 556–59; see also *Chronique catalane* 1941; Palacios Martin 1975.
28. *Missale* 1893, II:673.

Fig. 50   The wooden tribune of Lord Pier Maria Rossi in the castle of Torchiara (now in Milan, Castello Sforzesco, Museo di Arti Applicate).

Fig. 51   The Léver du Roy, engraving from A. Danchet, *Le sacre de Louis XV. . . .* The caption says:
"Léver. Le roy, vêtu d'une longue robe de toile d'argent, par dessus une camisole satin
cremoisi, reverte de même que la chemise, aux endroits mênagés pour les onctions, est
sur le bord de son lit, l'Eveque de Laon soulève Sa Majesté par le bras droits, et l'Evêque
de Beauvais par le bras gauche" [Léver. The king, dressed in a long robe of cloth-of-
silver, with a crimson cloak under it, pierced like his shirt to facilitate the anointment, is
on the side of his bed, supported by the bishop of Laon on his right hand and the bishop
of Beauvais on his left].

keep vigil, praying for part of the night, if he wishes."[29] This ceremony was later modified
to allow the king to remain in the nearby abbey, where a room was prepared for the occasion. The same *Ordo* prescribed that the next morning the bishops of Laon and Beauvais,
wearing relics around their necks, should come to the door of the king's room ("in Camera magna" [the great hall]), where he would await them, lying on a bed.[30] But it was only
with the coronation of King Charles IX (1561) that the feigned sleep and reawakening of
the king was fully elaborated. On coronation day the twelve peers of France came to the

29. "la nuit assez tot le roy doit venir a la dicte eglise pour faire s'orison, et veillier illuecques en orison une piece se il
veult": *Coronation Book* 1899, 5.
30. Jackson 1984, 126.

door of the great chamber asking, "[O]ù estre nostre nouveau Roy, que Dieu nous a donné pour nous réger et gouverner?" (Where is our new king, who God has given us to rule and govern us?) The response of the great chamberlain was, "Il repose" (He sleeps), and the peers demanded, "Esveillez le, afin que nous le saluoions, et luy faisons la révérence" (Awaken him, so that we can salute and revere him).[31] M. C. Leber has even tried to associate feigned sleep with the investiture of a knight,[32] although his interpretation is dubious, since a vigil was supposed to occur, rather than sleep. I think that the feigned sleep was meant to emphasize two things: death and resurrection, that is, a rite of passage from one state to another: surgens coruscat (it sparkles as it rises).

The *léver du roi* (the morning ceremony that we will shortly discuss) was always distinguished by an insistence on white clothing (Fig. 51). An anonymous description of the 1561 coronation ceremony says that the king "was brought to the said church in triumph, dressed all in white, with a great cloak of cloth-of-silver, a hat of white velvet with a white feather, and flesh-colored stockings, so that his legs seemed to be naked."[33] The insistence on the color white, as well as the nakedness of the legs and feet of French kings, reminds us of a papal coronation and of the perennial association of *rex* and *sacerdos*. Was this another sacrificial victim? Here again it seems so, although we are dealing with messages with multiple meanings and thus with many explanations, which changed with the passage of time and the point of view of the observer. For Jean Golin, our witness of the event, it seemed to be both a purification and a rite of passage: "And when the king takes off his clothes, it means that he abandons everyday dress to put on the religious dress of kingship, and if he does this with the devotion he should, I hold that he is washed of his sins, as those who take on religious orders are purified."[34] Golin thus confirms that we are confronted with a rite of passage and that the anointed one of God is stripped of his "everyday condition," "cleansed of sin," and received into the "religion of kingship."[35]

The prescriptions for the kings of Aragon did not differ much from the French ceremonials. These also, besides prescribing that the king arise at dawn and go to church to hear a private purifying Mass before the ceremony, minutely describe the garments he was to wear. These were episcopal garments, from the mantle to the tunic, from the stockings "of velvet worked with pearls" to the shoes and gloves "of red velvet woven with gold, pearls, and precious stones" to the maniple hanging from the left arm.[36]

If the night before the coronation received a particular emphasis, the continual daily succession from night to day was a further occasion to celebrate the solar cult of the monarch and at the same time to create gradations among courtiers and to admit petitioners to his presence.

The *cubiculum* was one of the most important rooms of state. At the château of Versailles the king's bedroom looked out directly onto the great courtyard (*cour de marble*). One approached it through a hall called the Oeil-de-Boeuf. The bedroom was dominated on one side by a true *momento mori*—a clock with the hands stopped at the time of death of the previous sovereign. The bed was placed beyond a gilded balustrade to protect the occupant from the crowd. Beside this room was the cabinet, the meeting

31. Godefroy 1649 (Charles IX), 312. See also *Le sacre des rois* 1985.
32. Leber 1825, 156ff.; see also Jackson 1984, 134, and Le Goff 1990a, 51.
33. Jackson 1984, 130.
34. Golain 1969, 315.
35. Golain 1969, 315. On him, see Nepote 1976.
36. For a full description, see *Coronación y consagración* 1849.

room of the king's council, and beside the door that led to the grand gallery was a little cabinet, the *cabinet de perruques* (wig closet). Then there was the king's real bedroom, with walls painted blue. A secret exit from this opened onto a corridor that led directly to the apartments of the queen.

There was a series of entrées, each distinguishing among those who had the right to attend. The ceremony of the *lever* was not necessarily connected with the true moment of the king's arising. Louis XVI, for instance, got up between seven and eight in the morning, while the ceremony of the *lever* was set in the court schedule for eleven, unless a hunt or some other activity had been planned, so that it had to be done earlier. Thus we should not take Michel Marion's *Dictionnaire des institutions* literally when he says it happened in the early morning.[37] The court schedule also gave time for the arrival of the courtiers, who waited in the *chambre de parade*. "Outside in the gallery everyone awaited the movement of the *lever*."[38]

On a signal of the first *valet de chambre,* who had slept at the foot of the king's bed, a series of six distinct entrées began. First was the *entrée familière (enfants de France,* princes and princesses of the blood, the first doctor, the first surgeon, the *valets de chambre*). This was followed by the *grande entrée* (great officials of the chamber and wardrobe who were to be received that day). After this came the *première entrée* (which in fact was the third), for the king's lectors, the intendants of *menus plaisirs,* the decipherer of secret documents. Fourth was the *entrée de la chambre,* to which were admitted the great eleemosynar, ministers, secretaries, and councilors of state, the captains of the guard, marshals of France, the master of the hunt, and the *grand louvetier* (there was a special official for the hunting-down of wolves). This was the entrée to which foreign ambassadors were admitted. The fifth entrée was reserved for those courtiers to whom the king had conceded entry for that day through the first gentleman of the chamber. The sixth was reserved for the king's familiars, including his bastards and their families, not through the main door, but through a side door. There was no distinction here; the side door provided direct access to the king's private rooms, although not to the council chamber.

The king's retiring at night was divided between the *grand coucher,* of no less importance than the morning ceremony, and the *petit coucher,* which followed the first and was the true moment when the king retired to his private rooms. There is a description in the *Mémoires* of the duc de Saint-Simon. A coveted honor was to carry the light, a two-branched candelabrum on a platter. One evening in 1702, after prayers, the chaplain of the day gave the light to the first *valet de chambre,* who presented it to Louis XIV. "He looked around and pronounced the name of one of those in attendance, to whom the first *valet de chambre* consigned the candelabrum. This was a favor and distinction that counted, so much did the king possess the art of making value out of nothing." Saint-Simon adds that the choice always went to persons of rank, rarely to ambassadors (except for the papal nuncio, and later to the Spanish ambassador). "One took off one's gloves and stood there holding the candelabrum for the remainder of the *coucher,* which was brief. Then it was given back to the *premier valet,* who, in his turn, gave it to someone assigned to the *petit coucher*."[39] Thus the sun set on the court of Versailles, at the beginning of the Age of the Enlightenment.

37. Marion 1923, s.v. "Etiquette."
38. Hezecques n.d., 151ff.
39. Saint-Simon 1983–88, II:174; see also Brocher 1934.

9

ON THE NIGHT OF 27 SEPTEMBER 1601, at Fontainebleau, Marie de' Medici delivered the heir to the throne to King Henry IV. It was midnight when the queen began to feel labor pains. The king sent for the midwife, Louise Bourgeois, called Boursier.

I slept in the queen's wardrobe, with the chambermaids, where often, in jest, they sent me false alarms, so that I didn't believe it when I was called by a certain Pierrot from the queen's chamber. I didn't give myself time even to lace my clothing, I was in such a hurry. The king asked, "Is it the midwife?" he was answered, "Yes." "Come in, midwife; my wife is ill. See if these are the labor pains; she is in great pain." Since I recognized that they were, I responded positively. Immediately, he said to the queen: "My life, you know well what I have told you several times. The princes of the blood must be present at the delivery. I beg you to receive them, for your greatness and that of your child." At this the queen answered that she was always resolved to do what the king wished. "I know, my life, that you wish what I wish; but I also know your timid and bashful nature; I fear that if you do not make this decision, you will be embarrassed at the moment of delivery. And for this I beg you to remain firm, because it is the custom observed at the queen's first birth.". . . About one o'clock, the king, overcome with impatience, seeing the queen's suffering, and fearful that she was about to deliver, and fearing that the princes would not arrive in time, sent to summon them, and these were the princes de Conti, de Soissons, and de Montpensier. . . .

In the meantime, the great hall at Fontainebleau near the king's chamber, called the Ovale, had been prepared for the queen's delivery with a great bed covered with crimson velvet and gold. Fixed around the bed were two baldacchinos, one large and the other smaller. They were anchored to the pavement and raised up. Now they were lowered. A curtain with rope-pulls was attached to the four corners of the large baldacchino, and this was a fine Dutch tapestry. In the center, under this, was placed the small baldacchino, of the same cloth, and under this the bed was placed, where the queen was made comfortable when she came out of her chamber. The ladies chosen by the king to assist at the delivery were called for. Monsieur de la Rivière, the king's first doctor, Monsieur de Lorens, the queen's first doctor, Messire Héroard, another of the king's first doctors, Monsieur Guide, the queen's second doctor, and Messire Guillemeau, the king's surgeon, were called to see the queen, and they stepped back to wait. A chair, some folding chairs, and some stools were brought under the baldacchino for the king, along with madame his sister and Madame de Nemours. The birthing chair was also brought up, covered with crimson velvet. . . . There were two elderly Italian ladies from the queen's household, who had had many babies and had assisted many deliveries. . . . The relics of Saint Margherite were on a table in the chamber, and two religious from St. Germaine-des-Près prayed to God continually. . . . The queen's labor pains lasted for twenty-two and a quarter hours.

Because of the long labor, the mother and child were very weak, and the midwife wanted to blow wine into the child's mouth, but did not dare.

The king pushed the bottle against its mouth and said to me: "Do as with any other child.". . . The king raised his eyes to heaven and with clasped hands gave thanks to the Lord. Tears flowed down his cheeks, as big as peas. . . . The queen suddenly clasped her hands and raised her eyes to heaven, shedding a quantity of tears, but she was overtaken immediately by weakness. . . . The king hastened to embrace the princes, without minding the queen's swoon. He went to open the doors of the chamber to let in all those who were waiting in the antechamber and the great room. There were at least two hundred persons, so many that it was impossible to lift the queen [from the birthing chair] and have her lie down on the bed. I was concerned to see her in that condition, and said that there was no need to let in so many people until the queen was in bed. The king heard me and struck my arm, saying: "Be quiet, midwife. Don't interfere. This child belongs to the whole world; let all rejoice." It was ten-thirty in the evening of Thursday, 27 September 1601, the feast of Saints Cosmos and Damian, nine months and fourteen days after the queen's wedding."[1]

The account of the midwife can be compared with that of the court doctor, Jean Héroard, who kept a detailed diary of the birth and infancy of Louis XIII. From this we learn that François de Bourbon, prince de Conti, Charles de Bourbon, comte de Soissons, and Henri de Bourbon, duc de Montpensier, "were commanded by His Majesty" to come up to the midwife to see the newborn, with the umbilical cord still attached, before it was cut.[2]

A contemporary print shows the dignitaries called to verify the sex of the baby (Fig. 52). They are shown seated in a square before the bed on which the queen was now reclining (at the foot of the bed the birthing chair is still visible). At the center of the square a female figure was standing (Catherine de Bourbon, the duchesse de Bar and sister of the king? Anne d'Este, the duchesse de Nemours?), showing the naked infant. Comparing the midwife's memory with the engraver's depiction, we must conclude that the latter shows a conventional scene that did not reflect the reality of the delivery, with the irruption of the crowd of courtiers while the royal mother was still in the birthing chair. But the conventional ceremonial scene is better shown in the painting by Eugène Devéria (Salon 1827—now in the Louvre; Fig. 53) that shows the birth of Henry IV himself (at Pau on 13 December 1553). The delivery of Jeanne d'Albret took place in much the same way as that

1. Bourgeois [1626] 1826, 103ff.
2. Héroard 1989, 1:370. See also Witckowski 1892.

of Marie de' Medici. While the mother was abandoned, swooning on the bed, the infant was shown by the father to the crowd of courtiers before being placed in the cradle. Was this a fantasy of a painter of historical pictures under the Restoration, or a scrupulous documentation of a ceremony still observed by the court? Certainly the custom of indiscriminately admitting any who presented themselves to view the queen's delivery remained at least until a delivery of Marie Antoinette on 19 December 1778. On the announcement of the doctor, Vermond, "The queen is giving birth," the crowd rushing into the chamber was so numerous and disorderly that "at that moment we feared to lose the queen."[3]

In 1610, along with the dagger of Ravaillac, the cradle of Henry Bourbon at Pau became a relic, after the martyrdom of the king who had occupied it as an infant. It became the object of a true and proper cult, exhibited on feast days and venerated like the fragments of the manger that had held the Baby Jesus. It was made from the shell of a great African turtle, and when, during the French Revolution, revolutionaries wanted to destroy it, someone quickly substituted another shell. The valueless one was what the revolutionary crowd destroyed on 1 May 1793.[4]

In a later restoration of the royal cult, under the First Empire, another important cradle with political/religious functions was the one prepared for Napoleon I's son, the king of Rome. It was designed by the painter Prud'hon and was supported at the corners

Fig. 52   *Der Dauphin in Franckreich wird geböhren. Anno 1601 den 27. September.* The birth of Louis
XIII, German broadside.

3. Kohn and Dalsace 1987.
4. Kohn and Dalsace 1987, 35–36.

Fig. 53   Dévéria, *Naissance de Henri IV* (1827), Paris, Louvre.

by four horns of plenty held up by personifications of the Genius of the Nation and of Justice. The sides were adorned with golden bees. A great *N,* the emperor's initial, crowned by a triple wreath of laurel, was mounted on top of it, while Glory was poised in flight above, bearing the crowns of triumph and immortality, and above that twinkled Napoleon's star. A small eagle at the cradle's foot opened its wings and turned its head in the act of taking flight. If it was impossible to consider such a cradle a relic—and it was practically impossible to return to the old cult of the sovereign, lost forever with the regicides of 1649 and 1793—nevertheless the message projected for the birth of the infant

Bonaparte still recalled the ancient model. Moreover, a statuette of Napoleon I holding up a naked king of Rome at his birth (1811),[5] and a medal coined by Bertrand Andrieu that showed the same scene,[6] demonstrate that the ceremony of the display of the baby's genitals was still performed.

Christomimèsis created a situation in which the births of heirs to thrones were perceived like the *dies natalis* of the divine infant.[7] But were the "dauphins" imitations of Jesus, or were representations of the Christ Child modeled on the births of kings? That all parties were alerted to a sacred event is shown, in the case of Napoleon, by the instructions given on the eve of the delivery of Marie Louise. In the empress's chamber all those in attendance were required "to wear the same dress as on Sundays at Mass."[8] At the moment of birth there were twenty-two persons.[9] The etiquette for French royal births was explained to Doctor Deneux, the gynecologist of the duchesse de Berry, at the court of Louis XVIII. He had inquired of the master of ceremonies so as to know how he should act. He received a note with the following instructions:

> 1. At the moment of feeling the first labor pains, the prince should be informed, so that he in turn could inform the family, the princes, the princesses, and the witnesses. 2. At the moment when the child was about to appear, the obstetrician should announce with a loud and clear voice, "Her Royal Highness is about to give birth." 3. At the moment of birth there should be the further announcement: "Her Royal Highness is giving birth." 4. When the child had appeared: "Her Royal Highness has given birth." 5. After cutting and tying the umbilical cord, the obstetrician should present the child to His Majesty, so that he can see its sex.[10]

The delivery should take place in the following manner: "During labor the princess is to be surrounded by a large screen; people can stand around this, but only the princesses called to assist her can enter. On the announcement of the obstetrician that the birth is about to occur, the screen will be taken away. The king enters the chamber, followed by all those designated to attend, and after having stopped at the foot of the bed, facing the princess, they take their places according to the rank assigned them, to the right and left of the bed, so as to form a semicircle."[11]

Let us now add to the representations of the deliveries of Jeanne d'Albret and Marie de' Medici two other illustrations of princely births: Marie Louise watching over the sleeping king of Rome (1811; Fig. 54), and the birth of Henri de Chambord, duc de Bordeaux (1821), the posthumous child of the duc de Berry. In the first instance the mother reveals the sex of the child by lifting a fold of the veil covering it, in a gesture that faithfully reproduces one of Raphael's paintings of the Holy Family (Fig. 55). In the second instance, Marie Caroline de Bourbon shows Marshal Suchet the uncovered genitals of the baby (Fig. 56).

If we return to examine more closely Dévéria's painting of the birth of Henry IV, it is

5. Dayot 1896, 202.
6. Kunsthistorisches Museum, Wien, *Führer durch die Sammlung,* Vienna, 1988, inv. no. 135.168.
7. See Blumenfeld-Kosinski 1990.
8. Kohn and Dalsace 1987, 125.
9. Kohn and Dalsace 1987, 128. See *Le Moniteur,* 21 March 1811.
10. Cabanès 1923, 82–83.
11. Cabanès 1923, 86. For Spain, see Cortés Echanove 1958.

Fig. 54   Marie Louise revealing the king of Rome, engraving after Franque. Paris, Boussod,
Valadon et C.e., 1894.

clear that the gazes of the two persons on the left, as of the two we see in front from the
rear, are looking toward the uncovered genitals of little Henry. They, along with Antoine
de Navarre, are the central figures in the painting. We should conclude that Dévérià knew
well the details and significance of the ceremony.

A Burgundian miniature showing the *Presentation in the Temple* from the *Book of Hours*
(1454–55) of Philip the Good shows the well-known custom for princely and kingly fami-

Fig. 55   The Holy Family, after Raphael, engraving of the sixteenth century.

lies. We only need to substitute the father of the infant for the priest in the miniature, who shows the sex of the Christ Child, and imagine figures in the court of Burgundy among the group waiting before the altar, to have an illustration of the *ostentatio genitalium* that followed every royal birth. Martin Schongauer, ca. 1480, engraved a similar *ostentatio* showing the infant Jesus (*regis puer*) with the attributes of an imperial *pallium* and a globe in his right hand ("the World has been spoken"—an equivalent of the *lex animata*). The

Fig. 56   The birth of the duke of Bordeaux. The duchess of Berry reveals the sex of her son to the marshal Louis-Gabriel Suchet (Paris, Musée Carnevalet).

pallium is open to exhibit the penis. Did the royal baby imitate the Divine Child, or had an earthly custom been transferred to religious iconography? Another painting suggests the wide diffusion of such symbolism. In Giovanni Maria Butteri's sixteenth-century portrait of the Medici family (Uffizi), commissioned by Isabella de' Medici, the daughter of duke Cosimo I, all the figures are shown dressed in the clothing and holding the symbols of their patron saints. The duchess Eleonora di Toledo, the family genitrix, exhibits the Divine Child (the only person in the portrait not recognizable as a member of the Medici family), exposing his penis in a way that could be read as a Medicean *vix generatrix* or, even better, as a personification of Medicean *fecunditas*.

The same meaning is projected in another official canvas, that of the Swedish royal family, painted by Ehrenstrahl in the seventeenth century (Gripsholm; Fig. 57). Under the protection of King Charles X, who looks down from a portrait hung on the wall, and Charles XI, who stands at one side of the central table, opposite Queen Ulrica Eleonora, the queen dowager Hedrig Eleonora points to the undressed baby prince Charles XII. He is seated on the table, and beside him the young princess Hedrig Sophia is standing, supported by Charles X's sister, Maria Euphrosque.[12]

12. Ellenius 1966, fig. 55.

Fig. 57   Ehrenstrahl, *The Swedish Royal Family* (from A. Ellenius, *Karolinska bildidéer,* Uppsala, Almquist & Wiksells, 1966).

If we accept this hypothesis of the derivation of sacred iconography from the practice of European courts (a projection of the court into the Christian Olympus), we must also change the parameters of our iconographic inquiry. As James I of England wrote, "[I]f we consider well the attributes of God, we will discover how well they are harmonized in the person of the king."[13] Royal attributes were being projected toward heaven! In an *Adoration* by Ghirlandaio (1487, Uffizi; Fig. 58), as in an *Adoration* painted by Titian for the first chapel of the Escorial, the Madonna is painted as if performing a duty, assisting the Magi kings in their inspection of the sex of the Christ Child, by opening his legs for them.

From this point of view the account of the childhood of King Louis XIII left by the physician Héroard has a different interpretation than the one presented by Philippe Ariès.[14] Héroard says that the baby Louis XIII "regularly touched and exposed himself, and invited handling."[15] Steinberg's judgment is that "the record of these proceedings was locked in a doctor's diary; no artist in 1602 would have depicted the Dauphin in such extremity."[16] But in my mind this exhibitionism was, rather, a reiteration of the *ostentatio genitalium* at birth, and of the assurance (to be exhibited!) of the good reign to come for which the child was destined. Courtiers at the time thought the baby king was showing them his ability to procreate, assuring them of his *vix generatrix*.

If, however, the penis of the Baby Jesus (often exhibited erect) was that of Christ as the eternal virgin,[17] the meaning would be different. The older king among the Magi might have been verifying—as Steinberg suggests—the human nature of God, after a circumcision that, for preachers of that time, anticipated the shedding of blood on the cross ("this most precious blood which today our Lord spills for us for the first time").[18] In the words of Saint Bonaventure: "[A]s you can see, I have not hesitated to scatter my blood for thee."[19] Was it a circumcised penis? The question is not irrelevant, due to the reluctance of painters to depict the circumcision. Steinberg gives us the theological interpretation of the circumcision of Christ as the first blood offered for mankind. But he is obliged to admit that in none of the many paintings he recollects does the penis appear to be circumcised.[20] Thus a theological interpretation appears to be lacking. On the other hand, in the miniature in the *Book of Hours* of Philip the Good, may we not imagine that the illustrator was showing a real ceremony performed at the Burgundian court, as in many other parts of Europe?

Two similar paintings by Orazio Gentileschi of the finding of Moses (1632–33) are relevant to this argument. Both have a dynastic connotation. The first, done for Charles I of England,[21] refers to the dynastic pretensions of the Stuarts to be descended (the incredible genealogies!)[22] from a pharaoh's daughter whose name was supposed to be "Scota." The second painting (in the Prado) was offered to Philip IV of Spain on the occasion of the birth of the heir to the throne, Baltasàr Carlos. At any event, in both pictures, but

13. McIlwain 1918, 307.
14. Ariès 1960, 102ff.
15. Héroard 1989, I:418; see also Marvick 1975, 213–14.
16. Steinberg 1996, 118.
17. Steinberg 1996, excursus XXIX:180–84.
18. Steinberg 1996, 61.
19. Bonaventura 1926, 92 (*Il legno di vita*, 5).
20. Steinberg 1996, excursus XXIII:165–67.
21. Finaldi 1999, table 8.
22. Bizzocchi 1995.

Fig. 58   Domenico Ghirlandaio, *Adorazione dei Magi* (1487), Florence, Uffizi.

more emphasized in the second, the pharaoh's daughter is clearly indicating to the maids present the sex of the infant Moses, whom she had saved.[23]

In the official portraits of monarchs—for instance, of Henry VIII (National Gallery, London), Philip II by Titian (Madrid, El Prado), and Henry II of France by François Clouet (1559, Uffizi)—the sexual organs of the king are emphasized within a turgid "codpiece" (Fig. 59). "Is not the codpiece the principal article of a warrior's armor?" Rabelais's Panurge asks Pantagruel (*Pantagruel* III:7). Shown as an instrument of power and strength (*signum victoriae*), the male organ was interpreted as a symbol of immortality in Christ,[24] but this meaning was perhaps derived from another, better-known *ostentatio:* that of the king.

The Sala di Amore e Psiche in the Palazzo del Tè in Mantua was certainly a public room meant to celebrate the "honest leisure" of Duke Federico II Gonzaga, as the inscription along the frieze that runs below the ceiling reads: "FEDERICVS GONZAGA II MAR. V.S.R.E. ET REIP. FLOR. CAPITANEVS GENERALIS HONESTO HOCIO POST LABORES AD REPARANDAM VIRT. QVIETI CONSTRVI MANDAVIT" (This palace was built by Marquis Federico Gonzaga II, standard-bearer of the Holy Roman Church and captain general of the Florentine republic, for his honest leisure and to reward his labors). At the top of the western and southern walls, along with the nuptial banquet of Cupid and Psyche taken from Apuleius's *Golden Ass,* Giulio Romano painted some small mythological scenes. Beginning at the left, just under the name of the duke (which occupies the whole space above, almost as a *titulus*), is a scene depicting the love of Jupiter, transformed into a triton, for the wife of Philip of Macedon, Olympia (Fig. 60). The husband looks over the scene from a window, distracted by an eagle. It is well known that the *Romance of Alexander* has the great king of Macedon born of this union, and it is curious to note that the iconography of the scene also reflects the story, well known in the Middle Ages, of Alexander himself, who through a window looks at the degradation of his master, Aristotle, coupling with Phillidis the prostitute. But the artist did still more: he gave Jupiter the face of the duke of Mantua, and painted his own self-portrait as Philip. We wonder if the woman did not have the physiognomy of Isabella Boschetto, married but unfaithful, whose love for Federico Gonzaga was contested by Isabella d'Este, in the guise of Venus, in the same fresco of the *Marriage of Psyche and Cupid* in the Palazzo del Tè. In the *Romance of Alexander,* the great priest Nectanebus, prophesying her destiny to Olympia, says that Jupiter-Ammon "is a young man with golden hair, blond beard, and two golden horns as well."[25] Except for the two horns, we can easily say that the young duke acted out his part as a deity very well.

Federico/Ammon, thus, like the philosopher, is surprised in the midst of carnal love (and thus is rendered more human?). But the god has an erect penis and is shown in the act of penetrating the queen. This was a bit of realism missing from the medieval scene. The courtiers and illustrious guests who were admitted to the villa probably admired the scene and without embarrassment recognized the portrait of their lord. This was not

Fig. 59   *(opposite)* The codpiece of a warrior: Cristóbal de Morales, *Prince Don Carlos* (1565), Madrid, Monasterio de las Descalzas reales.

23. See Weston-Lewis 1999, 47–49. For Philip IV, see Elliot 1894 and Elliott 1977.
24. Steinberg 1986, 90ff.
25. Centanni 1988, 14.

Fig. 60   Giulio Romano, *Jupiter, Olympia, and Philip of Macedon* (1527–28), Mantua, Palazzo del Tè.

only the "honest leisure" and *"virtù"* of the prince but also an *ostentatio* of his virility, which alone could assure the continuity of the dynasty.

And this is not the only representation of the *vix generatrix* in the Renaissance, which represented some lovers of princes as true and proper divinities. There was Isotta degli Atti, to whom Sigismondo Pandolfo Malatesta dared to dedicate one of the chapels in the Tempio Malatestiano, to the horror of Pope Pius II Piccolomini. There was Bianca Pellegrini, whom Pier Maria Rossi publicly celebrated both in the vault of the Camera d'Oro (as a "pilgrim" traveling around the Rossi state, looking at the territory of her lord) and in the chapel of the Castello di Torchiara, even while his legitimate consort was still living. There was Diane de Poitiers, to whom Henry II of France dedicated a true and proper cult, playing on her baptismal name to compare her to the pagan goddess.

Already in late antiquity heroic nudes (statues of the Achillean type, with realistic physiognomy) were widely diffused, although reproved by healthy-minded individuals such as Cicero and Seneca.[26] But heroic nudes in the Renaissance had another meaning.

26. Frova 1961.

Bronzino, depicting the admiral Andrea Doria as Neptune (in the Brera, Milan), hesitated between prudery and ostentation by choosing a compromise for showing the male organ. He has lowered the drapery around the loins to the level of the penis so that the drapery seems certainly to be falling (another example is the *Ecce Homo* by Antonello da Messina in the Prado, Madrid). The drapery does not prevent exhibition of the penis, just as certain pictures of the Madonna and Child show the Child's genitals.

For a portrait of Duke Cosimo I de' Medici, Bronzino preferred an allusive posture. He painted the duke in the guise of a nude Orpheus, but showed only his back.[27] The male organ was alluded to, but not exhibited.[28] On the other hand, we do not know how Cardinal Giovanni Salviati was depicted in the painting that showed him as Adam the Progenitor,[29] but perhaps, since he was a cleric, the *vix generatrix* was left out. To be sure, it is difficult, as has often been observed, to show Adam banished from the Garden of Eden, as in the fresco by Masaccio (Carmine, Florence), with all the virility that he should have had. How could the great progenitor show his own *fortitudo* while he was being punished by God?

But it could also happen that a prince was subjected to an official proof of his virility, as happened to Vincenzo Gonzaga, the husband chosen for a daughter of Grand Duke Francesco I de' Medici. After a long diplomatic negotiation, a virgin girl was chosen, and he had to sleep with her under medical observation before the marriage contract was concluded.[30]

Nor do we need to interpret the engraving of the *Holy Family* (1511; Fig. 61) by Hans Baldung Grien—where Saint Anne is touching the center of the penis of the little Jesus—as a "deeper insight into popular customs believed to possess magic powers,"[31] and all the less do we need to speculate whether Saint Anne was being represented as a witch in the depiction,[32] wracking our brains to find some possible Lutheran interpretation of the engraving. More likely, Saint Anne, like all nursemaids, was masturbating the little one to make him fall asleep! But we should certainly associate the *Cristo risorto* in Santa Maria sopra Minerva (1514–20), sculpted completely nude by Michelangelo, and the *Sorrowing Christ* (1525–30) by Maerten van Heemskerck as royal *ostentationes genitalium*. We should also associate the male organ, so often emphasized by painters of the Infant Jesus, Christ on the Cross, or the Deposition,[33] with the scepter, and thus with the ability to reign.[34]

In conclusion, the body of the sovereign was a fetish that contained a particular vision of the "low life" of sexual reproduction. If we associate the male organ with the scepter and with the ability to reign, then the exhibition of nude eroticism in the Renaissance acquires meaning. Was the scepter not the phallic symbol *par excellence?*

Another way of representing the prince was to identify him with a seminude Hercules,[35] whose club might refer to the phallic scepter. The reference was obvious for Ercole I d'Este, duke of Ferrara, for whom Dosso Dossi was commissioned in 1545 to

---

27. Forster 1977; Simon 1981; Langedijk 1981–87.
28. On the symbolic significance, see Vanggard 1969.
29. Hurtubise 1985, 307.
30. "Parentado" 1887.
31. Coch quoted in Steinberg 1996, 8.
32. Wirth 1978.
33. Steinberg 1986, excursus xxx:173–76; Rancour-Laferrière 1979.
34. An unacceptable interpretation of the scepter as an "attribut d'un itinérant, qui s'avance avec autorité, non pour agir, mais pour parler," is in Benveniste 1969, 32.
35. Banach 1984; Polleross 1998.

Fig. 61   Hans Baldung Grien, *Holy Family* (1511).

Fig. 62   Bosse, Louis XIII as Hercules Gallicus.

paint a group of tapestry cartoons with the theme, precisely, of the labors of Hercules. Less obvious was the fact that the walls of the Tribune of the Uffizi in Florence, crowned by an octagon to symbolize the vault of heaven and containing Grand Duke Francesco I de' Medici's cabinet/temple, were painted with the same scenes.[36] But representations of the seminude prince were particularly common in France. Perhaps the first comparison between Hercules and a French king was the one by Symphorien Champier (1509) that likened the struggle of Hercules with the lion to Louis XII's war with the lion of Saint Mark (Venice).[37] For the entrée of Henry II into Paris in 1549, the arch erected at Port Saint-Denis showed the monarch nude, a lion's skin covering "only those parts which nature commanded," as we read in a pamphlet printed at the time.[38] The medals coined and thrown to the crowd for the coronation of Henry IV had on their reverse a representation of Hercules surrounded by the motto: "IN VIRTUTI NVLLA EST VIA."[39] Louis XIII was represented by Abraham Bosse in the costume of a French Hercules, with a club on his shoulder and the cock of France at his feet (Fig. 62). For the marriage of Louis XIV, Cardinal Mazarin commissioned the opera *Ercole amante,* by Francesco Cavalli, with the libretto by the Abbé F. Buti. And one could add still further examples.

36. Heikamp 1984, 1989b, 1997. For Francesco's other *studiolo,* in the Palazzo Vecchio, see Berti 1967.

37. "Hercules en son temps aut plusieurs victoires contre ses ennemis . . . Hercules tua ung lyon, mais ledit Roy a plus fait, car il n'a point seulement tué ung lyon, mais en a tué quatorze mille de ses subgetz et le grand lyion engraigé il a rendu si doulx et si traictable que contre luy ne peut bouger." Champier 1977, 52.

38. Bryant 1992, 137.

39. Panofsky 1930.

For the continual equation of *rex sacerdos* with *sacerdos rex,* as was said, prelates also wanted to have a scepter: the pastoral staff. Admittedly, the shepherd's pastoral alluded to the bishop as shepherd of his folk, but, as Villette said at the beginning of the seventeenth century, "the staff in the hand of a prelate is the sign of his dignity," because David said that God in majesty has a staff: "Virga regni sui" (the staff of his reign).[40] Thus every king of the earth, following the example of the kings of Israel, held a scepter in his hand. As for French kings, who always wanted to be first among monarchs, they had two scepters. "Our most Christian kings of France have two: one the scepter of power in their right hand, the other the scepter of justice in their left hand," a unique prerogative among earthly kings, "like prelates of the church," who also had two scepters: one of mercy in the right hand, and one of censure in the left hand.[41]

The *testimonium fortitudinis* (proof of sexual power), so important for denoting the *plenitudo potestatis* (full power), was expressed, however, in ways besides pictorial representations. The king's body was always associated with the fertility of the land over which he ruled,[42] and proofs of fecundity were associated with the relationship leader/land/people. It was not by chance that the motto and symbol chosen by Duke Cosimo I de' Medici for his wife Eleonora di Toledo were "CVM PVDORE LAETA FECVNDITAS" (with modesty, happy fertility) and a peahen protecting her little ones under her wing. Cosimo had eleven children from her, and three from Camilla Martelli.

As for fecundity, we can remember that among the Medici dukes, Giovanna d'Austria gave Francesco I six daughters and one son, who died at her last delivery; Christina di Lorena gave Ferdinando I nine children, including five sons; and Maria Maddalena d'Austria gave Cosimo II five sons and three daughters.[43]

Other sovereigns did no less. Among the Hapsburg-Lorraine, Duke Leopold of Lorraine had fourteen children, Emperor Francis I and Maria Theresa sixteen, Emperor Francis II thirteen, and Maria Carolina seventeen.

The problem of *fortitudo* was also posed for two queens, who, due to lack of male heirs in the first case and an unexpected widowhood in the second, were brought unexpectedly to the throne: Elizabeth I of England and Marie de' Medici of France. The solutions were different, but nonetheless original, for each. Elizabeth was the Virgin Queen, or Astraea, whose cult approached, in Anglican England, that of the Virgin Mary. Marie, instead, was the Great Sage, not only as mother of the little Louis XIII (who certainly did not reciprocate her maternal love) but also as the reigning regent for all of France.[44] The choice was even physically appropriate. Elizabeth I was thin, with a youthful face, a small bosom, and long flowing hair (in a portrait that was perhaps exhibited at her funeral).[45] Marie was massive, with large and reassuring bosom and hips.[46] The English queen was presented as Diana, the Florentine-French queen as Minerva.

The symbol of the virgin Astraea was tied to the return of the Golden Age ("Iam redit et virgo, redeunt Saturnia regna" [Now the virgin also returns, and the rule of Saturn]

40. Villette 1611, 178–79.
41. Villette 1611, 179. But see also Hanley 1983.
42. Enright 1985, 52–53.
43. Pieraccini [1924–25] 1986, II:57, 251, 345.
44. On her, see Saward 1982.
45. Woodward 1997, 89.
46. See Morgues 1643, 7, "Ne vocetis me Noemi (id est pulchra), sed vocate me Maria (id est amara)" (Don't call me Noemi [that is, beautiful], but rather Marie [that is, bitter]).

Virgil, *Eclogue* 4, line 6). This was chosen by Elizabeth on her ascent to the throne and lasted through her long reign (Sir John Davies's *Hymns to Astraea* date from 1599).[47] It was an important step in the process of deification of the English monarchs, who were both spiritual and temporal leaders of their people. A print with the mark of a Phoenix (derived from the mark of the Venetian printer Gabriel Giolito de Ferrari, "Semper eadem" [always the same]) had the subtitle "This Virgin Queen came into the world on the eve of the birth of the Holy Virgin Mary, and died on the eve of the Annunciation of the Virgin Mary, 1603." It had a further caption:

> She was, She is (what can there more be said?)
> In earth the first, in heaven the second Maid.[48]

In a land where faith remained after the schism from Rome, to have Elizabeth ascend to heaven as a second Virgin was surely not a blasphemous comparison. Regardless, it accentuated a cult that had developed openly during her lifetime. Even Protestants who had escaped the persecutions under Bloody Mary turned to her. In 1559 John Awdelay, in *The Wonders of England,* said that a lamp had been lit in the darkness and that the very voice of God commanded Elizabeth to reign:

> Up, said this God with voice not strange,
> Elizabeth, thys real nowe guyde!

In his turn, Richard Mulcaster sang to her in a ballad:

> The God sent us your noble Grace, as in dede it was highe tyme
> Which dothe all Popery cleane deface, and set us forth God's trewe devine—
> For whome we are all bound to praye, Lady, Lady.
> Long life to raigne both night and day, most dere Ladye.[49]

As queen of the night, Elizabeth was compared to Diana and to Venus, "Queen of Love," "Queen of Beauty," following the concept of "beauty and love united in chastity."[50]

The guardian of religion and patron of peace were attributes that popular theater assigned to Elizabeth-Judith and Elizabeth-Deborah.[51] But like Marie de' Medici, Elizabeth could also be both virgin and mother (in the *Hypnerotomachia Poliphili* did not Venus appear as a *Mater dolorosa?*).[52]

> A Phoenix rare she is on earth amongst us,
> A mother of her people she doth nourish,
> Let us all therefore, with one heart, pray Iove that
> Long she may flourish.[53]

47. Yates [1975] 1978; Strong 1977.
48. O'Donoghue 1894, 79.
49. Wilson 1966, 7–8; Orgel 1974.
50. Wind [1958] 1971, 92.
51. Wilson 1966, 120.
52. Wind [1958] 1971, 29.
53. Wilson 1966, 148.

At the base of this mental structure where a Virgin could also be a Great Mother, Elizabeth brought out all of the thematics of the *vix generatrix,* so far as they could refer to a woman.

On the other hand, she who, despite appearances, did not wish to appear as a mother was Marie de' Medici. The series from the Palais de Luxembourg that was commissioned from Peter Paul Rubens on 26 February 1622 was a political statement thought up by the queen herself (on consultation with the erudite Nicolas-Claude Peiresc). In the contract she reserved the right to intervene at any moment in the execution of the twenty-four paintings foreseen (three were never executed), where "the histories and heroic accomplishments of the said lady queen" were to be portrayed.[54] Rubens thus worked under strict control for a series that was to be a response to the declining power of Marie during the preceding five years. In the depiction of the marriage ceremony at Lyons, the king is portrayed as Jupiter, with an eagle at his feet, while Marie, who has two peahens at her shoulders, shows her right breast bare, as a sign of virginity.[55] But more interesting are panels 10, 11, and 15, which were the center of the whole series. The first has the coronation in Saint-Denis, the second the apotheosis of Henry IV and Marie's assumption of the regency, the third "the happy state of the regency." But the reference to her own royal destiny was earlier announced in the second panel of the series, showing her birth, where Marie's *Genius natalis* holds a cornucopia from which emerge a crown, a scepter, and a hand of justice. The choice of Minerva as her protectress appears in the third panel: *The Education of Marie.* The goddess guides the education of the little girl, the Graces stand at her shoulder, and one of them holds a crown of roses and laurel. Apollo is present, playing a violin, while Mercury descends, tearing through the curtain that lines the cavern where the scene is placed, allowing the light to burst in (he is thus in a role opposite from that of the Mercury *psychopompus* in Botticelli's *Primavera* [Uffizi], who opens the clouds to allow the soul to ascend to heaven).[56] Minerva returns in the panel showing the "assumption of the regency" (the goddess in armor beside the throne), again in a prominent position, paired with Apollo; in the twelfth panel (*The Queen Governs*); and in the fifteenth, where the goddess, with the scales of justice, bends over Marie, seated on the throne, counseling her. But Rubens developed this still more, in another panel, giving Marie the helmet of Minerva in the *Triumph of Juliers* (or Jülich), and he gives Minerva the features of Marie ("Marie de Medicis sous la forme de Minerve déesse des arts") in another picture, "dedicated to the king," that was intended as a double of the Luxembourg series. This last painting says everything, besides also depicting a patron of the arts. The goddess-queen, with the helmet on her tresses, holds a scepter in her right hand and a *victoriola* in her left; two cherubs crown her; at her feet are the *spolia* of the defeated; and a canon is in the background. Marie, truly, was the *securitas* of the kingdom,[57] whether her son who had reached maturity wanted it or not, or that traitor Richelieu.

54. "les histoires et gestes heroiques de ladite dame Royne." "Ladite dame Royne s'est reserve le pouvoir d'augmenter ou diminuer les subjects des dits tableaux avant qu'ilz eront commancés et de faire retoucher et changer les figures que ne luy seront agréables lorsque lesdits tableaux seront par deca." Thuillier and Foucart 1967, 95. For this series, see also Simson 1979, 7–35; Saward 1982.

55. Paris, Louvre. See Bertelli 1997a.

56. Wind [1958] 1971, 141ff.

57. A reproduction of the panel, engraved by I. Masse, is in the copy of the whole series by Nattier (1710).

10 Spurious Offspring

SUCH PREOCCUPATION WITH THE *vix generatrix* of the prince could not help but burden his sexual life with ceremonial observances. The grand duke of Tuscany, Cosimo III de' Medici, had fixed occasions for sleeping with the grand duchess. The *abate* Bonsi wrote to Nicholas Fouquet on 18 July 1661: "The prince has only slept with her three times, and when he doesn't plan to do so, he sends a *valet de chambre* to tell Madame not to wait for him." In 1664, when the grand duke was twenty-two years old, Bonsi wrote to Princess Sophie of Hannover: "He sleeps with his wife only once a month, and then with a doctor in attendance to rouse him from the bed so that he will not damage his health by staying too long."[1] Of one night of Louis XV and Marie Leszczynska at Versailles (4 September 1726—the year following their marriage) it was said: "The evening come, the ceremony of the *coucher* unfolded according to etiquette. The king lay for a moment on his bed, and then was accompanied to the queen's by Monsieur le Duc, M. de Mortemard, M. de La Rochefoucault, and the maréchal de Villars, who would return the next morning at ten o'clock to pay their complements to the queen."[2]

But we may presume that other royal sexual intercourse was distant from the rigidity of ceremonial, even if not infrequently concubines were openly guests at court. For example, Marie de' Medici's delivery of Louis XIII preceded by only fifty days the delivery of a baby by the marquise de Verneuil, Henriette d'Entraigues, the mistress of Henry IV, who had been presented to Marie the very day of her arrival in the Louvre. Both of them, queen and favorite, must have lived together in the same palace, and this was not the first time in the history of the French monarchy that a king publicly kept near him both a consort and a concubine and recognized the progeny of both. The duc de Saint-Simon, in his late-seventeenth-century *Mémoires*, lashed out against "royal bastards," calling them "mud mixed with double adultery" and a "reversal of all the rules and of all the most ancient, most holy, most fundamental, and most important laws of the realm."[3] But he was looking at the problem from the wrong angle, although there is no doubt that the nobility, obsessed as it was with primogeniture and the entail of estates, posed legitimate descent as an ethical law.

The Ferrarese count Annibale Romei, in a dialogue entitled *Della nobiltà* (1586), pre-

---

1. Pieraccini [1924–25] 1986, II:648–49.
2. Kohn and Dalsace 1987, 87; see also Barbier 1857; De Nolhac 1900 and 1912.
3. Saint-Simon 1983–88, v:593.

sented a discussion involving Ercole Varano, Francesco Patrizi da Cherso, Count Guido Calcagnini, and Count Annibale Turchi. This last affirmed that a drop of blood was enough to make a noble, but Varano answered him that "to make a perfect noble" required that "his parents" be "pure, illustrious, and spotless of vice. The bastard, thus, cannot claim to have had a father and mother spotless of the vice of intemperance, having coupled dishonestly. . . . He must confess that he is not perfectly noble, and even that he has an impediment against being perfectly noble."[4] More or less the same argument was made by Giovan Battista de Luca in his book of etiquette *Il cavaliere e la dama,* when he explained that "above all other defects should be counted that of birth; the others—ugliness, age, good sense—end with the woman, but ignobleness from illegitimate birth produces a certain stain in the progeny, which lasts a while, and as long as the memory lasts, the stain is alive in the house and its progeny."[5] The 1532 statutes of the Republic of Lucca spoke openly of "damnation through coitus."

But for the monarch (and this surely must have been the point of view that led Louis XIV to father five illegitimate children) it was enough for there to be one drop of royal blood in the body of a descendant for this person to be *ipso facto* legitimated. As Voltaire wrote in the *Siècle de Louis XIV,*

> [D]eprived of almost all his children, his tenderness redoubled for the duc de Maine and for the comte de Toulouse, his illegitimate sons, inducing him to declare them and their descendants heirs to the Crown, if there were no princes of the blood, through an edict registered without any objection in 1714. Thus he tempered, through natural law, the rigor of the conventional laws that deprive sons born outside of matrimony any right of inheritance from the father. . . . Later, in 1715, he declared his bastards equal to princes of the blood.[6]

Louis-Auguste was created duc du Maine, and Louis-Alexandre, comte de Toulouse. One married Anne-Louise Bénédicte de Condé (from a lateral Bourbon line), niece of the Grand Condé; the other married Marie Victoire-Sofie de Noailles, the daughter of one of her father's generals. As for the illegitimate daughters, Marie-Anne, called Mademoiselle de Blois, was given to Louis-Armand I, prince de Condé; Louise-Françoise, called Mademoiselle de Nantes, to Louis III, prince de Condé; Françoise-Marie to Philippe, duc d'Orleans.

Whatever Saint-Simon said about it, Louis XIV had an ancient royal tradition behind him. The Merovingians did not even recognize a difference in the order of succession. Royal bastards were never diminished by their maternal origins. As Gregory of Tours said (*Histoire* IX:34): "[E]xcept for the exclusion of inheritance to women, all the men sired by the king are recognized as [free] sons." This was a *genus purpuratum;* the Merovingian kings inherited their capacity to rule through their father's blood. Among them, "even if the mother were known to be a royal concubine or a queen, it was not always certain that the child would be accepted as the offspring of the king. The suggestion that a prince was not of royal blood could have political repercussions. . . . The attack on concubinage,

4. Romei 1586, 211–12.
5. De Luca 1675, 160.
6. Voltaire 1947, II:42–43.

when it came, was a moral one."[7] Later, the Capetians, at least up to Philip Augustus, as-sured their descent by associating their successors with the throne, thus avoiding the dan-ger of an elected monarch. As the chronicle of Morigny recorded, in 1128 "at Reims, most noble city of Gaul, King Louis (VI) had his eldest son, Philip, anointed and crowned along with himself."[8] If the choice fell on the firstborn, it was because this was always possible, but not customary or obligatory.[9] In this sense one could say that even in France dynastic history was initially a family succession involving personal adventures. There was a simi-lar custom in Byzantium, whose dynastic history tended to involve an alternation of dy-nasties that received their legitimacy through proclamation by the divinely inspired people, just as in ancient Rome the heavens guided the Praetorian Guard when they elected (*acclamatio*) the emperor.[10] In western Christendom during the early Middle Ages there was but one, although fundamental, distinction between the king, his blood rela-tives, and members of other noble families: anointing, but not primogeniture.

Emperor Frederick II Hohenstaufen kept both legitimate and illegitimate sons near him and elevated both. He took more joy in the illegitimate ones (King Enzo, Frederick of Antioch, and Manfred) than he did in his legitimate heir, Emperor Conrad IV. These were not just offshoots of the Waiblingen tribe, the *regis stirps;* they were sons of Frederick's own *stirps caesarea*.[11] Other famous bastards recognized as such were Theodoric the Great, Genseric, king of the Vandals, Charles Martel, Arnulf of Carinthia, and William the Conqueror.[12]

In England during the period 1066–1485 there were with certainty between forty and fifty illegitimate sons of English kings, but there must have been many more, considering that Henry I (1100–1135), the youngest son of William the Conqueror, alone had about twenty (and perhaps twenty-three). Henry II had three: Morgan, who became provost of Beverly and bishop of Durham; Geoffrey, who became chancellor to his father and arch-bishop of York; and William Longsword, who was made count of Salisbury. King John (1199–1216) had at least seven bastards. Many of them were made counts, one became archbishop of York, and another was made abbot of Westminster.[13]

Of Richard the Lion-Hearted, a contemporary chronicle claimed that the king "car-ried off the wives, daughters and kinswomen of his freemen by force and made them his concubines; and when he had sated his lust on them, he handed them over to his knights for whoring."[14] Another chronicler, William of Malmesbury, although he confesses that Henry I had twenty illegitimate children, insisted that the king had no impure desires. "He was wholly free from impure desires for, as we have learned from those who were well informed, he partook of female blandishments not for the gratification of his lust, but for the sake of issue; nor did he condescend to casual intercourse unless it might pro-duce that effect."[15]

7. Wood 1979, 15.

8. "Apud Remim, nobilissimam Galliae metropolim, rex Ludovicus primogenitum suum Philippum ungi faceret in regem secumque coronari." Marlot 1846, III:265; Lewis 1981.

9. Wood 1979; Lewis 1981.

10. Dagron 1996, 34 and 43.

11. Kantorowicz 1988, 573.

12. Kern [1914] 1939, 23; Wallace-Hadrill [1962] 1982, 204.

13. Given-Wilson and Curteis 1984, 17.

14. Given-Wilson and Curteis 1984, 14.

15. Given-Wilson and Curteis 1984, 61.

If one looks at the later destinies of so many illegitimate sons of kings, one cannot but recognize that an ample family was useful for creating a wide network of relationships, both inside and outside of the kingdom, and also for finding loyal and faithful executors of the royal will. The most famous of Henry I's bastards was undoubtedly Robert of Caen, who was count of Gloucester through marriage with Mabel, the heiress to this title. On the death of his father (1135), he was the strongest supporter of the cause of his half sister Matilda, the widow of the emperor Henry V and legitimate heir to the English throne, and then of his nephew King Henry II, against the usurpation of King Stephen.

The use of illegitimate sons to reinforce ties with the great families of the kingdom and to serve as faithful agents was not abandoned later. Philip, the illegitimate son of King Richard I, married Emily, daughter of the lord of Cognac. John "de Southeray" (or Surrey), illegitimate son of Edward III, married the sister of Lord Percy and was knighted along with the future King Richard II in April 1377. Arthur Plantagenet, illegitimate son of King Edward IV, became one of the favorites of his nephew Henry VIII. In 1523 he was made viscount of Lisle, two years later vice-admiral of England, and in 1533 lord deputy of Calais. But the same Henry VIII directed most, if not all, of the hopes for a male succession to the person of Henry FitzRoy, who was born in 1519 from a relationship of the king with one of the ladies-in-waiting of Queen Catherine of Aragon. Within six years he was made a Knight of the Garter, count of Nottingham, duke of Somerset, and duke of Richmond, thus gaining first place in the line of succession to the throne. In 1529 he was made lord lieutenant of Ireland and Keeper of the Five Ports, and he was married in 1533 to Mary, a daughter of the duke of Norfolk. He predeceased his father in 1536, at the age of only seventeen years, but by that time Henry VIII had already fathered Mary from Catherine of Aragon and Elizabeth from Anne Boleyn, and there was no longer need to look to FitzRoy for an heir to the throne. The fact remains, however, that at least for a time Henry VIII thought of making his illegitimate son heir to the throne.

Otherwise, even in heraldry, royal descent, even if illegitimate, was a mark of honor to be appropriately exhibited; at the end of the fifteenth century a bend sinister began to appear in England as a distinctive blazon of royal bastards (Fig. 63).

After returning to the Continent, Philip the Good, duke of Burgundy (1419–67), had at least fifteen bastards, among whom was Antoine, "The Great Bastard of Burgundy." His great-great-nephew Emperor Charles V (the grandson of Marie of Burgundy and Maximilian Hapsburg) had two illegitimate daughters and one illegitimate son—Margerite, Taddeo, and John—in addition to his three legitimate children from Isabella of Portugal. Margerite was first given in marriage to Alessandro de' Medici, duke of Florence, and after his assassination, to Paolo Farnese, duke of Parma, that is, to two vassals of the empire. In her maturity, she served as governor of the Low Countries, one of the most important charges in the government of the empire. John was a loyal servant of his father, who gave him important military commands. He was captain general of the Mediterranean fleet, generalissimo in the war against the Moriscos, a victor of the battle of Lepanto, lieutenant general of Italy, and from 1576 governor and captain general of Flanders.

In Italy, Niccolò III d'Este, the natural son of Alberto V, the lord of Ferrara, Modena, Reggio, and Parma (1393–1441), had eleven illegitimate sons and seven illegitimate daughters, among whom were Lionello (ruled 1441–50) and Borso (ruled 1450–71), who inherited

The bifcount lifle   artf ur

Fig. 63   The bend sinister of English bastards. Coat of arms of Arthur Plantagenet, viscount of Lisle († 1542). London, Society of Antiquaries, ms. 442, Garter Roll 16, Henry VIII.

their father's signoria with all its titles. Borso, in the last year of his life, was even invested in it as duke. Among their half brothers, Meliaduce became abbot of Pomposa, and after his death (1450) his half brother Rinaldo succeeded to this benefice.[16] Gurone became abbot of Nonatola; Margherita married Galeotto II Malatesta, lord of Rimini; and Genevra married Sigismondo Pandolfo, Galeotto's successor. Lucia was given in marriage to Carlo Gonzaga; Isotta to Oddantonio di Montefeltro and, after his death, to Tristano Sforza. A younger Margherita married Galeazzo II Pio, lord of Carpi; Camilla married Rodolfo III of Varano, the lord of Camerino; Bianca Maria married Galeotto I Pico, lord of Mirandola; Orsina married Aldobrandino Rangoni, from one of the most eminent patrician families of Bologna; another half sister, Lucrezia, married Annibale II Bentivoglio, lord of Bologna. As for the legitimate daughters, Isabella married Francesco II Gonzaga, duke of Mantova; Beatrice married Lodovico Sforza, duke of Milan. Another illegitimate son, Cardinal Ippolito, followed an ecclesiastical career, but despite his vow of chastity, he also had a son and a daughter, the latter of whom married Gilberto Pio, lord of Sassuolo. A similar tale of the success of illegitimate offspring could be told about Francesco I Sforza, duke of Milan.[17]

Here again the network of important alliances woven by the lord of Ferrara is evident. But there was a distinction between the legitimate and illegitimate offspring: while the first were married among lordly or sovereign houses of about the same rank, natural children married downward to diffuse the blood of their house into the children of vassals. The same was true of the illegitimate daughter of Charles V, Margherite of Hapsburg, who was successively married to two vassals of the empire, while one of her legitimate half sisters was married to a cousin, the emperor Maximilian II, and the other to John Prince of Portugal.[18]

To conclude, the *vix generatrix* of the sovereign had many different ways to assure the continuity of the ruler's dynasty, for the sake of his subjects.

---

16. See Gandini 1891.
17. Giulini 1916.
18. See Da Costa Kauffmann 1978.

11

Ostentatio Genitalium

THE STORY I WISH NOW TO EXAMINE began with Jean de Mailly, author of a *Chronicon universalis* in 1255/56, which told of a woman who became pope.[1]

The first coronation conducted by clergy took place at Byzantium when the emperor Marcian was crowned by the patriarch in 450.[2] It is highly probable that Visigothic Spain borrowed the Byzantine ceremony in the seventh century, and then developed it in a more elaborate and liturgical manner, based on biblical tradition. In France, after the Merovingian *reges criniti* were deposed and Pepin required a liturgical legitimization in 751 that would be recognized with the same divine prerogatives that his predecessors had received by birth, the rite revived and reached its climax. Nonetheless, the Caesaro-papism of Byzantium was the model.[3] As was said of Charles the Bald (in 869), the king was "graecisco more paratus et coronatus" (dressed and crowned following the Greek custom).[4]

The revival of anointing was also an acknowledgment of the church's importance. In fact, its fragile origins compelled the new French dynasty to grant concessions to the clergy, as an indispensable intermediary with the heavens. The competition between the two powers was thus reinforced.

This competition can be demonstrated by observing that the rite of anointing a bishop's head cannot be found earlier than the age of Bishop Hincmar and of the Pseudo-Isidorian *Decretals* (ca. 865). For the clergy, we should recognize that the anointing of bishops "followed, rather than preceded, the ritual of the royal anointing. It implied that bishops, by their unction, became the king's peers, that they too, and in their way, became representatives of the idea of *rex et sacerdos.*"[5]

If the anointing of bishops followed, rather than anticipated, the king's rite, the same could be said for the papal coronation ceremony, which was even more elaborate than that for bishops. But when did this rite begin to be performed? The first pope said to have worn a headdress was Constantine I (708–15), who borrowed the *kamelàukion* from the inexhaustible store of rites and ceremonies at Byzantium. The *Liber pontificalis* testifies that

---

1. *Chronicon universalis* 1879.
2. Kantorowicz 1946, 78.
3. See Dagron 1996.
4. Kantorowicz 1946, 63.
5. Kantorowicz 1946, 63–64.

Fig. 64 The emperor Constantine offers the *kamelàukion* to Pope Sylvester. Rome, Basilica dei SS. Quattro Coronati, oratory of St. Sylvester (1246).

"apostolicus pontifex cum camelaucum, ut solitus est Romae procedere" (the pope, with the *kamelàukion* as usual when in Rome), entered into Constantinople in the year 708. The *kamelàukion* was a tall conical white silk cap used as the insignia of a Byzantine emperor but also used later by the Ostrogoth king Totila: "camelaucum lapidibus pretiosis ornatum" (*kamelàukion* decorated with precious stones), says the *Ducange Glossarium*. If we consider that between the years 640 and 772 twenty-four Roman pontiffs came from the Greek world, it is highly possible that the *kamelàukion* was used even before Constantine I. As an imperial *signum* it is possible that such a *dignitas* was used "as a nonliturgical headgear at the papal procession."[6] Was it related to papal sovereignty? Kantorowicz wrote that until the eleventh century a papal coronation did not exist, "for the simple reason that originally there was no crown he could have worn."[7] But on the obverse of two *denarii* of Pope Sergius III (died in 911), the pope appears with a kind of *regnum*.[8] We should admit that the pope was consecrated even before the tenth century and that a kind of ceremony was

6. Kantorowicz 1946, 136. See also Muntz 1897.
7. Kantorowicz 1946, 136.
8. Fioravante 1738; Muntoni 1972.

performed. May we assume that from the beginning the *kamelàukion* was a sign of his worldly power? Unfortunately, the frescoes of the Oratory of S. Silvestro in the Roman church of the SS. Quattro Coronati, where the pope is clearly depicted with the *kamelàukion* as a royal dignity, are too recent (1246) to testify to its earlier use (Fig. 64).

The coronation rite became a *conditio sine qua non* for the series of honors given to a pope, as they were to a king. In one of his decretals, Pope Honorius III (1221) affirmed the reservation of *laudes hymnidicae* to anointed kings.[9] In a narrow sense, these chants of welcome marked the *apàntesis* of the *missus Domini*,[10] emphasizing his holiness. Despite the relatively recent account of the first papal coronation, one section included in the elaborate ceremony was not only regarded as incomprehensible by onlookers but also found its roots in a much more ancient rite: the *ostentatio genitalium*.

I hope I have already demonstrated the importance of the *ostentatio genitalium* for the birth of the male heir of a kingdom. It was a *testimonium fortitudinis*. But what about elected sovereigns? These were men chosen to occupy thrones only in adulthood. Particularly for popes, this involved accession to full religious authority. If the Dalai Lama was discovered through divine inspiration as a baby, this was certainly not the case for Roman popes, who were elderly men elected by a gerontocracy within the clergy.

We need carefully to reexamine the statuette of Napoleon I holding up the king of Rome at his birth, showing his penis, and the same scene as shown on a medal of the time sculpted by Bertrand Andrieu. The emperor is shown standing on a small rug. Before him is a marble table, on which one can see a metal box, a thurible, and an oak branch with leaves. On the floor is a breviary (or a Mass book?). But more interesting for us is the marble throne with two winged lions, from which, we presume, the emperor has just risen. It was modeled on another marble throne that Napoleon himself ordered transferred from the basilica of St. John Lateran to the Louvre. The throne is the problem that confronts us.

At St. John Lateran, in Rome, three thrones were exhibited: a Carrara marble cathedra and two porphyry thrones used for the papal coronation rite (Fig. 65). The first, called the *sedia stercoraria,* was located on the porch. After the *Possessio,* the new pope, sitting in this chair, threw out some coins, saying: "Aurum et argentum non est mihi, quod autem habeo, tibi do" (I have no gold or silver, but what I have I give you). The name of the chair comes from the First Book of Samuel (2:8): "He raiseth up the poor out of the dust and lifteth up the beggar from the dunghill [*de stercore*], to set them among princes."[11]

We can now follow the description in the *Ordo Romanus*, written by Cencius Camerarius (1192), which explains how, on reaching the porch of the cathedral, the pope "ducitur a cardinalibus ad sedem lapideam, quae sedes dictur Stercoraria" (is brought by the cardinals to the marble seat, called *Stercoraria*), where the *jactum pecuniae* (the scattering of money) was observed. Then the pope entered the basilica, where two porphyry thrones stood, one on each side of the Chapel of S. Silvestro (Fig. 65). They were used for two different rites. When seated on the first of the two *sedes porphyreticae* the pope received the *ferula* (whip) and the keys from the prior of the basilica, to signify his power over the Roman cathedral, and then a belt holding a purple bag, in which were musk and

---

9. Potthast 1874–75, no 6584; Kantorowicz 1946, 74 n. 17.
10. See Eberlein 1982.
11. "Suscitat de pulvere egenum et de stercore elevat pauperem."

Fig. 65   A porphyry throne. Rome, Vatican Museum.

twelve seals made of precious stones. For the rite of the second throne, the elected pope should sit, or better *lie* between the two *beds;*[12] Cencius explains the ceremony as alluding to the two *principes apostolorum,* that is, Saints Peter and Paul.[13] The author of the *Codex caeremonialis* of 1437 simply passes over the embarrassing ceremony, and says that the pope was brought through the Lateran Palace to the door of the Chapel of S. Silvestro, to the two porphyry thrones ("ubi sunt duae sedes porphyreticae"). He specifies that while the pope was seated on the throne located on the right side of the entrance of the chapel, the prior of the basilica offered him the *ferula* and the keys, both of the cathedral and of the palace. Then the dignitaries of the palace came to kiss the papal foot ("recipit officiales palatii ad pedem et osculum"). Finally, the pope moved to the other throne, on the left, where he sat or, better, lay ("ut videatur potius jacere, quam sedere").[14] Paris de' Grassi, in recording the coronation of Pope Leo X (19 March 1513), confirmed these acts and yet again concluded with same verb: *jacere* (to lie: "et deinde illico papa surgens ivit ad aliam sedem et jacerit").[15] The self-censorship of the two ceremoniaries is symptomatic: neither the author of the *Codex caeremonialis* nor Paris de' Grassi says what the pope did while he was *lying* on the second chair, located on the left. The *Ordo Romanus* and the papal ceremoniaries describe the first of the two rites, that is, the submission of the Lateran chapter to papal authority, but they pass over the second rite in silence. In fact, while the pope was lying (rather than sitting) on the second throne, a deacon verified the testicles of the pontiff, informing the audience: "pontificalia habet et bene pendentes, dignum est papali coronae!" (he has pontifical equipment, and they are hanging well; worthy is the papal crown!). (In fact, thanks to this ceremony, testicles were sometimes called *pontificalia.*) Of course the censorship of details is understandable; only the Protestant Banck dared to dwell on such an embarrassing rite (Fig. 66).[16]

After Pope Leo X (1513) and Pope Pius IV (1560), who received the keys on the porch of the basilica, on the *stercoraria,* Pope Pius V abolished the whole ceremony. As we are told by the new papal master of ceremonies, Cornelio Firmiano, the order was made "reiectis superstitionibus aliorum pontificum" (rejecting the superstitions of the previous popes).[17] Also, at the beginning of the seventeenth century Pope Clement VIII requested that the head of Pope Joan in the frieze of popes' heads in the nave of the cathedral of Siena be renamed Pope Zacharias (741–52), who had perhaps been omitted from the original frieze that extended in time from Christ to Pope Lucius III.[18]

I do not know whether the coronation ceremony was wholly observed by the popes at Avignon, in France, that is, for the crowning of Popes Clement V and John XXII (at Lyon in 1305 and 1316), of Benedict XII and Clement VI (Avignon, Dominican church, 1335 and 1342), of Innocent VI (Avignon, cathedral, 1352), or of Urban V and Gregory XI (Avignon, papal chapel, 1362 and 1371). To be sure, Bertrand de Got (Pope Clement V) followed the Roman rite even to the extent of repeating the cavalcade of the *Possessio,* as before him Celestine V had done when he was crowned at L'Aquila (1294). Innocent VI and Urban V

12. "Qui siquidem electus in illis duabus sedis sic sedere debet, ac si videatur inter duos lectos jacere."
13. "id est ut accumbat inter principis apostolorum primarum Petri et Pauli." Mabillon 1687, ii:411–12.
14. Gattico 1753, 97.
15. Gattico 1753, 384; Cancellieri 1802, 65.
16. Banck 1656.
17. Cancellieri 1802, 65ff.
18. Haskell 1993, 41–42.

Fig. 66   "Pontificalia habet," engraving from Banck, *Roma triumphans.*

were the only popes who refused the cavalcade, as a sign of humility. The *Ordo xiv,* attributed to Cardinal Jacob Caetani,[19] provides some interpolations (e.g., *De coronatione papae extra Urbem*) that show the effort of the court of Avignon to maintain the Roman ceremonies. "When the Curia established itself on the banks of the Rhone, it became necessary to make some changes in the old Roman liturgy. Away from the place where it had developed, it became partly unexecutable. The work of adaptation was carried out by commentators at Avignon. They proceeded with a great sense of tradition and did everything possible to maintain the venerable customs transmitted by earlier centuries."[20] Did they even preserve the ceremony of the *ostentatio genitalium?* To be sure, Caetani recorded the ceremony of the *stercoraria,* and that of the two *sedes porphyreticae* as well, with the usual self-censorship: "[A]ccedit ad aliam sedem similem, quae est ad sinistram . . . et incipit sedere in illa secunda sede. Et postquam aliquantulum sederit, idem prior cingit eidem domino papae zonam" (He comes to another similar throne on the left side, . . . where he sits, and then the prior fastens a belt onto the pope).[21]

Now we need to pose another question: when did these "superstitions" begin? We open here another problem related to the papal coronation. Who was this Joan, recalled by Jean de Mailly, whom pope Clement VIII was so anxious to cancel out from the frieze

19. Mabillon 1687, ii:243–443.
20. Andrieu 1924, 375.
21. Mabillon 1687, ii:176.

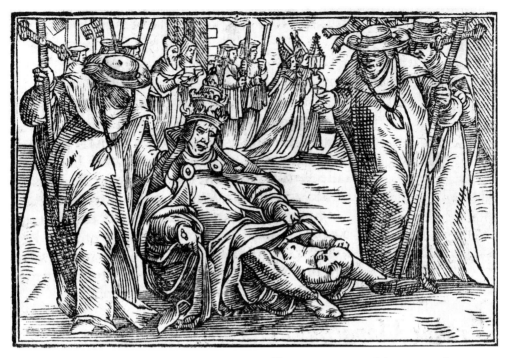

Fig. 67   Pope Joan's delivery, engraving from I. Wolff, *Lectionum memorabilium et reconditarum centuriae xvi,* Lauingen, Reinmichel, 1600.

of papal heads in the cathedral of Siena? We read in the Baronio *Annales ecclesiastici* (for the year 878) that Photius, patriarch of Constantinople and brother-in-law of Empress Theodora, accused Pope John VIII of having lost all virility ("abiecta penitus omni virilitate") and thus of not being a pope, as his predecessors, Nicholas I and Adrian II, but instead a *papissa* ("non papa ut Nicolaus et Hadrianus, sed papissa"). It is difficult to associate such an accusation in the ninth century with a legend that began only centuries later. For an explanation of the rite of the *ostenatio genitalium* it seems that we must look in a different direction.

The first record of an elaborate papal coronation dates from the time of Pope Paschal II (1099), that is, more or less two centuries after the *denarium* coined for pope Sergius III (904), showing the pope with a headdress similar to a *kamelàukion*. Was Paschal truly the initiator of the rite of the two porphyry thrones? This was recorded in the *Liber pontificalis* (II:327) for the coronation of Pope Honorius II (1124), and it was recorded yet again in Cardinal Cencio Savelli's *Ordo* of 1192. But, to be sure, a hundred and fifty years later it seems that the ceremony of the *ostentatio* was no longer understood. In fact, Jean de Mailly, in his *Chronicon universalis Mittensis,* tried to explain the curious rite by saying that in the mid–ninth century a woman named Agnese, born in Ingelheim of a British father, educated both in imperial and ecclesiastical right (*in utroque* [both kinds]) and disguised as a male, arrived in Rome. There, thanks to her wisdom, she attained the honor of the cardinalate and, later, the papacy. She sat in the chair of St. Peter for two years. Finally, she was delivered of a baby during a procession from the Vatican basilica to the Lateran, in the neighborhood of the Basilica of S. Clemente (Fig. 67). She was stoned by the people of Rome. From that time the place was considered a *locus infamis*. During the *Possessio* it was carefully avoided, and a small chapel was built at a corner near it.[22] We may presume that Jean de Mailly was not the inventor of the legend, because in more or less the same years Robert d'Uzès (died 1296), in the chapter "De futuro statu ecclesiae et quibusdam pontificibus" of his *Liber trium vivorum et trium spiritualium virginum,* told of a pertinent dream he had in the year 1291. From Orange, he was transported to Rome, where, in the porch of the Lateran basilica, he saw the porphyry thrones ("spiritus Domini assumpsit me in spiritu et statuit civitate Romana. . . . Et ecce posuit me in porticu ante sedes porphyrii ubi dicitur probari papa an sit homo" [the spirit of God took my soul and brought me to Rome . . . and brought me to a porch before some porphyry thrones, were it is said that they prove whether the pope is or is not truly a male]). At the end of the century, the legend was repeated by the Dominican bishop Martinus Polonus, in his *Chronicon summorum pontificum imperatorumque de septem aetatibus mundi.*

The same explanation of the rite is given in a *Mirabilia Urbis Romae* (1375): "In Laterano . . . supra palatium ante Sancta Sanctorum sunt due sedes, in quibus consideratur papa, an masculus sit an femina" (In the Lateran Palace, in front of the Sancta Sanctorum, there are two seats where they determine whether the pope is a man or a woman).[23]

The legend that a woman sat in the chair of St. Peter was accepted by Bartolomeo Platina, who wrote, in his *Vitae summorum pontificum* (1479), that after the reign of Pope Leo IV, "Ioannes anglicus, Maguntiaco oriundus, malis artibus (ut aiunt) pontificatum adeptus est" (the English John [Joan?], from Maguntian stock, cunningly, as it is told, reached the papacy).[24]

But at the beginning of the sixteenth century, even this explanation of the rite was no longer accepted. Some even joked about it, like the Venetian ambassador Antonio Giustinian. Referring to the coronation of Pope Julius II (26 November 1503), he wrote that after seeing so many cardinals surrounded by concubines, the scandal of a woman as pope seemed very far-fetched. "However they no longer perform the ceremony, vulgarly said to be that of putting a hand underneath; I think it is because the present times show that there is so much evidence of the virility of popes that it is not necessary to solemnly seek further evidence in that quarter."[25]

In Protestant propaganda, the story supported the image of Rome as the new Babylon. Pierpaolo Vergerio, the heretic bishop of Capodistria, affirmed that "a prostitute" had been seated on the papal throne; thus the cardinals "provided that a stone seat be placed in St. John Lateran, called the *stercoraria* because it is in the form of a shit hole [*sic!*],"[26] where an inspection could be made, to avoid such a danger in the future. As we will soon see, Vergerio merged the two different ceremonies associated with the papal coronation, but oddly enough the list of the many misunderstandings of the rite was opened by Bartolomeo Platina himself. In the introduction to his biography of Pope John XII we read:

Someone writes two things, that when the pope goes to the Lateran basilica, he runs away from that street where the childbirth occurred, and that, to avoid a second forgery

22. D'Onofrio 1978 and 1979. A different explanation is in Boureau 1989.
23. D'Onofrio 1978, 59.
24. Platina [1479] 1568, 134.
25. Giustinian 1876, II:330.
26. Vergerio 1556, n.p.

and mistakes, at the outset, when installed on St. Peter's seat, for that purpose perforated, he displays his genitals to the younger of the deacons. About the first explanation I am not sure; but there is a second, in my opinion: that this seat is prepared to allow the pope, before sitting in such high magistracy, to know that he is not God, but a man, constrained by the necessities of nature to defecate, and for this the seat is called *stercoraria*.[27]

The *stercoraria* and the two imperial porphyry thrones were henceforth confused.

Lutheran propaganda forced the Catholic polemicists to react. In 1568 Onofrio Panvinio, editing Platina's *Vitae pontificum* with additions and comments, explained the legend away thus: not a woman, but a lascivious and debauched man sat on the pontiff's throne, Pope John XII, who was removed by a Roman council in the year 963. This pope had a mistress, called Johanna.[28] Whether the pope was John XII or, as Photius affirmed, John VIII, this was not an explanation for the ceremony, but it put a softer spin on the legend.

Panvinio did not observe that in de Mailly's story the delivery of a child took place during a procession. This could not have been anything other than the cavalcade of the *Possessio*, performed after the pope's coronation to take possession of the Roman cathedral. The procession he describes started from the Vatican basilica and halted at the Basilica of S. Clemente, near the Coliseum, along the route to the Lateran. Saint Clement, the martyr, was the third Roman pope, and his tomb was always regarded as a place of regeneration for newly elected popes. Thus the *mana* of the apostle, the founder of the papal line, which had been captured by the pope-elect at the Vatican, was reinforced. The route was held to be sacred, and was followed only for papal coronations. When Giovanni de' Medici (Pope Leo X) was elected, he soon performed the duty of praying in the Roman cathedral, but postponed the solemn ceremony of the *Possessio* until the feast of Saint John. In his journal, Paris de' Grassi wrote that "causa devotionis . . . noluit facere viam papalem Monte Jordani, quia asseruit velle facere pompam solitam ad Lateranus die S. Johannis proxime futuri" (for devotion . . . the pope [Leo X] refused to pass along the pontifical route of Monte Giordano, affirming that he would observe the usual cavalcade to the Lateran in the near future, on the feast day of St. John).[29] The route was a *via sacra* that could not be taken a second time.

In Roman ceremonial there is only one other comparable procession, which was recorded in two *Ordines Romani*, the eleventh (1143) and the twelfth (1192). This second procession might have been associated with another papal ceremony, the distribution of the Agnus Dei, but it is not to be confused with the *Possessio*. It followed part of the route of the *Possessio*, but started from the Basilica of Santa Maria Maggiore, passed under the Roman arch at St. Eusebius, past the Trophy of Marius, and proceeded along Via Merulana finally to reach the Lateran Palace. But there is no record, in this itinerary, which accompanied the festivities of Easter, of the papal train halting at the Basilica of S. Clemente.

We must thus assume that there was a close connection between the delivery by the female pope and the first Lateran ceremony. Let us return to the porphyry thrones. On the second, situated at the left of the chapel gate, the Roman *Ordines* say that the pontiff must *jacere* (lie down); and as we noted, the same verb is used by the *Codex caeremonialis* of 1437 and by the master of ceremonies Paris de' Grassi.

27. Platina [1479] 1568, 134–37.
28. Platina [1479] 1730, 1:174–77.
29. De' Grassi 1753, 382.

As we have seen, the first mention of this rite is in the *Liber pontificalis* that referred to Popes Paschal II (1099) and Honorius II (1124). Can we penetrate backward to an even remoter time? Or, rather, can we discover, if not the origin, at least the mentality that provoked the initiation of this ceremony? I think we can do so and thus reach a "farthest point of navigation."

In his search for acknowledgment of full sovereignty, the Roman pontiff aspired to be a *vicarius Christi,* as the emperor pretended to be a *vicarius Dei.* This was a process that started about the eighth century with the forgery of the Donation of Constantine and reached its apex in the iconographic program in the oratory of S. Silvestro of the Church of the SS. Quattro Coronati. This last has been described as "one of the great monuments in the propaganda war waged by the papacy against the Emperor Frederick II."[30] But how would it be possible to compete with the imperial dignity without claiming similar origins? (And we should remember that precisely Frederick affirmed his "divine" origins, celebrating his *dies natalis.*) There could be only one solution: to affirm descent from a divine mother. If the *Ecclesia* was perceived to be a mother,[31] there was only one possibility in the Christian world: to assimilate this image to another even more important mother— Mary as *Mater Dei* or, definitively, the Great Mother.

Before the Council of Ephesus (431), Mary as *Theotokòs* or *Sancta Dei Genitrix* was central in the debate between Nestorians and Monophysites.[32] A fundamental aspect of her cult was identification with the Great Mother. In Byzantine iconography, the *nikopoia* is seated on a birthing throne, legs apart, with the Christ/Emanuel on her stomach. Centuries later, Guillaume Durand (1237–96) even compared the sacristy of a church to Mary's womb: "Sacrarium, in quo sacerdos sacras vestes induit, uterum sacratissimae Mariae significat, in quo Christi se veste carnis induit" (The sacristy, where priests dress themselves in holy garments, signifies the holy womb of Mary, where Christ assumed a corporeal body).[33] In the Zulu religion, "the hut is itself the image of the womb."[34] But in her cult, as in paleo-Christian iconography, Mary was something more than the pregnant Virgin. As with a large river, many different pagan cults flowed into her own cult, from Cybele to Artemis, from Diana to Juno, from Demeter to Coré, from the Mater Matuta to her double, Bona Dea (two goddesses strictly related to the delivery). But the river did not merge the waters of these different tributaries. Paleo-Christian iconography maintained the differences and repeated the original pagan typologies. The many ways in which Mary was depicted were fundamentally derived from two earlier typologies: the woman seated and the woman standing up. Usually, as mother, she was portrayed seated (with thighs spread wide apart). This portrayal was a consequence of *steatopigia,* the accentuated behind being a fundamental attribute of the Great Mother in primitive cultures. Alfred Neumann reminds us that the Great Mother was the "throne in itself" and that Isis had a symbol of the throne on her head. As the Earth's mother, she was intended to be the Great Mother in her seat:

30. Krautheimer 1980, 218.
31. Rahner 1943.
32. Jameson 1857, xxi and 59.
33. Quoted in Réau 1955, 1:63.
34. Heusch 1986, 89.

As the mother and lady of the earth, the Great Mother is the "throne in itself." It is typical that the female body is not restricted to the genital, but also includes the widely extended thighs of the seated woman, on which the child, born from that belly, sits as if on a throne. . . . Properly speaking, the name of the biggest goddess, mother of the primordial cults, is Isis, that is, the seat, the throne. Isis carries on her head the symbol of the throne. The king, when he takes possession of the Earth, of the Divine Mother, does this literally, by sitting on her belly. The goddess sitting on the throne lives as the sacred symbol of the throne. The king takes power by ascending to the throne, and he takes his place in the belly of the Great Mother, the Earth, when he becomes her son.[35]

In A.D. 431 the Council of Ephesus proclaimed Mary "Mater Dei, Thronus Dei" (the Mother of God, the Throne of God). Some of the iconographic representations of her as mother are of particular interest. When she is seated on a throne and holding up her son, she reiterates the model of Isis feeding Horus.

In her book *The Christ Child*, D. C. Shorr lists numerous types of Byzantine Madonnas:[36] *hodegetria, glykophilousa, galaktotrophousa, elousa, oumilenie, nikopoia, platytera.* Let us examine carefully the last two. As *nikopoia,* the seated Virgin is holding Christ / Emanuel in the center of her lap. As *platytera,* the pregnant Virgin is standing up, while the child is represented inside a mandorla, on her chest, symbolizing her womb. *Nikopoia* was the characteristic representation of the Romanesque age (before the thirteenth century), although this typology was still depicted in the seventeenth century (for instance, in the Church of S. Prudenziana in Rome). On the other hand, the *nikopoia* seems to have been none other than a development of the original *platytera,* the Diana type (the Virgin is standing on the globe with a crescent at her feet). The iconography gradually changed through the centuries, without changing its implicit meaning: the Virgin was delivering a particular child, the King of Heaven.

Basically, only two or three types of seats were used in these representations. One type—that we should perhaps consider the original—was a birthing chair, as can be discerned in a fresco of the third century (Rome, Catacombs of St. Priscilla) if we compare it with a scene of a birth from the Roman cemetery at Ostia. One may wonder whether the throne on which Mary is seated in a Christian sarcophagus in Rome[37] is another birthing chair, and even more whether the throne of the Mater Matuta from Chianciano (fifth century B.C.)[38] and the many thrones of the Matres Matutae from Capua[39] are birthing chairs (*sellae obstetriciae*). One might ask the same of the marble statues of Demeter and Coré, from Thebes and Boeotia, that are now in the Louvre,[40] and even if Peter Paul Rubens referred to a similar throne, with lion's feet, when painting the birth of Louis XIII (Louvre).

There was no necessary continuity among all these representations, from the Roman Matres Matutae to the Virgin and Child. But there was a general cultural and religious framework in the West (with deep Eastern influences) that produced similar images over

35. Neumann 1981, 100–101. See also Barb 1953.
36. Shorr 1954.
37. Rome, Museo Nazionale delle Terme, Alinari 28323.
38. Florence, Museo Archeologico.
39. Capua, Archaeological Museum. See *Matres matutae* n.d.
40. Neumann 1981, pl. 147.

Fig. 68   *Mater Ecclesia, Exultet,* Vatican Library, Barb. Lat. 592, fol. 1.

a long period of time. And it is worth noting that the meaning of these different thrones had not been forgotten in the Italian Renaissance. About 1447 Cosimo Tura and other painters prepared the Belfiore *studiolo* for Lionello d'Este, following a program thought up by Guarino Veronese that involved the fertility of the hearth. The muses—Erato, Terpsichoré, Thalia, Calliopé—are shown seated on luxurious thrones, pregnant; and just like the Madonna del Parto that Piero della Francesca painted about the same time in the cemetery of Monterchi, each shows a prominent belly and is dressed in a *cioppa,* a tunic open down the middle to facilitate pregnancy.[41]

In the twelfth-century *Exultet* roll of the Vatican Library, Mater Ecclesia is represented as a Byzantine Augusta, dressed in an *imation* covered by a *dalmatica* that is belted with a *loros,* and with *brachiola* over her arms (Fig. 68).[42] She is standing with her arms outspread, as in the *platytera* typology, but this time her son is not present. Her hands support a colonnaded porch, with a tympanum and two small towers symbolizing the church. In the same century as the *Exultet* roll, an inscription emphasizing the primacy of the Lateran was added to the pediment above its porch: "DOGMATE PAPALI DATVR AC SIMUL IMPERIALI QVOD SIM CVNCTARVM MATER ECCLESIARVM/HIC SALVATORIS CELESTIA REGNA DATORIS/NOMINE

41. For such dress in antiquity, see Bertelli 1589.
42. For this ceremonial dress, see Constantin Porphirogénète 1967 and Pertusi 1976, fig. IV.

Fig. 69   Gian Lorenzo Bernini, the delivery, the next to last panel at the base of the baldacchino of the Altare della confessione (1625–33), Rome, Basilica of St. Peter.

SANXERVNT CVM CVNCTA PERACTA FVERVNT / QVAESVMVS EX TOTO CONVERSI SVPPLICE VOTO / NOSTER QVOD HEC SEDES TIBI CHRISTI SIT INCLITA SEDES" (By papal and imperial order I am the mother of all churches. Here are the heavenly kingdoms of the Savior. I was consecrated in the name of the giver when all was complete. We ask all believers to worship with prayer that this, our seat, be known to you as the seat of Christ).[43]

We cannot look on such lavish stone seats as the ones located beside the Chapel of S. Silvestro as merely *sellae obstetriciae:* their function was primarily liturgical, not obstetrical. But even the birth of a son of a Roman emperor had been a public ceremony. As indicated above, I am not assuming a continuity of worship or cult. But I hope to have demonstrated that there was a deep connection between the birth of a king and the birthing chairs that so frequently appear as an indispensable attribute of the Great Mother.

And then, too, when the papacy came to regard *Christomimèsis* as a fundamental element in its claim to supremacy over the emperor, the pope was compelled to appear as the *filius Ecclesiae,* or Pope-Deus.[44] When Mary was perceived and assimilated into the Roman Church as the Great Mother, the two stone chairs reverted to an earlier function, as birthing chairs. Now, for the pope-elect, a rebirth was an obligatory rite of passage. On

43. See D'Onofrio 1979, 202.
44. Rivière 1924.

Fig. 70   Gian Lorenzo Bernini, the child of the church, last panel at the base of St. Peter's
baldacchino.

the birthing throne, the pope performed none other than a dramatic representation of his
own birth: a royal birth.

A final bit of evidence suggesting my hypothesis is to be found at the base of the great
baldacchino by Bernini in St. Peter's. On the base of the four pilasters a story was sculpted,
partly hidden by the pontiff's coat of arms: the face of a woman progressing from the joy
of pregnancy to the pains of delivery (Fig. 69). On the last pilaster, the smiling face of a
child announces that a son of the Roman Church is born (Fig. 70).

12   The Lord's Dinner

ONE FUNDAMENTAL ACTIVITY tied to the body is surely the act of eating. However, this act of basic nutrition has always been perceived as a moment of extreme peril. One could be persecuted by the spirit of an animal one had hunted, or by the gods for not sharing the meal with them. One could be contaminated by the food (or by the impurity of something cooked by someone unknown and somewhere other than where it was eaten).[1] One could choke on the food and suffocate or be poisoned by ingesting it. In the act of eating, man is the most exposed to dangers of impurity.[2] Taboos and totems were the religious underpinnings of the dinner table. Appropriate rites were elaborated to meet such contingencies, rites that differed from society to society, from culture to culture, and from one age to another. But nothing is better than food in codifying social events, and this code "will be found in the pattern of social relations being expressed."[3] This observation becomes particularly pertinent when we deconstruct the rituals constructed around the meals of the sovereign, which were loaded with an innumerable sequence of multiple messages.

If eating together has been seen as a great promoter of solidarity, of community,[4] if the sacrifice has been seen to be the central moment in the collective consumption of meat,[5] with the sovereign we must instead speak of solitude. Hercules, by nature half man and half god, did not share the sacrificed meat; the sovereign shared the meat, but not the table. Like the "big man" studied by Geertz in Bali, he was the dispenser; but as the one conducting the sacrifice, he did not mingle among the eaters.

What did the term "food of the king," *vyande royalle,* mean? Jack Goody writes: "A salient feature of the culinary cultures of the major societies of Europe and Asia is their association with hierarchical man."[6] This was true, above all, of the "king's food." Some types of food were particularly associated with divinity. Ambrosia was the nectar of the pagan gods; some totemic animals were associated with royalty, such as the griffin (a lion with the head of an eagle) in Egypt,[7] the bull in Asia Minor, the eagle and the horse in

1. Dumont 1966, 176ff.
2. Dumont 1966, 75.
3. Douglas 1970b.
4. Vernant and Vical-Naquet 1976, 121ff.; Detienne and Vernant 1979; Burkert 1983; Sanday 1986; Heusch 1986; Grottanelli and Parise 1988.
5. Goody 1982, 12.
6. Goody 1982, 99.
7. Bisi 1965.

classical Rome, the boar among the Lombards, the swan in England, the stag both among the Lombards and in England.[8] But the stag was part of royal symbolism in France as well: a winged stag was presented in the entrée of Louis XII into Paris in 1498;[9] another winged stag pulled the triumphal chariot (a boat with its steersman, symbolizing France and its king) for the entrée of Francis I into Lyon in 1515;[10] further flying stags, decorated with fleurs-de-lys, clearly alluding to royalty, were present in the miniatures illustrating the chronicle of Guillaume de Gangis.[11] Like the eagle, the more edible peacock was also associated with royalty. Since its spread tail feathers symbolized the sky in ancient Rome (Ovid, *Metamorphoses* xv, 385), it became the attribute of the apotheosis of an empress. When a peacock was served at the Spanish court with its tail feathers spread out, "around its neck [was] placed a kind of little mantilla of gold cloth or heavy silk on which [was] painted the king's coat-of-arms."[12] The same custom is documented for the court of Ferrara. At the carnival dinner cooked by Cristoforo di Messi Sbugo for the duke and the court (1548), a peacock was served in the second course "in pieces, garnished with white sauce and golden mustard, the colors of His Excellency."[13]

However, other foods were banned. Onions, garlic, scallions, and anchovies, for instance, were foods associated with peasants and the countryside. "Onions, garlic, scallions, and such things, although thought ingenious additions by some, are not honorable, because, beside their smell, they show that the diners are peasants or their offspring; they are nauseating and disgusting."[14] In the mid–seventeenth century, Vincenzo Tanara thought eggplants were food meant for servants and Jews—"eggplants (*melanzani*) are called *Mala insana* (sick-insane), because when eaten they disturb the mind and make people go mad . . . they can be served at home, and among Jews"[15]—and he thought garlic "the breath of villains."[16] Little birds, however, were much esteemed. "They make very delicate dishes, adapted to the tables of kings and princes more than to [those of] humble or middle-class people. Thus the plebes, the lower classes, and any, as Satiro says, who haven't the ability to choose better things, shouldn't desire or, even worse, eat such food."[17] A bird banned from the table, however, was the starling, called "flesh of the Devil."[18] The same was said of the gosling, reserved for dinner on the second of November, the day of the dead, from the popular belief that it carried souls to the hereafter.[19] Another ritual bird was the blackbird; in Florence it was reserved for brickmakers.[20]

But even the cut of meat was subjected to rules that reflected the hierarchy of the body. The head, heart, and liver were held in great esteem, whatever they tasted like. Manuals of cookery dedicated to the carver (the highest-ranked attendant at the lord's

8. For the bull, the eagle, the raven, the swan, and the wolf, see Chapter 6 above; for the stag, Chaney 1969, 131–32.
9. Godefroy 1649, 59.
10. Mourey 1930, 23.
11. Hindman and Spiegel 1981.
12. Villena 1965, 106.
13. Messi Sbugo 1557, 37v.
14. Evitascandolo 1609, 6.
15. Tanara 1665, 275.
16. Tanara 1665, 239.
17. Platina 1985, 105. See also Henisch 1976.
18. Platina 1985, 112.
19. This information was provided by Allen Grieco. See also Saly 1980.
20. Goldthwaite 1980, 281.

Fig. 71   Hackhofer, the coronation banquet of Emperor Joseph I, with the exhibition of the
regalia and the *Capilla regis* (from *Erbhuldigung . . .*, 1705).

table) showed the hierarchy of what was to be served when cutting up animals or birds
brought to the table whole and covered with their skin, fur, or feathers.[21]

Although the consumption of food in company has always contributed to the solidarity of a community, the solitude of the sovereign's table always emphasized his "highness," his distance from the others. But this was understood above all as a precaution dictated by the need to avoid impurity.[22] Only exceptionally (for instance, at a coronation
feast; Fig. 71) did the queen sit next to him. On some occasions, the queen presided over
an all-female table, as in a gynaeceum, in another hall. Normally, if allowed, the women
watched from a secluded place, like a balcony. Given the often elevated position of the
lord's table, in Italy it was often called the *tribunale*.

This solitude seems to have been a constant. Of the Emperor Otto III it was said:
"Solus ad mensam quasi semicirculus factam loco caeteris eminenciori sedebat" (He sat
alone at a semicircular table, in an upper part of the room). A table of this type was called

21. A somewhat different hierarchy, which is nonetheless important for the development of taste, is in Courtin [1671]
1682, 107–10.
22. Dumont 1966, 178.

Fig. 72   Bosse, *Festin des chevaliers du St. Esprit* (1633), Paris, Bibliothèque Nationale, Cabinet des étampes.

sigma and probably derived from a Byzantine model.[23] An engraving by Abraham Bosse of a banquet of the Order of the Holy Spirit at Fontainebleau (1633) shows Louis XIII eating alone, separated from the two "lower" tables of knights, while a train of servants, escorted by armed guards, presented all the courses to the king before distributing them to the other diners (Fig. 72). Pietro Giannone, who took refuge in Vienna after the scandal provoked by his *Istoria civile del regno di Napoli* (1723), received an invitation to attend a dinner of the emperor, and recorded this experience in his book of recollections, *L'Ape ingegnosa:* "The most solemn way for the emperor to show himself to his subjects was for him to eat in public, attended by ambassadors, princes, and the nobility, and with such a great crowd of spectators as to fill a great hall, with people pressing in and going out so that it always remained full. It was as if they saw their sovereign at the head of a great army or a great council."[24] A painting by Luis Parret y Alcázar (now in the Prado in Madrid), shows Charles III of Bourbon, king of Spain, seated at the center of a long table, completely alone, surrounded by numerous servants. Here one detail deserves mention: the presence, in a room all lined with tapestries, of dogs. This was also a constant that dated from Homeric times. One easily remembers from the *Odyssey* the scandal of the suitors seeking the hand of Penelope, who insulted Ulysses, the sacred guest, by reducing

23. Thietmar 1935, IV:47. See also Eberlein 1982, 115; Schramm [1929] 1960b, I:110ff.
24. Giannone 1993, 68.

him to the rank of an animal. They threw him bones to chew, meaning that Ulysses was present at the banquet, but among the humblest of the guests. Francesco Doni, in his *La zucca* (1551), tells a story about Dante Alighieri when a guest of the lord of Verona: "Dante dined one day in the household of Messer Cane della Scala. His sons and the rest of his family threw bones at Dante's feet (provoking him, waiting to hear some witticism) when they got up from the table, as was customary. Dante immediately said: 'This shows that I am not a dog [*cane*] like you; because I haven't chewed on the bones as you did.'"[25] With this response, Dante thus avoided being treated like Ulysses. But it confirms how constant the presence of dogs was; they were at the lowest level of a social hierarchy, below the kitchen scullions.

It is well known that the emperor Napoleon ate alone. So did later dandies, like the Italian poet Gabriele d'Annunzio at the Vittoriale (the splendid villa on Lake Garda where he kept his court). He always ate apart from his guests, for whom he reserved a dining room lined with red and black lacquered paneling.

The king's royal table was considered to be a sacred place. At the court of England, if the king preferred to eat in his private chamber, his place in the public hall was nevertheless laid as usual, the courses carried to the royal table even *in absentia* and then redistributed to the lower tables of his courtiers. A Venetian ambassador, at the time of Queen Anne, wrote: "When the king sometimes eats privately, the officials [of the table] nonetheless appear to do their tasks at the usual table of the king, with their heads uncovered and in the same way as if the king were present; and after the food has remained on the table for a while, they take it away and depart, making the same bows to the table as if the king were there, and they do the same for the queen."[26] Since the food for the "household" descended directly from the mouth of the lord, it would not have been possible to distribute it without its having been on his table long enough to be infused with his *mana*.

A truly singular way of presenting food was implemented by the signoria of Siena during the visit of Emperor Charles V (1536), to which I have referred several times:

Just after the return of the *signori* to the Palazzo [Pubblico], they ordered the presentation to His Majesty to begin, everything being ready, and in good order all the porters issued from the palazzo. They took the wider street and turned left, entering the duomo through the Porta del Perdono and leaving it through the front door. The emperor, informed, had taken his place at a window to see them pass. They went in the following order: first forty live calves carried on the backs of forty peasants.

Fifty sheep followed, carried like the calves.

Then a hundred baby goats carried by fifty men.

Then tied up or in cages, 250 pairs of chickens, geese, and pigeons came after the goats.

A hundred sacks of grain and barley followed, carried by a hundred men; and two hundred *staia* [bushels] of white bread in long baskets.

The wine followed the bread in bottles and casks of all kinds, white and red, carefully carried; there were two hundred *staia* of this.

Seventy white candles followed;

25. Doni 1979, 1:644.
26. Alberi 1839–63, ser. I, II (1840): 395.

fine cheese, three hundred pounds;

marzipan, one hundred pieces;

a hundred boxes of sweets of different kinds;

twenty-five baskets of sugar;

six great baskets filled with beautiful artichokes;

and finally quantities of wild boars, roebucks, hares, peacocks, pheasants, and other game available at this time of year.

    They all filed into the palace and the presentation was graciously accepted. His Majesty asked that the torches burning everywhere in good number be extinguished, although it was night. Everything was sacked by the court and anyone who could. The crowd immediately rushed up in disorder and confusion and overturned, sacked, and wasted everything.[27]

Three things are revealed by this long description: the display of wealth by the signoria, the passage of the food through the cathedral to acquire a particular sanctity, and, again, the violence and waste of the ritual sack, without regard of the value.

    For coronations, despite the different structure of the rite, the banquet varied little from earlier to later ones, and the solitude of the sovereign (or the royal couple) was respected, even when, in 1760, King George III of England and Charlotte of Mecklenburg-Strelitz celebrated their coronation. On this occasion they were joined at table by the duke of York, the duke of Cumberland, and Her Royal Highness Princess Augusta. But these diners were placed at the two extremities of the table, the men on the side of the king and the woman on the side of the queen.[28] One can say the same about the banquet for the wedding of Emperor Joseph II and Isabel of Parma, immortalized by Martin von Meytens (Vienna, Schönbrunn): bride and groom are isolated at the middle of a table next to two longer tables where are seated six gentlemen and six ladies, the companions of the royal couple. The hall is crowded with hundreds of courtiers, while a group of musicians (a harpsichord, two trumpets, a cello, a double bass, and a singer) are in the left corner of the picture, playing.

    Can it be possible that papal banquets were a model for medieval courts? The pope also ate alone. He sat at a square table ("quadratus thalamus") under a baldacchino. The sideboard was arranged to the left, "with gold and silver vessels for the water and wine, and the other usual things." The master of ceremonies Patrizi Piccolomini compared it to an altar ("similiter in divinis").[29] The pope was dressed "cum paramentis pontificalibus," the miter on his head, a red mantle open at the chest, and sandals on his feet.[30] If he was host to an emperor or king, a second table was set up to the right of the pontifical one: "If the emperor should attend, a place would be prepared for him on the pontiff's right; the table would be placed on a platform, and the emperor would eat alone there."[31]

    The hierarchy of the table was always considered one of the most important aspects of court life. It had the same meaning (from Byzantium to the Escorial) as that of the frequent processions inside the palace, which were regulated minutely by rules of prece-

---

27. *Descrittione delle cerimonie* [1884] 1968, 35–37.
28. Taylor 1820, 295.
29. Dykmans 1980–82, 1:85.
30. Dykmans 1980–82, 1:85.
31. Dykmans 1980–82, 1:85. But see also Dykmans 1968a, 1968b, and 1977.

dence. The gradations of places at table were the means *par excellence* of daily verifying one's prerogatives. Once again the rule of proximity measured and denoted favorites.[32]

As Bronislaw Malinowski observed, "the center of gravity of the feast lies, not in the eating, but in the display and ceremonial preparation of the food."[33] Appropriate officials took their functions from service in the kitchen: from the dispenser and cork drawer to those who were directly concerned with the lord's table, beginning with the carver and the cupbearer. The basic structure of the meal was implicit in the preparation of a royal banquet. Preachers recommended that the table be amply supplied with meat that could be successively redistributed. "When thou art at table / Thinkest thou first of the poor and needy; / For, when thou feedest the poor, thou feedest thy Lord / Who will feed thee, after thy death, in the eternal bliss."[34] The first advice of Thomasin von Zerclaere in his treatise *Der Wälsche Gast* (The Italian guest) was "[t]o think of the poor first of all."[35]

The structure of the lord's banquet was based on the distribution of food according to fixed norms and observed rigid precedents. We have already noted that all the dishes were first presented to the prince, who tasted them in moderation to imbue his own power. From the lord's mouth, the food thus descended—ideally and really—to those of his guests and courtiers who were seated at "low tables" awaiting the distribution. Figuratively, the food was transformed into the body of the *dominus* before it passed to the lower tables. At the court of Ferrara, the *Ordinario per el piato de S. Ex.tia* informs us, the remains from the table of Duke Alfonso were carried to two lower tables, sometimes called troughs, that were expected to serve some ninety persons: "From what is taken from the said table, ninety mouths can eat abundantly, which at present are the number served at the two smaller dining tables (*tinelli*)."[36]

The remains from the dining hall then passed still further to courtiers of inferior rank who also awaited the remains from the first table. Great vessels of copper were filled with scraps that were passed on to the scullions in the kitchens; the bones were thrown on the floor for the dogs. Vincenzo Cervio refers to these vessels when he reserves for the carver the right to a plate of meat from the piece reserved for the lord (since he had carved it): "at least to avoid the heavy hand of those who pass out the remains from the lord's table in certain copper vessels all mixed together, so that even thinking about it, not to mention chewing such food all mixed together, makes one's stomach turn."[37] It is not superfluous to remember here that the office of carver was seen by Antonio da Colle as the last refuge of an impoverished nobleman.[38] The abundance of food and profusion of different dishes described in cookbooks should not mislead us. All those dishes were not consumed at the first table: courtiers, guests, even servants and kitchen scullions, were dependent on that food.

The distribution of food was, naturally, of particular importance when a new sovereign ascended to the throne. I have already indicated how, for the coronation of Emperor Matthias, the imperial banquet began at the same time as the sacking of the oats deposited as a *congiarium* in a nearby square. Not much different is recorded in the chronicle of

32. Brocher 1934, 28.
33. Malinowski 1922, 171.
34. Rossetti 1869, 16, vv. 5–8.
35. Rossetti 1869, 32.
36. *A tavola con il principe* 1988, 74.
37. Cervio 1581, 5.
38. Colle 1520.

King Pere III of Catalonia in the thirteenth century. The day of the coronation "and the two following, we kept open house for any man who wished to eat, and according to the scribe *de racio* [dispenser] and others of our officials, some ten thousand persons ate there the first day."[39] A similar liberality was observed for the coronation banquet of King Louis XII of France in 1498: "Item, the said hall was draped all around very richly, and also the pillars. And all about were tables, at which to sit and eat and drink, for the notables invited to court. They were so well served with meats of all kinds that no man alive remembered such a sumptuous supper for the entrée of a king."[40]

During the Renaissance, the midday meal was eaten in private, whereas ceremonial banquets were arranged for the late afternoon or the evening, following the norms enunciated by Bartolomeo Platina (1474/75): "Contrary to what is said of our ancestors or men-at-arms, who ate their dinner before noon, we eat our main meal toward evening, when we can rest from any strenuous bodily activity."[41] The physician Michele Savonarola (1384–1468) gave the same advice.[42] But King Louis XIV dined about one o'clock, after the work of attending the Council of State: "One o'clock was the usual hour," the duc de Saint-Simon tells us. However, in the evening the king preferred to eat alone: "Supper was always *au petit couvert,* that is to say, alone in his chamber, at a square table in front of the central window."[43] Bartolomeo Platina had a series of rules. "Dinner should be set out in the manner most appropriate to each season: in winter in a closed warm room, and in summer in open air where it is cool. In springtime scatter flowers on the seats and tables; in winter burn incense. In summer strew the pavement with sprigs of sweet-smelling herbs or olive and willow branches, which refresh the air. In autumn hang ripe grapes, pears, and apples from the ceiling. The napkins should be white, the tablecloth spotless."[44] This advice reminds us of the festoons of fruit that often adorn fifteenth-century altarpieces. For the Sforza-Aragon marriage banquet at Pesaro in May 1475, the whole hall was festooned "with balm from Cyprus and Neapolitan perfumes."[45]

Since the banquet was a rite, there was an obsession with purity. The ceremony began with washing the hands, since, as Mauss observed, water "separated" different states of purity.[46] At the time of Homer one washed the whole body; in the Gospel of Saint Mark (7:1–5) the Pharisees were astonished by the way the disciples of Jesus ate: "And when they saw some of his disciples eat bread with defiled, that is to say, with unwashed, hands, they found fault." The *dominus* washed his hands before and after touching the food.

Since pure and impure were religious concepts,[47] we have to free ourselves from any notion of hygiene. Ablution of the hands was a ceremony dense with solemn meaning. At a papal banquet, the first act was to purify the hands. If an emperor or king was present, he would be the one to serve the pope. This rite, which underscored the moment of contamination represented by the food, was emphasized by all those present, kneeling. "When the pope washes his hands, laymen and any who are not prelates genuflect; cardi-

39. Pere III 1980, para. 15, 198–99.
40. Guenée and Lehoux 1968, 135.
41. Platina 1985, 13.
42. Savonarola 1508, 57v–59r.
43. Saint-Simon 1983–88, v:607.
44. Platina 1985, 20.
45. De Marinis 1946.
46. Hubert and Mauss 1929. But see also Mauss 1950.
47. Dumont 1966, 70; Douglas 1970b.

nals and prelates stand with their heads bared."[48] The same respect was owed to cardinals: "When cardinals wash before dinner and after, it is customary for all the lay servants to genuflect and for others to remove their hats."[49] Patrizi Piccolomini added that this was the custom in his own time, although he could find no reference to it in earlier books of ceremonies ("quod servari nostris temporibus vidimus, quamvis in nullo ceremoniarum libro id legerimus").[50] One understands why Gregorio Leti, in his *Vita di Sisto V,* reported that one day a Venetian ambassador, coming out from a papal banquet, had to observe that "eating with the pope is an ideal honor and a bodily labor."[51]

Even pouring liquid into goblets was an act that obeyed rules. As Francesco Liberati recommended, "what is drunk one offers with the left hand on the left side of the lord, holding the carafe of wine with the right hand and the water with the left, keeping the goblet on its saucer underneath at the bottom point of the triangle; observe the usual reverence when coming and going, always with the head bared and serving with a firm hand."[52] Similar rules of etiquette seem to have ruled the tables of kings, cardinals, and princes. Bonvesin de la Ripa, in his *Zinquanta cortexie da tavola* (ca. 1290), says of dinners with bishops that one should stop chewing when the prelate drank: "Mangiando appreso d'un vescho, tan fin ch'el beve dra copa, / usanza drita prende: no mastegar dra bocha"[53] (when you eat with a bishop, be careful: don't chew while he is drinking). But why should all the diners pause? This rule of etiquette seems not to have any explanation, although we still find it at the beginning of the seventeenth century, at the court of the cardinal of San Giorgio, Pietro Maria Borghese (died 1624). All the diners and spectators were supposed to take their hats off when the cardinal drank:

> The way of serving this lord was thus: the cupbearer poured the water onto the hands of His Eminence; the steward gave him a napkin, which he then retrieved and folded in two. When he came to the table, the carver adjusted his chair, the steward uncovered the dish, which the carver held in his left hand, and the cupbearer offered what was to be drunk. The other servants poured water for the hands of the prelates or others who were dining with His Eminence, and passed napkins to dry their hands . . . and while all this was done, everyone remained with bared heads, and the servant to whom each had returned his napkin remained to serve him for the rest of the meal. And all remained bareheaded while His Eminence ate, except for the servants, who were always bareheaded and standing. In offering what was to be drunk, the gentleman who brought the saucer with the goblet remained bareheaded until [His Eminence] had finished drinking, and when the cardinal drank, everyone took off his hat except for some who were eating with him . . . and after he had drunk, the steward presented him with a white napkin between two plates, and the cardinal took it and put the napkin he had been using on the other plate; thus every time he drank, he changed napkins.[54]

48. Dykmans 1980–82, 1:87.
49. Dykmans 1980–82, 1:457.
50. Dykmans 1980–82, 1:90.
51. Leti 1669.
52. Liberati [1658], 71.
53. Furnivall 1869, II:25, vv. 115–16.
54. Lunadoro 1650, 192–93.

Thus there was a series of rules of etiquette that differed for gentlemen who served the *dominus* or his guests. But even here the act of drinking received a special emphasis. At first sight it might seem that kneeling at a papal dinner derived, through imitation, from the elevation of the chalice during the Mass; but why stop chewing or take off one's hat in the presence of bishops and cardinals? In fact, the same norms were observed for lay princes. Antonio Frugoli, in his *Pratica e scalcaria,* says in reference to a "great prince" that every time he drinks, the steward, as a sign of respect, bares his head, as do "all the other gentlemen around the room."[55] This "great prince" is transformed in Antoine de Courtin's manual of etiquette into a "person of rank," but the norm remains nearly identical to what had been enunciated by Bonvesin de la Ripa four hundred years previously. De Courtin writes: "If it happens that you are responding to a person of quality, you must, when he holds up his cup to drink, remain quiet and wait for him to finish drinking before continuing the conversation."[56] This seems to exclude a reference to the elevation of the chalice during the Mass. Are we confronted merely with complicated gestures or petty signs of prestige, or is something else hidden behind this norm of etiquette?

If we extend our inquiry to distant times and spaces, we are surprised to discover not dissimilar norms in the Bamum Empire, a mountainous part of what is now the Congo, an empire whose history began in the seventeenth century and ended with the nineteenth-century German colonial occupation. The ceremony of the court required all the courtiers to cover their eyes when the emperor drank.[57] Marcel Mauss has observed that "to know the motive for why an individual makes a certain gesture, one needs to know the traditions that impose it."[58] If we return for a moment to our rules of etiquette, we must also reflect on how one drank in the Middle Ages: not just touching the cup to the lip, but in gulps. The "farthest point of navigation" that our inquiry can touch is again the king's body: kneel, stop chewing, take off one's hat, wait before speaking, cover one's eyes are all acts intended to underline a perilous situation. These rules of etiquette were in fact aimed at preventing one from seeing the inside of the sovereign's body. They were not valid for all the diners, but specifically for the *dominus,* whose presence descended gradually into that of the "person of rank" of de Courtin.

Another one of the chief rules of etiquette was to wait for the host to invite the guest to purify himself, as Antoine de Courtin also wrote in his *Traité de la civilité.* "If it happens that a person of quality invites you to dine, it is uncivil to wash with him, without an express command, and seeing that there is no servant to take the napkin with which one has dried oneself, one should keep hold of it and be sure it does not pass into the hands of someone of greater rank."[59]

Another detail: the way in which the table was set. This reminded those in attendance that a rite, like the Eucharistic one, was about to be celebrated. We know well that a Eucharistic feast is being celebrated in the Mass. The altar, covered with a white cloth, is readied, with a lectern, missile, chalice, paten, while two ampullae with water and wine are put on a small table to the side. These objects were also symbols. In the same way, the table of the king was laid with objects that were also symbols. The regalia were often ex-

55. Frugoli 1631.
56. Courtin [1671] 1682, 125.
57. Tardits 1985, 195.
58. Mauss 1965, 397.
59. Courtin [1671] 1682, 105. See also *Manger et boire* 1984; *La sociabilité à table* 1992.

Fig. 73   The ship for the table of Napoleon.

hibited, on a small side table, if not directly on the table of the king; insignia (banners and oriflammes) were carried by standard-bearers behind the prince; a collection of gold, silver, pewter, and glass objects was exhibited on the sideboard, or *dressarium,* as a reminder of the lord's greatness. This sideboard had the same meaning as the exhibition of *spolia* in a triumph. It is worth noting that when the emperor took part in a papal banquet, a personal sideboard had to be added at the left side of the pope's *credentia* ("similiter parabitur pro eo credentia iuxta credentiam pape a sinistris").[60] The addition of a table not only permitted the stewards to perform their duties better ("ibi erunt familiares imperatoris pro suo servitio"), the table also served, with its gold and silver ornaments, to embellish the grandeur of the occasion. The additional sideboard symbolized the greatness of the prince; like an ideal "repose of the warrior," he was accompanied by his trophies.

Another symbol often present to indicate an eminent table was a silver ship (Fig. 73).[61]

60. Dykmans 1980–82, 1:86.
61. Oman 1963.

Fig. 74 Hackhofer, the courtiers' table at the coronation banquet of Emperor Joseph I.

Usually it held knives, spoons, and napkins for the prince's mouth, but Cristoforo di Messi Sbugo says that the ship was also used to hold gifts later to be distributed to the guests. At a dinner offered by the archbishop of Milan, Ippolito d'Este, on 20 May 1529, a silver ship was filled with bracelets, earrings, and rings and carried to the prelate's table so that he could distribute them to the diners.[62] At the French court the ship was considered to be a personification of the sovereign. Wherever it was located, all had to render homage to it. When it was carried to the table, to a place at the right of the king, one of the fourteen guards who accompanied him was specifically charged with looking after it. The master of the house bowed to it, and it was uncovered when the servants in attendance needed to refresh the napkins used to wipe the royal mouth. But they did not approach the ship without bowing to it.[63]

What did these precious, and often jeweled, objects represent? A sacramental value is indicated by a comment provided in Pietro Delfino's Italian translation (1379) of the romance of Robert de Boron, where there is a reference to a revelation made to Joseph of Arimathea: "Our lord God revealed to him that he should lay a table for his supper, and place a vessel onto it, and cover this with a white cloth. And that vessel was given by Jesus Christ, and it divides good men from bad."[64] Now, in Italian, *vascello* means "ship," while in the French text the word *veissel* (*vaisseau*/*vaisselle*) has the double meaning of "ship" and "pot," and as Merlin subsequently revealed, it was the Holy Grail: "Know that this table will not be set in your time, and he who will complete it is not yet born. And before he is knighted by his father, who rules the perilous seat [the *sitio perillo,* which was taken as the heraldic sign of Aragon], he will acquire that holy vessel which Joseph brought to these parts, and it will be called by all the Holy Grail."[65] Elsewhere, the translation of *veissel* as "ship" could be reinforced by the fact that the ship was a symbol of the Savior: "The wooden cross becomes a ship to guide you safe through all the storms of the world."[66] The ship on the lord's table, then, assumed the same function as the monstrance on the altar.

Careful attention was given even to the napkins. Not only were they used at several junctures during the meal (at the Sforza-Aragon wedding banquet "thirteen linen napkins were provided for each table because they had to be changed twice, and at the head table they had to be changed still more often").[67] Starched, these could be folded into little fantastic shapes (birds, fish, flames, and so on), using an art that Mattia Giegher tried to pass on.[68] Sometimes, napkins of this kind, when made of Rhemish cloth, were used by diners to take away little morsels from the table, as one can see in Jean Baptiste Greuze's painting *Le bonbon du Roy* (Montpellier).

The royal table was a table of order, confronting the disorder and (relative) impurity of the lower tables of courtiers and the household (Fig. 74). Enrique de Villena (1384–1434) recommended that the carver observe the king's face: "When the carver is not cutting, he should watch the king, and if there is any food on his face or chest, make a secret sign to

62. Messi Sbugo 1557, 14v.
63. Marion 1923, s.v. *Etiquette.*
64. Boron 1884, 197.
65. Boron 1884, 205; see also Paris and Ulrich 1886, 1:98.
66. Rahner 1943, 69; Bertelli 1992, 26–27.
67. De Marinis 1946.
68. Giegher 1639; Garbero Zorzi 1985.

him to remove it, so that he always looks neat and clean."[69] John Paston, who attended the wedding banquet of Charles the Bold, duke of Burgundy, compared that court with the court of King Arthur: so much magnetism emanated from the ducal person.[70]

The procession carrying the food from the kitchen to the lord's table seemed like a triumph. Guards walked alongside the line of servants and pages, which was led by the master of ceremonies or some other great official with his staff. The procession proceeded cautiously, opening its way through the spectators, while soldiers kept the part of the room reserved for the meal free from the crowd.

The temporal order of the meal was governed by rules that we can see in a description of a papal banquet. It began with the order of precedence for washing the hands.[71] The blessing of the table by the pontiff followed.[72] The way for the carriage of dishes to the papal table was opened by armed soldiers, who cleared the crowd from the route, and they were followed by the servants carrying the barrows loaded with dishes of food. The order of service followed the order of precedence. "The first barrow was carried to the most noble prince, either emperor or king. The second went to the next in precedence, and so on in succession."[73] "For the pontiff and emperor," the dishes were presented covered with napkins; "for others, including kings, they were uncovered; the same was observed for the wine." Except for great princes, the dishes could be covered "up to the dining hall," but then they were uncovered "in conspectu pape" (in the pope's sight)[74] to allow him to make his choice.

The habit of carrying dishes and wine covered with napkins was universally observed. Fusoritto da Narni warns that "the dishes destined for the pope, king, or princes [the pages] must carry covered with a napkin folded in the middle."[75] Enrique de Villena adds the following: "When the king drinks wine, remove the plate he was eating from, so that no drops will fall into it. Hold it up at his side, making way for the cupbearer so that he can perform his task. When he is finished, put the plate down again before the king, so long as the food has not gotten cold; if so, change the plate."[76] The same advice was given by Cavalier Lunadoro. While the cardinal of San Giorgio, Pietro Maria Borghese, drank, the carver "covered the meat he had before him with a plate."[77] Should we imagine that this was done only to keep the food warm, or that more was involved? Can we suppose that it was to keep some ill-intentioned person from putting poison into the food?[78] But if the food of the lord had already been tested in his presence ("nisi in presentia pontificis nulli omnino publice fit pregustatio sive proba" [nobody dares publicly to taste the food except in the pontiff's presence]),[79] why take further precautions? And why were dishes covered for the pontiff and, if present, the emperor, but not for a king or other diners? Not only this: why were dishes for kings or great princes covered until they reached the hall,

69. Villena 1965, 105.

70. Cartellieri 1970, 163.

71. "Stabunt ante mensas laantes eo ordine quo debent sedere in mensa." Dykmans 1980–82, 1:88.

72. "Postquam omnes laverint, pontifex benedicit mensam stans sine mitra, et tunc diaconi assistunt. Finita benedictione sedet, imponitur mitra, et diaconi vadunt ad loca sua." Dykmans 1980–82, 1:89.

73. Dykmans 1980–82, 1:89.

74. Dykmans 1980–82, 1:89. On the use of napkins, see Garbero Zorzi 1985.

75. See Cervio 1593.

76. Villena 1965, 104–5.

77. Lunadoro 1650, 192.

78. Wheaton 1983, 52.

79. Dykmans 1980–82, 1:90.

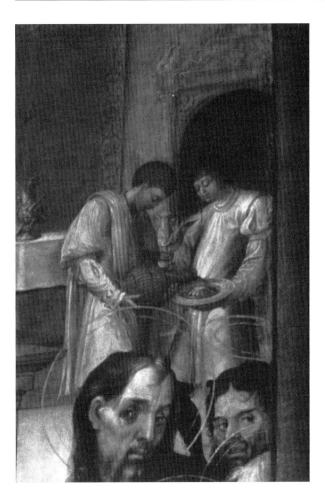

Fig. 75   The *Salva* ceremony, from Gregorio Lopez (second half of the sixteenth century), *The Last Supper*, Tomar, São João Batista.

but then uncovered? We should presume that this was to make subtle distinctions among the guests, that the covered plate was what Norbert Elias calls "a fetish of prestige."

Later, the napkins used to cover plates were transformed into lavish silver lids, as can be seen in the treasury of plates once owned by the Portuguese Crown.[80]

Another important moment in the banquet was the act of the taster, who poured a little of the wine to test it, as well as the vessel in which it was carried, for traces of poison. In Spain, the ceremony was defined: *la Salva*. The seventeenth-century dictionary by Bestián de Covarrubas says this was done "to signify that the king was safe from any treason or betrayal." But he adds that the vessel of silver or gold that held the goblet was an object of value similar to the paten (*diskos*) used by a priest in the Mass, kept along with the chalice (*potèrion*) in the tabernacle.[81] The *Salva* ceremony is illustrated in the background of a *Last Supper* in the cathedral of Tomar (Fig. 75).

During the banquet, a lector read edifying texts from a pulpit (Livy's decades, passages from the New Testament). Silence was strictly observed.[82] For the Sforza-Aragon marriage banquet, "everything was done in silence."[83] The banquet ended with a second

80. D'Orey 1991.
81. Bertelli 1992, 28–29.
82. "Interim cum silentio et sine strepitu omnia administrentur quam diligentissime." Dykmans 1980–82, 1:90.
83. De Marinis 1946, 31.

washing of hands ("secunda lotio manum") and the words pronounced by the lector: "Tu autem Domine miserere nobis." From the manuscript collection *Etiquetas de corte* of Sebastián Gutiérrez de Párraga (1651) we learn that the chief eleemosynar read the prayer of thanks. During the prayer the sovereign listened standing, while the carver used a napkin to dust him off and then kissed his hand.[84]

The whole ceremony was thus immersed in the sacred. A nun's etiquette book of two generations ago held that dinner was as sacred as the Mass in a monastic institution![85] From the papal banquet, women were tacitly excluded. When Queen Christine of Sweden, the famous convert to Catholicism of the late seventeenth century, was in Rome, the problem of her dining with the pope was brilliantly resolved: as we can see in a drawing by P. P. Sevin (in Stockholm), the queen was accommodated at a smaller table beside the pope, although both were covered by the same baldacchino.

As for other ceremonies, those for the prince's table were differentiated for different occasions. A book of etiquette from the Spanish court at the time of King Philip IV in the seventeenth century distinguishes royal meals for different occasions, especially those linked to different religious festivals.

Coronation was certainly the most solemn occasion for a royal banquet, and all the rites connected with the royal table were modeled on the coronation banquet. The rules were quite complicated so as to transform the act of eating into a series of prescriptions proceeding from purifying the hands to the arrival of the barrows laden with food, to the exhibition of the regalia, and ending with the prayer of thanks. We are not wrong if we speak of *drama* (following the definition of Karl Young) or of *theater of State* (following Clifford Geertz) of the medieval monarchy.[86]

Let us follow a description of the coronation banquet for King William of Orange and Mary Stuart in Westminster Hall after their return from the abbey in 1689:

> Their Maiestyes having ascended the Throne retyred till their Table was served, and then returned, where the Lord Great Chamberlain preceded by the Chiefe Gentleman Usher and followed by the Cupbearer, the Earle of Bridgwater, and his assistants, the Viscount Weymouth and the Lord La Ware goe to the Cupboard and from thence the Lord Great Chamberlain brought the Basin and Ewer to their Maiestyes, the Earle of Bridgwater poured out the water while their Maiestyes washed their hands, and his two assistants held the Towell. . . .
>
> The Earle of Bristoll was Cupbearer of the Queene, his Assistant the Viscount Hatton and Lord Berkley.
>
> The Earles of Sussex and Radnor, Sewers [Stewards].
>
> The Earle of Stamford, the Earl of Kingston, Carvers.
>
> Their Maiestyes Sewers did goe to the Kitchen, and the Hot meale was carryed to their Maiestyes Table by the Gentlemen Pensioners, as followeth.
>
> The 2 Clerks Comptrollers.
>
> The two Clerks of the Greencloth.
>
> The Master of the House, and Cofferer.

---

84. Bertelli 1992, 41.
85. Ceccarelli 1956.
86. Young 1933; Geertz 1980.

The Earle Marshall, Lord High Steward, Lord High Constable, all on Horseback.

Sergeants at Armes.

The 2 Earles Sewers.

The Meate carried by the Gent. Pensioners.

The first and second Clerks of the Kitchen.

A Messe [porridge] of Gruell was then presented to his Maiesty [and the person's] . . . claim was allowed.

The first cup of drinke was presented to his Maiesty on the behalf of Lord Allington in minority in a silver Cup Gilt, for the Mannor of Wymondley, his claime being allowed, and the Cup was his Fee.

Toward the end of the first course the Champion repaired to the Hall.

First the Knight Marshall cleared the way to the steps going up to the Throne. Then entered the Trumpets. The Sergeant Trumpeter with his Mace. Two Pages, the one carrying a Target of the Champion's Armes, the other a lance upright. A Herald with his Coat of Arms.

The Champion mounted on a goodly horse in complete armor being come within Westminster Hall doore was there received by the Earle Marshall and the Lord High Constable on Horseback in their robes, their coronets on, the first on the left the other on his right hand.

The Trumpets sounded thrice, and the Herald having called silence, said. If any person of what degree soever, high or low, shall denye or geine say Our Sovereigns Lord and Lady William the third and Mary, King and Queene of England, France, and Ireland, Defenders of the Fayth to be rightfull and undoubted King and Queen of the Imperiall Crowne of this Realme of England, or that they ought not to enjoy the Imperiall Crowne of the same. Here is their Champion who sayth, That he lyeth and is a false Traytor, being ready in person to combate with him, and in this Quarrell will adventure his life against him on what soever he shall be appointed.

Then the Champion threw doun his Gantlet, which having layne a little while the said Herald took it up, and delivered it to him againe.

From thence they advanced into the middle of the Hall, where the same Challenge was againe made in like manner.

Lastly they repaired to the bottom of the steps leading to the Throne, where the Herald did ascend the steps, and stayde about the middle of them, where he pronounced the Challenge in like manner, and the Champion having received his Gantlet as before, made a low obeissance to their Maiestyes, and a silver Cup Gilt being filled with wyne was brought by the Cupbearer to their Maiestyes, they drinke to the Champion, and the same Cup and wyne being delivered to the Champion, he there drinks the wyne makes a low obeissance to their Maiestyes and returnes, in the same manner as he came into the Hall doore, carrying the Cup in his hand as his Fee.

The Hall was then cleared againe as before, and Garter Principall King of Armes followed by the other Kings, Heralds, and Pursuivants, with his Coronet on his head repaired to the lower end of the Hall, where they made their obeissances to their Maiestyes, from thence they advanced to the middle of the Hall, where they did the like, then proceeded to the foote of the steps, where they againe did the same, then they ascended the said steps leading to the Throne where Garter repairing to the middle of the

Table (the other officers of Armes being behind him), made their reverence to their Maiestyes and there Garter having thrice cryed Largesse, proclaimed their Maiestyes style in the word following:

Serenissimorum, Potentissimorum et Excellentissimorum Monarcharum Gulielmi tertij et Mariae, Dei gratia, Regis et Reginae, Angliae, Franciae et Hiberniae, Fidei Defensorum.

Du treshaut trespuissant et tres excellent Monarques Guillaume tierce et Marie, par la grace de Dieu, Roy et Reigne d'Angleterre, France et Irlande, Defenseurs de la Foy.

Of the most high, most mighty, and most excellent Monarques William the third, and Mary, by the grace of God, King and Queene of England, France, and Ireland. Defenders of the Fayth.

Then the other Officers cryed Largesse thrice made their obeissances to their Maiestyes retyred going backwards, their faces towards the Throne.

From thence they retired in the same posture to the middle of the Hall where Garter proclaimed againe their Maiestyes style, and Largesse was also cryed as before.

Lastly they did in like manner at the lower end of the Hall, and repaired to their Tables provided for them.

This being done the second course was carried up to their Maiestyes Table, and the same solemnity should have been observed as was at the first, but was omitted for want of time, it growing late.

Then William Rider Esquire in pursuance of his claime allowed for the Mannor of Bilsington presented their Maiestyes with three Maple Cups.

Lastly the Lord Maior of London attended by the Aldermen, Sheriffs, and the twelve Citizens in pursuance of their claime allowed to be assistant of the Duke of Norfolke Cheife Butler of England presented their Maiestyes a Cup and Cover of gold and wyne in it, who having dranke a little thereof, gave the said Cup and Cover to the Lord Maior, who carried it away as his Fee.

Their Maiestyes having dined, the Basin and Ewer with water was brought to their Maiestyes by the Lord Great Chamberlain, who having washed as before dinner, they received their scepters, and the Regalia are delivered to the Deane of Westminster to be preserved in that Cathedrall, and the rest were committed to the custody of the Master of the Jewell House, and from thence their Maiestyes departed privately to Whitehall.[87]

In this English case, the coronation banquet was also an ordeal, and at the same time it prefigured the recognition of the court, with the acts of submission of officials and knights. The cry of "Largesse" reinforced the proclamation of the new royal couple and referred to the *congiarium*. From this description is missing the final moment of the sack of the remains of the banquet, which is documented for the English court from other sources. We will return to this point later.

As to the service, every banquet had two or three courses with many dishes each, interrupted by musical interludes or representations (*intermezzi*). For each course, the food had to be presented according to a conventional order, regarding quality, taste, and cooking (roasting, frying, boiling).[88]

---

87. *Three Coronation Orders* 1900, 108–11.
88. Romoli n.d. [1560?]; Calvi and Bertelli 1983, 208.

Even the moments for lifting food or drink to the mouth were regulated by temporal successions. The diners could not eat or drink until the *dominus* had eaten or drunk (but there were further norms of etiquette, particularly for drinking). The occasion for drinking did not follow only the initiative of the lord, but happened at times and in ways that were predetermined. A spy may have provided the description by Pierre Du Chastel of the feigned postmortem dinner offered the king during the obsequies for Francis I: "The three courses of the meal were carried out with the same forms, ceremonies, and samplings as they were wont to be during the life of the seigneur, without forgetting those of the wine, with the presentation of the cup at the places and hours that the seigneur had been accustomed to drink, twice during each of his meals."[89] This account can be compared with one regarding Queen Christine of Sweden. When she took refuge in Italy, she was offered sumptuous banquets in the cities she visited. Outside of the halls, cannons shot off salvos every time the queen raised her goblet to drink.

At the court of Vienna, the royal dinner remained one of the most important moments of the sovereign's day as long as the Burgundian ceremonial, originally imported by Emperor Charles V, lasted.[90] Even at the beginning of the last century the norms of etiquette made Emperor Franz Joseph a celebrant, rather than a diner. The guests could eat and drink only when the emperor ate and drank. Since the emperor was quite abstemious, the many wines poured into the series of different wine glasses with different sizes and shapes that were arranged in a half-moon around the diner's plate remained untouched, just like the food presented during the successive courses.[91] At the emperor's table, the companions were not invited to satisfy their appetite but to participate in a rite.

I have mentioned the difference between the royal table, set like an altar, and the "low" tables of the courtiers. We would be wrong, however, to think of disorder, or an absence of rules of etiquette. On the contrary, even the trencher, who distributed food to the low tables, observed precise norms of etiquette, which assimilated the tables of courtiers to the table of the prince. It is enough to glance at the *Règlement de Monsigneur le Prince de Conti* (the governor of Languedoc), which was printed by Claude Fleury, to understand how similar a court was to a monastery.

> In the morning, all gathered for Mass in the chapel and to hear the brief sermon; the same happened for evening prayers and for catechism on Saturdays. After the evening prayers all retired to their chambers, before six o'clock in winter and before eight in summer, and they did not go out in the morning without hearing Mass, except when they were obliged to do errands. In winter the Swiss Guards closed the gates at six o'clock in the evening and consigned the keys to the porter before ten; in the morning they only received the keys after dawn.[92]

For England, we could refer to the rules of the Abbey of Saint Edmund, in Suffolk, for lack of rules of the court, to see how the etiquette of the table operated in a royal palace

89. Du Chastel 1649, 280–81.
90. See Rodriguez Villa n.d. and 1904.
91. Cacciaglia 1975. For the sequence of wines that was characteristic of French meals, see Douglas 1975, 259.
92. Fleury 1688.

of the fifteenth century. In this abbey, when a guest was called to the abbot's table, much attention was given to the rules of precedence.[93]

A huge folder in the Florentine Archives assists us further in understanding how a court functioned. When the Lorraine dynasty was transferred to the grand duchy of Tuscany after the death of the last Medici duke, Giangastone, in 1737, a whole bundle of documents was transported to Florence. This contains a *Règlement général pour l'hôtel de S.A.R.,* approved on 27 April 1730, only thirty years after construction of the Château de Lunéville, and the last personnel registers of the Lorraine from their previous state.[94] They clearly intended to use this material for the organization of their new court in Florence. The *Règlement* makes it clear that much attention was given to control of the kitchen and bakery. The distribution of food to the many members of the household extended to many rubrics. Thus, each member of the household was assigned a specific and immutable portion of the vessels of leftovers; everything was under the control of the *maître d'hôtel.* There was strict oversight also of the distribution of candles and firewood. The daily menu was specified for everybody, from the prince to courtiers and minor functionaries. From the *Liste de tout ce qui se doit servir des cuisines aux différents répas sur la table de l'Hôtel de S.A.R. matin et soir, pour un jour ordinaire* we learn that in 1731 the ducal table was served two courses, arranged as follows:

At midday:
> *First course*
>> 2 great soups
>> 2 little ones
>> 1 great entrée
>> 8 entrées, 6 of meat and 2 of poultry
>> 2 meat hors-d'oeuvres
>
> *Second course*
>> 1 entremet [a side dish: vegetables, sweets, or other]
>> 6 dishes of roast
>> 6 entremets

For the table of the duchess:
> *First course*
>> 4 medium soups
>> 2 great entrées
>> 6 entrées, 4 of meat and 2 of poultry
>
> *Second course*
>> 2 great entremets
>> 4 medium dishes of roast
>> 6 entremets

In the evening the menu had a different two courses:
> *First course*
>> 4 soups

93. Grandsen 1973, 20–21.
94. Now AS, Florence, Guardaroba mediceo, Filza 1300.

1 medium entrée

10 entrées, 6 of meat and 4 of poultry

Second course

6 dishes of roast

6 entremets

Confronted with such a diet, it is not surprising that gout was a common malady among the upper classes! But this was a menu that one might easily deconstruct using the method indicated by Mary Douglas.[95]

As with ecclesiastical ceremonies, which were punctuated with concerts and cantatas, a particular type of music punctuated royal meals. "Table music" (*Tafelmusik, musique de table*) became a distinct musical genre. Played by a small band of musicians who accompanied singers (all borrowed from the royal chapel), this underlined the sacred character of the banquet. This kind of music gave particular prominence to slow movements: the andante, largo, or grave. The *Musique de table* published in 1733 by Georg Friedrich Telemann provided two overtures, two quartets, two concerti (short pieces with alternating parts), two trios, and two solos. The movements of the overtures were: (1) *Lentement, vite, lentement;* (2) *Réjouissance;* (3) *Rondeau;* (4) *Loure;* (5) *Passe-pied;* (6) *Air;* (7) *Gigue.* The first quartet began with a largo followed by an allegro, and then another largo followed by an allegro, a grazioso, and another allegro. In short, Telemann's program fulfilled Angelo Berardi's requirement of fifty years before: "Finally, music is needed by great princes, who find justice and mercy in it; it sweetens their souls, dissolves anger and resentment, and keeps them calm to exercise clemency."[96] One should remember that in antiquity and the Middle Ages music "was primarily a musical-mathematical theory"[97] meant to elevate the spirit. At the Parisian banquet for the entrée of King Louis XII, musicians on three platforms erected for them played "trumpets, clarinets, and violins; they made such a beautiful sound that one thought to be in paradise."[98]

Cristoforo di Messi Sbugo has left an account of one of these performances. Music composed by Messer Alfonso della Viola was performed during the intervals between one course and another at the banquet offered to the duke of Ferrara by his son Ercole on Saturday, 24 January 1539. The orchestra was composed of "five viols, a clavecin with two keyboards, a lute, a great flute, and a smaller one." The singer was Madonna Dalida. In the interval between the fifth and sixth courses the famous comedian Angelo Beoloco performed, and "Ruzante sang songs and madrigals 'alla pavana,' with five men and two women, beautifully." At the end of the banquet, "music was played with five viols in five voices, a plucked instrument, a great flute, a lyre, a trombone, and a German flute."[99]

As a manifestation of the exterior of the royal person, the banquet was a public ceremony with overlapping spectacles. Nonetheless, the recondite meanings of the lord's dinner (a potlatch, but also a distribution of the king's body; a celebration of his power, but also a defense of his body against innumerable dangers) remained intact through the centuries. The persistence of the sack of the table at the end of the meal also indicates its

95. Douglas 1975.
96. Berardi 1681, 110; see also Stefani 1974, 192ff.
97. Ladner 1988, 19.
98. Godefroy 1649, 63.
99. Messi Sbugo 1557, 15ff.

special character. André Félibien, in *Les divertissemens de Versailles,* tells us that at the end of the banquet celebrating the annexation of Franche-Comté by Louis XIV, after the king and queen had finished their meal, "all was put to sack, as is customary on such occasions."[100] Thus also, at the end of the coronation banquet for King George IV in England, as soon as the king retired, the crowd set to sacking the royal table: knives, forks, plates, goblets were all carried away by the diners. Meanwhile, those in the gallery rushed down the stairs to participate. People drank what remained in the wine bottles, they grabbed pastry in their hands and devoured it. Trophies, ornaments, garnishes, and baskets were torn to pieces. The pewter plates inscribed "George IV" were a particular prize. One woman who had gotten hold of a spoon, when asked by one of the attendants to give it up, refused indignantly, thus blocking his efforts to restore order: "Sir, put one finger on me and I will scream with all my might."[101]

Precisely this last incident helps us to understand the sacred meaning of banquets when they were closely connected with the physical body of the *dominus.*

100. Félibien 1674.
101. Jones 1883, 507.

PART III | The End of Sacredness

THE KING'S SOLITUDE CONTINUED beyond the grave. His place of burial was distinct from that of his subjects. If Hadrian's Tomb became the sepulcher of Roman emperors, the emperor Constans wanted his father's mausoleum to become the burial place for the imperial family of the East.[1] Chinese emperors were buried with their soldiers and horses, but Leon Battista Alberti surrounded the Church of San Francesco in Rimini with a marble outer shell that transformed it into the mausoleum of Pandolfo Malatesta, providing niches on the exterior fitted with sarcophagi designed to hold the bodies of the knights of the lord of Rimini. In France, the *valets de chambre* of the king were often buried at the foot of the royal tomb.

It is difficult to speak of a necropolis for the Merovingian kings. When Clovis received the title of Augustus from the emperor Anastasius I and moved his residence from Soissons to Paris (Lutetia Parisiorum), the Church of the Saints-Apôtres, which he founded, was chosen for the royal sepulcher. Indeed, when his daughter Clotilde died, returning from Spain in 531, her body was taken to Paris for burial.[2] However, this first burial place was soon abandoned, and Childebert preferred to found a new sacred spot outside the walls: Saint Vincent, to which he gave a relic of a tunic of the saint and in which he had himself buried in 558. A third choice seems to have been made by the last Merovingians: Saint Étienne at Choisy, a basilica founded by Dagobert I.[3]

The first king to be buried at Saint-Denis was Dagobert I (639). But the designation of this basilica as the royal necropolis occurred only after the burial of Hugh Capet. Charlemagne, with an act of January 769,[4] also chose Saint-Denis, where his ancestors were buried, but forty-five years later his wishes were forgotten. We know little of his tomb. Einhard says simply that "his body, according to the rite, was washed and wrapped, carried into church and buried amid the desolation of the whole people."[5] It is not clear whether this was a religious funeral rite or an already elaborated royal ceremony. Richer speaks of the funeral of Lothair II as a ceremony where the regalia were carried;[6] Suger,

---

1. Dvornik 1966, II:649.
2. Erlande Brandenburg 1975, 80.
3. Erlande Brandenburg 1975, 57; Beaune 1986.
4. Erlande Brandenburg 1975, 72.
5. Eginhard 1947, 50–51.
6. Richer 1930–37, II:140–43.

in turn, refers to funerals for Louis VI, the Fat, and for Philip I as burials "more regio,"[7] implying the same ceremony described for Louis VI.[8]

The importance given to uniting all the kings of France in one sepulcher is demonstrated by the decision taken by Saint Louis in 1263–64 to construct at Saint-Denis a series of cenotaphs, or "commemorative effigies,"[9] to demonstrate the continuity of the dynasty. This was a series of statues sculpted as if the persons, when standing, were destined to decorate and fill niches on the façade of a cathedral. Reclining, however, they were placed onto tomblike blocks. They show how far funeral monuments still had to evolve.

The French necropolis thus transformed the church into a great cemetery. The Angevin kings of Naples would soon do the same for the Neapolitan church of Santa Chiara, and their Aragonese successors for the Church of San Domenico.

For the German emperors, Byzantine influence appeared through the marriage of Otto II and Theophano (972).[10]

The experience of the Iberian Peninsula was quite different, more like the fragmented choices of the Merovingians, probably because of the changes of allegiance of kings to different sacred places and the relics found there. In contrast to French ceremonial, Castile seemed to emphasize succession rather than burial. In the manuscript *Etiquetas generales* (from the time of Philip IV), the paragraph on the *Entrada de los SS.re Reyes despues de heredados* emphasizes the reception of the new monarch more than the burial of his predecessor: "When a king of Spain dies, his successor retires to the royal monastery of San Jeronimo, where the funeral ceremony will take place, and in the meantime he makes preparation for this entry. His councilors are advised to come on the day of entry to kiss the king's hand. . . . The bishop of Toledo, in pontifical vestments, awaits the king under the portico of the Church of Santa Maria, in hand the cross with the relic of the True Cross that is kept in the royal treasury." Then the Te Deum began, following the Roman ritual.[11]

The kings of Aragon preferred burial in monastic cemeteries as more humble and respecting of the ancient custom of avoiding burial in churches.[12] The preferences of the kings of Asturias, León, Castile, and Navarre varied between monasteries and cathedrals, which were reserved particularly for burials of royal children. In Castile, they preferred the Franciscans (at least ten Franciscan monasteries contain royal burials), and numerous kings and queens were buried in the habit of Saint Francis in the Capilla des Reyes Nuevos of the cathedral of Toledo.[13] It was exceptional for Henry II to be buried (1374) in the habit of Saint Dominic.[14]

In Toledo the Church of the Virgin received the remains of the first kings, and the cathedral (used for the coronation of King Sancho IV, 1284) was preferred only later. From the beginning of the twelfth century, a royal sepulcher began to emerge at Santiago de Compostela, in the Chapel of St. Lawrence; another at Sahagún with Alfonso VI; a third

7. Suger 1964, 83–85.
8. Erlande Brandenburg 1975, 13.
9. Vitry and Brière 1908, 83; on the basilica, see Guilhermy 1848.
10. Gros 1965–66.
11. *Etiquetas generales que han de observar los criados de la Casa de S. Mag. En el uso y exercicio de sus oficios*, BAV, Barberini Indice I. 1098:140ff.
12. Arco 1954, 45–46.
13. Arco 1954, 53.
14. Arco 1954, 105.

was begun by Alfonso VIII, the founder of the monastery of Santa María la Real at Burgos (1187 / 1199).[15] Another burial place was the royal chapel in Seville. For Navarre there were two burial places: the monastery of San Salvador at Leire (thirteenth century) and the monastery of Santa María la Real at Nájera.[16]

Spain was an exception, due in large part to the fragmentation of its kingdoms and to the particular *pietas* of being buried in Franciscan cemeteries. However, again, these were burials in sacred places with a tendency to concentrate on one monastery or church for the members of the family reigning at the time, although there was not a true and proper dynastic concentration.

Even for the Roman Church one cannot say that the choice of St. Peter's as a sepulcher for popes was rigid, even though from the time of the emperor Constantine the Vatican basilica was known as the site of the remains of Saint Peter. Tombs were located mostly in the colonnaded forecourt, but some were in interior chapels. They were all removed in the sixteenth century during the construction of the new basilica, a clear sign of the lack of a dynastic awareness such as that shown by Saint Louis at Saint-Denis. Pope Celestine V was buried at L'Aquila. The popes at Avignon were buried in the palace chapel (and their tombs were profaned during the French Revolution); in the sixteenth century the mausoleum designed by Michelangelo for Pope Julius II della Rovere was located in the Church of San Pietro in Vincoli. This vacillation in the choice of burial sites continued into the eighteenth century. Pope Benedict XIII was buried in the Chapel of San Domenico in the Church of Santa Maria sopra Minerva on 21 February 1730. Thus it was only later that the Vatican basilica and its underlying Holy Grotto became the fixed place for papal burials. Here, the earliest was that of Innocent VIII Cybo in the tomb designed by Antonio Pollaiuolo (1492–98).[17]

Thus in the fourteenth century the sacred precinct of the Scaligeri at Verona was an absolute novelty. This was a signoria that between the thirteenth and fourteenth centuries seemed destined for several generations to control a vast area in the Venetian hinterland and the Po valley but that disappeared instead suddenly in the midst of a fratricidal struggle. The Scaligeri signoria began when Mastino I obtained the office of podestà of the Domus Mercatorum of Verona (1261–69) and was followed in this office by his brother. When Mastino was murdered on 27 October 1277 through a plot, he was buried in a red marble tomb covered by a ciborium that was formed by a stone-vaulted archway, which dominates the external north wall of the Church of Santa Maria Antica. He was the first of the lords of Verona to rule over the city from his tomb. As was the custom, his brother Alberto (died 1301) and Alberto's sons, Bartolomeo and Adriano, had simple sarcophagi with sculpted decorations or coats of arms inside the church. The innovation came with Cane, the son of Mastino I. His marriage to Johanna of Swabia, the great-niece of Frederick II, elevated him to the rank of imperial vicar. His expansionist policy then justified his appellation *grande*. The taking of Treviso (18 July 1329) was his crowning act of aggression. "Signor Cane entered [the city] with a thousand soldiers and his captains and was welcomed joyfully by the people of Treviso. The same day he received the scepter in hand as the sign of his true domination of Treviso, and the citizens swore their alle-

15. Arco 1954, 93–94.
16. Arco 1954, 115–26.
17. D'Achille 1867; Muñoz n.d., 57ff.

giance."[18] The triumph sealed his brief but intense career; some prophesied that "he would be king of Italy in a year."[19] In fact, Can Grande died on 22 July, and his embalmed body ("aromatis arte refectum")[20] was taken secretly to Verona. Dressed in a dark blue tunic with a pattern in gold brocade of swans, lions, and rabbits, his sword in his hand and boots up to his knees,[21] he was deposited temporarily in Santa Maria Antica, to await the construction of a mausoleum outside. Thus the triumph was soon followed by a funeral, in which his regalia were exhibited.[22]

Cane had no offspring and—following a procedure also practiced by Merovingian kings—he associated his nephew Alberto with his rule. At his uncle's death, Alberto in turn associated his younger brother Mastino II, who was the true ruler up to the Black Death of 1348. Foreseeing his own death, Mastino II ordered a sepulcher, and when he died, at the age of forty-four years, on 3 June 1351, the lordship went to his sons, Cangrande II, Cansignorio, and Paolo Alboino. The attempt by Cangrande II to associate his own bastards with the government provoked Cansignorio, who ordered the murder of his brother in December 1359. Concerned for the safety of his own two bastards, Bartolomeo and Antonio, Cansignorio arranged a second fratricide, imprisoning and then killing Paolo Alboino in early October 1375. On the nineteenth of the same month, Cansignorio himself died: he had inaugurated his lordship with one fratricide and had concluded it with another.

The sculptor Rigino di Enrico made the sarcophagus of Alberto I. His son Giovanni had the task of constructing the arches for Can Grande and Mastino II.[23] Like Mastino I, Can Grande was put outside of the sacred interior, on the left external wall of the church. He was not put into a tomb, but instead into a monument covered by a ciborium and a gilded gable. This was the first step in the construction of a true necropolis, a precinct outside and independent of the church, in the immediate vicinity of the signorial palace. Red marble pillars and four dogs holding the Scaligeri coat of arms supported the platform with the urn. Above the urn, as on a bed, lay the body of the lord, but the arch and gable over it supported an equestrian statue of Cane, with his sword in his fist and his helmet on his shoulder (Fig. 76). It was the first representation of the double image of a dead and an immortal body. Ferreto de' Ferreti (died 4 April 1337) spoke of it as a "marmoreus dux," and although the model may have been the tomb of the bishop and lord of Arezzo Guido Tarlati da Pietramala (1330), this provides a sure *ante quem* to date it. One might note, though, that in the Dussàimi arch (Verona), in the Castelbarco one (Verona, Santa Anastasia, 1320), and in those of the *glossatori bolognesi* (the jurists who wrote the *glossae* on the Justinian Code) in the Churches of San Francesco and San Domenico at Bologna, the dead person does not appear at all. Or where he does appear (in the Tarlati and Castelbarco arches, and the Rigati-Negri arch in Sant'Antonio in Padua) he is only presented lying down, in eternal sleep.

When Cansignorio, the last of the Scaligeri, died in 1375, "there was a great funeral, with horses, banners, and three hundred members of his household dressed in mourning. At two o'clock at night he was accompanied to his mausoleum by all the clergy, citizens,

18. Saraina 1649, 39r.
19. *Sonetto di Niccolò de'Rossi da Treviso*, in Cipolla Pellegrini 1902, 48.
20. Ferreto de' Ferreti 1908–20, III, *De Scaligerorum origine*, v. 532.
21. Sangiorgi 1922, 443–57.
22. *Cantare*, in Cipolla Pellegrini 1902, 73.
23. De Mattei 1955; Mellini 1971. The ground plan is also in Litta 1819–93: *Scaglieri di Verona*.

Fig. 76   The Cangrande arch at Verona (from P. Litta, *Famiglie celebri italiane*,
Milan, 1819–83).

soldiers, and people. The bier was carried by the four most famous doctors of the city."[24]
While still living, he had constructed an arch for himself in the dynastic sepulcher, which
he commissioned from Bonino da Campione (Fig. 77). At his funeral, a cleansing rite had
to be performed to free his soul from ecclesiastical censorship as a fratricide who had also
robbed property and taxes from the church. The bishops of Verona and Vicenza circulated around the tomb, sprinkling it with holy water.[25]

24. Saraina 1649, 53v.
25. Simeoni 1929, 151.

Fig. 77   The arch of Cansignorio Scaligeri at Verona (from P. Litta, *Famiglie
celebri italiane,* Milan 1819–83).

Another example of a sculpted portrait of a lord in the Po valley standing erect is on
the outside of a church (in this case the cathedral of Ferrara) across from the signorial palace: the marchese Alberto d'Este. The statue, signed by "Henricus de Colonia aurifex,"
was placed there by a public decree of 25 March 1393. The marchese is shown in the guise
of a pilgrim, as he presented himself when leading four hundred noble Ferrarese at the
jubilee of Boniface IX in 1391. But this was not a tomb, and only in the Scaligeri arches are
there the two bodies of the lord.

Some of the same themes from the Verona arches were present about the same time

in the monument for Carlo, duke of Calabria, in the Church of Santa Chiara in Naples. A
son of King Roberto, who died before his father (in 1328), his tomb was sculpted by Tino
da Camaino in 1333–38. It was a tomb of the type of Arnolfo di Cambio, with a canopy and
the body *gisant* lying on a sarcophagus. This was held up by four columns resting on lions, in front of which were four angels, and the front of the sarcophagus showed the duke
in majesty, with scepter in hand, receiving the homage of dignitaries and churchmen of
the kingdom. This might be a representation of the *lex animata,* since the bas-relief tells a
story, recalls an action, tells a fact. Carlo had been made Vicar of the Realm by his father,
and had administered justice with an almost proverbial wisdom. We remember that Cino
da Pistoia, in his *Lectura in Codicem* (1312–14), had distinguished between the bosom of the
king ("princeps debet habere omnia iura in scrinio sui pectoris" [the prince must have the
law safeguarded in his breast]) and his "court," rich in jurists "through whose mouth[es]
the most law-abiding Prince himself speaks."[26] Above the sarcophagus was a niche with
the *gisant,* for whom angels opened the curtains of heaven. Above the niche was the presentation of the defunct to the Virgin and Child, which later served as a model for the
arch of King Roberto. We find this theme also on the sarcophagus of Mastino II Scaligeri,
sculpted by Giovanni di Rigino.

   Tino da Camaino had previously executed a tomb monument in 1325–26 in another
Neapolitan church, Santa Maria Donnaregina, for the mausoleum of Maria of Hungary,
the wife of King Carlo II. But in this case the front of the sarcophagus showed the figures
of the eleven sons of the queen, put there to guard her eternal rest. A quite different
theme appeared, also in the Church of Santa Chiara in Naples, a few years after the arch
for Can Grande and the funeral monument for Carlo di Calabria, on the tomb of Roberto
of Anjou, king of Naples (who died in 1343). This monument was commissioned from
Giovanni and Pacco Bertini by Queen Giovanna (ca. 1343–35; Fig. 78). In comparison with
the simple double message of the Scaligeri tomb (the image of the body lying below and
the victorious warrior on the canopy), there were multiple themes in this last tomb. On
the canopy was sculpted the Majestas Christi, with Christ sculpted within a mandorla (a
theme we have already seen in the apotheosis of Emperor Otto III). The lower, internal
scenes were divided into four levels. At the bottom the dead man was shown kneeling and
being presented by Saint Francis and Saint Clare to the enthroned Virgin, who supports
the Christ Child standing on her right knee in a posture of benediction. On the next
higher level, the king was shown alive, enthroned, in the ceremony of the *prokypsis,* with
the *katapetàsmata* raised. On the base of the throne was the Petrarchesque inscription
"CERNITE ROBERTVM REGEM VIRTUTE REFERTVM" (see King Robert rich in virtues). On the
next higher level was another *prokypsis* (but now with the ecclesiastical symbolism of the
gates of heaven opening). The king was shown lying on his deathbed, dressed in a
Franciscan habit, holding a globe and scepter in his hands, and looked over by allegorical
figures representing the *trivium* and *quadrivium* (the liberal arts). Then, at the highest
level, on the front of the urn, the king appeared on a faldstool, a chair supported by lions,
surrounded by eight members of his family. The central focus of the whole arch was the
central panel, which showed the Angevin king in majesty, and the model for this panel
seems to me to have been the triumphal portal showing the emperor Frederick II at
Capua (Fig. 79).

26. Kantorowicz [1957] 1981, 154 n.

Fig. 78   Giovanni and Pacco Bertini, King Robert d'Anjou's arch (1343), Naples, St. Chiara.
Above, the king seated on a faldstool; below, the *prokypsis:* the king is lying down, and
the curtains of heaven are opened by two angels.

Fig. 79   Capua, the niche over the royal gate, with the statue of Frederick II seated on a
faldstool, his head and hands mutilated.

The bas-reliefs on the urns of Maria of Hungary (King Roberto's mother) and Carlo di Calabria (her grandson, the son of King Roberto) were thus both different from the one for King Roberto and also from the one for Can Grande in Verona. The first omitted the figure of the defunct lying on the sarcophagus; the second omitted the figure of the deceased in majesty. Only the monuments of Can Grande and King Roberto have a true contradistinction between the mortal body, lying down, and the ideal political body. This last became the typical arrangement in the later Angevin tombs in the Neapolitan church of San Giovanni at Carbonara.

We must finally consider another monument by Tino da Camaino, erected in honor of the emperor Henry VII (died 1313) in the Camposanto at Pisa. Here the emperor was shown enthroned (perhaps with a scepter and globe, which have disappeared with the statue's deterioration through time), surrounded by four personages of his court. We might accept the hypothesis advanced by W. Valentiner, although it is not fully proved, that under this group was an urn showing the emperor lying behind curtains. The relevance of this example would, of course, also depend on this truly being a tomb and not just a memorial monument.

Regarding this widespread representation of the monarch sitting enthroned, we can refer to "The lord our king shall sit forever," a sermon in memory of King Carlo I of Naples by the Neapolitan monk Federico Franconi, prior of St. Pietro a Castello (1337–39): "For after a prince has had a triumph, he sits."[27]

A hundred years later, in a quite different context, the contradistinction of the two bodies (or rather the doubling of the body of the deceased) was represented as a *memento mori* in England. It appears in the tombs of Henry Chicheley, the archbishop of Canterbury (died 1424; Fig. 80); of Richard Fleming, the bishop of York (died 1431), in Lincoln cathedral; of the seventh earl of Arundel, John Fitzalan (died 1435); and of Thomas Bekington, the bishop of Wells (died 1451). These attracted the attention of Kantorowicz, who did not know of the Neapolitan examples, but they are quite different from the Italian tombs. They all show a skeletal body lying inside a lower Gothic loggia, with the dead person dressed in episcopal robes or knight's armor on the slab covering the tomb. As the inscription along the sides of the Chicheley tomb reads:

> Pauper eram natus, post primas hic elevatus
> Iam sum prostratus et vermibus esca paratus
> Ecce meum tumulum . . .

> (I was born poor, but later was elevated.
> Now I am prostrate and food for worms.
> See here my grave . . .)

This macabre image also appears on the tombs of Margherita of Austria and Filberto of Savoy, in the chapel at Brou (Bourg-en-Bresse) by Michel Colombe and Girolamo da Fiesole (1499).[28] It is, of course, possible, as Kantorowicz suggested, that these double tomb images derived from funerals with the figure of the dead person carried in effigy.[29]

27. D'Avray 1994, 90.
28. Nodet 1906.
29. Kantorowicz [1957] 1981, 435–36.

But it is difficult to find a political message here, or a distinction between the *dignitas* and the person in whom the dignity was invested ("Tenens dignitatem est corruptibilis, Dignitas tamen semper est, non moritur" [He who has dignity is corruptible, but dignity itself always exists; it does not die]).

After Verona and Naples, the double body of the king returns in the monument for Pope Innocent VIII by Antonio Pollaiuolo (1492) in St. Peter's. The Cybo pope is seated on a throne, wearing the triple crown, surrounded by virtues in bas-relief, and is in the act of giving benediction. Below, his mortal remains lie on an urn.

It is difficult to find the clearly political message of the Scaligeri and Angevin tombs, or even of that of Pope Innocent VIII, with the second ideal body of the monarch represented alive and in majesty, in the now lost tomb of King Charles VIII of France (died 1498), where a statue of the king, kneeling in prayer, was placed over the sarcophagus. This second theme was repeated at Saint-Denis on the three tombs for Louis XII and Anne de Bretagne (Jean Juste, 1517–31), Francis I and Claude de France (Philibert Delorme and Pierre Bontemps, 1548–58), and Henry II and Catherine de' Medici (Primaticcio and Germain Pilon, 1565–70). The difficulty arises from the resemblance of the praying kings and queens to the donors painted into religious pictures. In fact, the royal couples are shown on their knees, praying on the top of the burial chamber (or chapel), while the *memento mori* below shows the bodies *en transis,* without omitting, for Louis XII and Anne de Bretagne, the realistic details of embalming, with their stomachs cut open and hastily sewn up (Fig. 81). This macabre sentiment disgusted Catherine de' Medici, who rejected

Fig. 80   The tomb of Archbishop Henry Chicheley (1424), Canterbury cathedral.

the statue by Girolamo della Robbia that showed her old and skeletal. She preferred to be shown in the flower of her youth, sleeping beside her husband (on a marriage bed rather than the cold marble of a sarcophagus), her nakedness prudently covered by a sheet rather than a shroud. Henry is shown with the veins in his neck swollen, in his death agony, while Catherine has her eyes closed; she is more a beautiful woman asleep than a dead body.

Erwin Panofsky, followed by Kathleen Cohen,[30] saw in these monuments, on the basis of the cliché of increasing paganism in the Renaissance, the passage from an agonized concern for the salvation of the soul to a pagan glorification of one's past. Even though the tomb of Francis I clearly shows a triumphal arch with three openings, it seems to me that all three of the tomb chambers at Saint-Denis still kept the *memento mori* intact in meaning. If one is looking for a different kind of monument, showing the earthly glory of the prince, it is to be found more in the clear distinction between the natural and political bodies in the Scaligeri and Angevin tombs. It is to be noted that in the tombs at Saint-Denis the *gisants* cover their genitals in the same way as in the Deposed Christ in the Tomb sculpted by the same Pilon (ca. 1540–54),[31] which was perhaps modeled on the nude *Pietà* by Rosso Fiorentino, now in the Louvre.[32] "Surprisingly constant is the gesture of the self-touch in many figured scenes of the Entombment or Lamentation. That the

Fig. 81   Antonio and Giovanni Giusti, the tomb of Louis XII and Anne de Bretagne (1515–31), showing where the two corpses were opened and then sewn up after embalming, Abbey of Saint-Denis.

30. Panofsky 1964; Cohen 1973.
31. Steinberg 1986, fig. 117.
32. Steinberg 1986, 134.

placing of the hand in these instances is a gesture seems to me indeed undeniable."[33] Steinberg even indicates the first funeral monument where touching the genitals was attributed to a dying person: the tomb of the doctor Guillaume de Harcigny at Laon, who died in 1393, after having cured King Charles VI several times.[34] We are, thus, far from an exaltation of the glories of the earth.

To escape the desperate sense of death represented by bodies in a state of decomposition, we must turn to the family members praying around and with the kings sculpted by Pompeo Leoni for the tombs of Charles V and Philip II in the Escorial (1595–98), or to the tombs of two cardinals, Georges d'Amboise (died 1510) and his son Georges d'Amboise (died 1550), at Rouen sculpted by Rouland de Roux. Within sculpted enclosures of incredible richness, the statues of the defunct, in the latter instances, are shown kneeling in prayer in all the splendor of their pontifical vestments.[35] But still, in all of these cases the doubling of the body we were looking for, with the contradistinction between *dignitas* and *tenens dignitatem,* is missing. The defunct are still faithful Christians praying on their knees.

Interest in the royal necropolis at Saint-Denis lessened during the seventeenth and eighteenth centuries. It is surprising to see, for example, how simple and low-key was the sepulcher of the king who compared himself to the sun. The tomb of Louis XIV is not even located at the level of the nave of the basilica, but instead in the wall of the crypt. This forgetfulness showed the dawning Enlightenment's disrespect for the Middle Ages. Contempt for the "Gothic" even infected the religious of the Abbey of Saint-Denis (just as it infected the canons of the cathedral of Valladolid, who, in 1809, glorified the destruction of what—judging from the ruins—must have been a splendid church, by the architect of the Escorial, with the erection of a stone marker inside their new building).[36] At Saint-Denis in 1781, the prior, D. Maleret, submitted a proposal to comte d'Angivilier, the royal director of monuments, to free the main altar from the tombs that surrounded it and to move those in the choir.[37] A few years later the iconoclastic French Revolution did even worse. A decree of the National Assembly on 14 August 1792 ordered the destruction of "all the statues, bas-reliefs, inscriptions, and any other kind of monument, in bronze or any other material," that recalled the monarchy "in public places, churches, gardens, parks, or their environs," and the destruction as well of all the monuments of feudalism. This decree was followed by the sacrilege committed by the Convention on 1 August 1793, following a report prepared for the Committee of Public Safety by Bertrand de Vieuzac Barère. To justly commemorate the *journée* of 10 August, when the monarchy had been overthrown, the Convention ordered destruction of the French royal tombs.[38] Thus sentence was pronounced on the necropolis, and the expiatory ceremonies ordered by Louis XVIII under the Restoration, which were followed by the attempt to restore the tombs, could not replace the destroyed monuments. Nor did the work subsequently commis-

33. Steinberg 1996, 94.
34. Steinberg 1996, 202–9. But see also Cohen 1973, fig. 1.
35. Pilon 1887, 230–37; Blunt 1954, 17.
36. See Bertelli 1990a, 19.
37. Vitry and Brière 1908, 88–89.
38. "Dans la monarchie, les tombeaux mêmes avaient appris à flatter les rois. L'orgueil et le faste royale ne pouvaient s'adoucir sur ce théâtre de la mort, et les porte-sceptres qui ont fait tant de maux à la France et à l'humanité, semblent encore, dans la tombe, s'enorgueillir d'une grandeur évanouie. La main puissante de la République doit effacer impitoyablement ces épitaphes superbs et démolir ces mausolées qui rappelleraient encore des rois l'effrayant souvenir." Vitry and Brière 1908, 91–93.

sioned to the architect François Debret have any more success.[39] As the comte de Montalembert complained in the Chamber of Peers on 26 July 1847: "The interior of Saint-Denis is now only an unsightly hodgepodge of monuments, the rubble of different times and styles in incredible confusion: a museum of jumbled bric-a-brac, where anachronisms are countless."[40]

The theme of the defunct in majesty on a prayer stool, with two angels opening the gates of heaven, was resolved genially (it could not have been otherwise) by Michelangelo for the tombs of Lorenzo and Giuliano de' Medici in the sacristy of San Lorenzo in Florence. Away with the dead bodies of Christian piety; away with prayer stools and devout figures praying! But this was not simply a return to the majesty of King Roberto of Anjou in Naples. Lorenzo and Giuliano de' Medici are seated, leaning slightly forward in thought; their faces have neither the joy of victory of the lord of Verona nor the immobile and haughty glance of the Angevin king. War and glory are in their armor. But even the curtains of heaven have disappeared, to be replaced by volutes on the covers of the sarcophagi.[41] At the lower level, close to the spectator, instead of angels are the nude figures of Night, Day, Dawn, and Dusk. This typology was repeated in the funeral monument for Pope Paul III Farnese by Guglielmo della Porta (1549), at least in its last relocation by Urban VIII (1628), and also in a monument for this same Barberini pope by Gian Lorenzo Bernini, who has allegories of Justice and Charity descending from the volutes they are leaning on.

But in Florence, while Michelangelo was still living, there was a further replication of the royal theme of the Scaligeri and Angevins. The construction of a third sacristy for San Lorenzo, the church of the Medici family that had been elevated to a basilica to make it equal to the cathedral, had already been planned under Grand Duke Cosimo I de' Medici. It was to contain the tombs of the grand dukes. Instead, in 1602 a competition was announced, not for a sacristy, but instead for a mausoleum independent of the church. It was said that the greatest ambition of this project was to transfer "the sepulcher of the Redeemer with the assistance of Faccardino [Fakhr ad-Din II], grand emir of the Druze, . . . from the capital of Judea, and bring it here."[42] That the grand duke Ferdinando I would have entertained such a sacrilegious project (of putting the Medici tombs in the empty tomb of Christ) is doubtful, and not believed even by the chronicler Moreni. But to the Florentine popular mind this seemed symptomatic of the grandeur of the project. Another plan was to build a great ciborium in the midst of the basilica.

The final plan was drawn up by the architect Bernardo Buontalenti with assistance from Don Giovanni de' Medici in 1602–4.[43] One reads in the chronicle of Francesco Settimanni:

On the day 6 August 1604, the grand duke, having selected the place near the Church of San Lorenzo for building a sumptuous chapel, at 14 ½ o'clock, Friday, the day of the passion of Our Lord, S.A.S., went to the place with the court, and gave his firstborn son,

39. Vitry and Brière 1908, 99.
40. Vitry and Brière 1908, 101. On the restoration by Viollet-le-Duc in 1847–67, based on the documentation of Baron Roche, see Guilhermy 1848.
41. Battisti 1966, 1:517–30.
42. Moreni 1813, 201.
43. Moreni 1813, 330 and passim.

Prince Don Cosimo, a golden pick, with which he broke the ground, and taking a golden
trowel, he put some earth into a gilded basket, thus beginning the work on the foundations. And the ceremony finished, the grand duke said, "This will be our end."[44]

But the previous grand duke, Francesco I, whose interest in magic and alchemy are
well known, had in addition thought of an edifice decorated with "precious stones, chalcedony, quartz, sardonyx, agates, and jaspers of different colors,"[45] to capture the occult
powers contained in such gemstones. He also wanted porphyry, an emblem of imperial
dignity,[46] which he had secretly discovered how to work. In 1609 Costantino de' Servi was
sent to eastern Europe and Asia to procure jaspers from Bohemia and lapis lazuli from
Persia;[47] other Medici agents searched for jaspers from Corsica and Sicily; Oriental trans-
parent chalcedony was sought in Spain; agates from Goa were imported from Portugal.
Inlaid onto black marble, these semiprecious stones were worked in a laboratory that was
first organized by Francesco I in the Casino di San Marco and then moved in 1588 by
Ferdinando I to the first floor of the Uffizi.[48] The best artisans for inlaying precious stones
were employed. Teofilo Gallaccini wrote in a letter to Niccolò Tornioli that "in Florence
at the time of Grand Duke Ferdinando I the art of inlaying precious stones was invented,
using gems, precious stones, lapis lazuli, jasper, amethyst, and others. . . . They make land-
scapes, figures, historical scenes, the arms of the principal cities of the grand duchy, to be
placed among the ornaments in the Chapel of Their Highnesses of Tuscany in San
Lorenzo."[49] The collection of precious stones was not used only for the burial chapel. The
Church of SS. Annunziata was also paneled with them, since the icon of the Virgin Mary
preserved there had a particular sacredness associated with the dukes.[50] One sees what
value was attributed to the possession, working, and display of precious stones. A further
occult aspect of this work was discovery of the *mana* contained in each stone, which was
outlined by its imperfections. Constantino de' Servi was charged with the work of "dis-
covering imperfections to adapt [the stones] to the marvelous works of art made from
them . . . by seeking to find" what "nature had done for itself."[51] Thus one might capture
the fantasies of nature. The importance of this industry is indicated by a ducal proclamation of 10 July 1602 (at the same time as the proclamation of the competition for the de-
sign of the burial chapel) prohibiting subjects from dealing in semiprecious stones, which
were to be reserved "for the honor of God."[52] This was not only to establish a ducal mo-
nopoly but also to find out the deep secrets of nature that made one enter into contact
with divinity and to prevent others from having access to the occult powers involved.
Prince Don Lorenzo de' Medici on one occasion gave to an assistant of the painter Cigoli,
the Flemish master Giovanni Bilivert, "a tawny-colored silken cloak, as a vow, for his
liberation from sickness,"[53] as if wearing it would increase the painter's already remarkable artistic ability.

44. Zobi 1841, 94–95.
45. Berti 1957, 123. See also *Splendori* 1989.
46. Lucci 1964, 237ff.; Zobi 1841, 103ff. For the significance of porphyry, see M. C. Marchei in Borghini 1989, 274.
47. Baldinucci 1702–28, I:5–6; Giusti 1989.
48. Zobi 1841, 89–92.
49. Cited in Zobi 1841, 25. See also Macchiori 1984, 219–26.
50. Fantoni 1994, 171ff.
51. Baldinucci 1702–28, I:8–9.
52. Zobi 1841, 177–80.
53. Baldinucci 1702–28, II:71.

The ciborium for the altar of the chapel was designed to be the center of a mandorla that recalled the earlier constructed Tribune in the Uffizi. This had the form of an octagonal temple (a profane *sancta sanctorum*), planned by Duke Francesco I with the assistance of Buontalenti to hold the most valuable works of art.[54] Cabinets extended along the lower part of the walls, with drawers where "the most precious jewels and other fine objects of the grand duke"[55] were kept, that is, the medals and cameos of the Medici collection, a magical treasure that included the collection of Lorenzo the Magnificent, who dared to engrave on each one of them the inscription "LAV.R." (Laurentius rex),[56] an ambitious title that he had found otherwise unattainable under a republic. On the walls of the Uffizi Tribune, Gianbologna had depicted the Labors of Hercules, and statues were arranged all around, depicting the four elements (earth, water, air, and fire). The Tribune, in short, was "a sacred place where the dignity of the prince *dei gratia* was celebrated, an aspect of the cosmological system designed by God."[57]

The construction of the burial chapel became a grandiose undertaking, one on which the Medici lavished the resources of their state to enhance its occult power.[58] Those who have interpreted it as a waste of resources, as a Renaissance folly, as a merchant family's conspicuous consumption, or even as a revival of antiquity, miss this essential feature. Such great expenditure is not made without a political and religious motive, which was already present in the earlier burial chapel designed by Michelangelo.[59] To heap up, in the city center, in the place most sacred to the Medici family, so many precious stones—to find the secret "imperfections" in them that were understood to be the occult virtues of the stones themselves, their secret natures—was an ambitious project meant to ensure the long life of the dynasty. It was not by chance that the Medici dukes were presented in the interior, standing and dressed in their ducal mantles in effigies of gilded bronze (*tenentes dignitatem*) above sarcophagi, from which the *momento mori,* however, had disappeared.

When the Medici were replaced by the Hapsburg-Lorraine, who were culturally quite distant from them, the last Medici, Anna Maria Luisa, a daughter of Grand Duke Cosimo III, petitioned Francis Stephen of Lorraine for the use of all the materials stored up in the Uffizi awaiting completion of the burial chapel. On her death, in 1743, she directed in her will that a part of the revenue from her estate be used "and should be used to continue, finish, and perfect . . . the said famous chapel with the same nobility and priority employed up to the present." Thus the last Medici felt upon her shoulders the weight of saving the project by which her ancestors had been known for generations. Not to complete the chapel would have endangered the eternal repose of her family.

The Hapsburg-Lorraine, a quite bourgeois dynasty, saw the laboratory for working precious stones merely as a workshop for luxury items and did not (or did not want to) understand the religious and occult imperatives that stood behind its initial foundation. In the twenty-eight years of his reign (1737–65) Francis Stephen only visited the workshop once, in 1739. His son, the archduke Peter Leopold, who was influenced by the severe

54. On the octagonal shape, consider the Castel del Monte of Emperor Frederick II in Puglia. For the chapel, see Moreni 1813; for the Tribune, Heikamp 1984, 1989a, 1989b, 1997.

55. Del Riccio [1597] 1996, 144.

56. Dacos 1973, 137.

57. Heikamp 1989b, 53.

58. On this, see De Tolnay 1934 and 1969.

59. See Tietze-Conrat 1954; Ettlinger 1978; Przyborowski 1982.

Jansenism of the bishop Scipione de' Ricci, did not even want to hear mention of ciboriums or altars for a necropolis, which for that matter was not even his. In 1779 he disbanded the laboratory for working precious stones in the Uffizi[60] and dispersed its various elements, each one of which earlier had a precise value within a predetermined discourse: the formation of a mandorla for the Medici grand duchy.

Of the many reliquaries that filled the Palazzo Pitti, he had some melted down for their precious metals and gave some to churches, especially those made of wood, according to the adage "chiacchiere e tabacchiere di legno, il Monte non dà pegno" (the Monte [pawnshop] does not make loans on gossip or wooden snuff boxes).

60. For more on the workshop, see Ricci 1597; in general, Chastel 1983; Cresti 1989.

The Body Denied

JUST AS A COMMUNITY RECOGNIZED itself in a mystical body, it could also reject that body when it was perceived to be a danger to the community's cohesion. In ancient Greece a leader who did not have royal blood in his veins was called a *tyrannos*. In the Middle Ages in the West, the term changed its meaning, shifting the emphasis rather to the contract, the relationship that tied the prince to his subjects. The Visigothic maxim "rex eris si recte facias, et si non facias, non eris" (you will be king if you rule rightly, otherwise not) was translated by the Aragonese *fueros* in the oath of fidelity to the Crown: "y si no, no" (yes, if no, no).[1] Aristotle justified revolt against a tyrant in his *Politics* (1311a). Saint Thomas Aquinas admitted in the *Summa theologie* (II, *Quaesito* 42) that "sedition is a mortal sin, but revolt against a tyrant cannot be called sedition, because this revolt aims to preserve the common good" (*bonum commune*), while a tyrant aims only to fulfill his own interest (*bonum privatum*). "Regimen igitur tyranni est iniustissimus" (the government of a tyrant is the most unjust). The jurist Bartolo da Sassoferrato, in his *De tyrannia,* defined a tyrant as someone who kept the city divided. Such a one was to be held guilty on the basis of the Roman *lex Julia majestatis*. Coluccio Salutati, at the beginning of the fifteenth century, spoke of tyranny *ex exercitio,* which he distinguished from tyranny *ex defectu tituli* (which was closer to the ancient Greek concept). King Alfonso X (the Wise) of Leon and Castile, in his *Partidas,* returned to the Italian jurists' concept of a *bonum privatum* contrasted with a *bonum commune*. He explained that "a cruel lord is called a tyrant, one who takes possession of a realm or city with force, trickery, or betrayal: and the nature of such men, when they have taken power, is to follow their private interest, even if it damages the city, rather than the common good."[2]

Thus the tyrant was someone who threatened the social group. To repair the broken unity, it was necessary to carry out a series of rituals opposite and contrary to those of coronation: a dethronement. The translation of this violent process into an expulsion always resulted in a catharsis.[3] But if rites of expulsion are widespread throughout almost all regions and cultures of the world, they do not always present themselves or persist in the same form. For example, it is telling that in an American context, influenced by frontier vigilantism, the verb "lynch" was often the equivalent of "hang." A newspaper

---

1. Giesey 1968.
2. *Las Sietes Partidas* 1807, II, para. 1, ley X, II:11.
3. Girard 1972, 431; see also Mousnier 1964, 47–90.

account of the barbarous assassination of four young blacks in Shubuta (Mississippi) in December 1918 says they were "lynched on a bridge."[4] In the Far West at the time of the Gold Rush, lynch law was basically capital punishment by hanging. In the deep South, the lynching of a black person could take two forms: one was summary justice by hanging of the guilty or suspects taken from a prison, as in the case of the vigilantism of the West;[5] the second was a burning that completely expelled the victim from the social body. In January 1911, at Shelbyville (Tennessee), as reported in the *Chicago Tribune,* two young Negroes accused of insulting white women were taken from jail, together with another black convict who was awaiting a death sentence. "All three Negroes pleaded for their lives but the lynchers paid no attention to them. The lynching was devoid of the minor brutalities that frequently mark such occasions. There was no abuse of the prisoners. The mob was made up of quiet, determined men whose mission was to execute but not to torture."[6] Again, in 1904, in an incident that seems to hark back to medieval European violence of the seventeenth century, a Negro from Doddsville (Mississippi) who had killed a white planter in a dispute was taken with his wife, and both were lynched. As the *Evening Post* of Vicksburg reported:

> They were tied to trees, and while the funeral pyres were being prepared they were forced to suffer the most fiendish tortures. The blacks were forced to hold out their hands, while one finger at a time was chopped off. The fingers were distributed as souvenirs. The ears were cut off. . . . The most excruciating form of punishment consisted in the use of a large corkscrew in the hands of some of the mob. This instrument was bored into the flesh of the man and woman, in the arms, legs, and body, and then pulled out, the spirals tearing out big pieces of raw, quivering flesh every time it was withdrawn.[7]

An act of Congress in 1941 defined lynching as follows:

> Any assemblage of three or more persons which shall exercise or attempt to exercise by physical violence and without authority of law any power of correction or punishment over any citizen or citizens or other person or persons in the custody of any peace officer, or suspected of, charged with, or convicted of the commission of any offense, with the purpose or consequence of preventing the apprehension or trial or punishment by law of such citizen or citizens, person or persons, shall constitute a "mob" within the meaning of this Act. Any such violence by a mob which results in the death or maiming of the victim or victims thereof shall constitute "lynching" within the meaning of this Act.[8]

Despite the many similarities, we must be careful not to compare lynch law too closely with the behavior of European crowds in the Middle Ages and early modern period. In a context dominated by Roman law, which rarely knew vacancies of authority like those in American mining camps (the refuge of many convicts escaped from Australia), the verb

---

4. NAACP 1969, 27.
5. See Garnett and Williams 1910 and 1911; Raper 1969.
6. Shay n.d., 134. See also McGovern 1982 and Masur 1989.
7. Shay n.d., 104.
8. Ames 1942, 22. See also Cutler 1905.

"lynch" often meant something quite different from "provide for the lack or delay of justice," its original meaning.

Orest Ranum, in studying the active participation of the people of Paris in the torture and capital execution of Ravaillac (the assassin of King Henry IV in 1610), understood intuitively (although he had been anticipated by Natalie Z. Davis)[9] that the crowd followed a precise ritual. But we cannot accept his hypothesis that this ritual resulted from "the tradition of sermons and iconography about the deaths and triumphs of martyrs." Ranum continues: "The scenes I have just described have their graphic and literary foundations in the experiences early Christians suffered at the hands of centurions and the Roman populace. If Ravaillac's body had not been consumed by fire, I think that—by paralleling with martyrologies—we might also predict how the ritual would have terminated. Every piece of the corpse would have been collected carefully and venerated in churches as a relic."[10] Aside from the cliché about Christian martyrs (Ranum seems not to have known of the study by Jean Bayet),[11] how far he is from the truth can be easily understood by considering that crowds usually destroyed the body of the "tyrant." Nor can these violent acts be explained as sympathetic acts. "Official acts of torture and official acts of desecration of the corpses of certain criminals anticipate some of the acts performed by riotous crowds."[12] If we deconstruct the particular actions of crowds in the different time sequences they occurred, I think that we will be able to see that these followed a precise ritual that was culturally acquired.[13]

Ravaillac, who had committed the crime of regicide, had in a certain sense captured the *mana* of the king, and consequently the crowd was motivated to collaborate with the executioner and his assistants in completely destroying the body of one who had attacked the *bonum commune*. Ravaillac, in this lynching, appeared both as a tyrant and as a scapegoat. His body had to be completely destroyed, and it was irrelevant if in this process some parts of it were symbolically eaten. The dismemberment of his body was similar to what happened to the ancient Christian king Oswald of Northumbria after the battle of Maserfeld (5 August 641). Oswald was slain by the pagan king Penda of Mercia; "caput et manus cum brachiis a corpore recisas, iussit rex qui occiderat, in stipibus suspendi" (his head and his hands and arms cut from the body, the king [Penda] ordered that they be hung from the stirrups).[14]

The more a community recognized itself as a mystical body, the more the community was called to repudiate the body of a leader when he was perceived to be a danger to its cohesion. "Dead pagans shall be cast out from the places of saints," intoned Theodore, archbishop of Canterbury (ca. 668–90).[15] The bodies of pagans would have profaned a Christian cemetery! We know that Sulla profaned the tomb of the consul Marius, to expel his body from Rome;[16] a similar fate, after a macabre trial, was applied to the remains of Pope Romanus Formoso in 897.

The tyrant was thus someone who threatened social cohesion. But, as Alfonso the

---

9. "[C]rowds do not act in a mindless way." Davis 1973, 91.
10. Ranum 1980.
11. Bayet 1957.
12. Davis 1973, 62.
13. See Detienne and Vernant 1979; Burkert 1983; Burkert, Girard, and Smith 1987.
14. Beda 1930, 1:386 (*Historia*, II, 12).
15. Canon 6 in McNeill and Gamer 1938, 216.
16. See Calore 1995. In general, on the forms of exclusion and rejection in ancient Rome, see Crifò 1985.

Wise, king of Leon and Castile, wrote, a usurper was also to be considered a tyrant, someone who deprived the *polis* of its legitimate sovereign or who lacked divine investiture. To repair the broken unity, a series of countermeasures had to be set in motion, which we can recognize as a reversal of the coronation rites. Paraphrasing Theodore of Canterbury, we could say that anyone who threatened the *bonum commune* could no longer remain within the community.

Naturally these rites did not remain the same through the centuries. In Homeric Greece, the most ancient example is that of *aikìa,* the expulsion of the enemy's body to completely cancel its memory. Achilles performed on the body of Hector a series of rites that reversed burial: he dug him up to disfigure him, to deprive him of power, of sex (Homer speaks of "devoured sex"), of his facial features. Instead of purifying the body, washing and anointing it, *aikìa* involved dirtying it, taking off the skin, destroying its individuality.[17] When the emperor Commodius was murdered (A.D. 192), the Roman crowds and the senate significantly changed the laudatory chants that accompanied an imperial enthronement into cries such as "The enemy of the fatherland, the murderer, the gladiator. Let him be mangled in the *spoliarium* [the place in the amphitheater where wounded gladiators were eliminated]! Let the murderer be dragged! Let the slayer of citizens be dragged! Let him be dragged by a hook!"[18] These rites, tied particularly to ceremonies of dethronement, were inherited, in more elaborated forms, by European crowds of the Middle Ages.

In A.D. 415, when Priscus Attalus, a usurper and agent of the Visigoths, was captured, he was presented to the emperor Honorius at Ravenna. His punishment was to have his right hand cut off, the hand that held the scepter, the baton of command. The same fate was suffered by another usurper, Johannes, at the beginning of the reign of Galla Placida and Emperor Valerian III. In the arena at Aquileia his hand was cut off, and he was ritually insulted with the kind of cries used by crowds along the route of a *triumphus infamantis.*[19] A more vehement triumph of this type was enacted at Constantinople in 488, when the emperor Zeno celebrated his victory over his colleagues Illus Isaurius and Leontius with a parade of severed heads that ended in the Hippodrome, after which the heads were exhibited before the Church of St. Conone in Syca.[20] In 602, when Phocas rebelled against the emperor Maurice, the bodies of the sovereign, his sons, and his closest followers were dragged through the streets of Constantinople and burned in the form used for slaughtering cattle.[21] Another cruel parade of infamy was the one suffered by a thousand Archemenides who rebelled against the emperor Constantine VI. On 24 June 793 they were marched through Constantinople with the words "archemenus conspirator" cut onto their disfigured faces.[22] The idea of disfiguring the face was easily linked to a culture like that of Byzantium, which gave such importance to iconographic representation. When the emperor Justinian II was deposed after a popular revolt in A.D. 695, and before his exile in the Crimea, his nose was cut off to signify his loss of power (so that he received the nickname Rhinotmetus [nose cut off]). Still, this was a less cruel fate than the one suf-

17. Vernant 1989, 78ff.
18. SHA, Commodus, 18. See Aldrete 1999, 131.
19. Johannes Malalas 1940, 8–18.
20. McCormick 1986, 60.
21. Nicephorus of Constantinople 1837, 5.3–7; *Chronicon paschale* 1832, 700. 12–13; McCormick 1986, 70.
22. Theophanes 1883, A.M. 6285, 469. 11–14; Speck 1978, 1:249–50.

fered in the twelfth century by Andronicus I Comnenus, who was castrated and then mur-dered by his subjects.[23]

Another parade of infamy occurred on 13 April 989, in the Forum of Constantinople, after the triumphal entry of Basil II and Constantine VIII to celebrate their defeat of Bardas Phocas. The head of the usurper was exhibited in procession and exposed to the ritual insults of the people.[24] In 1042, when the eunuch Stephanus Pergamenus defeated the usurper Georgios Maniakes, he sent the head to the emperor Constantine IX, who had it carried in procession through the streets of Constantinople. But even in this case hierarchy and rules of precedence were respected: the head of the usurper came at the end of the procession, after the heads of his defeated companions.[25] Another different punishment for usurpers that was frequently used was blinding. The emperor John IV Lascaris was deposed and blinded in 1259.

In many of these cases, as we see, the crowds in Constantinople pressed to participate in these events, although their participation seems to have been limited to shouting ritual insults. The medieval and early modern European masses had a more active role in the dethroning of usurpers (or those who represented them or bore their insignia). A few ex-amples will suffice to illustrate these particular rituals of violence. But in reading them, keep in mind the salient points of an enthronement:

1. Investment.
2. Placing a miter or crown on the head.
3. Consignment of the insignia of rule: a pastoral staff or scepter.
4. Presentation to the people (*acclamatio*).
5. Sitting on a gestatorial chair (*anàtellon*).
6. A cleansing procession recognizing territory.
7. The true and proper seating on the throne.

From the medieval and early modern period, let us examine a few episodes of dethrone-ment among those that are the best documented.

In September 1342 Walter de Brienne, duke of Athens, was named signore of Flor-ence for life. But on 26 July of the year following, the city rebelled against his domination, and the duke was obliged to surrender to the crowd, in his stead, his own "protector of the laws," Guglielmo d'Assisi, and his son Gabriele.

Cola di Rienzo was certainly someone with whom Romans identified at a moment when the absence of the pope (it was in the time of the "Babylonian Captivity" of the popes at Avignon) had left the city leaderless, creating a political/sacred vacuum. Be-tween May and August of 1347, the notary Cola di Rienzo proclaimed himself "Candidatus Spiritus Sancti miles, liberator Urbis, Tribunus augustus" (Soldier of the Holy Spirit, Liberator of Rome, August Tribune). This last adjective, *augustus,* expressed his presumption of sacredness, which Cola attempted to enhance by pretending to be the (illegitimate) son of the emperor Henry VII. His "classical" triumph, celebrated in August 1354 on his return from Avignon, was to have completed his recognition as a *divus*. But at

23. There is a miniature of this scene in the Boccaccio of the BNP, reproduced in Ducellier 1986, 167.
24. McCormick 1986, 177.
25. McCormick 1986, 180–82.

this point the Roman plebes refused further recognition of him, exasperated as they were by the fiscal burdens that Cola, in his megalomania, had continually increased.

In 1476 the duke of Milan was murdered by a group of conspirators, including Andrea Lampugnani and Girolamo Olgiati. In this case, the attackers were the ones who suffered the rite of expulsion, and we will see why presently.

In 1478 the Pazzi, with the support and encouragement of Pope Sixtus IV, conspired against Lorenzo and Giuliano de' Medici, the leaders of the faction that dominated Florence. Giuliano was murdered in the cathedral; Lorenzo saved himself by taking refuge in the sacristy. Immediately, a vendetta of the Medici party was unleashed against the opposing faction, with active participation of the Florentine plebes.

Girolamo Riario, nephew of Pope Sixtus, had bought the signoria of Imola from Galeazzo Maria Sforza in 1473. But this was a purchased lordship; he was not the natural lord. Nor did his subsequent marriage with the daughter of Sforza, Caterina, modify this "usurpation" of the lordship. When a series of external factors—the death of his papal uncle and the hatred of Lorenzo the Magnificent from Florence for his having been the one to organize the Pazzi conspiracy—brought on his isolation, it did not take much on the part of the local nobility and the people of Imola to conclude that he was a "tyrant."

Pier Luigi Farnese, the son of Pope Paul III, was also considered a tyrant by the local nobility: the Anguissola, Landi, and Pallavicino families. Strengthened by the external support of Ferrante Gonzaga and the consent of Emperor Charles V, on 10 September 1547 these stabbed Farnese at Parma and threw his body from a window into the moat.[26]

Again in Florence, Giuliano Buonaccorsi made an assassination attempt on Duke Cosimo I de' Medici. He was discovered and condemned to die after being tortured and burned with hot irons along the route from the Bargello (the Palace of Justice) to the scaffold (the so-called trip),[27] and after the execution his body was desecrated by the Florentine plebes, who thus completed the act of dethronement.

After the assassination of King Henry IV, Concino Concini, the favorite of Marie de' Medici, assumed nearly absolute power due to the minor age of Louis XIII. In 1610 he bought the marquisate of Ancre, and three years later the queen made him maréchal de France. He was thus a foreigner and minister to a foreign queen (from the same family as the execrated Queen Catherine, who had been tainted by the massacre of the night of Saint Bartholomew in 1572!). When the young king found no better means to end the regency than to order the murder of the maréchal d'Ancre, the people of Paris took revenge on his body and carried out a complete rite of dethronement.

Johan de Witt had been the grand pensioner of Holland in the Republic of the United Provinces of the Low Countries, and governed in the terrible times of the Dutch War with England under Cromwell and with France under Louis XIV. But he had to resign in 1672 because of the rise of the Orange party. Not able to strike against him personally, his opponents accused his brother Cornelius of plotting against Prince William. A compliant tribunal condemned him to exile. But the crowd of Orange supporters besieged the prison, and when Johan went there in his carriage to rescue Cornelius, hoping to carry him to safety, he was surrounded by the lynch mob and killed along with his brother.

26. Gosellini 1864.
27. Fineschi 1995, 39–51.

I will give some different attention also, at the end of the chapter, to the case of the Neapolitan fishmonger Tommasso Aniello, who was involved in the 1647 revolt at Naples that bears his name.

Let us begin to examine witnesses to these episodes of popular violence, which we will compare with others of equal value but less historical importance.

In Florence, on 26 July 1343, the crowd pressed its assault on the priors' palace, with Walter de Brienne, duke of Athens, enclosed within. At the same time, functionaries and ministers of ducal justice, who had not taken refuge in the palace, were being hunted down. The chronicler Marchionne di Coppo Stefani writes as follows:

> While the Florentine people besieged the duke and fought for the palace for the liberty of the city, some officials of the duke were found, among whom were a notary and some of the household of the *conservatore* [of laws], who were put to death through the fury of the people. Messer Simone da Norcia, a justice who had condemned many citizens from his bench, and in his punishments had seemed crueler than was needed and had decapitated many, met the same fate. The captain of the duke's household, a Neapolitan who was a notary, when taken, was cut to bits. Ser Arrigo Fei, who had been the duke's deputy in the tax office, an astute man who sought out fraud, fled dressed as a friar, but was recognized at the city gates and killed. Then the youths of the city got hold of him, tore off his clothes, and dragged him through the city until they reached the piazza, where the low people hung him by the feet from a gallows and stuck him like a pig. And some of his followers were treated badly.[28]

Giovanni Villani writes: "A *notaio* of the *conservatore* for the Altoviti, a murderer and criminal, was cut to pieces. And then Messer Simone da Norcia, who had been an accountant for the commune and had cruelly tormented and condemned many citizens, some rightly and some wrongly, was found and likewise cut to bits. A Neapolitan notary called Filippo Terzuoli, a criminal and felon, who was captain of the foot soldiers of the duke, was taken at the ditch by Por Santa Maria and cut to bits by the people."[29] The lynching of Ser Arrigo Fei occurred on 30 July and was also described by Giovanni Villani: "fleeing up [Via] de' Servi dressed as a friar," he was recognized at Porta San Gallo, "dragged naked through the city by youths, and then in the Piazza dei Priori he was hung by the feet, stuck like a pig, and left there."[30] Other details are added by an anonymous chronicler from Pistoia: "He was dragged by youths through the city, and then tied in the Piazza del Palagio del Duca [Piazza della Signoria] by the feet, like a pig, and hung from a hitching post, and stuck through; his heart was torn from his body and carried on a lance point throughout Florence."[31]

We deduce from this that during the rebellion, while Walter de Brienne was closed within the palace/fortress of the priors, the people carried out a series of vendettas against his officials, as if these were the very person of the duke. Note that the bodies were taken over by youths, dragged through the city streets to the Piazza della Signoria,

28. Marchionne di Coppo Stefani 1903, 208.
29. Villani 1823, VII:51.
30. Villani 1823.
31. *Storie pistoresi* 1907, 190–91.

the sacred ground of civic authority. Note also that there occurred a reversal of the *anàtellon* (the hanging by the feet) and a dismembering of the body.[32] I will discuss this further below.

After five days of siege, the duke was obliged by his Burgundian soldiers to abandon to the Florentines—led by the families who had most suffered from ducal persecution—his own *conservatore delle leggi* (protector of the laws) Guglielmo d'Assisi and his son Gabriele. We can follow the testimony of Giovanni Villani:

> On the first of August, about dinnertime, the Burgundians took Messer Guglielmo d'Assisi, called the protector of the duke of Athens's tyranny, and his son called Messer Gabriello, an eighteen-year-old recently knighted by the duke but also a criminal and felon for tormenting the citizens, and pushed him [Gabriello] out the door of the palace into the hands of the enraged people and the relatives and friends of those his father had sentenced, Altoviti, Medici, Oricellai, and the relatives of Pettone Cini above all, and others. And in the presence of the father, and to his sorrow, the son pushed outside was dismembered and cut into little pieces. And this done, they pushed out the protector and the same was done, and some carried bits on lances, and some on swords through the city; and some were so cruel and animated by bestial fury that they ate their flesh raw.[33]

The *Vita di Cola di Rienzo,* written by an anonymous author in Roman dialect, contains one of the most detailed accounts of a lynching, which is worth quoting almost in its entirety:

> Now I will tell of the death of the tribune. . . . He was a rather virtuous man who wanted the Lordship of the People; and they cut off his head pitilessly without any reason. His death disturbed all of Rome. . . . It was the eighth of September. Cola di Rienzo was in bed. . . . Suddenly voices cried, "Long live the people! Long live the people!" At this cry people ran here and there in the streets. The cries got louder and the crowd increased. Armed men came to the crossroads at the market, from Sant'Angelo and from the Ripa, and others from Colonna and Trevi.. When they came together, the voices changed: "Death to the traitor Cola di Rienzo! Death!" Now youths rushed up without reason. . . . They ran to the palace of the Campidoglio. Now many people were in action, husbands and wives, youths. They threw stones; there were clamorous cries; they surrounded the palace on all sides, in front and back, crying: "Death to the traitor who made the *gabelle* [taxes]!" "Death!" Their furor was terrible. The tribune made no response to this; no bells were rung, he didn't protect himself with his people. . . . When, finally, he saw that the voices were against him, he was uncertain. Especially since he was abandoned by all the living beings at the Campidoglio. Judges, notaries, soldiers, nobody wanted to lose his life. . . . When the tribune saw the tumult of people growing, he saw himself abandoned and unarmed and was very uncertain. . . . At first he wanted to die honorably, armed, with his sword in hand among the people, like a magnificent and imperious person. And he showed this when he put on his helmet and armor. The second thought was

---

32. But see Muir (1984), who confuses it with cannibalism. See also Estebe 1975.

33. Villani 1823, VII:51. There is another witness in Francesco di Giovanni Durante, *Memorie,* BNF, Magliabechiano II.III.280m.ff, fol. 22v.

to save his person and not die. And he showed this when he took off his helmet. These two thoughts fought in his mind. He willed to survive and live. He was a man like others; he feared death. Having decided for the best, to live in whatever way he could, he sought the means and the way, shameful and down-spirited. Already the Romans had set fire to the outer door. . . . There were horrible screams. The tribune thought to pass through the fire, mix with the others and survive. This was his last thought. He saw no other way. Thus he ripped off his baronial insignia; he put down his arms. Sad to relate! He cut off his beard and smudged his face with black. . . . Someone came up and recognized him, taking his hand and saying: "Don't go. Where are you going?". . . Now that he was seen to be the Tribune, he showed himself. He couldn't turn back. There was no remedy but to seek mercy from the will of others. Bodily, he was led unmolested up the stairs to the "Place of the Lion," where sentence was pronounced and where he had sentenced others. There all were silent. No man dared touch him. He stood for less than an hour. . . . In the silence his head turned to look here and there. Then Cecco dello Viecchio took a sword in hand and stuck it into his stomach. He was the first. . . . Then one and another of the others struck him, doing it or crying that they would. He said no word; at the first stroke he died, feeling no pain. Someone came up with a rope and tied it around both feet. He was on the ground, stripped; they stabbed him, passing through him like a sieve. They joked with him, pretending to be at the ceremony of remission of sins. This way he was dragged to San Marcello. There he was hung by the feet from a loggia; his head was missing. Part of his thigh had come off in the street. He had so many wounds that he seemed like a sieve. There was no place without a wound. His greasy intestines hung out. Horribly greasy. White as milk tinged with blood. He was so fat that he seemed like a big buffalo or cow in the slaughterhouse. He hung there two days and a night. Youths threw stones at him. The third day . . . he was dragged to the "Campo dell'Austa." There all the Jews collected, a great multitude; no one stayed away. A fire was made of dry straw; he was put into the fire. He was fat; with the fat he burned quickly. The Jews stood around, abusing him in a crowd, stirring the straw to make it burn. Thus the body was burned and reduced to ashes; not a bit remained.[34]

To summarize the essential points of this terrible description of a lynching: Cola was not killed as soon as he was recognized, but bodily taken to the hall of the Campidoglio, where "sentence" was usually pronounced (that is, where authority was exercised). Killed, he was dragged through the streets of Rome, and when his body was hung from the loggia, he had already been decapitated; his legs had been torn from his body. Youth gangs (*zitelli*) were present. After two days of exhibition, the miserable remains were consigned to the Jews to be burned.

I will analyze these facts later. Let us go on to the third example, where it seems that some kind of "power" remained, one might say, "attached" to the perpetrator of the tyrannicide after he failed in his bloody task. In 1476 the body of Andrea Lampugnani, who, along with Girolamo Olgiati, had attempted to assassinate the duke of Milan, Galeazzo Maria Sforza, underwent a true and proper "dethronement." His body was dragged by youths through the streets of the city, hung by one foot, cut to bits, and given as food to pigs, but not without some cannibalism: "Quum aliqui cives, res est horrenda

---

34. Anonimo Romano 1981, 193–98.

relatu, / Dentibus heu mordent cor jecur atque manus" (some citizens, horrible to tell, with their teeth bit heart and hands), as Gabriele Paveri Fontana expressed it in verse.[35]

This same pattern was repeated in the incident that occurred two years later in Florence. After the failure of the Pazzi conspiracy in 1478, the bodies of the conspirators were hung from the windows of the Bargello. On 17 May the body of the leader of the clan, Jacopo de' Pazzi, was dug up by a band of youths. "They tied the neck of the wicked leader to an ass, and in this way disinterred him, and tied him to a stake . . . dragging him through Florence naked as he was born."[36] The chronicler Landucci adds: "When they reached the portal of his house, they put the wicked leader beside the entrance and raised him up, saying: 'Knock on the door.' Then they took him to the Rubaconte bridge, and being in a good number, all youths under fourteen years, they used stakes and timbers to push him into the Arno."[37]

Now let us turn to the fourth episode, at Forlì. On 14 April 1488, Checco and Deddo d'Orso and Lodovico Pansechi, with the assistance of a soldier (and on the instigation of Lorenzo the Magnificent in Florence, who sought revenge on Riario for the aid he had given to the Pazzi), killed Count Girolamo Riario in his audience chamber. "Dead as he was," the Florentine commissioner at Castrocaro wrote, "they stripped him and threw him from a window." The same information is provided in the chronicle by Leone Cobelli, a painter from Forlì, who adds that after the defenestration, Simone dei Fiorini and a partisan attacked the count's body, while Pagliarino Ronco took it by one foot and began to drag it along. When they took away the body, it was "naked and pissing blood." The crowd that rushed up with the cry "Liberty, Liberty!" not only continued to attack the body but also assaulted his steward, killing him under the eyes of Caterina Sforza-Riario, who cried from the window: "Don't do it, don't kill him!" The steward was also dragged through the streets; "they dragged him for a piece" and also denuded him; "someone took his shoes, another stripped him, another took his shirt." The countess and her children were taken prisoner to the house of Messer Lodovico d'Orso. "Then the palace was sacked."[38]

In this incident the salient points were the stripping off of clothes, the defenestration, the mutilation of the two bodies (the phrase "pissing blood" suggests that the count had been castrated), the dragging through the streets, and finally the sack of the palace. The castration assumes a particular value, since chroniclers often censored their accounts to omit some horrifying detail. Géza Roheim has studied the castration phobia associated with Phrygian kings and their scepters, whips, and clubs, which gave off "light" and had "voices" and whose "vital fluid" might refer to that of the penis and its seminal fluid.[39] Roheim goes further, hypothesizing that "the king is a phallic divinity, the crown represents the union of the sexes, of Father and Mother, and by way of solar symbolism it stands for incest . . . the king's head stands for the phallus and the head in the crown is the penis in the vagina."[40] We could associate this bloody rite also with that of cutting off the nose (as something that protrudes from the body), which I have already cited in the case of the Byzantine emperor Justinian II. This also could occur in a lynching.

35. Fontana 1477; see also Barbaro 1574; Corio 1978, 1400–410; Casanova 1899; Bellotti 1929.
36. Poliziano 1856, 94.
37. Landucci 1883, 21. See Zorzi 1993.
38. Cobelli 1874; Bernardi 1895.
39. Roheim [1930] 1972, 224ff.
40. Roheim [1930] 1972, 230; see also Moret 1902.

Similar in ferocity was the murder of Altobello di Chiaravalle, who was briefly tyrant of Todi. In 1500, while he was being besieged in Acquasparta by Vitellozzo Vitelli and Giovanpaolo Baglioni, he attempted to flee in disguise but was captured. He was "immediately set on by a great crowd of enemies . . . because they all wanted to dirty their hands with his blood," as Pompeo Pellini writes.[41] But the incident is described more fully by the chronicler Francesco Maturanzio: "Every man came up to take some of his flesh, eating it raw like dogs and pigs; so many [of them] that nothing was left of his evil miserable body. And if he had been a giant, there would not have been enough for his enemies to eat. And for any willing to sell an ounce of that flesh, it would have been easy for him to find buyers ready to pay a golden ducat for it; but there was no more, and those who could not get his flesh threw fire onto his blood."[42]

In this lynching one might note the comparison of men to "dogs and pigs," and the reduction of human flesh to an object (which one could even buy). There is also the detail of the burned blood, to which I will return.

A few decades later Florence was the scene of another summary execution of a usurper, Giuliano Buonaccorsi.

There was a great show in our city of a certain Giuliano Buonaccorsi, a Florentine citizen who was said to have tried to assassinate Duke Cosimo by means of a servant called Il Moretto. . . . He was put on a wagon, with pincers and burning coals and a sign that indicted him for wanting to assassinate the duke of Florence. And thus he was shown throughout the city, and at every major crossroads he was tortured with the coals, a pitiable sight. But the evil plebes of Florence wanted to pull him from the wagon to do worse to him, and they continued to shout insults so that the miserable wretch begged for death. Thus suffering, he was taken to the place of execution and there hanged by the neck and then by one foot. As soon as the *bargello* [jailer] had left, the plebes cut him down, cut off his hands, and tied him by one leg to drag him in the dirt. And first they dragged him around the fortress, then more in the dirt till they reached the place of the lions, and they cut him open and gave his heart to the lions. And then they went to beat on the door where a sister of his lived, and, knocking, said, "Open, Giuliano is here." And then they dragged him to the Arno and threw him in, where he remained for three days.[43]

In this incident we note the hanging by the feet (like a pig); the cutting off of the hands; the route around the Fortress of San Giovanni (the great symbol of Medici power in the city); the throwing of his heart to the lions (who were kept caged as the living symbols of the Florentine Marzocco); the beating on the door of his sister, which recalled the lynching of Jacopo de' Pazzi (the reference: "Giuliano [Buonaccorsi] is here"); and the throwing of his remains into the river.

Let us go on to the eighth in our series of lynchings. On 24 April 1617 Concino Concini, maréchal d'Ancre, was killed by a courtier of King Louis XIII, Jacques de Vitry, while Concini was entering the Louvre. His body was immediately stripped, and the clothes were divided among his assassins.[44] He was left inside the palace gates, in sight of the crowd. It

41. Pellini 1664, 7.
42. Maturanzio 1851, II:150.
43. *Cronaca di anonimo,* 7v–9v.
44. See Marillac 1937, 465, and *Destinée* 1617.

was not until ten o'clock at night that the maréchal's servants were allowed to take the body for burial at St. Germain-de-l'Auxerrois. But this burial interrupted the dethronement ritual. What was missing was the consignment of the body to the local youth gangs. This is why, on the following day, a crowd of youths and women went to the church, opened the sepulcher, and dragged out the body, crying: "Long live the king, the tyrant is dead!" The maréchal's body was again stripped,[45] and his remains were then dragged to the Pont Neuf to be hoisted up where Concini had erected a gallows. The body was made to kneel before the statue of Henry IV to make an *amende honorable* (to beg pardon).[46] In France this was a rite required of anyone condemned to death (especially any guilty of witchcraft),[47] and it reminds one of the knocking at the door during the lynchings of Jacopo de' Pazzi and Giuliano Buonaccorsi in Florence. The mutilations of the body began at this point;[48] finally he was castrated.[49] Then the body was carried in a cleansing procession from one square to another through all the quarters of the city in a kind of reversal of a triumph, where shop signs were used in place of banners.[50] There was some cannibalism. One man pushed his hand into the body to suck blood off it. The heart was taken out, and before being eaten publicly, it was roasted on naked coals (a kind of roasting used for the remains of butchery).[51] The process of expulsion of the tyrant's body proceeded along the route of this infamous triumph. At the Bastille the guts were torn out and burned. The remains were dragged to the palace of the maréchal, near the palace of the prince de Conti, where another rite of cooking was performed, "around the courtyard."[52] Thus there was a complete expulsion of the tyrant's body.[53] Some wanted to feed what remained to the dogs.[54]

All the ritual elements we have noticed in the previous incidents returned in this lynching: stripping, exhibition, deprivation of symbols of power (the head, the right hand, the virile member), the reduction of the body to the level of a butchered animal, finally the complete expulsion of the body from the community that had previously recognized it, and its consignment to elements not part of the community (Jews, lions, dogs). The insults hurled by the crowd ("death to the traitor," "liberty," "the tyrant is dead") clearly indicate the community's refusal to further recognize this person as their lord. A Parisian broadside said clearly that God had inspired the crowd to drag the maréchal from his tomb.[55] As with a parricide, the earth could not receive his body.

45. "luy despouillerent sa chemise de manier que tous ses membres et sa turpitude parurent a nud": *L'enterrement* 1617, 4–5. See also *Histoire générale* 1617; *L'Honteuse cheute* 1617.

46. "on luy fit faire une amende honorable": *L'enterrement* 1617, 6.

47. Mousnier 1968, 111.

48. "d'autres creverent les yeux, d'autres luy couperent le nez et les oreilles, et autres parties de son corps": Marillac 1937, 467.

49. "on luy couppe les parties vergogneuses": *L'enterrement* 1617, 5–6.

50. "pour ses trophées et en mémoires des victoires qu'il avoit eues en ses batailles imaginaires, estoient devant luy portez des bouchons ou mais de taverne, des insignes de brasseries": *L'enterrement* 1617, 5–6.

51. "il y eut en homme vestu d'éscarlat si enragé, qu'ayant mis sa main dans le corps mort, il en tira sa main toute sanglante et la porta dans sa bouche, pour succer le sang, et avaller quelque petit morceau, eu'il en avoit arraché . . . un autre eut le moyen de luy arracher le coeur; et l'aller cuire sur les charbons et manger publiquement avec du vinaigre": Marillac 1937, 467.

52. "à la Bastille, on ils luy osterent les entrailles, et en ayant bruslé un partie, traisserent le reste au fauxbourg S. Germain, devant sa grande maison, et devant celle de monsieur le prince, où ils arracherent quelqu'autre partie d'autour du coeur, et la bruslerent": Marillac 1937, 467.

53. "on vient à la Greve ou sont ordinairement punis les criminels de leze majesté, là on brusle une partie de ce qui restoit de ce colasse d'orgueil et de presomption": *L'enterrement* 1617, 7.

54. "d'autres les veulent faire manger aux chiens": Phelypeaux de Pontchartrain 1837, 390.

55. "de l'arracher du tombeau, don't il estoit indigne et de la terre qu'il estimoit bien indigne de le porter": *Actions de graces* 1617, 11–12.

Fig. 82   The murder of Concino Concini, German broadside (Paris, Bibliothèque Mazarine).

News of the assassination and of the example made of Concini spread throughout
Europe. Broadsides were printed, many as propaganda favorable to the coup d'état of
King Louis XIII. Two seem particularly interesting. A German broadside faithfully reproduced the scenes of the lynching and the rite of dethronement (Fig. 82). This engraving
adds as a detail the opening of an aviary and the releasing of birds, a symbol that must
have been immediately recognizable to seventeenth-century eyes. Another broadside, this
time French, transformed the body of Concini into an animal (a squirrel that had over-
turned a vase filled with French fleurs-de-lys and thus had to be punished; Fig. 83). A
wheel of fortune recalled a symbol much diffused in the Middle Ages and Renaissance.
"Fortunae rota volvitur: cescendo minoratus / Alter in altum tollitur, nimis exaltatus /
Rex sedet in vertice, caveat ruinam" (The wheel of fortune turns: he who rises to the top
is pushed down, while another is raised; the overly exalted king sitting at the summit
should fear his ruin). Here also the details of the lynching are fairly well shown: the dragging of the killed beast, the hanging by the feet, the cutting up of the body, the gallows.[56]
A third *avis,* also French, illustrated the narrative with a man-fish (also a common Renaissance monster; Fig. 84), showing readers an image of Concini's soul in hell, guarded by a
comic devil-bat (Fig. 85).[57] Soon, Marie de' Medici's unfortunate favorite was spoken of as
a talisman to use against pistol shots.[58]

56. *Tableav et emblèmes* n.d.
57. *Dialogue* 1617.
58. *Charmes* 1655; *Relazione* 1617.

Fig. 83   *Tableav et emblèmes de la detestable vie et malhevrevse fin dv maistre Coyon* [Concini], French
broadside (Paris, Bibliothèque Mazarine).

Let us pass on to our last incident, following the testimony of Abraham de
Wicquefort, a Dutch historian employed by de Witt, who was himself ruined by his
protector's fall and was condemned to life imprisonment but died in exile after a hair-rais-
ing escape. When Johan de Witt went to the prison to save his brother Cornelius, he had
not understood that the true victim the crowd wanted to destroy in his brother was himself, or rather the old state of affairs symbolized by the grand pensioner. By going to the
prison, he was directly offering himself in sacrifice, and he did not succeed in saving his
brother. Incited by one of the city aldermen and by the treasurer, the crowd seized both
of them. After the de Witt brothers were killed, their bodies were stripped naked, and
their noses, ears, toes, and fingers were cut off. A jeweler, Henry Verhoef, cut open the
chest of the grand pensioner and took out his heart. Finally, the two desecrated bodies
were hung by their feet from the prison gallows (Fig. 86). Here again, the salient ritual elements were repeated and transposed: the cutting off of the nose symbolized castration;
the cutting off of the fingers stood for cutting off the hand; the hanging by the feet was
the same public exhibition suffered by Arrigo Fei, Guglielmo d'Assisi, Cola di Rienzo,
Jacopo de' Pazzi, Giuliano Buonaccorsi, and Concini, and similar to the defenestration of
Count Riario (this last incident having the double meaning of exhibition and consignment to the people).

Similar in typology to the killing of officials of the duke of Athens and the steward at
Forlì was a lynching of an *eletto* of the Seggio del Popolo (a municipal tribunal) at Naples,
Giovan Vincenzo Starace, in 1585. The *eletto* was taken in the place where he exercised his
office, the Seggio, and dragged through the city streets. His body was mutilated in the
way we have observed, and then left in front of the royal palace, as if the crowd were
"consigning" it to the viceroy, of whom Starace was a friend and in a certain sense the

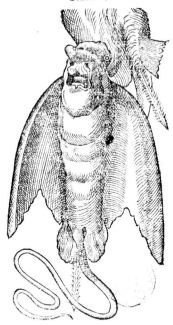

Fig. 84   *Fantosme de Conchini*, engraving in
           Dialogue de la Galligaya . . . , 1617 (Paris,
           Bibliothèque Mazarine).

Fig. 85   *Portraict du mauuais demon,*
           gardant Conchini, in *Dialogue de*
           la Galligaya . . . , 1617 (Paris,
           Bibliothèque Mazarine).

agent. This also was a transposition: the representative of the sovereign for the sovereign himself.

One could associate another Neapolitan lynching with these last incidents: the tearing apart of the body of the cavalry captain Niccolò Fiani di Torremaggiore, a Jacobin in the period of the French Revolution who was hanged during the Bourbon reaction, on 29 August 1799. "The people began to attack the body, to pull and shake it; they stripped it naked and began to cut it to pieces with knives, leaving only the bones hanging from the gallows. And with the pieces of flesh on their knifepoints, the low people began to go through the city crying out, as if they were selling meat: 'Who wants to see the meat and liver of a Jacobin?' They even carried pieces of flesh on sword points, and some fried the liver and ate it."[59] More information on this lynching is provided in the "Frammenti di una inedita storia della rivoluzione napoletana" edited by Benedetto Croce: "the low people cut him to pieces and carried his genitals in triumph through the street on a pick."[60]

In this lynching Captain Fiani, because of his military office in the Jacobin regime, was taken to personify that government and thus was not only deprived of the attributes of power but completely expelled from the social fabric, thus marking the Jacobin government as completely foreign to the Sanfedist (Bourbon and clerical) reaction. We could

59. Fortunato 1884.
60. "Frammenti" 1932, 314.

De 2. Broeders Jan en Cornelis de Wit in den Hage vermoord en daar na aan de galg by de beenen opgehangen &c den 20. Aagasti 1672.

Fig. 86   Pwart, *De 2 Broeders Jan en Cornelis de Wit in den Hage vermoord en daar na aan de galg by de beenen opgehangen &c. den 20 Augusti 1672* (1728), from J. Le Clerc, *Geschiedenissen der Vereenigde Nederlanden*, Amsterdam, Z. Chatelain 1730.

note that in this incident as well ritual elements appear that we noticed in the earlier examples: hanging was, in a certain sense, an *anàtellon;* the body was denuded of flesh in the same position as that of the notary Arrigo Fei when he was "stuck like a pig" (although Giuliano Buonaccorsi was hanged by the feet, as were Cola di Rienzo, Concini, and the de Witt brothers); his flesh was made salable (and so made edible), as was that of the tyrant of Todi. In all these cases the body was cut up as if it were being butchered. The pig is at the same time "man" and "animal, "friend" and "enemy."[61] This was, in fact, a hybrid creature in constant contact with medieval man, to whom it was one of the principal nutrients. It lived off his garbage, ate many of the same things, was naked like man (and even had pink humanlike skin!).[62] The degradation of the victim to the status of an animal was to emphasize his expulsion, and the proximity of swine to humans facilitated the transposition.

There are other cases where a dethroning was, so to speak, mimicked. In the absence of the king (or one of his ministers), his statue was attacked.[63] This is easily understandable when one thinks of the value the image of the prince assumed in the eyes of his subjects, for whom the *imago personae* had his very *numen* within it. Among the ancient

---

61. "friendly and hostile transgress major oppositions and coordinates in the cultural grid." Lerch 1964. But see also Evans [1906] 1987, 155ff.

62. Stallybrass and White 1986, 44ff.

63. See *Destruction* [1776?].

Babylonians, the destruction of the statue of a god and the temple where it was kept led naturally to a kind of divine death.[64] At the time of Rome under Constantine, the cult of imperial statues was particularly widespread. In the periphery of the empire, the *adventus* was celebrated by going to meet the *imago imperatoris,* as substitute for the sovereign, at the gates (and we have already seen how a person coming in triumph tried to imitate the statue of Jupiter). Saint John Chrysostom said in a homily: "When the statue of the emperor or his image is invited to enter a city, the magistrates and people come to meet it singing lauds. In so doing, they are not venerating wooden images, but the emperor himself."[65] Once *imago* and *numen* were so closely united, it is not surprising that an image could be considered the very person of the sovereign.

Precisely for this reason it was held in the early Middle Ages that portraits should not be made that were not representations of Christ, the Virgin, or saints. The first great representation of a sovereign was that of the emperor Frederick II sitting above the triumphal gate at Capua (1234); but when the people of Orvieto, in 1297, erected two statues of Pope Boniface VIII on their walls—one on the principal gate and one on a back gate—to indicate their allegiance to him, the Christian world spoke of idolatry.[66]

This is what the Bolognese thought when, on 30 December 1511, they destroyed a bronze statue of Pope Julius II that had been placed on the façade of the Cathedral of San Petronio three years earlier. It was a statue by Michelangelo (and three years earlier the Bolognese had destroyed another statue of the pope, made of plaster). We know that the statue by Michelangelo was hacked to pieces and that the duke of Ferrara used these to cast a cannon, called out of disrespect "The Julia." We also know that the head of the statue was kept for a time in Ferrara, and from this we know indirectly that the destruction of the statue involved a decapitation. It is possible that the face was disfigured and the nose was hacked away. Certainly, the fact that the statue was hacked to pieces is enough to indicate that the crowd vented its anger on the "body" of the pope. In turn, the recasting of the pieces had the same meaning as the consignment of the remains of Cola di Rienzo to the Jews to be burned, or the abandonment of the body of Concini to the dogs.

On 18 August 1559 a similar fate befell a statue of Pope Paul IV that was located on the Campidoglio in Rome. In this case as well, the head was cut off, and a Jew was summoned to put his yellow cap on it. The body of the statue was dragged through the city and thrown into the Tiber (another ritual expulsion from the community). The riot ended on 22 August, and many palaces were fortified and armed out of fear of an interregnum.

Less than a hundred years later, in 1644, a statue of Pope Urban VIII sculpted in marble by Bernini ran the same risk. Repulsed by the guards of the constable Prospero Colonna (one of his daughters had married a nephew of the dead pope), the crowd went on to the Collegio Romano, where they destroyed another, plaster statue of the pope.

In Paris, in the winter of 1589, during the Wars of Religion, wax statues of King Henry III were placed before altars in churches, and for forty days people stuck them with knives, nails, and other pointed instruments in a seeming paroxysm of witchcraft.[67]

When French troops took Naples during the period of the French Revolution, they came upon the *porta triumphalis* in Capua. They (rightly) saw the statue of Emperor

64. Cassin 1986, 75.
65. In John of Damascus, *De imaginibus,* Or. iii, PG, xciv:1408ff.; Dvornik 1966, ii:652ff.
66. Sommer 1920.
67. L'Estoile 1621, 280.

Frederick II as a royal symbol and disfigured it in a typical way by cutting off the head and the hands (see Fig. 79).

One would be wrong to call the incidence of eating human flesh simply "cannibalism" in these lynchings.[68] Two things should attract our attention: first, the reduction of these bodies to an animal level (they "stuck him like a pig," it was said of Arrigo Fei; the low people of Naples "were selling meat"), and second, the distribution of the remains to pigs (Lampugnani), to lions (Buonaccorsi), or to dogs (Concini). As the Jesuit Leonardo Leys wrote in 1606, "what is eaten must always be in its nature lower than the one who does the eating."[69] But we have also noted that in the case of Altobello the crowd proceeded to burn the blood remaining in the street; purifying fire was to destroy completely any residual of the mortal remains of the tyrant. In these cases we are not confronted with "cannibalism" (understood, for instance, as a means of taking possession of the force and power of the person killed); this was rather the bloody ritual of total expulsion of the tyrant from the social body. Eating pieces of flesh had the function of accelerating this expulsion, in the same way as in the Asian world relatives of a dead leader ritually eat pieces of his dead body so as to accelerate the separation of the flesh from the bones and permit the deceased to be admitted more quickly into the world of the dead.

A dethroning thus obeyed a series of ritual norms that were "learned" by the crowd and permit us to construct pairs of symmetrical opposites:

Investment	Divestment
Acclamation	Defenestration
Crown/tiara	Beheading
Pastoral staff/scepter	Castration
The hand of justice	Cutting off the hand
Anàtellon	Hanging the body
Enthronement	Expulsion
Cleansing procession	Dragging through the streets

A French engraving illustrates this sequence very well (Fig. 87). On 25 April 1562 the Catholic governor of Dauphiné, La Motte-Gondrin, was assassinated by the soldiers of Baron François Beaumont des Adrets and by the Huguenots of Valence.[70] The broadside shows almost all the stages of the ritual of dethroning, except for the final ones of dragging through the streets and expulsion. It begins with the invasion of the house adjoining his habitation (A), where the governor had taken refuge (B), passes on to illustrate his murder (C), then the expulsion of the body from a window (D), then the cutting of the rope from which the body was hung (E), "ut cadaver ad terram delapsum populus agnoscat" (the corpse . . . dropped to the ground to let the people recognize it). In the last stage the soldiers set fire to the door of the governor's house (G), a ritual that reminds one of the *amende honorable*.

---

68. Besides the shocking simplification of Torraca 1949–50, 113–25, see Pagden 1982, 50 (where Lampugnani is confused with Duke Galeazzo Maria Sforza!), and Muir 1984 (whose author compares the eating of human flesh in dethronings to cannibalism in the New World, on which, see Sanday 1986).

69. Lessius 1605, 674–75.

70. Briard [1770] 1890; Haag and Haag 1877–78.

Popular broadsides like this, or like the broadsides and *avis* showing the fate of Concini, helped to confirm a "culture of lynching" in the crowd.

There remains something to be said about those who carried out these macabre rituals. One notes a constant presence through the Middle Ages and early modern period of a role played by "youth gangs" ("youths under fourteen years," Landucci says). The research on historical demography carried out by M. Reinhard, A. Armengaud, and J. Dupaquier, and for fifteenth-century Florence by David Herlihy and Christiane Klapisch Zuber,[71] indicate that youths under age fifteen were more than a third of the population and that youths under age twenty were some 43 percent. This large mass of population included *trovatelli* (babies abandoned while they were still in swaddling clothes), children *iti con Dio* (who had left their natural families), orphans, and mendicants. It is obvious that such a large segment of the population would be represented in urban disturbances. However, one notes that in these incidents of lynching, the youths (*fanciulli*) did not mix with the adults (*uomini fatti*), but carried out precise roles: dragging through the streets, throwing a body into the river.

The world of the Middle Ages and early modern period had rituals that channeled youth violence (*mos iuvenis*). One proceeded from the Italian *mattinate* or *chiariugioli* (in

Fig. 87   *Valentia vrbs Delphinatus capta, D. Mottae Gondrinae occiditur 25 Aprilis 1562* (Assassination and lynching of La Motte-Gondrin, 25 April 1562), broadside. (Providence, Hay Library, Anne S. K. Brown Military Collection). The caption explains the different acts of the murder. Under letter *E* it reads, "The rope cut, the corpse is dropped to the ground to let the people recognize it."

71. Herlihy 1960; Herlihy and Klapisch Zuber 1985.

French *charivari,* in English *rough music*) to *sassaiole* (rock throwing), to religious confraternities for youths (in Florence the Compagnia di San Giovanni and the Natività were for youths from thirteen to twenty-four years),[72] to associations (*societates iuventum*) that organized sacred representations and also *armeggiarie* (joists) and carnival festivities (in Florence the *Potenze,* in Venice the *Scuole*).[73] But children (*fanciulli*), as already noted, were also needed for processions because they represented purity. In Florence, the *priorista* of Paolo di Matteo Pietrobuoni, describing a procession for the feast of San Giovanni (the patron of the city) on 23 June 1428, says that the Compagnia dei Magi of San Marco, among its "very rich and beautiful arrangements," had "eight horses draped with silk bearing eight pages dressed in silk with angelic faces," and, "in a cloud, a child about three years old." He adds significantly, "God appeared in the guise of this child's body."[74] At Orvieto, in 1496, the millennial sermons of a Corsican friar put the whole city into panic. "He always prophesied disasters, that is, death, famine, and war that few would survive. He cried in all his sermons 'Jesus! Jesus!' and led solemn processions with the cross in front and little children behind, crying, 'Jesus! Jesus! God help us!'"[75]

Richard Trexler has justly observed that during the fifteenth century "adolescence became a new fetish of a deeply religious society" and that "the 'little angel' or *giovanangelo* slowly became a societal ritual object, one whose correct manipulation could result in the preservation, even salvation, of the natural and civil order."[76] And we must ask these "angelic faces," the divine presence in puerile bodies, for an explanation. Did not God speak *ex ore infantium,* through the mouth of the *episcopus puerorum?*[77] There is no doubt that, in medieval ritual, adolescents had a specific role that could not be performed by adults. This was the part of society, in a world tinged with sin, that took on the most serious task in the dethronement ritual: the complete expulsion from the urban social fabric.

The tyrannicide at Foligno on 28 September 1377 was an incident about which one would certainly like to know more. A bastard from the Brancaleoni family killed the lord, Trincia Trinci, and threw his body from a balcony of the palace. The historian Pompeo Pellini writes, "In order that the people might have greater hope of liberty, he threw the body, lacerated with wounds, into the piazza, where, as it is told, it remained for several days without being touched or taken up by anybody."[78] The Trinci family, as Pellini remembers, had dominated Foligno for seventy-two years. In this case it seems clear that the city continued to recognize the family's lordship and refused to "accept" the mutilated body of the lord so as to carry out a rite of expulsion. (In fact, the people of Foligno recalled the Trinci family as soon as Count Lucio di Lando, a Florentine general who had supported the conspirators, left the city.)

We need to examine one final incident because the previous examples are reflected in it and also because of its triple meaning: a community's self-recognition in a leader, the rejection of his body, and finally its reintegration and divination. This was the life on earth of the fishmonger Masaniello (Tommaso Aniello), who rose up at a moment of crisis to

72. Trexler 1980, 368ff.
73. For Venice, see Crouzet Pavan 1984; Casini 1996; for France, Rossiaud 1976.
74. Cited in Hatfield 1970, 146.
75. Tommaso di Silvestro 1922, 50–51.
76. Trexler 1980, 368f.
77. Grinberg 1993.
78. Pellini 1664, 1188. See also Dorio 1638, 170–71.

represent the people of Naples. Like Cola di Rienzo he also became drunk with power and was rejected by his followers. A dispatch of 16 July 1647 tells us that, "zealous and humble as he had been," he was transformed into a "proud tyrant, no longer listening to advice, governing himself capriciously, going enraged through the city with a few followers and stopping carriages and with harsh words directing persons of high rank to do reverence to him, giving blundered orders, cutting off the heads of many only on his verbal accusation, raising gallows in many places."[79] With this attitude Masaniello "came to concentrate the fear and hatred of the whole people, who took fright at this tyranny." The same morning of 16 July, when this dispatch was sent, Masaniello had gone to the Church of the Carmine, where the cardinal was to officiate. He climbed into the pulpit and babbled out in a fit of passion. Calmed, he retired to the convent, where he was joined by "some gentlemen of courage and spirit accompanied by some of the people" (as another witness, Alessandro Giraffi, tells us), "who had first entered the Church of the Carmine crying, 'Long live the king of Spain.' They each shot four musket balls into him."[80]

Masaniello's body was immediately mutilated. "A butcher came up who cut off his head with a great knife and put it on a stake. The first assassins carried it through the Church of the Carmine, which was filled with eight thousand souls. . . . His assassins went freely through the city with his head on the stake; meanwhile youths dragged his body through the streets and piazze." But it was precisely at this moment that the process of reintegration began. People ran to the houses of three bakers, among whom was Salvatore Cattaneo,

> and sought him out to kill him, calling him a parricide because he had killed Masaniello. . . . Toward the Carmine there were no less loud cries from another crowd of frenzied men and women running up to look for Masaniello. And finding him, some kissed his hand, some his feet, some the sheet. There were many women who, not being able to get up to him, lacerated their heads and faces out of grief over his death. Some were seen who adored him as a saint and touched him with rosaries that they had kissed, and touched his eyes, his forehead; others scattered flowers and leaves over the body and honored and blessed him.[81]

Francesco Capecelatro writes that, in succession, the mutilated body was gathered together; "the head was put back on the body, which was carried in procession with many candles to the Church of the Carmine and placed nobly before the main altar; and it was hard to believe what numerous crowds of people came up, for the most part women and low people, touching the corpse with their rosaries, some taking locks of his hair to keep as if he were a saint."[82]

The act of rejoining the head to the body was in itself an act of reintegration. But now the people accomplished a second operation: they restored the "sacredness" of the leader by showing that they took parts of his body for relics. The testimony of Francesco Fuidoro concurs: "The crowds of plebeian low women rushed up, rosaries in their hands,

79. Donzelli 1647, 101ff.; Fuidoro 1647.
80. Giraffi 1648. See also Fuidoro 1647.
81. De Santis 1770, 116.
82. Capecelatro 1830.

and genuflected, and prayed to God for this soul, with tears that would melt any rock. These crowds canonized the innocence of Masaniello, the defender of his country, and they never tired of circulating around the body with sobs, sighs, cries, and even howls."

Masaniello was now a saint; we are witnessing the first steps of his canonization. No better or more appropriate term could be found to indicate the deep meaning of this re-integration. As Romeo de Maio has noted,[83] we are confronted with the beginning of the process of a Baroque canonization: the pious transit, the apotheosis, the *Passio Christi*. His prophecy of his own death to his enemies is not even lacking ("climbed up onto the market fountain," Giraffi notes, "he said to the people that what he did, he did for the good of his city, and he knew well that when he had done it, within three days he would be killed and dragged through the streets of Naples"). His death was followed by his resurrection and by the reintegration of the community of his believers. In the solemn funeral given in tribute to the dead leader, the drums of the people's militia played *scordati* (out of tune) to signify the break of the cosmic harmony, the suspension of the social order.

This is why Masaniello is the best summary of the examples earlier presented. His body was above all the body of the leader, recognized and made divine by the community that recognized him, repudiated him, and then reintegrated him. He was the true scapegoat for the anomie of a community undergoing a deep crisis of identity.[84]

83. De Maio 1980, 155. On the preliminaries of the revolt, see Villari 1976; on the figure of Masaniello, Musi 1989.
84. Girard 1982.

"IN THE YEAR FOUR HUNDRED, less one, a king will be judged in a triangular castle after having reigned for twenty-two years with his fullest powers." This prophecy of Merlin seemed to be realized on 1 September 1399, when the people of London went to meet Henry of Lancaster, conqueror of England. The king went directly to Saint Paul's Cathedral; he prayed at the high altar; then filled with emotion, he turned to the tomb of his father, "where he wept exceedingly." Early the following morning another small cavalcade passed through London: King Richard II, accompanied by the young duke of Gloucester and earl of Arundel, was returning to the Tower, where he was a prisoner. He rode a small charger and was followed by a youth who cried: "Honor King Richard, who has done so much good for the Kingdom of England!" But others seeing the little procession pass said: "Now we are rid of the miserable bastard who governed us so badly."[1] Despite the fact that the abdication had been made by the king directly, the constitutional problems regarding his deposition were by no means simple ones. The agreement was that Richard II would save his life in exchange, and receive a pension for himself and for six others of his court whom he would designate, and that awaiting the convening of Parliament, he would remain closed up in the Tower of London. But the archbishop of Canterbury immediately objected that at the moment of the abdication Parliament was also dissolved. New writs in the name of Henry were required, which were sent out on 30 September for a convening on 6 October. That same day, nonetheless, both chambers, Lords and Commons, met in the Great Hall of Westminster. At the back of the hall was placed the empty throne, or Chair of State ("absque praesidente quocunque" [without anyone presiding]), flanked by the seats of the high clergy. A commission of bishops, lords, and members of the Commons was elected and sent to the Tower of London to receive the act of abdication.[2] The chief problem that seemed to concern Parliament was Richard's "very willing" absolution, for all his subjects—"dukes, marquises, earls, barons, vassals and valvassors and all and every my liege people whatsoever, ecclesiastics or secular"—of their oaths of fidelity.[3] They wanted the king also to recognize his own inability: "I do confess, acknowledge, repute, and truly and out of certain knowledge do judge myself to have been and to be utterly insufficient and unuseful for the rule and government."[4]

1. *Chronique de la traison* 1846, 64.
2. Cobbett 1806, 1:241ff.
3. Cobbett 1806, 1:252.
4. Cobbett 1806, 1:253.

He was accused particularly of having adhered to the concept of the *lex animata*. Among the charges was that of having said publicly "that his laws were in his mouth," "that they were in his breast," and that he alone could dictate or change the laws of the realm.[5]

On 6 October the two houses of Parliament met together again, and Henry of Lancaster took his place on the throne. But still there were those who challenged him. The Benedictine bishop of Carlisle, Thomas Merks, denied that anyone could sit on the throne without having undergone coronation: "No lord may sit in the chair of justice except the king of England, duly crowned."[6] The bishop was immediately arrested and shut up in St. Albans. As for the complained-of impediment, it was soon removed by a new coronation, preceded on the eve by the creation of fifty-four knights, among whom were the four sons and two younger brothers of the new sovereign, who then went in procession to Westminster all dressed in the same way, "and they looked like priests."[7] Beyond the continuing preoccupation with obtaining the assent of Richard II to his abdication, the juridical formula that permitted his deposition ("for the greater security and tranquillity of the people, and benefit of the kingdom") was based on his failure to observe his coronation oath to uphold social peace. The act of Parliament stated that the deposition of a king was justified when the duties he had sworn to observe were unattended. Richard had acted "to publicly erect his standard against the peace which he had sworn to keep," and "the said king very often commanded many things to be done against such statutes unrepealed; acting therein expressly and knowingly against his oath taken in coronation."[8] The breaking of this pact, in short, freed his subjects from obedience: "Y si no, no," the Aragonese would have said had they been in the place of the English.[9]

Mary Queen of Scots was accused of a much more serious crime in 1587: that of having conspired to damage her cousin Queen Elizabeth I. But her beheading seemed a wound in the cult of monarchy. "What law of God," her son King James I would exclaim, "can permit that justice shall strike upon them whom he had appointed supreme dispensators of the same under him, whom he hath called gods"?[10]

No one would have imagined that sixty years after the accusation of Mary Queen of Scots, an accusation of felony would touch a king of England. The accusation of failing to fulfill his oath was taken up again against King Charles I. The successful and rapid deposition of Richard II, despite the protest of the duc d'Orleans, who accused Henry of Lancaster of having no pity for "our liege king and sovereign lord" ("You lie falsely and wickedly," Henry IV replied). This was not a legal argument.[11] The presumed murder of Richard II in prison might be explained by the need to eliminate a second contemporaneous anointed king on English soil, the first being a living challenge to the sacredness of the second. For Charles I the explanation has to be sought elsewhere. It was more complicated, even if Cromwell eventually presented himself as a deuteragonist (in Greek drama, the second actor) with respect to the Stuarts, to the extent that he aspired to be not only Lord Protector (his provisional title) but also the founder of a new Protestant dynasty.[12]

5. Cobbett 1806, 1:259.

6. *Chronique de la traison* 1846, 71.

7. *Chronique de la traison* 1846, 74.

8. Cobbett 1806, 1:255 and 259; *Rotuli Parliamentorum* 1935, 316–26; Baumer 1940, 13. For the doctrine of nonresistance, see the third draft of the sermon by Bishop Russell in Chrimes 1936, chap. 2, excursus 6:189–90.

9. Giesey 1968. See page 231 above.

10. Letter of 16 January 1587 in Akrigg 1984. For the decapitation of Mary Queen of Scots, see Woodward 1997, 67ff.

11. Williams, preface to *Chronique de la traison* 1846, lxxiii.

12. See Sherwood 1977.

Peter Lombart well understood this when he engraved Charles and Oliver as doppel-gänger.[13] But one wonders how dangerous the precedent of Mary Queen of Scots had been.

In the first half of the sixteenth century the English monarchy reached the highest summit of its power, reuniting in the person of the king both temporal and spiritual authority, extracting this from the earlier priestly sphere.[14] This reinforcement of the Crown occurred with the Reformation Parliament of King Henry VIII. The king attained a position of preeminence, now also in the ecclesiastical realm, that was unknown to his predecessors. The Act of Proclamations gave the king *plenitudo potestatis,* the right to publish laws also in matters of faith.[15]

When Bishop Stephen Gardiner, in his *De vera obedientia* (1535), which appeared after Henry VIII's death, proclaimed the absolute spiritual sovereignty of the king of England, he was only emphasizing an already-made decision. But the pamphleteers among Henry's supporters also detached themselves from the political theory of the fourteenth and fifteenth centuries on another important point: they proclaimed the doctrine of non-resistance to the sovereign, thus reversing the juridical concepts that had been at the base of the deposition of Richard II. At a moment when the absolutist state was being consolidated, they affirmed that nonresistance was essential for the state's unity. In doing this, they emphasized the cult of the king as Vicar of Christ on earth. Rebellion became a sin, a sin against God.[16] Hobbes took this same line in his *Leviathan* (1612), where he sustained the idea of unlimited sovereignty.

Naturally such theories encountered opposition, especially among Catholics. Cardinal Reginald Pole, for example, in the third part of his *De ecclesiasticae unitatis defensione* (1536), sustained to the contrary the constitutional right of insurrection against a king who trampled on the rights of his subjects. But these were Catholic opponents. Anglicans pushed instead for an absolutism that would defend them against a return to Rome and would not question their faith, and they found support in the Crown. One must wait until the second half of the seventeenth century for there to appear in England theories of a right to rebellion,[17] which had already appeared on the other side of the English Channel, in France, among Huguenots and monarchomachs during the Wars of Religion. During the Fronde these theories gained a new impulse from the French Parlements' opposition to the absolutist tendencies of Mazarin.

In the first half of the sixteenth century, the Reformation Parliament had thus given the sovereign such power in the ecclesiastical sphere that his person was inevitably involved in religious disputes. But by doing this, it sowed the seeds of a future revolt, since the king was now drawn into the vortices of religious schisms, whereas his absolutism earlier had precise limits in the law of nature and in respect for the rights of Parliament.[18]

With the opening of the new century, the parliament of 1604–10 and the Addled Parliament of 1614 showed that a religious party was being formed to resist the court. The parliaments of King Charles I were even more independent of control by the royal

---

13. Roberts 1999, figs. 37 and 38.
14. Baumer 1940, 22.
15. Baumer 1940, 58.
16. Baumer 1940, 85; Janelle 1930.
17. Baumer 1940, 118.
18. Baumer 1940, 152–53.

entourage,[19] and the opposition was even gaining practical experience; it "had captured the new mechanism" and was becoming organized as a party.[20]

This experience was reflected in William Prynne (1600–1669) and his book *Soveraigne Power of Parliamente and Kingdomes . . . Wherein the Superiority of Our owne and most Other Foreine Parliaments is Abundantly Evidenced* (1643). Parliament, Prynne said, was the single source of law, the single supreme authority, on the basis of the Magna Carta, not subject to the laws, but the source of law. "The parliament is the absolute sovereign power within the realm, not subject or obliged by the letter of interment of any laws, being in truth the sole law-maker and having an absolute authority over the laws themselves, yea over Magna Charta . . . to repeal, alter, determine and suspend them when there is cause."[21]

One must add that Prynne referred to the particular current parliament, which now had a Puritan and Presbyterian majority that stood in opposition to the Episcopal Anglicanism of Archbishop Laud and that identified the religious enemy precisely as King Charles I ("the Capital Enemy"). Those who became Roundheads could not overthrow the Anglican Church without overthrowing the monarchy along with it. This iron logic brought Charles I to the bar of justice and to the scaffold. The religious conflict was clear, and if the juridical terms of the deposition of Richard II were taken up again to legitimize the new judgment, one must recognize that whereas three hundred years earlier there was a preoccupation with dissolving oaths of fidelity before the king could be judged, now in the mid–seventeenth century both sides stood on a common ideological ground. That is, no one had the courage to challenge the sacredness of the king's person. The ideas of those who dared, among Levellers such as John Hare and John Lilburne, were too dangerous to follow.[22] When Charles was arrested at Holdenby, he said to the young officer who commanded the troop of five hundred infantry, George Joyce: "If I should refuse yet to go with you, I hope you will not force me? I am your King and you ought not to lay violent hands upon your King, for I acknowledge none here to be above me but God."[23]

Those who would try King Charles I had first to strip him of his divine powers by accusing him of breaking his coronation oath, thus degrading him to the status of a tyrant. The *Ordinance for the Trial of the King* was quite clear.

> Whereas it is notorious that Charles Stuart, the now king of England, not content with the many encroachments which his predecessors had made upon the people in their rights and freedom, hath had a wicked design totally to subvert the ancient and fundamental laws and liberties of this nation, and in their place to introduce an arbitrary and tyrannical government; and that, besides all other evil ways and means to bring his design to pass, he hath prosecuted it with fire and sword, levied and maintained a civil war in the land, against the parliament and kingdom; whereby this country hath been miserably wasted, the public treasure exhausted, trade decayed, thousands of people murdered, and infinite other mischiefs committed; for all which high and treasonable offenses the said Charles Stuart might long since have justly been brought to exemplary and condign punishment.

19. On this, see Aylmer 1974.
20. Mitchell 1957, 121.
21. Baumer 1940, 154; see also Allen 1938, 443.
22. See Frank 1955, 83ff., and Bertelli 1973, 247–48 (1984, 177–96).
23. Carlton 1983, 315.

If the parliament had rejected a trial up to this point, it had done so to preserve public tranquillity; but its clemency had only encouraged the tyrant and his accomplices in their schemes. Thus now a court of justice had been formed "for the charging of him, the said Charles Stuart, with the crimes and treason above-mentioned."[24]

A high court, as John Cook suggested, should be regarded as an image and anticipation of the Last Day of Judgment, when the saints would judge the powers of the earth.[25]

As with King Richard II, the problem of the legitimate convocation of Parliament presented itself. Edward Montague, earl of Manchester, supported by Algernon Percy, duke of Northumberland, held that on the basis of the fundamental laws of the kingdom Parliament was composed of three groups (or estates), among which the king was the first. He alone had the power to convoke or dismiss the assembly. Without him no parliament of any kind existed, and it was thus absurd to claim that the king was a traitor with respect to Parliament. Thus the House of Lords rejected the proposal of the House of Commons. The earl of Denbigh, William Fielding, who had been assigned a place on the high court, declared that he would rather be cut to pieces than be involved "in so infamous a business."[26] At the beginning of January, Prynne himself, the defender of parliamentary sovereignty, dissented from the majority with a pamphlet in which he no longer recognized Parliament's authority: *A Brief Memento unto the present unparliamentary junto, touching their present intentions and proceedings to depose and execute Charles Stuart, their lawful King.* When a parliamentary delegation went to ask him to withdraw the work, Prynne said that he would reply only to a legitimately constituted authority.

The constitutional objections were thus strong, but this time there was no recourse even to a pretended reconvocation. In the name of what new supreme authority, now, would it be possible to reconvene Parliament? The Gordian knot was cut by the House of Commons, which declared itself to be the supreme court of the nation. When the new high court was constituted, it was made up of 133 persons, among whom only seventy actively took part in the trial.

John Cook, named "solicitor general for the English commons," read the heads of the accusation, and John Bradshaw as lord president asked the king to respond to them. Charles disdainfully replied that he wanted first of all to know by what authority ("I mean lawful") he had been brought to the bar: "there are many unlawful authorities in the world, there are robbers and highwaymen. . . . Remember I am your king, your lawful king, and what sins you bring upon your heads and the judgment of God upon his land."[27] Then he recapitulated the legal arguments that we have already noted: "Let me know by what lawful authority am I seated here, and I shall not be unwilling to answer."[28]

Again the secretary of the court turned to the king: "Charles Stuart King of England, you are accused in the behalf of the Commons of England of diverse high crimes and treasons which charge hath been read unto you. The court now requires you to give your positive and final answer by way of confession or denial of the charge." And the king: "Sir, I say again unto you so that I might give satisfaction to the people of England of the clearness of my proceedings—not by way of answer, not in this way, but to satisfy them that I

---

24. Cobbett 1809–26, III:1254–55.
25. Walzer [1974] 1989, 111.
26. Cobbett 1809–26, III:1256.
27. Cobbett 1809–26, III:1260.
28. Carlton 1983, 350.

have done nothing against that trust that hath been committed to me—I would do it. But to acknowledge a new court against their privileges, to alter the fundamental laws of the kingdom—Sir, you must excuse me."[29]

Thus there was no compromise. The high court did not succeed in assuming the appearance of legality. It derived its right to judge from the assertion that Charles Stuart was no longer king but instead a tyrant and a traitor; but it did not succeed in obliging the sovereign to collaborate in his own degradation. It did not even challenge the divine characteristics derived from the king's anointing. During his imprisonment Charles continued to exercise his thaumaturgic powers against the "king's evil," touching coins that were passed through the prison windows to be made into "cramp rings," talismans against apoplexy.[30]

On the scaffold, the distance maintained by soldiers between the condemned man and the crowd prevented the king from being heard. He spoke nonetheless to those around him, and the press soon undertook the publication of his last words.[31] To Bishop Juxon, who comforted him by saying that before him would soon open a great highway that would lead him to heaven, where a crown of glory awaited him, Charles I replied: "I go from a corruptible crown to an incorruptible one."[32] It was 30 January 1649, and a crown of martyrdom would soon be placed upon his head by enflamed partisan pamphlets. One must add that he also presented himself as a martyr to his own people. After the interminable discussions with parliamentary commissions, when a delegation from parliament had left Newport on 27 November 1648 to return to confer in Westminster, Charles expressed his agony to them: "I thank God I shall make my peace with him, and shall not fear whatsoever He shall suffere men to do unto me. You cannot but know that in my fall and ruin you see your own, and that also of those near unto you."[33]

On the scaffold, when Fairfax displayed the king's head, the crowd ran to soak handkerchiefs in his blood: "the blood of that sacred body."[34] An instant demand arose for such relics when miracles "wrought by his blood" were reported.[35]

During the days of his captivity, the king himself threw down some notes to prepare his own martyrology. Dr. John Gauden, dean of Worcester, brought them together in a small volume: *Eikon Basilike: The Pourtraiture of his sacred Maiestie in his solitude and suffering,* published by Richard Royston at the beginning of February. Quite soon a new edition followed, produced by William Dugard, with the king's prayer appended, and between June and December 1649 John Williams issued a series of miniature editions of the book, which could be hidden more easily (Dugard and Williams were both arrested).[36]

The text was written in the first person, as if by the king himself. The frontispiece too, engraved by Guillaume Marshall, was partly inspired by Charles with an elaborate symbolism (Fig. 88). The king is shown kneeling in front of a table, on the top of which a lectern holds a book open to "IN VERBO TUO SPES MEA" (In Your Word my hope), and a sheet

29. *Calendar of State Papers* 1883, DXVII:350–53; Cobbett 1809–26, IV:1099. See also *A Perfect Narrative* n.d. Another contemporary chronicle is the *Discours ample* 1649.

30. Carlton 1983, 331. On "cramp rings," see Jones 1883, 474–75; Thomas [1971] 1973, 235–36.

31. Marsys 1649; *L'execvtion* 1649; *Lettre de consolation* 1649; *Lettre du prince de Galles* 1649; *Les memoires* 1649; *The pourtraicture* 1648. There is more bibliography in Muddiman n.d. and Roberts 1999.

32. Cobbett 1809–26, III:1265, *Reliquiae sacrae Carolinae.*

33. Carlton 1983, 339.

34. *Remonstrance* 1649, 12v.

35. See Howarth 1997.

36. See Roberts 1999, 30. Other editions of the *Eikon Basilike* were published in 1662, 1681, 1685, and 1687.

Fig. 88   Guillaume Marshall, Charles I, martyr of the *religio regis,* engraving from
The Pourtraicture . . . , London, Royston, 1648.

on which was written "Christi Tracto." His right foot rested on a globe. The earthly
crown *splendidam et gravem* (bright and heavy), but related to *vanitas,* lay at his feet. Following the symbolism of *Christomimèsis,* the king held a crown of thorns (*asperam at levem*
[harsh but light]) while gazing at a celestial crown of glory (*beatam et eternam* [beatific and
eternal]).[37] The royal face was lit by a sunray (*coeli specto* [heaven's gaze]). A second ray
penetrated through a black cloudy sky, *clarior e tenebris* (more brilliant in darkness). In the
landscape the tempest of the revolution was shown breaking against a solid rock *immota
trimphans* (still and triumphant). In the foreground was shown the martyr's weighted
palm: *crescit sub pondere virtus* (virtue increases under weight). One might note that this
palm was a reproduction of the printer's mark of John Wolfe, a palm with a scroll in Italian: "Il vostro malignare non giova nulla" (Your malignity will gain nothing).[38]

This print was reproduced in France in *Les memoires du roy d'Angleterre* of the same
year,[39] but with a modification of the political meaning of the original: the storm-battered
rock was removed, thus better emphasizing the theme of martyrdom (Fig. 89).

Another print was produced by William Faithorne some years later, showing the king

37. *The pourtraicture* 1648.
38. Bertelli and Innocenti 1979, sec. XVI, 171.
39. *Les memoires* 1649.

Christe iubes, pereat gemmis onerata corona,
Spinea nobilior sanguine facta tuo est.

Fig. 89   *Christe iubes, pereat gemmis onerata corona, spinea nobilior sanguine facta
tuo est*, engraving from *Les Memoires du roy d'Angleterre*, Paris, E.
Pruveray, 1649.

with his head covered by the cap he wore on the scaffold, his arms in the gesture of prayer, a sunray bringing down to him the celestial crown. "Religion played a crucial part in Charles I's downfall and the cult of the Martyr King that arose soon after his death was based on the belief that he died a martyr for the Anglican Church."[40]

What shock was produced in Europe by the Roundheads' regicide is indicated in the words of the anonymous author of a letter of consolation to the queen of England that was printed in Paris by G. Sassier. There was no hesitation in comparing the royal execution to the crucifixion of Christ: "Madame, after God died on the cross by the hand of the most infamous of executioners, such sufferings must be received by pious souls as acts of grace; to imitate the Creator in his death and participate in his innocence is to give posterity the assurance of an imperishable glory . . . and it is not surprising that the greatness of this virtue has obtained from heaven a divine diadem, which a bloody court could not take from him."[41] Another pamphlet compared the sufferings of the king directly to those of the Savior.[42] And further: "The barbarians . . . can no longer act against him whom they have made more brilliant than a sun."[43] "Barbarianism" is the concept that appears most frequently in these works. Another pamphlet spoke of "that barbarous act" for which there were no examples in antiquity and which future centuries would find difficult to believe.[44]

In his apocryphal lamentations, the Prince of Wales addressed the soul of his father, saying that the cruel sword of the executioner "immolated you like an innocent victim to the fury of an enraged people."[45] A further tract repeated the comparison with the passion of the Savior.[46] Another work took up instead the theme of the *lex animata*. England was a cursed isle that had violated all fidelity by dethroning its own king and by giving laws rather than receiving them. "You have killed your prince, your lord; you have emptied upon him the traces of your barbarity; you have covered this innocent prince with your blackest propaganda; you have set law upon him, you who should have received it from him."[47] But the day of restoration of the son of the martyr was already foreseen: "Your Majesty will prevail over the ruins of this wild and bloody people and with a Christian and faithful council will counter the power of their inhuman judgment for taking the life of their lord."[48]

The anonymous author of the remonstrance to the sovereigns of Europe said that "the whole earth must rise up against these rebels, who dared to aspire to independence and who sought sovereignty in the greatest of all crimes, and they must be lowered and humbled by the greatest of punishments."[49] Contagion seemed to be what was feared the most. Now one must remain continually alarmed and suspicious; this example showed libertines the simplicity of the crime: "The ease of the crime has presented to the imagination of libertines how to commit it without reflecting on the consequences."[50] For this the sovereigns of Europe should be moved to act before it was too late. "Rise up thus ye

40. Roberts 1999, 33.
41. *Lettre de consolation* 1649, 3–4.
42. *Consolations* 1649.
43. *Consolations* 1649, 5.
44. *Relation veritable* 1649, 4.
45. *Lettre du prince de Galles* 1649, 5.
46. *Consolations* 1649.
47. *Sanglots pitoyables* 1649.
48. *La reception* 1649, 7.
49. *Remonstrance* 1649, 11r.
50. *Remonstrance* 1649, 11r.

illustrious avengers of divine wrath; this blow struck all of Christendom; it is a toxin against which all the monarchs of Europe should act."[51]

We must now go on to examine the two chief texts of this pamphlet literature: the *Defensio regia pro Carolo I,* by Claude Saumaise, and the *Regii sanguinis clamor,* by Pierre Du Moulin. The authors were among the most celebrated scholars of the seventeenth century, and it is symptomatic that both were Protestants. The first was the son of the erudite Benigne Saumaise, whose fame he surpassed; the second was the son of a famous theologian who bore the same name. Both help to demonstrate to what extent the cult of kingship permeated European society (the *Defensio* was reprinted nine times in three years!) and how unrealistic it is to speak of the cult of kingship as a belief confined to the lower classes.

The horrible news of the regicide not only reached the ears of Saumaise, it wrenched his soul. This was a parricide of a king committed by a sacrilegious conspiracy of nefarious men. They were beasts with human faces ("belluae tam immanes sub humana facie"); he thought he was confronted with enemies of the human race ("communes generis humani hostes iudicadi sunt").[52] They were *cacodaemones,* parricides worthy of being sewed up in a *culleus.*[53] But Saumaise said something much more important (which certainly would have pleased a scholar of kingship like Kantorowicz had he noted it): "At the time of King Edward II two Despensers, to maintain their own power [*ut proditionem suam regerent*], wanted to distinguish between the political and the natural body of the monarchy. This did great harm to both kings and kingdoms because, when the subjection due to the king was directed more to his political body than to his physical body, it became permissible for subjects to remove the sovereign, if he was weak or unjust or if he violated the law; and this could be done just as well through force. This was the worst possible conclusion and one deduced from a false proposition, thought up and invented with specious pretexts, since now, at the subjects' will, the king could put down his scepter along with his life. So long as royal power was inseparable from the person of the monarch, the sovereign, even if he committed a crime, could not be punished like a private person, because his majesty and person were inseparable. Whoever offends his person cannot remain unpunished, but must be hunted down instead for the crime of lèse-majesté, since whoever offends him violates his majesty.[54] From this derived the affirmation in English common law, that 'the king cannot commit a crime.'. . . The king can act freely with impunity because his actions cannot be considered as crimes, as they would be for others. The king is not obliged to consider the crime of adultery, homicide, or other capital offenses to which others are subjected, who are bound by the law [*legibus solutus*]."[55]

The reference of Saumaise was to Hugh Le Despenser the elder, earl of Winchester, and to his son Hugh the younger, earl of Gloucester, favorites of Edward II who were decapitated in 1326.[56] Hugh the younger, particularly, had theorized in the parliament of 1322 about the right of the assembly to control the royal will and *in extremis* the right of rebellion against the monarch, since the fidelity of subjects was directed to the Crown

51. *Remonstrance* 1649, 13r.
52. Saumaise 1651, "Prefatio."
53. Saumaise 1651, 2 and 9.
54. See Sbriccoli 1974.
55. Saumaise 1651, 179.
56. Stubbs 1882, 1:322 (*Annales Paulini*); *Chronicles* 1886.

(to the *dignitas*) and not to the *persona* of the sovereign.[57] But it is probable that Saumaise, even though indicting the two Despensers, meant to include in his polemic also the more recent Tudor jurists who had developed this concept into a true and proper constitutional theory.

Pierre Du Moulin also concerned himself with parricides and deicides,[58] who were guilty of having committed violence against a sovereign who represented a legitimate line of succession extending through ten centuries.[59] Du Moulin repeated the same objection of the House of Lords to the legitimacy of the House of Commons' sitting in judgment over what was an integral part of that assembled body.[60] With a dialectical leap, he also objected to any judgment in the name of the people. This was, in fact, a "most atrocious crime against the people, as well as an unworthy assassination of the king. If the king rules not for himself but for the people, it is a still worse crime for the people to violate his person. For this reason it is imprudent, even mad, to say that the killing of a king and the abolition of a monarchy are done in the name of the people."[61]

John Milton took it upon himself to reply both to Saumaise and to Du Moulin. Turning upside down the concept of the divine origin of the monarchy, he departed from the fundamental premise that the monarchy was given to the people by God or that the people had asked God to receive a monarch ("Qui Regem non ivito Deo unquam petivimus, nec ispo dante accepimus"). To the contrary, the people constituted the monarchy through their own laws, based on the *jus gentium,* neither following a command nor disobeying a prohibition of God ("sed jure gentium usi, nec jubente Dio nec vetante, nostris legibus constituimus").[62] Two horns of a dilemma thus logically followed: if kings reign in the name of God, the people can also claim freedom in the name of God ("Si ergo Reges hodie per Deum regnant, etiam populi per Deum in libertatem se vindicant"). And if the people could establish a king without God's doing, through the same right they could also reject a king ("Populus ubiqunque sine Deo manifesto Regem creavit, potest eodem jure suo Regem rejicere").[63] As for the *Regis sanguinis clamor,* Milton thought it might have been written by the churchman Alexander More (1616–70) ("Est Morus quindam, partim Scotus partim Gallus" [This More is part Scotsman, part French]), and this pamphlet truly annoyed him, leading him to a vulgar attack. He accused More of having committed adultery when he was a teacher of Greek in Geneva, and of having raped a woman in the house of Saumaise in Holland. To poor More, who had gotten Nieupoort, the ambassador of the Low Countries, to intervene in an attempt to keep Milton from publishing his book, there remained only the recourse of publishing two series of acts and attestations in his own defense.[64]

The true respondent to Milton ("non Anglus, sed Anglorum dedecus" [he is not English, but the disgrace of Englishmen]) was John Rowland, who spoke of the "useless word 'people.'"[65] He repeated the thesis that parliament could not be convened without

57. Stubbs 1906, II:368ff.
58. Du Moulin 1652, preface to Charles II.
59. Du Moulin 1652, 2.
60. Du Moulin 1652, 57–59.
61. Du Moulin 1652, 82–83.
62. Milton 1651, 13.
63. Milton 1651, 15.
64. Milton 1654; More 1655. Another pamphlet, *The Life and Reigne of King Charles,* London: W. Raybald, 1651, attributed to Milton, was probably the work of the Calvinist Hamon L'Estrange.
65. [Rowland] 1652, 20.

being presided over by the monarch ("Absque rege Parlamentum ullum nec esse nec vocari potest"),[66] denying that it was possible freely to degrade a king into a tyrant ("tua perfidia omnes reges tyrannos redderes")[67] and asking what remedy remained to the people against a parliamentary tyranny ("Remedium contra regis tyrannidem dicis Parlamentum, sed quod remedium restat populo contra tyrannidem Parlamenti?").[68]

What I wish to emphasize from this polemic is the persistence of the cult of kingship among cultivated people and intellectuals of note on the seventeenth-century scene. This was still while Milton, the monarchomachs, and soon figures of the Enlightenment were beginning to gnaw at the foundations of a system that, as Du Moulin wrote, had continued for more than a millennium. What Milton could not foresee was that, despite the solemn vote of Parliament condemning the Stuart king to death, and despite the threat of a restoration, England would soon be drawn toward the constitutional settlement of a new reigning house. Had it not been for the weakness of his son Richard, Oliver Cromwell would probably have installed a new dynasty. The ceremonial of his court (including a *lever*)[69] suggests the direction that the revolution of the Roundheads was taking. That Cromwell (compared to a new Moses)[70] was increasingly taking on the role of a monarch is confirmed, for example, by his granting of a barony to one of his cousins, Edmund Dunch, made Baron Burnell of East Wittenham (26 April 1658). The letters patent were addressed to all "Dukes, Marquises, Earls, Viscounts, Barons, Knights, Prevosts, Freemen, and to all the officers, ministers and subjects" of the realm, using the same formula of a feudal monarch.[71] But it was above all his funeral in effigy, modeled on those of the preceding monarchs,[72] that showed how little England had succeeded in liberating itself from the royal cult. "Cromwell's funeral procession imitated that of James I but was even more elaborate and costly."[73] What was now impossible to restore, even by King Charles II, was its sacred character. In the new climate created by the Puritan Revolution, the divinity of kingship had now definitely dissolved.

It remained across the English Channel in the France of the Grand Siècle. But precisely Voltaire wrote in his *Essai sur les moeurs:* "The gods of the earth were both the horror and the divinity of Catholic Europe."[74] "Divinity" referred directly to the *divus rex*. As for the peoples of Europe, who the leaders of the French Revolution later set themselves up to interpret and vindicate, Montesquieu, in *L'esprit des lois,* observed: "Machiavelli attributed the loss of liberty of the Florentine republic to the fact that the people did not judge crimes of lèse-majesté committed against it as a body, as in Rome."[75] And he introduced the concept of "nation" and spoke of the "way of thinking of a nation," of the "spirit of a nation" (what would become the *Volksgeist* of the Romantics).

The minds of the deputies in the National Convention during the French Revolution were full of such ideas when the deputies gave their vote (*opinion*) on the fate of Louis Capet (Louis XVI). As Robert Lindet declared in his report of 10 December 1792, "France,

66. [Rowland] 1652, 149.
67. [Rowland] 1652, 38 and 116.
68. [Rowland] 1652, 21.
69. Sherwood 1977, 70.
70. Sherwood 1977, 109; see also Burton 1974.
71. Sherwood 1977, 128.
72. Sherwood 1977, 61, 69 (dispatch of the Venetian ambassador Francesco Giavarini), 74–75, 127ff.
73. Woodward 1997, 200.
74. *Essai,* XIII, chap. 197, 176.
75. *Esprit,* VI, 5:75.

[has arrived at the point] where the general diffusion of enlightenment and awareness of the rights of man announced a coming regeneration."[76]

On 7 November 1792, the deputy from the Haute-Garonne, Jean Mailhe, presented the report that would be the basis for the approaching judgment on the fate of the king: "You have to make pronouncement on the crimes of a king: but the accused is not a king; he has resumed his natural title, he is a man. If he is innocent, let him justify himself; if he is guilty, his fate should serve as an example to all nations."[77]

Looking through the declarations concerning the vote,[78] some things strike one immediately: the reappearance of the idea of the breaking of an oath was one theme, and the reduction of the monarch to the status of a tyrant was another. Alexandre Deleyre (Gironde) said: "The monarch has become a tyrant because he exercises an absolute power, because he has questioned the recovered liberty of a people, because he wants to govern without a constitution, because he violated the constitution he had accepted. He is guilty in the eyes of the people of the excesses of arbitrary power and of the abuse of legitimate power. This monarch, as tyrant, can be punished by the law, or without the law." Another theme was the reduction of the monarch to the status of a man ("daring to judge a king like any other citizen," as the Jacobins of Auxerre expressed it, addressing the Convention).[79] Another theme was that the king's blood was now "impure." (Bordas from the Haute-Vienne said, "I have seen that the impure blood of Louis could become the pretext and fuel for a war carried out against all who wear crowns.)[80] A new concept, but derived from Montesquieu, made its appearance: *lèse nation*.[81] It was affirmed that the principle of the inviolability of the monarchy was a sham. ("Royal inviolability. . . . France, they say, cannot maintain itself without monarchy, nor the monarch without the principle of being inviolable; since, if the king were accused or judged by the legislative body, it would depend on him, and as a consequence the monarchy will be subdued to that body . . . it would be deprived of energy, of action to execute the law; in this case there would be no more liberty. . . . It is held, however, that this inviolability was a threat to liberty, but it is thought that a remedy might be the responsibility of ministers.")[82] But this was merely a political superstition ("My opinion is unequivocal on the stupid dogma of inviolability . . . a political superstition").[83]

In reality, the Jacobins spoke of *lèse nation* because they wanted to rid themselves of the monarchical regime, and thus they had to "kill" it as an institution. Although for the English Puritans Charles I was a religious adversary who had threatened the common good, thus making him a tyrant, they nonetheless had not thought of killing the system. The funeral granted to Cromwell was significant in this regard. But in the language of Saint-Just, for instance, there was "the dramatic denial that the king ever belonged to the French people. If he had never been a part of it, he could not be treated as a traitor, and there was no need to arrange a trial. The king should simply be considered an enemy of

---

76. Cited in Soboul 1973, 101.

77. *Rapport et projet de décret présentés au nom du comité de législation par Jean Mailhe, député de la Haute-Garonne* (session of 7 November 1792), in *Procès de Louis XVI* 1821 (reprinted in Soboul 1973, 63); Walzer [1974] 1989, 159ff.

78. *Convention nationale* 1793 (further references will be to the name of the deputy).

79. Soboul 1973, 52.

80. *Précis des opinions prononcées* 1793, 2–3.

81. Ibid., under J. Dusaulx, *Département de Paris*.

82. *Rapport*, in *Procès de Louis XVI* 1821, 5; see also Soboul 1973, 62.

83. Session of 13 November, motion by Petion.

France; his death did not need to follow from a lawful sentence; it was stupid to elevate him to the rank of a citizen so as to condemn him."[84]

Jean Mailhe reached much the same conclusion in his report:

> He will say that his person cannot be separated from the functions of royalty, that he is inviolable as king for all administrative acts, but an individual for personal acts. We reply that he is accused of depending too heavily on this separation. His inviolability as head of the executive power was based only on the fiction that he could pass crimes and punishments down onto the heads of his agents. Has he not forgone the benefit of this fiction if he truly hatched plots without the knowledge of his ministers or other visible agents, or put his ministers beyond the reach of effective surveillance? And since it is against the very premises of the constitution accepted by Louis XVI for the law to be broken with impunity, Louis XVI can naturally and necessarily be charged with all crimes with which it is impossible to charge his agents.[85]

Given the lack of "reciprocity between the nation and the king" and the inalienability of the sovereignty of the nation, "the nation is not tied by royal inviolability; it could not be, because there is no reciprocity between the nation and the king; Louis XVI was king only through the constitution; the nation had been sovereign without the constitution and without the king; it holds its sovereignty from nature; it cannot be alienated for a single second."[86]

As the deputy from the Département de la Yonne said with lucidity, "Accustomed to consider kings as sacred objects, the people will of necessity conclude: 'But the heads of kings are not so sacred, because the axe is ready and the avenging arm of justice knows how to strike them.' This way you show them the path to liberty."[87] The anointed one of God, in the words of a motion from the Commune of Paris, was now wittily called "the royal individual"; his health should be looked after so that he could be sent to the scaffold. "We must dissipate the concern expressed in some sections about the health of the royal person."[88] The contempt for the sovereign had reached such an extreme that two members of the Paris Commune, Colombean and Jacques René Hébert, held it "unworthy of a republican to occupy himself for a single instant with an individual whose only superiority over others is that of his crimes."[89]

However, an eyewitness account of the English ambassador George Monro, sent to Lord Grenville on 27 December 1792, shows that the cult of royalty was not yet totally extinguished: "His Most Christian Majesty made his appearance yesterday at the bar of the National Convention. . . . He appeared to me perfectly composed and in good health; his appearance and address had again a great effect upon the people"; this was enough to make Monro think the king's life would be saved.[90]

We know that the critical words in the debate were pronounced by Saint-Just in his first appearance on the tribune: "Citizens, it is my intent to prove that the king can be

84. Walzer [1974] 1989, 113, 202ff., 274ff.
85. *Rapport*, in *Procès de Louis XVI* 1821, 4, not in Soboul 1973; Walzer [1974] 1989, 163–63.
86. *Rapport*, in *Procès de Louis XVI* 1821, 6, not in Soboul 1973.
87. *Convention nationale* 1793, *opinion* of Jacques Boilleau.
88. Beaucourt 1892, II:129; Conseil Général de la Commune, session of 19 November 1792.
89. Beaucourt 1892, II:131, Conseil Général de la Commune, session of 20 November 1792.
90. Beaucourt 1892, II:238.

Fig. 90   *L'idole renversée,* French broadside (Providence, Hay Library, Anne S. K. Brown Military Collection).

judged . . . the king must be judged as an enemy."[91] One seemed to hear an echo from Rousseau's *Social Contract:* "kill the vanquished"!

At the following meeting on 3 December 1792, Maximilien Robespierre, for his own part, with words as sharp as a sword blade, removed any legalistic preoccupation of the Girondists:

> No trial is to be undertaken here; Louis is not a plaintiff, and you are not his judges. You are, and can be, none other than statesmen, the representatives of the nation. You are not here to pronounce sentence for or against a man, but must take a measure of public

91. *Convention nationale* 1793, 36ff., *Recueil . . . Appels nominaux faits à la Convention Naztionale;* Soboul 1973, 71.

safety, exercise an act of national salvation. . . . Louis was king; now a republic has been founded. The whole debate that has occupied you is resolved with these words. Louis was dethroned for his crimes. Louis has denounced the French people as rebels; he has appealed to the armies of his fellow tyrants to strike them. The victory of the people has decided that he is the only rebel. Thus Louis cannot be judged; he has already been judged. Either he will be condemned, or the Republic will not be absolved.[92]

Unlike Charles Stuart, Louis of France accepted the authority of his tribunal; he responded, asked for advice regarding his defense, was defended by his lawyers, and thus lost the grandeur maintained by his unfortunate predecessor.[93] He had accepted the constitution; he anticipated a sentence that respected the juridical norms that the revolutionaries themselves had set down. He put his faith in the principle of the inviolability of the sovereign, which the constitution accorded him, and in the nonretroactive nature of the laws. He did not understand what had been clear from the onset to Danton (at least according to what Théodore de Lameth said in his *Mémoires*): "Could one save a king through a trial? He was dead when he appeared before his judges."[94]

"Louis, the French people accuse you of having committed a multitude of crimes to establish your tyranny by destroying their liberty."[95] How could one defend oneself against such a political accusation? At the beginning of the whole process, the report on the conduct of the king, by Robert Lindet, said that Louis had been "denounced by the people as a tyrant who had constantly applied himself to prevent or retard the progress of liberty." He added that "in France, where the general diffusion of enlightenment and awareness of the rights of man announced a coming regeneration, an isolated despot, tottering on his throne, was no longer able to protect himself, if not supported by the force, faith, and enlightenment of the people."[96]

In this difficult atmosphere, the king's very defense judged it more profitable to emphasize the man and to forget his anointing: "Louis is not guilty."[97] After his defenders, the king took the stand:

Perhaps I speak for the last time. I declare that my conscience accuses me of nothing and that my defenders have spoken the truth. I have never feared a public judgment of my conduct, but my heart breaks when I find in the act of accusation that I wished to spill the blood of the people and, above all, that the tragic events of 10 August are attributed to me. I believe that the numerous proofs of my love for the people, which I have always given, and my whole conduct prove how little I feared exposing myself to protect their blood and to keep such an accusation far from me.[98]

92. *Convention nationale 1793*, 74–77; Walzer [1974] 1989, 219ff.

93. *Convention nationale 1793*, *Défense de Louis, prononcée à la barre . . . 1793; Arringa in difesa* n.d.; *Compendio istorico 1793*.

94. Soboul 1973, 24.

95. *Convention nationale 1793*, 124ff., *Interrogatoire de Louis XVI* (session of 11 December), and *Acte enonciatif des crimes de Louis XVI* (decree of 11 December 1792), 117ff.

96. *Convention nationale 1793*, 95ff., *Rapport sur la conduite de Louis XVI*.

97. *Convention nationale 1793*, 149ff., *Défense de Louis, prononcée à la barre . . . 1793*. On the trial and defense, see also Reinhard 1969; Mejan 1814; Lacouloumière n.d.

98. *Convention nationale 1793*, 201ff.

The outcome, however, was already decided. As Maximilien Robespierre would declare in the session of 28 December: "I demand that the National Convention declare Louis guilty and deserving of death."[99]

His last words to his family were quite timid, intimate. The figure of a private man emerges from them, not to say a bourgeois, but certainly a man stripped of all sacredness.

> I recommend to God my wife and my children, my sister and aunts, my brothers, and all those who are attached to me by blood or in whatever other way. I pray to God particularly to show mercy on my wife, my children, and my sister, who have long suffered with me. . . . I recommend my children to my wife; I have never doubted her maternal affection for them. I ask her above all to make them good Christians and honest men. . . . I recommend to my son, should he ever have the misfortune to be king. . . . I conclude by declaring before God, ready as I am to appear before him, that I am innocent of the crimes of which I am accused.[100]

What a misfortune to be king!

On 21 January 1793, the priest Jacques Roux presented the Commune of Paris with the following report:

> Jacques Roux, priest, one of the commissioners named by the Commune to attend the execution of Louis spoke. "We give account of the mission charged to us. We were taken to the Temple. There we told the tyrant that his hour of execution had come. He asked to be left alone for some minutes with his confessor. He had wanted to give us a packet [his testament] to give to you; we told him that we were charged only with taking him to the scaffold. He answered: 'That is just.' He gave the packet to one of our colleagues, recommended his family, and asked that Cléry, his *valet de chambre,* be assigned to the queen; in his haste he said 'my wife'. . . we did not take our eyes off of Capet till he reached the guillotine. He arrived at ten hours, ten minutes; it took him three minutes to descend from the conveyance. He wanted to speak to the people. Santerre denied this; his head fell. The citizens dipped their pikes and their handkerchiefs in his blood."[101]

The same acts of devotion were repeated as had occurred after the decapitation of Charles I. But in the three minutes that it took Louis Capet to descend the steps of his carriage, a thousand years of the *religio regis* ended.[102]

99. *Convention nationale* 1793, 245–64, *Discours de Maximilien Robespierre* (session of 29 December 1792).

100. *Convention nationale* 1793, 372–75, *Testement de Louis* (also printed in Beaucourt 1892, II:326ff.).

101. *Convention nationale* 1793, 370, *Rapport de l'execution de Louis Capet, fait à la commune de Paris, le même jour 21 janvier 1793* (also printed, in abridged form, in Beaucourt 1892, II:309–10).

102. For the posthumous cult of Louis XVI, see Combes 1872, 266–76; *La France en deuil* n.d.; Seguin 1829; Granel 1908; Delassus n.d.; Aulard 1921.

Bibliography

Abbreviations

AASS *Acta Sanctorum quotquot toto orbe coluntur . . .*, edited by J. Bolland, Antwerp, 1643–

AESC *Annales: Economie, société, civilisation*

AJA *American Journal of Archaeology*

AS Archivio di Stato (followed by the place)

ASI *Archivio storico italiano*

ASL *Archivio storico lombardo*

BAV Biblioteca Apostolica Vaticana

BHR *Bibliothèque d'humanisme et Renaissance*

BMP Bibliothèque Mazarine, Paris

BNF Biblioteca Nazionale Centrale, Firenze

BNNa Biblioteca Nazionale, Napoli

BNP Bibliothèque Nationale, Paris

Bullarium *Bullarium privilegiorum ac diplomatum romanorum pontificum amplissima collectio,* edited by C. Coquelin, Rome: Mainardi, 1739–58

DSP Deputazione di Storia Patria (followed by the city or province)

HBS Henry Bradshaw Society for the Editing of Rare Liturgical Texts, London, 1891–1940

JRS *Journal of Roman Studies*

JW *Journal of the Warburg and Courtauld Institutes*

MGH *Monumenta Germaniae Historica*

MGHEp. *Monumenta Germaniae Historica Epistolae*

MGHSS *Monumenta Germaniae Historica Scriptores*

MGHss *Monumenta Germaniae Historica Scriptores rerum germanicarun in usum scholarum ex monumentis Germaniae historicis*

MGHSSRMer. *Monumenta Germaniae Historica Scriptores rerum merovingicarum*

NDI *Novissimo digesto italiano,* Turin: UTET, 1959

PG *Patrologiae cursus completus . . . series graecae,* edited by J. P. Migne, 1857–62

PL *Patrologiae cursus completus . . . series latinae,* edited by J. P. Migne, 1844–64

RBMES *Rerum Britannicarum Medii Aevi Scriptores,* London: Longman, 1858–96

RE *Paulys Real-Encyclopaedie der classischen Altertums Wissenschaft,* edited by G. Wissowa, E. Kroll et al., Stuttgart, 1893–1919

RIS *Rerum Italicarum Scriptores,* edited by L. A. Muratori, Milan, 1723–51

RIS² *Rerum Italicarum Scriptores,* edited by G. Carducci and E. Fiorini, Città di Castello, 1900–

RSCI *Rivista di storia della chiesa in Italia*

SCJ *Sixteenth Century Journal*

SHA *Scriptores Historiae Augustae*

SSHByz. *Corpus Scriptores Historiae Byzantinae,* edited by B. G. Niebuhr, Bonn, 1828–

SSRA *Scriptores Rerum Anglicarum,* London: Longman, 1859–

ZfRG *Zeitschrift für Religionsgeschichte*

Accursio. 1939. *Glossa ad Institutiones Iustiniani imperatoris.* Bologna: Zanichelli.

Ackerman, J. S. 1954. *The Cortile del Belvedere.* Vol. III of *Studi e documenti per la storia del palazzo apostolico vaticano.* Vatican City: BAV.

Actions de graces et regiovissance de la France svr la mort dv Marqvis d'Ancre: Av Roy. 1617. Paris: Nicolas Alexandre.

Adami, A. 1636. *Il novitiato del maestro di casa.* Rome: Facciotti.

Ademollo, A. 1886. *Alessandro VI, Giulio II e Leone X nel carnevale.* Florence.

Adler, A. 1992. *La mort est la masque du roi.* Paris: Payot.

Akrigg, G., ed. 1984. *Letters of King James VI. and I.* Berkeley and Los Angeles: University of California Press.

Alberi, E. 1839–63. *Relazioni degli ambasciatori veneti.* Florence: Barbèra.

Albicante, G. A. 1541. *Trattato dell'intrar in Milano di Carlo V.* Milan: A. Calmum.

Aldobrandini, G. 1990. "Vittoria: L'imperatrice delle classi medie." In Bertelli and Grottanelli 1990, 101–19.

Aldrete, G. S. 1999. *Gestures and Acclamations in Ancient Rome.* Baltimore: Johns Hopkins University Press.

Alföldi, A. 1970. *Die monarchische Repräsentation im römischen Kaiserreich.* Darmstadt: Wissenschaftliche Buchgesellschaft.

Allen, J. W. 1938. *English Political Thought, 1603–1660.* London: Methuen.

[Alletz P.-A.]. 1775. *Cérémonial du sacre de rois de France.* Paris: G. Desprez.

Amalarius. *De ecclesiasticis officiis libri* IV. PL., CV.

Ames, J. D. 1942. *The Changing Character of Lynching: Review of Lynching, 1931–1941, with a Discussion of Recent Developments in This Field*. Atlanta, Ga.: Commission of Interracial Cooperation.

Ammianus Marcellinus. 1978. *Res gestae*. Edited by W. Seyfarth. Leipzig: Teubner.

Andreas Ungarus. 1882. *Descriptio victoriae Karolo Provinciae comite reportate*. Edited by G. Waitz. MGHSS, XXVI.

Andrieu, M. 1924. *Immixtio et consecratio: La consécration par contact dans les documents liturgiques du Moyen Âge*. Paris: Plon, 1924.

Annales Bertiniani. 1883. Edited by G. Waitz. MGHss.

Anonimo Romano. 1981. *La vita di Cola di Rienzo*. Edited by G. Porta. Milan: Adelphi.

Aragona, Enrique de. See Villena, Enrique de.

Arco, R. Del. 1954. *Sepulcros de la casa real de Castilla*. Madrid: Consejo Sup. de Investigaciones Científicas.

Ariès, Ph. 1960. *L'enfant et la vie familiale sous l'ancien régime*. Paris: Plon.

Ariosti, M. 1899. *Resoconto delle feste fatte in Reggio Emilia nell'anno 1453 per l'ingresso di Borso d'Este*. Reggio Emilia: Calderini.

———. 1901. *Le poesie latine e italiane di Malatesta A. precedute da notizie sulla sua vita*. Edited by A. Levi. Florence: Bencini.

Arringa in difesa del re Luigi XVI recitata da **** Deseze in nome de' suoi compatrocinatori alla sbarra della Convenzione Nazionale. . . . n.d. Milan: L. Veladini.

A tavola con il principe: Materiali per una mostra su alimentazione e cultura nella Ferrara degli Estensi. 1988. Amministrazione Provinciale di Ferrara. N.p.: G. Corbo.

Aubrey, J. 1881. *Remains of Gentilism and Judaism, 1686–87*. Edited by J. Britten. London: Satchell Peyton & Co.

Augspurg (Der hoch / heerte) wie solches . . . mit . . . der . . . Roemischen Kayserin und Roemischen Koenigs Eleonorae und Josephi Kroenungs-Festivitaet beglucket worde. . . . 1690. Augsburg: Jacob Koppmayer.

Aulard, A. 1921. "L'exécution de Louis XVI et la presse française." *La revue française* LXXXII:65–76, 153–62.

Aylmer, G. E. 1974. *The King's Servants: The Civil Service of Charles I, 1625–1642*. London.

Bachtin, M. 1965. *Tvorcestvo Fransua Rable i narodnaja kul'tura srednevekov'ja i Renessanza*. Moscow: Izdatel'stvo Chudozestvennaja literatura.

Bak, J. M., ed. 1990. *Coronations: Medieval and Early Modern Monarchic Ritual*. Berkeley and Los Angeles: University of California Press.

Balandier, G. 1982. "Ordre commun, pouvoir et inceste royal en Afrique Orientale." *Actions et recherches sociales* 6, no. 5.

Baldassarri, A. 1714. *I pontifici Agnus Dei dilucidati*. Venice: Poletti.

Baldinucci, F. 1702–28. *Notizie de' professori del disegno da Cimabue in qua, Che contengono tre decennali, dal 1580 al 1610*. Florence: Giuseppe Manni (then Tartini & Franchi).

Banach, J. 1984. *Hercules Polonus: Studien z ickonografii sztuki nowozytnej*. Warsaw: Panstwowe Wydawnictwo Naukowe.

Banck, L. 1656. *Roma triumphans, seu Actus inaugurationum et coronationum pontificum romanorum et in spetie Innocentii X . . . brevis descriptio*. Franeker: Typis Arcerii.

Barb, A. A. 1953. "Diva Matrix: A Faked Gnostic Intaglio in the Possession of P. P. Rubens and the Iconology of a Symbol." *JW*, XVI:193–238.

Barbaro, S. 1574. *Sommario delle vite dei duchi di Milano*. Venice: n.p.

Barbero de Aguilera. 1970. "El pensamiento político visigodo y las primeras unciones regias en la Europa medieval." *Hispania* XXX:245–326.

Barbier, E. J. F. 1857. *Chronique de la régence et du règne de Louis XV*. Paris: Champetier.

Barbier de Montault, X. 1886. *Un Agnus Dei de Grégoire XI, découvert dans les fondations du château de Poitiers*. Poitiers: Impr. Gén. de l'Ouest.

Bardon, F. 1974. *Le portrait mythologique à la cour de France sous Henri IV et Louis XIII*. Paris: Picard.

Baronio, C. [1588–1607] 1738–45. *Annales ecclesiastici*. Lucae Venturini.

Basin, Th. 1963. *Historiarum de rebus a Ludovico XI Francorum rege et suo tempore in Gallia gestis libri*. Edited by Ch. Samaran. Paris: Les Belles Lettres.

Battisti, E. 1960. *Rinascimento e barocco*. Turin: Einaudi.

———. 1966. "I coperchi delle tombe medicee." In *Arte in Europa: Scritti di storia dell'arte in onore di Edoardo Arslan*, I.

Baumer, F. Le van. 1940. *The Early Tudor Theory of Kingship*. New Haven, Conn.: Yale University Press.

Bautier, R.-H. 1989. "Sacre et couronnement sous les Carolingiens et les premiers Capétiens: Recherches sur la genèse du sacre royal français." *Annuaire-bulletin de la Société de l'histoire de France*: 7–56.

Bayard, J.-P. [1964] 1981. *Le sacre des rois*. Paris: La Colombe.

Bayet, J. 1957. *Histoire politique et psychologique de la religion romaine*. Paris: Payot.

Baynes, N. H. 1984. *Sacre et couronnements royaux*. Paris: Trédaniel.

Beaucourt, marquis de. 1892. *Captivité et derniers moments de Louis XVI: Récits originaux et documents officiels*. Paris: Picard.

Beaune, C. 1986. "Les sanctuaires royaux." In *Les lieux de mémoire*, edited by P. Nora, II:57–87. Paris: La Nation.

Beccadelli, A. ["il Panormita"]. 1646. *Speculum boni principis Alphonsus rex Aragoniae: Hoc est dicta et facta Alphonsi regis Aragoniae. . . .* Amsterdam: L. Elzevir.

Beda. 1930. *Historia ecclesiastica.* Edited by King. London: Heinemann.

Bellotti, V. 1929. *Il dramma di Gerolamo Olgiati.* Milan: Cogliati-Martinelli.

Benveniste, É. 1969. *Le vocabulaire des institutions indo-européennes.* Vol. II, *Pouvoir, droit, religion.* Paris.

Berardi, A. 1681. *Ragionamenti musicali.* Bologna: G. Monti.

Bercé, Y.-M. 1990. *Le roi caché: Sauveur et imposteurs: Mythes politiques populaires dan l'Europe moderne.* Paris: Fayard.

Bergeron, D. M. 1971. *English Civic Pageantry, 1558–1642.* Columbia: University of South Carolina Press.

Berlier, U. 1929. "Le droit de gîte épiscopale lors d'une joyeuse entrée." In *Mélanges Paul Fournier.* Paris: Recueil Sirey.

Bernardi, A. [Novacula]. 1895. *Cronache forlivesi dal 1476 al 1517.* Edited by G. Mazzatinti. DSP Bologna.

Bernardi, T. 1986. "Analisi di una cerimonia pubblica: L'incoronazione di Carlo V a Bologna." *Quaderni storici* 61.

Bernhardt, J. W. 1993. *Itinerant Kingship and Royal Monasteries in Early Medieval Germany, c. 936–1075.* Cambridge: Cambridge University Press.

Bertaux, E. 1902. "La mausolée de l'empereur Henri VII à Pise." In *Mélanges Paul Fabre: Études d'histoire du Moyen Âge.* Paris: Picard.

Bertelli, C., P. Brambilla Barcilon, and A. Gallone. 1981. *Il ciborio della basilica di sant'Ambrogio in Milano.* Milan: Credito Artigiano.

Bertelli, P. 1589. *Diversarum nationum habitus.* Padua: Alciati.

Bertelli, S. 1973. *Ribelli, libertini e ortodossi nella storiografia barocca.* Florence: La Nuova Italia. (Spanish trans., *Rebeldes, libertinos y ortodoxos en el Barroco* [Barcelona: Ediciones Península, 1984].)

———. 1978. *Il potere oligarchico nello stato-città medievale.* Florence: La Nuova Italia.

———. 1990a. "Quel brutto ceffo d'un longobardo." In *Le tenebre e i lumi: Atti del convegno . . . Ascoli Piceno,* edited by E. Menestò. Ascoli Piceno: n.p.

———. 1990b. "Rappresentare 'Il Principe,' rappresentare Machiavelli." In *Asmodée-Asmodeo,* vol. 2, *Rappresentare il principe: Figurer l'état,* 47–57.

———. 1992. *Il dramma della monarchia medievale, ovvero: Il pranzo del Signore.* In Profeti 1992, 22–41.

———. 1994. "Lex animata in terris," in Cardini 1994, 119–61.

———. 1995. "La gamba del re." In *Florilegium: Scritti di storia dell'arte in onore di Carlo Bertelli.* Milan: Electa.

———. 1997a. "Cortigiane sfacciate e sposi voyeurs." *Paragone arte* XLVIII, no. 567:3–33.

———. 1997b. "Rituals of Violence Surrounding the King's Body." In Kolmer 1997, 263–80.

———. 1998. "*Rex et sacerdos:* The Holiness of the King in European Civilisation." In Ellenius 1998, 123–46.

———, ed. 2000. *Il teatro del potere nel XX secolo.* Rome: Carocci.

Bertelli, S., and M. Centanni, eds. 1995. *Il gesto nel rito e nel cerimoniale dal mondo antico ad oggi.* Florence: Ponte alle Grazie.

Bertelli, S., and G. Crifò, eds. 1985. *Rituale, cerimoniale, etichetta.* Milan: Bompiani.

Bertelli, S., and C. Grottanelli, eds. 1990. *Gli occhi di Alessandro: Potere sovrano e sacralità del corpo da Alessandro Magno a Ceausescu.* Florence: Ponte alle Grazie.

Bertelli, S., and I. Innocenti. 1979. *Bibliografia machiavelliana.* Verona: Edizioni Valdonega.

Berti, L. 1957. "Nota alla pianta di don Giovanni de Medici per la cappella dei principi a Firenze." *Atti del 5 convegno di storia dell'architettura, 1948:* 383–86.

———. 1967. *Il principe dello studiolo: Francesco I de' Medici e la fine del Rinascimento fiorentino.* Florence.

Bertolotti, A. 1878. "La morte di Pier Luigi Farnese: Processo e lettere inedite." In *Deputazione di Storia Patria per le Provincie dell'Emilia, Atti e Memorie,* n.s., III, 1:25–53.

———. 1881. *Artisti lombardi a Roma nei secoli XV, XVI e XVII.* Milan: Hoepli.

Beskow, P. 1962. *Rex gloriae: The Kingship of Christ in the Early Church.* Stockholm: Almquist & Wiksell.

Bettelheim, B. 1976. *The Uses of Enchantment: The Meaning and Importance of Fairy Tales.* New York: A. Knopf.

Beverini, B. 1829. *Annales ab origine Lucensis urbis.* Lucca: Bertini.

Bevy, C. J. 1766. *Histoire des inaugurations des rois, empereurs et autres souveraines de l'univers.* Paris: Moutard.

Biagio da Cesena. 1877. *Carlo V a Roma nel 1536: Frammenti dal diario. . . .* Edited by B. Podestà. Rome.

Bickermann, E. 1929. "Die römische Kaiserapotheose." *Archiv für Religionswissenschaft* XVII:1–34.

———. 1972. "Le culte des souverains dans l'Empire romain." *Entretiens de la Fondation Hardt* XIX:7–37.

Bie, J. 1636. *La France métallique. . . .* Paris: Camusat.

Bisi, A. M. 1965. *Il grifone: Storia di un motivo iconografico nell'antico Oriente mediterraneo.* Rome: Bardi.

Bizzocchi, R. 1987. *Chiesa e potere nella Toscana del quattrocento.* Bologna: Il Mulino.

————. 1995. *Genealogie incredibili: Scritti di storia nell'Europa moderna*. Bologna: Il Mulino.

Blancas, G. de. 1641. *Coronaciones de los serenísimos reyes de Aragón*. Saragossa.

Blanchet, J. A. 1892. "Médailles et jetons du sacre des rois de France." In *Études de numismatique*, 1:191–220. Paris: Rollin-Fenardent.

Bloch, M. [1923] 1961. *Les rois thaumaturges: Étude sur le caractère surnaturel attribué à la puissance royale particulièrement en France et en Angleterre*. Paris: Colin.

————. 1989. *Ritual, History, and Power: Selected Papers in Anthropology*. London: Athlon Press.

————. 1998. *How We Think They Think: Anthropological Approaches to Cognition, Memory, and Literacy*. Boulder, Colo.: Westview Press.

Blumenfeld-Kosinski, R. 1990. *Not of Woman Born: Representation of Caesarean Birth*. Ithaca, N.Y.: Cornell University Press.

Blumenthal, F. 1913. "Der aegyptianische Kaiserkult." *Archiv für Papyrusforschung* 5:317–45.

Blunt, A. 1954. *Art and Architecture in France, 1500–1700*. Baltimore: Pelican.

Bober, P., and R. Rubinstein. 1986. *Renaissance Artists and Antique Sculpture*. London: Oxford University Press.

Boer, W., ed. 1972. *Le culte des souverains dans l'Empire romaine, sept exposés*. . . . Geneva: Fondation Hardt.

Boisserée, S. 1842. *Über die Kaiser-Dalmatika in der St. Peterskirche zu Rom*. Munich: Weiss.

Bonaini, F., A. Fabretti, and F. L. Polidori. 1850. *Cronache e storie inedite della città di Perugia*. . . . ASI, I, XVI.

Bonardo, V. [1586] 1621. *Discorso intorno all'origine, antichità e virtù degli Agnus Dei di cera benedetti*. Rome. (Also reprinted in 1700.)

Bonaventura, Santo. 1926. *Opuscoli mistici*. Milan: Vita & Pensiero.

Bonfante Warren, L. 1970. "Roman Triumph and Etruscan Kings: The Latin Word Triumphus." In *Studies in Honor of J. Alexander Kerns*, 108–20. The Hague: Mouton.

Bonne, J.-C. 1990. *The Manuscript of the Ordo of 1250 and Its Illuminations*. In Bak 1990, 56–73.

Borghini, G., ed. 1989. *Marmi antichi*. Rome: De Luca.

Borgia, S. 1775. *De benedictione Agnorum Dei opusculum*. Rome: n.p.

Boron, R. de. 1884. *I primi due libri della storia di Merlino ristampati secondo la rarissima edizione del 1480*. Edited by J. Ulrich. Bologna: Romagnoli.

Borsook, E. 1965–66. "Art and Politics at the Medici Court: The Funeral of Cosimo I de' Medici." *Mitteilungen des Kunsthistorisches Institutes in Florenz* 12: 31–54.

Boucher, J. 1982. "L'évolution de la maison du roi des derniers Valois aux premiers Bourbons." *XVIIe*

siècle XXXIV, no. 137:359–79.

Bouman, C. A. 1957. *Sacring and Crowning: The Development of the Latin Ritual for the Anointing of Kings and the Coronation of an Emperor Before the Eleventh Century*. Groningen: Diakart, J. B. Wolters.

Bouquet, S. 1572. *Bref et sommaire recueile de ce qui a esté faict et de l'ordre tenue à la joyeuse et triumphante entrée de . . . Charles IX . . . avec le couronnement de . . . princesse madame Elisabet d'Austriche*. Paris: Denis du Près. (Reprinted in Graham and McAllister Johnson 1979.)

Bourdieu, P. 1980. *Le sens pratique*. Paris: Les Éditions de Minuit.

————. 1982. "Les rites comme actes d'institution." *Actes de la recherches en sciences sociales* 43:58–63.

Boureau, A. 1988. *Le simple corps du roi: L'impossible sacralité des souverains français XVe–XVIIIe siècle*. Paris: Les Éditions de Paris.

————. 1989. *La papesse Jeanne*. Paris: Aubier.

Bourgeois, L. [1626] 1826. *Récit veritable de la naissance de Messeigneurs et dames les enfans de France avec les particularitez qui y ont esté*. . . . Paris: Foucault.

Boutier, J., A. Dewerpe, and D. Nordman. 1984. *Un tour de France royal: Le voyage de Charles IX (1564–1566)*. Paris: Aubier.

Bowersock, G. W. 1972. "Greek Intellectuals and the Imperial Cult in the Second Century A.D." In *Le culte des souverains dans l'Empire romain*, Entretiens sur l'antiquité classique, XIX:179–206. Geneva: Fondation Hardt.

Bowman, F.-P. 1977. "Le Sacré-Coeur de Marat 1793." In *Les fêtes de la révolution*, ed. J. Ehrard and P. Viallaneix. Paris.

Boyer, L. 1963. *Rite and Men*. Notre Dame, Ind.: University of Notre Dame Press.

Bracton, H. 1915. *De legibus et consuetudinibus Angliae libri quinque*. Edited by G. E. Woodbine. New Haven, Conn.: Yale University Press.

Bradford, C. A. 1933. *Heart Burial*. London: George Allen.

Braustein, P., and Ch. Klapisch Zuber. 1983. "Florence et Venise: Les rituels publics à l'époque de la Renaissance." *AESC*, 1110–24.

Brehier, L., and P. Battifol. 1920. *Les survivances du culte impérial romain*. Paris: Picard.

Brelich, A. 1938. "Trionfo e morte." *Studi e materiali di storia delle religioni* 14:189ff.

Briard, G. [1770] 1890. *Histoire du baron des Adrets*. Valence.

Brocher, H. 1934. *Le rang et l'étiquette sous l'ancien régime (à la cour de Louis XIV)*. Paris.

Bromato, C. 1753. *Storia di Paolo IV pontefice massimo*. Ravenna: Landi.

Brown, E. A. R. 1980. "The Ceremonial of Royal Succession in Capetian France: The Funeral of Philip V." *Speculum* 55:266–93.

————. 1981. "Death and the Human Body in the

Later Middle Ages: The Legislation of Boniface VIII on the Division of the Corpse." *Viator* 12:221–70.

Brown, J., and J. H. Elliott. 1985. *Un palacio para el rey.* Madrid.

Brown, P. 1982a. "Chrétienté orientale et chrétienté occidentale dans l'Antiquité tardive: La divergence." In *La société et le sacré dans l'Antiquité tardive,* 119–45. Paris.

———. 1982b. *The Society and the Holy in Late Antiquity.* London: Faber & Faber.

Bruhl, C. 1950. *Reims als Krönungsstadt des französischen Königs bis zum Ausgang des 14. Jahrhunderts.* Frankfurt am Main: n.p.

Bryant, L. M. 1986a. "La cérémonie de l'entrée à Paris au Moyen Âge." AESC, XVI:513–42.

———. 1986b. *The King and the City in the Parisian Royal Entry Ceremony: Politics, Ritual, and Art in the Renaissance.* Geneva: Droz.

———. 1990. "The Medieval Entry Ceremony at Paris." In Bak 1990, 88–118.

———. 1992. "Politics, Ceremonies, and Embodiments of Majesty in Henry II's France." In Duchhardt, Jackson, and Sturdy 1992, 127–54.

Buck, G. [1619] 1982. *The History of King Richard the Third.* Edited by A. N. Kincaid. Gloucester: Alan Sutton.

Burchard, J. 1883–85. *Diarium, sive rerum urbanarum commentarii (1483–1506).* Edited by L. Thuasne. Paris: Leroux.

———. 1906. *Liber Notarum ab anno MCCCCLXXXIII usque ad annum MDVI.* Edited by E. Celani. RIS², XXXII.

Burckhardt, J. 1951. *The Civilisation of the Renaissance in Italy.* London: Phaidon Press.

Burkert, W. 1983. *Homo necans: The Anthropology of Ancient Greek Sacrificial Ritual and Myth.* Berkeley and Los Angeles: University of California Press.

Burkert, W., R. Girard, and J. Z. Smith. 1987. *Violent Origins: Walter Burkert, René Girard, and Jonathan Z. Smith on Ritual Killing and Cultural Formation.* Edited by Robert G. Hamerton-Kelly. Stanford: Stanford University Press.

Burton, Th. 1974. *Diary of Thomas Burton: Member in the Parliaments of Oliver and Richard Cromwell from 1656 to 1659.* Edited by J. T. Rutt. New York: Johnson Reprint Co.

Bury, J. B. 1907. "The Ceremonial Book of Constantine Porphyrogenitus." *English Historical Review* XXII:209–27, 417–39.

———. 1920. "The 'Notitia Dignitatum.'" JRS, x:131–54.

Butler, A. 1803. *Travels through France and Italy, and part of Austria, French and Dutch Netherlands, during the years 1745 and 1746.* Edinburgh.

Bynum, C. W. 1987. *Holy Feast and Holy Fast.* Berkeley and Los Angeles: University of California Press.

Cabanès, A. 1923. *Moeurs intimes du passé: Enfances royales.* Paris: A. Michel.

———. 1938. *Le cabinet secret de l'histoire: Le premier accouchement à la cour de France.* Paris.

Cacciaglia, M. 1975. "Il cerimoniale spagnolo alla Corte di Vienna." *Studi trentini di scienze storiche* LIV, 3:354–59.

Cagnola, G. P. 1842. "Storia di Milano." Edited by C. Cantù. ASI, ser. 1, vol. III:126ff.

Calendar of State Papers, Domestic Series, of the Reign of Charles I, 1625–1649. 1883. London: Her Majesty's Stationery Office.

Calore, A. 1995. "Tactis evangeliis." In Bertelli and Centanni 1995, 53–99.

Calvi, G., and S. Bertelli. 1983. "La bocca del Signore: Commensalità e gerarchie sociali fra cinque e seicento, in Il linguaggio, il corpo, la festa: Per un ripensamento della tematica di Michail Bachtin." In *Metamorfosi* 7:197–218. Milano: F. Angeli.

[Camden, W.]. 1600. *Reges, reginae, nobiles et alii in Ecclesia collegiata B. Petri Westmonasterii sepulti usque ad annum 1600.* London: Bollifantes.

Cameron, A. 1973. *Porphirius the Charioteer.* Oxford: Clarendon Press.

———. 1976. *Circus Factions: Blues and Greens at Rome and Byzantium.* Oxford: Clarendon Press.

Camporesi, P. 1983. *La carne impassibile.* Milan: Il Saggiatore.

Cancellieri, F. 1802. *Storia de' solenni possessi de' Sommi Pontefici detti anticamente processi o processioni, dopo la loro coronazione dalla basilica vaticana alla Lateranense.* Rome: L. Lazzarini.

Cantimori, D. 1955. "La periodizzazione dell'età del Rinascimento nella storia d'Italia e in quella d'Europa." In *Comitato Int. di Scienze Storiche,* proceedings of the x Congresso Int. di Scienze Storiche, Rome, 4–11 September 1955, *Relazioni,* IV, Storia Moderna, 305ff. Florence: Sansoni.

Capecelatro, F. 1830. *Diario contenente la storia di cose avvenute nel regno di Napoli negli anni 1647–50.* Edited by A. Granito. Naples.

Carandente, G. 1963. *I trionfi del primo Rinascimento.* Rome: ERI.

Cardini, F. 1981. *Alle radici della cavalleria medievale.* Florence: La Nuova Italia.

———, ed. 1994. *La città e il sacro.* Milan: Scheiwiller.

Carlton, C. 1983. *Charles I the Personal Monarch.* London: Routledge & Kegan Paul. (Ark Paperbacks, 1984.)

Cartellieri, O. 1970. *The Court of Burgundy: Studies in the History of Civilisation.* New York: Haskell House.

Casanova, F. 1899. *L'uccisione di Galeazzo Maria Sforza e alcuni documenti fiorentini.* ASL, XXVI, no. 12:299–332.

Casini, M. 1996. *I gesti del principe: La festa politica a Firenze e Venezia in età rinascimentale.* Venice: Marsilio.

Cassin, E. 1986. "Forme et identité des hommes et des dieux chez les Babyloniens." *Le temps de la réflexion*, VII (*Corps des dieux*): 63–76.

Castagnoli, F. 1992. *Il Vaticano nell'antichità classica*. Vol. VI of *Studi e documenti per la storia del palazzo apostolico vaticano*. Vatican City: BAV.

Ceccarelli, P. 1956. *Il galateo della suora*. Milan: Ediz. Ancora.

Centanni, M., ed. 1988. *Il romanzo di Alessandro*. Padua: Arsenale Editrice.

Ceresole, A. [1845] 1887. *Notizie storico-morali su gli Agnus Dei*. Rome: Tip. Vaticana.

Ceruti, A. 1896. *Miscellanea di storia italiana*. Vol. II.

Cervio, V. 1581. *Il Trinciante, ampliato ed a perfettione ridotto dal Cavalier Reale Fusoritto da Narni*. Original ed. Venice: Heredi Tramezzini.

———. 1593. *Il Trinciante, ampliato ed a perfettione ridotto dal Cavalier Reale Fusoritto da Narni*. Rome: Gabbia.

Champeau, J. 1982. *Fortuna: Recherches sur le culte de la Fortune à Rome et dans le monde romain*. École Française de Rome.

Champier, S. 1977. *Le triumphe du tres chrestien roy de France Loys XII*. Edited by G. Trisolini. Rome: Ateneo & Bizzarri.

Chaney, W. 1969. *The Cult of Kingship in Anglo-Saxon England*. Berkeley and Los Angeles: University of California Press.

Charlesworth, M. P. 1936. "*Providentia* and *Aeternitas*." *Harvard Theological Review* 19:107–32.

———. 1939. "The Virtutes of the Roman Emperor: Propaganda and the Creation of Belief." *British Academy Proceedings* (London) 23.

Les charmes de Conchine, desquels il se devoit servir pour éviter les coups de pistolet. . . . 1655. Lyons: n.p.

Chartrou, J. 1928. *Les entrées solennelles et triomphales à la Renaissance*. Paris: PUF.

Chastel, A. 1983. "La Chapelle des Médicis." In *Firenze e la Toscana dei Medici nell'Europa del '500*, III:787–89. Florence: Olschki.

Chastellain, G. 1863–66. *Chronique*. Edited by Kervin de Lettenbrove. Bruxelles. (Reprint, Geneva: Slatkin, 1971.)

Chaula, Tommaso da. See Tommaso da Chaula da Chiaromonte.

Chevalier, U. 1900. *Sacramentaire et martyrologe de l'abbaye de Saint-Rémy*. Paris: Picard.

Chirat, H. 1945. "Psomia diaforà." In *Mélanges E. Podechard*, 121–26. Lyons.

Chrimes, S. B. 1936. *English Constitutional Ideas in the Fifteenth Century*. Cambridge: Cambridge University Press.

Chronicles of the Reigns of Stephen, Henry II, and Richard I. 1886. Vol. III. Edited by R. Howlett. London: Longman.

Chronicon parmense. 1902. Edited by G. Bonazzi. RIS², XI.

Chronicon paschale. 1832. Edited by L. Dindorf. Bonn.

Chronicon universalis Mettensis. 1879. Edited by G. Waitz. MGHSS, XXIV.

Chronique catalane de Pierre IV d'Aragon III dit le Cérémonieux ou del Puuyalet. 1941. Edited by A. Pagès. Toulouse: Privat; Paris: H. Didier.

Chronique de la traison et mort de Richart Deux Roy d'Engleterre. 1846. Edited by B. Williams. London: Bentley, Wilson & Fley.

Cionacci, F. 1682. *Storia della beata Umiliana de' Cerchi vedova fiorentina del Terz'ordine di S. Francesco*. Florence: Franchi.

Cipolla Pellegrini, C. M. 1902. "Poesie minori riguardanti gli Scaligeri." *Bull. Ist. St. it.* XXIV.

Ciseri, I. 1990. *L'ingresso trionfale di Leone X in Firenze nel 1515*. Florence: Olschki.

Clark, T. J. 1994. "Painting in the Year 2 (Marat)." *Representations* 47.

Clementi, F. 1899. *Il carnevale romano nelle cronache contemporanee*. Rome: Tip. Tiberina.

Clop, E. 1913. *Les Agnus Dei: Une des plus anciennes et des plus vénérables institutions de la Sainte Eglise*. Monte Carlo. (Extract from *Union Séraphique*, 1913.)

Coarelli, A. 1988. *Forio Boario*. Rome: Quasar.

Cobbett, W. 1806. *Cobbett's Parliamentary History of England from the Norman Conquest, in 1066, to the Year 1803*. London: Curson Hansard.

———, ed. 1809–26. *A Complete Collection of State Trials . . . from the earliest period to the year 1783*. London: Bradshaw-Longman.

Cobelli, L. 1874. *Cronache forlivesi dalla fondazione della città sino all'anno 1498*. Monumenti storici pertinenti alle provincie delle Romagne, edited by G. Carducci and E. Frati, I. Bologna.

Cock, H. 1863. *Relación del viaje hecho por Felipe II, en 1585, á Zaragoza, Barcelona y Valencia*. Madrid: Aribau.

Codex Carolinus. 1892. Edited by W. Gundlach. MGH, Ep. 3.

Codinus. 1839. *Codini Curopalatae De officialibus palatii Constantinopolitani et de officiis magnae ecclesiae liber*. Edited by I. Bekker. SSHByz.

Cohen, H. 1888. *Description historique des monnaies frappés sous l'Empire romaine*. Paris.

Cohen, K. 1973. *Metamorphosis of a Death Symbol: The Transi Tomb in the Middle Ages and the Renaissance*. Berkeley and Los Angeles: University of California Press.

Cohn, N. 1976. *The Pursuit of the Millennium* (in Italian trans.). Milan: Ed. di Comunità. (English original, London: Secher-Warburg, 1957.)

Colasanti, A. 1922. "Ritratti di principi estensi in un gruppo di Guido Mazzoni." *Boll. d'arte* I, no. II (April).

Colle, G. F. da. 1520. *Refugio di povero gentiluomo*. Ferrara: Lorenzo de Russi da Valencia.

Collins, A. J. 1953. *The Ordering of Coronation of*

Elisabeth I: Drawings and Descriptions from a Contemporary Official Manuscript. London.

Collins, R. 1977. "Julian of Toledo and the Royal Succession in Late-Seventh-Century Spain." In Sawyer and Wood 1977, 30–49.

Colombo, A. 1905. *L'ingresso di Francesco Sforza in Milano e l'inizio di un nuovo principato.* ASL, ser. IV, vol. VI, XXXII:229ff.; vol. VII:33ff.

Combes, L. 1872. *Fils de Saint-Louis montez au ciel (Episodes et curiosités) révolutionnaires.* Paris: Madre.

Comfort, A. 1967. *The Anxiety Makers.* London: Nelson.

Compendio istorico della condanna a morte data a Luigi XVI colle di lui accuse, difese e testamento. 1793. Assisi: Sgariglia.

Conciliorum oecumenicorum: Decreta. 1962. Edited by J. Alberigo. Basel: Herder.

Conrad, J. R. 1959. *The Horn and the Sword: The History of the Bull as Symbol of Power and Fertility.* London: Macgibbon.

Consolations à la Reine de la Grande Bretagne d'Ecosse et d'Irlande, tirées dv tableav de la passion de nostre Sauueur. 1649. Paris: C. Morlot.

Constantin Porphirogénète [Constantine Porphyrogenetos]. 1967. *Livre des cérémonies.* Edited by A. Vogt. Paris: Les Belles Lettres.

———. 1983. *Presagi di gloria nella "Vita di Basilio" di Costantino VII Porfirogenito.* Edited by E. Pinto. Messina: Ed. Dott. Antonio Sfameni (BNF NC.V.Mis.21412.13).

Convention nationale: Appels nominaux faits à la Convention Nationale. 1792–93. Paris: Imprimerie Nationale.

Convention nationale: Défense de Louis, prononcée à la barre de la Convention Nationale le Mercredi 26 Décembre 1792. 1793. Paris: Imprimerie Nationale.

Convention nationale: Inventaire des pièces par la Commission des vingt-un, concernant les crimes de Louis Capet. . . . 1793. Imprimé par ordre de la Convention National . . . (Premier . . . Quinzième recueil . . .). Paris: Imprimerie Nationale.

Convention nationale: Opinions. 1793. Paris: Imprimerie Nationale.

Coppini, W. 1988. "Il culto di un santo vivo nella Prato del seicento: Benedetto Bacci da Poggibonsi." *Ricerche storiche* XVIII:235–50.

Corazza. 1894. *Diario fiorentino di Bartolomeo del Corazza, anni 1405–1438.* Edited by G. Corazzini. ASI, ser. XIV.

Corio, B. 1978. *Storia di Milano.* Edited by A. Morisi Guerra. Turin: UTET.

Corippus, F. C. 1879. *In laudem Iustini.* Edited by Partsch. Berlin: Weidmann.

Coronación y consagración de reyes y ceremonias que en ella se guardan. 1849. Edited by R. Obispo. Collección de documentos inéditos para la historia de Espana, XIV. Madrid.

The Coronation Book of Charles V. of France. 1899. Edited by E. S. Dewick. HBS XVI.

The Coronation Order of King James I. 1902. Edited by J. Wickham Legg. London: Robinson.

Corpus glossatorum Juris civilis. 1969. Edited by M. Viora. Augsburg Taurinorum.

Cortés Echanove, L. *Nacimiento y crianza de personas reales en la corte de España, 1566–1886.* Madrid: Consejo Sup. de Investigaciones Científicas 1958.

Cortesi, P. 1511. *De cardinalatu.* In castro Cortesio.

Coulet, N. 1977. "Les entrées solennelles en Provence au XIVe siècle." *Ethnologie française,* n.s., VII.

———. 1979. "De l'intégration à l'exclusion: La place de Juifs dans le cérémonies d'entrée solennelle au Moyen-Âge." AESC, 672–81.

Courtin, A. de. [1671] 1682. *Nouveau traité de la civilité qui se pratique en France parmi les honnestes gens.* Paris: Jonet.

Cresti, C. 1989. "La cappella dei principi: Un pantheon foderato di pietre dure." In *Splendori* 1989, 62–73.

Crifò, G. 1985. *L'esclusione dalla città: Altri studi sull' "exilium" romano.* Perugia: Università di Perugia.

Cronaca della Novalesa. 1983. Edited by G. C. Alessio. Turin: Einaudi.

Cronaca di anonimo. BNF, MS Magliabechiano XXV, 660.

Cronichetta di Lodi del sec. XV. 1884. Edited by C. Casati. Milan: Dumolard.

Crouzet Pavan, E. 1984. "Violence, société et pouvoir à Venise (XIVe–XVe siècles): formes et évolution de rituels urbains." *Mélanges de l'École française de Rome: Moyen Âge—Temps modernes* 96:903–36.

Cruciani, F. 1983. *Teatro nel Rinascimento: Roma 1450–1550.* Rome: Bulzoni.

Cutler, E. J. 1905. *Lynch-Law: An Investigation into the History of Lynching in the United States.* New York.

D'Achille, A. 1867. *I sepolcri dei Romani Pontefici con breve ed istorica illustrazione.* Rome: Menicanti.

Dacos, N. 1973. "La fortuna delle gemme medicee nel Rinascimento." In N. Dacos, A. Giuliano, and E. Pannuti, *Il tesoro di Lorenzo il Magnifico,* I, *Le gemme,* 133–67. Florence: Sansoni.

Da Costa Kauffmann, Th. 1978. *Variations on the Imperial Theme in the Age of Maximilian II and Rudolf II.* New York: Garkland.

Dagron, G. 1974. *Naissance d'une capitale: Constantinople et ses institutions de 330 à 451.* Paris: PUF.

———. 1996. *Empereur et prêtre: Étude sur le "césaropapisme" byzantin.* Paris: Gallimard.

Dakhlia, J. 1988. "Dans la mouvance du prince: La symbolique du pouvoir itinérant au Maghreb." *Les annales ESC:* 735–60.

Davis, N. Z. 1973. "The Rites of Violence: Religious

Riot in Sixteenth-Century France." *Past and Present*, no. 59:51–96.

———. 1987. *Fiction in the Archives: Pardon Tales and Their Tellers in Sixteenth-Century France*. Stanford: Stanford University Press.

D'Avray, D. L. 1994. *Death and the Prince: Memorial Preaching Before 1350*. Oxford: Clarendon Press.

Dayot, A. 1896. *Napoleone nelle opere de' pittori, degli scultori, degl'incisori*. Milan: "Corriere della Sera."

de' Grassi, P. 1731. *Excerpta ex Diario Curiae Romanae ab anno MDXVIII usque ad MDXXII*. In *Nova Scriptorum ac Monumentorum . . . Collectio*, edited by Ch. G. Hoffmann. Leipzig: Haered. Lanckisianorum.

———. 1753. *Sacra processio ad Lateranum cum Pontifice Leo X*. In Gattico 1753.

———. 1805–6. "Diarium." In *The Life and Pontificate of Leo the Tenth*, by W. Roscoe. Philadelphia: Bronson. (Italian trans., Milan: Sonzogno, 1816–17.)

———. See also Cancellieri 1802; Döllinger 1862–82.

De Grazia, S. 1948. *The Political Community: A Study on Anomie*. Chicago: University of Chicago Press.

Delassus, A. n.d. *Louis XVI, roi et martyr, et sa béatification*. Paris: Oudin.

della Valle, P. 1650. *Viaggi di P. d. V. il Pellegrino, [. . .] in 54 lettere familiari [. . .] divisi in tre parti, cioè la Turchia, la Persia et l'India*. Rome: Vitale Mascardi.

Del Riccio, A. [1597] 1996. *Istoria delle pietre*. Edited by R. Gnoli and A. Sironi. Turin.

de Luca, G. B. 1675. *Il cavaliere e la dama: Ovvero discorsi familiari nell'ozio tuscolano autunnale dell'anno 1674*. Rome: Magoncelli.

De Maio, R. 1980. *Pittura e controriforma*. Rome-Bari: Laterza.

De Marinis, T., ed. 1946. *Le nozze di Costanzo Sforza e Camilla d'Aragona celebrate a Pesaro nel maggio 1475*. Nozze Ricasoli-Firidolfi Russo di Guardialombarda. Florence: Vallecchi.

De Mattei, F. [s.a.] 1955. *Le arche scaligere di Verona*. Verona: La Nave.

De Mause, L. 1974. "The Evolution of Childhood." *History of Childhood Quarterly* I.

Dennistoun, J. 1851. *Memoirs of the Dukes of Urbino, Illustrating the Arms, Arts, and Literature of Italy, from 1440 to 1630*. London: Longman.

De Nolhac, P. 1900. *Louis XV et Marie Leczinska*. Paris: Joyant.

———. 1912. *Louis XV: Vie privée: Le règne de l'amour: Reine et favorites*. Paris: Tallandier.

De Santis, T. 1770. *Istoria del tumulto di Napoli*. Naples: Gravier.

Descrittione delle cerimonie, pompa et ordine che si tenne per honorare Carlo V . . . entrando in Siena ne l'anno dell'Incarnazione del Divino Verbo 1536. . . . [1884]

1968. In *Scelta di curiosità letterarie inedite o rare . . .* , edited by P. Vigo. Bologna: Comm. per i testi di lingua.

Desplat, Ch., and P. Mironneau. 1997. *Les entrées: Gloire et déclin d'un cérémonial: Actes du colloque tenu au château de Pau les 10 et 11 mai 1996*. Biarritz: Société Henri IV.

Destinée du marechal d'Ancre, par Pub. Virgile de Mantoue Au neusiesme de l'Eneide. 1617. Paris: Fleury Bourriquaut.

La destruction de la statue royale à Nouvelle York. [1776?] Paris: Basset.

Detienne, M., and J.-P. Vernant. 1979. *La cuisine du sacrifice en pays grec*. Paris: Gallimard.

De Tolnay, Ch. 1934 and 1969. "Studi sulla cappella medicea." *L'Are* XXXVII, vol. v:5–44, 281–307; *Gazette des beaux-arts* 73:65–80.

Devisse, J. 1976. *Hincmar archevêque de Reims: 845–882*. Geneva: Droz.

———. 1985. "Le sacre et le pouvoir avant les Carolingiens: L'héritage visigothique." In *Le sacre des rois* 1985, 27–38.

Dewick, E. S. See *Coronation Book*.

Dialogue de la Galligaya et de Misoquin esprit follet, qui luy ameine son mary: La rencontre dudit esprit avec l'Ange gardien de monsieur le Prince. 1617. Paris: Iean Sara.

Diaz Cruz, R. 1998. *Archipiélago de rituales: Teorías antropológicas del ritual*. Barcelona: Anthropos Editorial.

Digard, G., ed. 1890. *Les Registres de Boniface VIII*. Paris: E. Thorin.

Di Marzo, G., ed. 1864. *Delle origini e vicende di Palermo di Pietro Ransano e dell'entrata di re Alfonso in Napoli: Scritture siciliane. . . .* Palermo: Lorsnaider.

Dio Cassius. 1970. *Roman History*. Translated by H. B. Foster. Harvard University Press.

Dionysius of Halicarnassus. 1968. *The Roman Antiquities. . . .* With an English translation by E. Cary. Cambridge, Mass.: Harvard University Press.

Discours ample, tovchant le procez dv roy d'Angleterre, en la sale de Westminster, Samdi le 30 Ianvier, lundi le I.et mardi le 2 de Fevrier 1649. 1649. n.p. [Paris?]

Diurnali [I] del duca di Monteleone. RIS², XXI, v.

Dölger, F. J. 1929–30. *Antike und Christentum, Kultur und religionsgeschichtliche Studien*. Münster in Westfalen: Aschendorfsche Verlag.

———. 1930 and 1932. "Christus im Bilde des Skarabaeus." *Antike u. Christentum* II:230–40, III:280ff.

Döllinger, J. J. 1862–82. *Beitrage zur politischen, Kirchlichen und Cultur-Geschichte der sechs letzten Jahrhunderte*. Regensburg: G. J. Mainz.

Doni, A. F. 1979. *Opere*. Edited by C. Cordié. Milan: Ricciardi.

D'Onofrio, C. 1978. *Mille anni di leggenda: Una donna*

sul trono di Pietro. Rome: Romana Soc. Ed.

———. 1979. *La papessa Giovanna: Roma e papato tra storia e leggenda*. Rome: Cassa di Risparmio di Roma.

Donzelli. 1647. *Partenope liberata o vero racconto dell'heroica risoluzione fatta dal popolo di Napoli*. Naples: Beltrano. (Facsimile reprint, Naples: Fiorentino, 1970.)

d'Orey, L. 1991. *A baixela da coroa portuguesa*. Lisbon: Inapa.

Dorio, D. 1638. *Istoria della famiglia Trinci*. Foligno: A. Alterii.

Douglas, M. 1970a. "The Healing Rite." *Man*, n.s., 5:302–8.

———. 1970b. *Purity and Danger: An Analysis of Concepts of Pollution and Taboo*. Harmondsworth, Middlesex: Penguin Books.

———. 1975. "Deciphering a Meal." In *Implicit Meanings: Essays in Anthropology*. London: Routledge & Kegan Paul.

Drabek, A. M. 1964. *Reisen u. Reisezeremoniell der Römischen-Deutschen Herrscher in Spätmittelalter*. Vienna: Geyer.

Ducellier, A. 1986. *Byzance et le monde orthodoxe*. Paris: Colin.

Du Chastel, P. 1649. "Le Trespas, Obsèques et Enterrement des très hault, très puissant et très magnanime Francois [. . .] Roys de France." In Godefroy 1649, 277–308.

Duchhardt H., R. A. Jackson, D. Sturdy, eds. 1992. *European Monarchy*. Stuttgart: Steiner Verlag.

Dumont, L. 1966. *Homo hierarchicus: Le système des castes en ses implications*. Paris: Gallimard.

Du Moulin, P., Jr. 1652. *Regii sanguinis clamor ad coelum adversus parricidas anglicanos*. The Hague: A. Vlacq.

XII *panegyrici latini*. 1911. Edited by W. Braehrens. Leipzig.

Dupont, F. 1986. "L'autre corps de l'empereur-dieu." *Le temps de la réflexion* VII (Corps des dieux): 231–52.

Du Puy, P. 1617. *Journal de ce qui s'est passé à la mort du marechal d'Ancre*. In *Histoire générale* 1617.

Durand, G. 1992. *Les structures anthropologiques de l'imaginaire*. Paris: Dunod.

Du Tillet, J. 1580. *Recueil des roys de France, leurs couronne et maison.* . . . Paris: Du Puys.

Dvornik, F. 1966. *Early Christian and Byzantine Political Philosophy: Origins and Background*. Washington, D.C.: Dumbarton Oaks Center for Byzantine Studies.

Dykmans, D. 1968a. "Le cérémonial de Nicolas V." *Revue d'histoire ecclésiastique* LXIII.

———. 1968b. "D'Avignon à Rome: Martin V et le cortège apostolique." *Bull. de l'Inst. Hist. Belge de Rome* XXXIX:203–309.

———. 1977. *Le cérémonial papal de la fin du Moyen Âge à la Renaissance*. Brussels and Rome: Inst. Hist. Belge de Rome.

———. 1980–82. *L'oeuvre de Patrizi Piccolomini ou le cérémonial papal de la première Renaissance*. Studi e testi 293–94. Vatican City.

Eberlein, J. K. 1982. *Apparitio regis—revelatio veritatis: Studien zur Darstellung des Vorhangs in der bildenden Kunst von der Spätantike bis zum Ende des Mittelalters*. Wiesbaden: Reichert.

Ebersolt, J. 1910. *Le Grand Palais de Constantinople et le Livre des cérémonies*. Paris: Leroux.

Eginhard. 1947. *Vie de Charlemagne*. Edited by L. Halphen. Paris: Les Belles Lettres.

Ehrle, F., and H. Egger. 1985. *Die vatikanische Palast in seiner Entwicklung bis zur Mitte des XV. Jahrhunderts*. Vol. II of *Studi e documenti per la storia del palazzo apostolico vaticano*. Vatican City: BAV.

Eichmann, E. 1942. *Die Kaiserkrönung im Abendland: Ein Beitrag zur Geistesgeschichte des Mittelalters*. Würzburg: Echter Verlag.

Eisler, R. 1910. *Weltenmantel und Himmelszelt: Religionsgeschichtliche Untersuchungen zur Urgeschichte des antiken Weltbildes*. Munich.

Eliade, M. 1957. *Mythes, rêves et mystères*. Paris: Gallimard.

Ellard, G. 1933. *Ordination Anointing in the Western Church*. Monograph of the Med. Academy of America, VIII. Cambridge, Mass.

Ellenius, A. 1966. *Karolinska bildidéer*. Uppsala: Almquist & Wiksell.

———, ed. 1998. *Iconography, Propaganda, and Legitimation*. European Science Foundation. Oxford: Clarendon Press.

Elliot, F. M. 1894. *Old Court Life in Spain*. New York: Scribner's Sons.

Elliott, J. H. 1977. "Philip IV of Spain, Prisoner of Ceremony." In *The Courts of Europe: Politics, Patronage, and Royalty*, edited by A. G. Dickens. London: Thames & Hudson.

Elze, R., ed. 1960. *Die Ordines für die Weihe u. Krönung des Kaisers u. die Kaiserin*. Hannover: Hahnsche Buchhandlung.

———. 1977. "'Sic transit gloria mundi': La morte del papa nel medioevo." *Annali dell'Istituto storico italo-germanico in Trento* III:23–41.

———. 1982. "'Sic transit gloria mundi': La morte del papa nel medioevo" (in the original German). In *Päpste-Kaiser-Könige und die mittelalterliche Herrschaftssymbolik*, IV. London: Variorum Reprints.

Enright, M. J. 1985. *Iona, Tara, and Soissons: The Origin of the Royal Anointing Ritual*. Berlin: W. De Gruyter.

L'enterrement, obsèques et funérailles de Conchine mareschal d'Ancre, dedié au Conchinistes. 1617. Paris: Bernard Hameau.

"Entrada d'Alfonso el Magnanim a Napols." 1932. Edited by R. d'Avalos-Moner. In *Autores catalàns antics*, 1:187ff. Barcelona.

Epifania, A. 1902. *Carlo VIII di Valois a Napoli*. Naples: F. Giannini.

Erb = Huldigung. See Gülich, L. von.

Erlande Brandenburg, A. 1975. *Le roi est mort: Étude sur les funérailles les sépultures et les tombeaux des rois de France jusqu'à la fin du XIIIe siècle*. Geneva: Droz.

———. n.d. *L'église abbatiale de Saint-Denis*. Vol. II, *Les tombeaux royaux*. Paris: Éd. de la Tourelle.

Escouchy, M. d'. [1863] 1976. *Chronique*. Edited by G. du Fresne de Beaucourt. Paris: Renouard.

Estebe, J. 1975. "The Rite of Violence: Religious Riot in 16th-Century France: A Comment." *Past and Present* 67:127–30.

Etiquetas generales que han de observar los criados de la Casa de S. Mag. en el uso y exercicio de sus oficios. BAV, Fondo Barberini, Indice I. 1098.

Ettlinger, L. O. 1978. "The Liturgical Function of Michelangelo's Medici Chapel." *Mitteilungen des Kunsthist. Inst. Florenz* 22:287–304.

Eugenio di Palermo. 1964. *Versus iambici*. Edited by M. Gigante. Palermo: Istituto Siciliano di Studi Bizantini e Neollenici.

Eusebio di Cesarea. *Vita Constantini*. PG, XX. (English trans., 1845.)

Evans, E. P. [1906] 1987. *The Criminal Prosecution and Capital Punishment of Animals*. London: Faber & Faber.

Evitascandolo, C. 1609. *Dialogo del Trenciante: Nel quale si legge quanto si si deve operare et osservare nel servitio del Trenciante*. Rome: Vullietti.

L'execvtion et la mort dv roy d'Angleterre Faite publiquement le 9. Febr.1649 à Londres en Angleterre, avec ce que le Roy a dit sur l'eschaffaut. 1649. Antwerp: M. Binnart.

Fabriczy, C. von. 1898. "Der Triumphbogen Alphonsos I. dem Castel Nuovo zu Neapel." *Jahrbuch des K. Preußischen Kunstsammlungen* XIX:146–47.

Facinger, M. F. 1968. "A Study on Medieval Queenship: Capetian France, 987–1237." *Studies in Medieval and Renaissance History* 5:3–47.

Facio, B. 1560. *De rebus gestis ab Alphonso primo Neapolitanorum rege commentariorum libri decem*. Lyons: Haeredes Sebast. Gryphii.

Fairbairn, W. R. D. 1936. "The Effect of the King's Death upon Patients Under Analysis." *International Journal of Psychoanalysis* XVII.

Fantoni, M. 1994. "La Madonna dell'Annunziata e la sacralità del potere mediceo." In *La corte del Granduca: Forma e simboli del potere mediceo fra cinque e seicento*. Rome: Bulzoni. (Originally in ASI, CXLVII [1989]: 771–93.)

Fears, J. B. 1977. *Princeps a Diis electus: The Divine Election of the Emperor as a Political Concept at Rome*. Rome: American Academy in Rome.

Febvre, L. 1968. *Rabelais, ou le problème de l'incroyance au XVIe siècle*. Paris: Albin Michel.

Félibien, A. 1674. *Les Divertissemens de Versailles, donnez par le Roy à toute sa cour au retour de la conqueste de la Franche-Comté en l'année 1674*. Paris: J.-B. Coignard.

Félibien, M. 1706. *Histoire de l'Abbaye Royale de Saint-Denys en France*. Paris: F. Leonard.

Fernandez, L. S. 1975. *Nobleza y monarquía: Puntos de vista sobre la historia castellana del siglo XV*. Valladolid.

Ferreto de' Ferreti. 1908–20. *Opere*. Edited by C. Cipolla. Ist. Storico Italiano, Fonti per la storia d'Italia. Rome: Forzini.

Filangieri, R. 1954. "L'arrivo di Ferdinando il Cattolico a Napoli: Relazione dell'oratore Giovanni Medina al cardinale d'Este." In *Estudios*, V Congreso de Historia de la Corona de Aragón, 311–14. Saragossa.

Finaldi, G., ed. 1999. *Orazio Gentileschi at the Court of Charles I*. London: National Gallery.

Fineschi, F. 1995. *Cristo e Giuda: Rituali di giustizia a Firenze in età moderna*. Florence: Bruschi.

Finkelstein, J. 1992. *Andare a pranzo fuori: Sociologia delle buone maniere*. Bologna: Il Mulino.

Fioravante, B. 1738. *Antiqui Romanorum Pontificum denarii*. Rome: Typis Bernabò.

Firmicus Maternus. 1907. *De errore profanarum religionum*. Edited by K. Ziegler. Leipzig: Teubner.

Fishwick, D. 1987. *The Imperial Cult in the Latin West*. Leiden: Brill.

Flodoardus. 1854–55. *Historia Remensis Ecclesiae*. Edited by M. Lejeune. Reims: Regnier.

Folz, R. 1973a. *Études sur le culte liturgique de Charlemagne dans les églises de l'Empire*. Geneva: Slatkine Reprints.

———. [1950] 1973b. *Le souvenir et la légende de Charlemagne dans l'Empire germanique médiéval*. Geneva: Slatkine Reprints.

———. 1984. *Les saints rois du Moyen Âge en Occident (VIe–XIIIe siècles)*. Brussels: Soc. des Bollandistes.

Fontana, Gabriel Paverus. 1477. *De vita et obitu Galeaz Mariae Sfortiae Vicecomitis Mediolani ducis Quinti*. Milan: n.p.

Forcella, U. 1885. *Tornei e giostre ingressi trionfali e feste carnevalesche in Roma sotto Paolo II*. Rome. (Reprint, Bologna: Forni, 1971.)

———. 1896. *Spettacoli ossia caroselli, tornei, cavalcate e ingressi trionfali*. Milan. (Reprint, Bologna: Forni, 1975.)

Foresi, F. 1885. *Il trionfo di Cosimo de' Medici: Frammento di un poema inedito del secolo XV*. Ancona: Morelli.

Foreville, R. 1978–79. "Le sacre des rois anglo-normands et angevins et le serment du sacre (XI et XII siècles)." Proceedings of the Brattle Conference.

Forster, K. W. 1977. "Metaphors of Rule: Political Ideology and History in the Portraits of Cosimo

I. de' Medici." *Mitteilungen des Kunsthistorischen Institutes in Florenz* XV, no. 1:65–104.

Forster, R., and O. Ranum, eds. 1982. *Ritual, Religion, and the Sacred: Selections from the "Annales: Economies, Sociétés, Civilisations."* Baltimore: Johns Hopkins University Press.

Fortes, M. 1968. "Of Installation Ceremonies" (presidential address, 1967). *Proceedings of the Royal Anthropological Institute for 1967:* 5–20.

Fortunato, G. 1884. *I Napoletani del 1799.* Florence: Barbèra.

Foucard, C. 1877. "Descrizione della città di Napoli e statistica del regno nel 1444." *Archivio Storico per le Provincie Napoletane* II.

"Frammenti di una inedita storia della rivoluzione napoletana del 1799." 1932. Edited by B. Croce. *La critica* XXX.

La France en deuil ou le vingt-un janvier, collection contenant les pièces officielle relatives à la translation des victimes royales, le détail des honneurs funèbres qui leur ont été rendus soit en France, soit en pays étrangers. . . . n.d. Paris: Lepetit.

Franchi de' Cavalieri. 1916–17. "I funerali e il sepolcro di Costantino Magno." *Mélanges d'Archéologie et d'Histoire* (École Française de Rome) XXXVI:265–361.

Frank, J. 1955. *The Levellers.* Cambridge: Cambridge University Press.

Frati, L. 1883. "Delle monete gettate al popolo nel solenne ingresso in Bologna di Giulio II per la cacciata di Giovanni Bentivoglio." In *Deputazione di Storia Patria per le Provincie di Romagna, Atti e Memorie,* ser. III, 1:474–87.

Frazer, J. 1911. *Taboo and the Perils of the Soul.* Pt. II of *The Golden Bough.* London: Macmillan.

Freistedt, E. 1928. *Altchristliche Totengedächtnistage und ihre Beziehung zum Jenseitsglauben und Totenkult der Antike.* Münster in Westfalen.

Frittelli, U. 1900. *Giannantonio de' Pandoni detto il Porcellio.* Florence: Paravia.

Froissart, J. 1869. *Chroniques.* Edited by S. Luce. Paris: Renouard.

Frova, A. 1961. *L'arte di Roma e del mondo romano.* Turin: UTET.

Frugoli, A. 1631. *Pratica e scalcaria.* Rome: Cavalli.

Fuidoro, F. 1647. *Successi istorici raccolti dalla sollevazione di Napoli dell'anno 1647.* BNNa, X. B. 12 bis.

Furnivall, F. J., ed. 1869. *Queene Elisabethes Achademy (by Sir Humphrey Gilbert): A Booke of Precedence: The Ordering of a Funerall etc.* London: Early English Text Society, Trubner & Co.

Gagé, J. 1933. "La théologie de la victoire impériale." *Revue historique* CLXXI:1–43.

Gandini, L. A. 1891. *Saggio degli usi e delle costumanze della corte di Ferrara al tempo di Niccolò III, 1393–1442.* Bologna: Fava & Garagnani.

Garbero Zorzi, E. 1985. "Cerimoniale e spettacolarità: Il tovagliolo sulla tavola del principe." In Bertelli and Crifò 1985, 67–83.

Gardiner, S. 1535. *De vera obedientia.* London: Berthelet. (See also Janelle, P.)

Garnett, P., and M. F. Williams, eds. 1910, 1911, and 1919. *Papers of the San Francisco Committee of Vigilance of 1851.* Acad. of Pacific Coast Hist., Publications, 1:285–353, II:121–39, IV.

Gattico, G. B. 1753. *Acta selecta Caerimonialia Sanctae Romanae Ecclesiae.* . . . Rome: Heredes J. L. Barbiellini.

Gaudemet, J. 1958. *L'Église dans l'Empire romain.* Paris: Sirey.

Geertz, C. 1980. *Negara: The Theatre State in Nineteenth-Century Bali.* Princeton: Princeton University Press.

———. 1983. *Local Knowledge: Further Essays in Interpretive Anthropology.* New York: Basic Books.

———. 1987. *Interpretation of Cultures* (in Italian trans.). Bologna: Il Mulino. (Original English, New York: Basic Books, 1973.)

Gerard, V. 1983. *Los sitios de devoción en el Alcázar de Madrid: Capilla y oratorios.* Archivo Español de Arte, LVII.

Gesta Stephani. 1976. Edited by E. R. Potter. Oxford: Clarendon Press.

Ghirardacci, Ch. 1933. *Historia di Bologna.* Edited by A. Sorbelli. Bologna: Zanichelli. (Also RIS², XXXIII, 1929.)

Giannone, P. 1993. *L'ape ingegnosa, ovvero raccolta di varie osservazioni sopra le opere di natura e dell'arte.* Edited by A. Merlotti. Rome: Istituto Italiano per gli Studi Filosofici.

Giegher, M. 1639. *Trattato sul modo di piegare ogni sorta di panni lini, cioè salviette e tovaglie e d'apparecchiare una tavola.* Padua: P. Frambotto.

Giesey, R. A. 1960. *The Royal Funeral Ceremony in Renaissance France.* Geneva: Droz.

———. 1968. *If Not, Not: The Oath of the Aragonese and the Legendary Laws of Sobrarbe.* Princeton: Princeton University Press.

———. 1986. "Modèles de pouvoir dans les rites royaux en France." AESC, 579–99.

———. 1987. *Cérémonial et puissance souveraine: France 15e–17e siècles.* Cahiers des Annales 41. Paris.

Gill, J. 1991. *Hidalgos y samurais: España y Japón en los siglos XVI y XVII.* Madrid: Alianza Universidad.

Ginzburg, C., et al. 1987. "Saccheggi rituali: Premesse a una ricerca in corso." *Quaderni storici* 65:615–36.

Giordani, G. 1842. *Della venuta e dimora in Bologna del sommo pontefice Clemente VII per la coronazione di Carlo V imperatore, celebrata l'anno MDXXX.* Bologna: Volpe.

Giovanni Crisostomo [Saint John Chrysostom]. 1862. *Homilia III ad Ephesisos.* PG, LXII.

Giovanni da Cornazzano. 1738. *Historiae Parmensis Fragmenta.* RIS, XII.

Giraffi. 1648. *Le rivolutioni di Napoli [. . .] con pietosissimo ragguaglio d'ogni successo e trattati secreti e palesi.* Ferrara: Gironi.

Girard, R. 1972. *La violence et le sacré.* Paris: Grasset.

———. 1982. *Le bouc émissaire.* Paris: Grasset.

Giulini, A. 1916. *Di alcuni figli meno noti di Francesco I Sforza.* ASL, 1:29–52.

Giusti, A. M. 1989. "Origine e sviluppi della manifattura granducale." In *Splendori* 1989, 10–23.

Giustinian, A. 1876. *Dispacci di A.G. ambasciatore veneto in Roma dal 1502 al 1505.* Edited by P. Villari. Florence: Le Monnier.

Given-Wilson, C., and A. Curteis. 1984. *Royal Bastards of Medieval England.* London: Routledge & Kegan Paul.

Gluckmann, M., ed. 1972. *Il rituale nei rapporti sociali.* Rome: Officina Ed.

Gobet, N. 1775. *Sacre et couronnement de Louis XVI, roi de France [. . .] précédé de recherches [. . .] depuis Clovis.* Paris: Vente.

Godefroi de Fontaines. 1924. *Le huitième Quodlibet.* Edited by J. Hoffmans. Les philosophes belges: Textes et études. Louvain: Inst. Sup. de Philosophie de l'Université.

Godefroy, T. 1649. *Cérémonial de France.* Paris: Cramoisy.

Goethe, J. W. 1864. *The Autobiography of Goethe: Truth and Poetry: From My Own Life.* Trans. J. Oxenford. London: Bell & Daldy.

Golain, J. 1969. "Traité du sacre." Edited by R. A. Jackson. *Proceedings of the American Philosophical Society* 113:305–24.

Goldthwaite, R. 1980. *The Building of Renaissance Florence: An Economic and Social History.* Baltimore: Johns Hopkins University Press.

Goody, J. 1961. "Religion and Ritual: The Definitional Problem." *British Journal of Sociology* XII:142–64.

———. 1982. *Cooking, Cuisine, and Class: A Study in Comparative Sociology.* Cambridge: Cambridge University Press.

Gorski, K. 1969. "Le roi-saint: Un problème d'idéologie féodale." AESC, XXIV:370–76.

Gosellini, G. 1864. *Congiura di Piacenza contro Pier Luigi Farnese.* Florence: Molini.

Grabar, A. 1936. *L'empereur dans l'art byzantin: Recherches sur l'art officiel de l'empire d'Orient.* Paris: Les Belles Lettres.

Graham, V. E., and W. McAllister Johnson, eds. 1974. *The Paris Entries of Charles IX and Elisabeth of Austria, 1571. . . .* Toronto: University of Toronto Press.

———, eds. 1979. *The Royal Tour of France by Charles IX and Catherine de' Medici: Festivals and Entries, 1564/6.* Toronto.

Grandsen, A., ed. 1973. *The Customary of the Benedictine Abbey of Bury St. Edmunds in Suffolk.* Chichester: Regnum Press.

Granel, A. 1908. *Louis XVI martyr de la foi: Mémoire pour servir à l'introduction de sa cause.* Toulouse: Privat.

Graus, F. 1981. "La sanctification du souverain dans l'Europe centrale des xe et xie siècles." In *Hagiographie, culture et société, ive–xiie siècles: Actes du colloque, 2–5 mai 1979,* 559–71. Paris: Études Augustiniennes.

Green, L. 1986. *Castruccio Castracani: A Study on the Origins and Character of a Fourteenth-Century Italian Despotism.* Oxford: Clarendon.

Greenhalgh, M. 1985. "Iconografia antica e sue trasformazioni durante il Medioevo." In Settis 1985, 45–93.

Gregory of Tours. 1881. *In gloria martirum.* Edited by B. Krusch. MGHSSRMer., 1.2.

———. 1885. *Liber vitae patrum.* Edited by W. Arndt and B. Krusch. MGHSSRMer., 3.2.

———. 1951. *Historiarum libri.* Edited by B. Krusch and W. Levison. MGHSSRMer., 1.1.

Grinberg, M. 1993. "L'Episcopus puerorum." In Niccoli 1993, 144–58.

Grisar, H. 1907. "Archeologia degli 'Agnus Dei.'" *La civiltà cattolica* 2:568–84.

Gros, P. 1965–66. "Rites funéraires et rites d'immortalité dans la liturgie de l'Apothéose impériale." *École Pratique des Hautes Études, ive sect.* "Annuaire": 477–90.

Grottanelli, C. 1993. "Bambini e divinazione." In Niccoli 1993, 23–72.

Grottanelli, C., and N. F. Parise, eds. 1988. *Sacrificio e società nel mondo antico.* Rome: Laterza.

Grottanelli, C., N. F. Parise, and P. G. Solinas. 1985. "Divisione delle carni: Dinamica sociale e organizzazione del cosmo." *L'uomo: Società, Tradizione, Sviluppo* ix, nos. 1–2.

Guenée, B., and F. Lehoux. 1968. *Les entrées royales françaises de 1328 à 1515.* Paris: Centre National de la Recherche Scientifique.

Guevara, A. de. n.d. *Aviso de privados y doctrina de cortisanos.* Antwerp: M. Nucio. (Italian trans., Venice: Tramezino 1544.)

Guidi, P. 1936. "La coronazione d'Innocenzo VI." In *Papsttum und Kaisertum: Forschungen zur politisches Geschichte und Geisteskultur des Mittelalters, Paul Kehr zum 65. Geburtstag dargebracht,* edited by A. Brackmann, 571–94. Munich: Münchner Drucke.

Guilhermy, F. M. Nolasque de. 1848. *Monographie de l'église royale de Saint-Denis, tombeaux et figures historiques.* Paris.

Gülich, L. von. [1705.] *Erb = Huldigung / so Aller = durchleuchtigist = Grossmachtigist = und Unuberwindlichsten Roemischen Kayser / durch Hungarn / und Boeheimb Koenig . . . Iosepho dem Ersten . . . durch Erst = wohlermelter Nid. Gest. Landschafft Syndicum.* Vienna.

Haag, E., and E. Haag. 1877–78. *La France protestante*. Paris: Sandoz-Fishbacher.

Hallam, B. M. 1982. "Royal Burial and the Cult of Kingship in France and England, 1060–1330." *Journal of Medieval Studies* VIII:359–80.

Halsberghe, G. H. 1972. *The Cult of Sol Invictus*. Leiden: Brill.

Hanley, S. 1983. *The Lit de Justice of the Kings of France: Constitutional Ideology in Legend, Ritual, and Discourse*. Princeton: Princeton University Press.

Hardt, H. von, ed. 1699. *Magnum oecumenicum Constantiniense Concilium*. Frankfurt and Leipzig.

Haskell, F. 1993. *History and Its Images: Art and the Interpretation of the Past*. New Haven, Conn.: Yale University Press.

Hatfield, R. 1970. *The Compagnia de' Magi*. JW, XXXIII:107–61.

Hedeman, A. D. 1990. "Copies in Context: The Coronation of Charles V in His *Grands Chroniques de France*." In Bak 1990, 72–87.

Heikamp, D. 1984. "La Tribuna degli Uffizi come era nel cinquecento." *Antichità viva* III:11–30.

———. 1989a. "Lo 'studiolo grande' di Ferdinando I nella Tribuna degli Uffizi." In *Splendori* 1989, 57–61.

———. 1989b. "Lo 'studiolo nuovo' ovvero il tempietto della Tribuna degli Uffizi." In *Splendori* 1989, 53–56.

———. 1997. "Le sovrane bellezze della Tribuna." In *Magnificenza alla corte dei Medici: Arte a Firenze alla fine del cinquecento*, exhibition catalog (Florence, 1997–98), 329–45. Milan: Electa.

Heisenberg, A. 1920. *Aus der Geschichte u. Literatur der Palaiologenzeit*. Munich: Sitzungsberichte der Bayerischen Akademie der Wissenschaften.

Helbig, W. 1903. "Le currus du roi romain." *Mélanges Parrot*: 167ff.

Henderson, J. 1994. *Piety and Charity in Late Medieval Florence*. Oxford: Oxford University Press.

Henisch, B. A. 1976. *Fast and Feast: Food in Medieval Society*. University Park: Pennsylvania State University Press.

Herklotz, I. 1985. "Der Campus Lateranensis im Mittelalter." *Römisches Jahrbuch für Kunstgeschichte* (Bibl. Hertziana) 22.

Herlihy, D. 1960. "Vieillir à Florence au quattrocento." *AESC*, XXIV:1338–52.

Herlihy, D., and Ch. Klapisch Zuber. 1985. *Tuscans and Their Families: A Study on the Florentine Catasto of 1427*. New Haven, Conn.: Yale University Press.

Hermanin, F. 1911. *Die Stadt Rom im 15. und 16. Jahrhundert*. Leipzig.

Héroard, J. 1989. *Journal de Jean Héroard*. Edited by M. Foisil. Paris: Fayard.

Herodian. [ca. 1550.] *The History of Herodian, a Greeke Author, Treating of the Roman Emperors*. London.

Herodotus. 1948. *Histoires*. Translated and edited by Ph. E. Legrand. Paris: Les Belles Lettres.

———. 1969–70. *Historiae*. Edited by C. R. Whittaker. Cambridge, Mass.: Harvard University Press.

Hertz, R. 1978. *Death and the Right Hand* (in Italian trans.). Introduction by E. E. Evans-Pritchard. Rome: Savelli. (English original, Glencoe, Ill.: Free Press, 1960.)

Heusch, L. de. 1982. *Rois nés d'un coeur de vache*. Paris: Gallimard.

———. 1986. *Le sacrifice dans les religions africaines*. Paris: Gallimard.

Hezecques, compte de [Felix de France]. n.d. *Souvenir d'un page de Louis XVI*. Brione: G. Monfort. (Reprint, Aubonne, 1983.)

Hillgarth, J. N. 1976–78. *The Spanish Kingdoms, 1250–1516*. Oxford: Clarendon.

Hindman, S., and G. M. Spiegel. 1981. "The Fleur-de-lis Frontispieces of Guillaume de Nangi's *Chronique Abrégée*: Political Iconography in Late Fifteenth-Century France." *Viator* 12:381–407.

Histoire de l'Abbaye Royale de Saint Denys en France [. . .] avec la description de l'Eglise. . . . 1606. Paris: Leonard.

Histoire générale du marechal et de la marechale d'Ancre, par le sieur D.P. 1617. Paris: I. Bouillarot.

Historiae Parmensis Fragmenta. See Giovanni da Cornazzano.

The History of the Coronation. See Sandford, F.

Hocart, A. M. [1927] 1969. *Kingship*. Oxford: Oxford University Press.

———. [1936] 1970. *Kings and Councillors: An Essay in the Comparative Anatomy of Human Society*. Chicago: Chicago University Press.

Hofmeister, A. 1938. "Puer, iuvenis, senex: Zum Verständnis der mittelalterlichen Altersbezeichnungen." *Papsttum und Kaisertum: Forschungen zur politisches Geschichte und Geisteskultur des Mittelalters, Paul Kehr zum 65. Geburtstag dargebracht*, edited by A. Brackmann, 287–316. Munich: Münchner Drucke.

L'Honteuse cheute du marquis d'Ancre par les prières des bons Francois, Faite le 24 jour d'Avril 1617. 1617. Paris: I. Beriou.

Hope, Sir W. H. St. John. 1907. "On Funeral Effigies of the Kings and Queens of England: With Special Reference to Those in the Abbey Church of Westminster." *Archaeologia* LX.

Howarth, D. 1997. *Images of Rule: Art and Politics in the English Renaissance, 1485–1649*. London.

Howell, T. B. See Cobbett, W., ed.

Hubert, H., and M. Mauss. 1929. *Essai sur la nature et la fonction du sacrifice*. Paris: Alcan.

Huntington-Metcalf, R. 1985. *Celebration of Death: The Anthropology of Mortuary Ritual* (in Italian trans.). Bologna: Il Mulino. (English original, Cambridge: Cambridge University Press, 1979.)

Hurtubise. 1985. *Une famille témoine: Les Salviati.* Studi e testi 309. Vatican City.

Inauguratio, coronatio, electioque aliquot imperatorum: Nempe a D. Maximiliano I ad D. Matthiam Austriacum Augustum. . . . 1613. Hannover: Welchelianis.

Infessura, S. 1890. *Diario della città di Roma.* Edited by O. Tommasini. Rome: Forzani.

Ingersoll, R. 1993. "The Possessio, the Via Papale, and the Stigma of Pope Joan." In *Urban Rituals in Italy and the Netherlands,* ed. H. de Mare and A. Vos, 39–50. Assen: Gorcum.

Inghirami, B. n.d. *Vita del padre Venerabile Benedetto Bacci da Poggibonsi dell'Osservanza di san Francesco.* Florence: Archivio Provinciale dei Frati Minori.

La intrata del re christianissimo Henrico II nella città di Rems et la sua incoronatione et consecratione. 1858. Ferrara.

Izard, M., and P. Smith, eds. 1979. *La fonction symbolique.* Paris: Gallimard.

Jackson, R. A. 1969. *The Sleeping King.* BHR, 31:525–51.

———. 1984. *"Vivat Rex": A History of the French Coronation Ceremony from Charles V to Charles X.* Chapel Hill: University of North Carolina Press.

———. 1994. "Who Wrote Hincmar's Ordines?" *Viator* xxv:31–62.

———, ed. 1995. *Ordines Coronationis Franciae: Texts and Ordines for the Coronation of Frankish and French Kings and Queens in the Middle Ages.* Vol. 1. Philadelphia: University of Pennsylvania Press.

Jacquot, J. 1956–60. *Les fêtes de la Renaissance.* Paris: Édit. CNRS.

James, M. E. 1983. "Ritual, Drama, and the Social Body in the Late Medieval English Town." *Past and Present* xcviii:3–29.

———. 1986. *Society, Politics, and Culture: Studies in Early Modern England.* Cambridge: Cambridge University Press.

Jameson, Mrs. 1857. *Legends of the Madonna as Represented in the Fine Arts.* London: Longman.

Janelle, P. 1930. *Obedience in Church and State: Three Political Tracts of Stephen Gardiner.* Cambridge: Cambridge University Press.

Jarnut, J. 1982. *Geschichte der Langobarden.* Stuttgart: Kohlhammer.

Johannes Malalas. 1940. *Chronographia.* Edited by M. Spinka and G. Downey. Chicago: University of Chicago Press.

John of Damascus. *De imaginibus.* PG, xciv:1408ff.

Jones, W. 1883. *Crowns and Coronations: A History of Regalia.* London: Chatto & Windus.

Jordan, D. 1979. *The King's Trial.* Berkeley and Los Angeles: University of California Press.

Jouguet, P. 1942. "L'arrivé de Vespasien à Alexandrie." *Bulletin de l'Institut d'Egypte* xxiv:21ff.

Journal d'un bourgeois de Paris. [1881] 1990. Edited by A. Tuctey. Paris: Soc. de l'Hist. de Paris, Champion. Reprint, edited by C. Beaune, Paris: Librairie Générale Française.

Julian of Toledo. 1910. *Historia Wambae regis.* Edited by B. Krusch. MGHSSRMer., v.

Kantorowicz, E. 1944. "The 'King's Advent' and the Enigmatic Panels in the Doors of Santa Sabina." *Art Bulletin* xxvi:207–31. (Reprinted in Kantorowicz 1965, 37–75.)

———. 1946. *Laudes regiae: A Study in Liturgical Acclamations and Mediaeval Rules Worship.* Berkeley and Los Angeles: University of California Press.

———. 1951. "Dante's Two Suns." In *Semitic and Oriental Studies Presented to William Popper,* University of California Publications in Semitic Philology, xi:209–30. Berkeley and Los Angeles: University of California Press.

———. 1963. "Oriens Augusti: Lever du Roi." In *Dumbarton Oaks Papers* xvii. Washington, D.C.

———. 1965. *Selected Studies.* Locust Valley, N.Y.: J. J. Augustin.

———. [1957] 1981. *The King's Two Bodies.* Berkeley and Los Angeles: University of California Press.

———. 1988. *Kaiser Friederick der Zweite: Ergänzungsband* (in Italian trans.). Milan: Garzanti. (German original, Berlin: G. Bondi, 1931.)

———. 1989. *Kaiser Friederick der Zweite* (in French trans.). Paris: Gallimard. (German original, Berlin: G. Bondi, 1927.)

Kern, A. 1956. *Die Handschriften der Universitätsbibliothek.* Vienna: Staatsdruckerei.

Kern, F. [1914] 1939. *Kingship and Law in the Middle Ages.* Oxford: Blackwell.

Kirigin, M. 1976. *La mano divina nell'iconografia cristiana.* Vatican City: Pontificio Ist. di Archeologia Cristiana.

Klapisch Zuber, Ch. 1985. "Childhood in Tuscany at the Beginning of the Fifteenth Century." In *Women, Family, and Ritual in Renaissance Italy,* 94–116. Chicago: University of Chicago Press.

Klauser, Th. 1971. *Die Cathedra in Totenkult der heidnischen u. christlichen Antike.* Münster in Westfalen: Aschendorfsche Verlag.

Klewitz, H. W. 1941. *Die Krönung des Papstes.* ZfRG, xxx:97ff.

Knowles, Ch., ed. 1983. *Les enseignements de Théodore Paléologue.* London: Modern Humanities Research Association.

Kohn, R., and R. Dalsace. 1987. *Naissance royales et princières.* Paris: Trédaniel.

Kolmer, L., ed. 1997. *Der Tod des Mächtigen: Kult und Kultur des Todes spätmittelalterlicher Herrscher.* Pedeborn: Schöningh.

Krautheimer, R. 1980. *Rome: Profile of a City, 312–1308*. Princeton: Princeton University Press.

Labarge, M. W. 1982. *Medieval Travellers: The Rich and the Restless*. London: Hamilton.

Lacouloumière, G. n.d. *Procès de Louis XVI: Role exact de Oardoux Bordas-Darnet*. Paris: Libr. gén. de droit.

Ladner, G. B. 1942. "The Portraits of Emperor in Southern Italy: Exultet Rolls and the Liturgical Commemoration of the Emperor." *Speculum* XVII:194ff.

———. 1979. "Medieval and Modern Understanding of Symbolism: A Comparison." *Speculum* LIV: 224–56. (Reprinted in *Images and Ideas* I:239–82.)

———. 1988. *L'immagine dell'imperatore Ottone III*. Rome: Unione Int. degli Ist. di archeologia storia e storia dell'arte.

Landucci, L. 1883. *Diario fiorentino*. Edited by I. Del Badia. Florence: Sansoni.

Landwehr, J. 1971. *Splendid Ceremonies: State Entries and Royal Funerals in the Low Countries, 1515–1791: A Bibliography*. Nieuwkoop: De Graaf; Leiden, Sijthoff.

Lanec. 1981. *The Rites of Rulers: Ritual in Industrial Society: The Soviet Case*. Berkeley and Los Angeles: University of California Press.

Langedijk, K. 1981–87. *The Portraits of the Medici: 15th–18th centuries*. Florence: Spes.

Lapini, A. 1900. *Diario fiorentino dal 252 al 1596*. Edited by O. Corazzini. Florence: Sansoni.

Lasi, D. 1974. *De vita et operibus S. Iacobi de Marchia: Studium et recensio quorundam textum*. Falconara Marittima: Bibl. Francescana.

Lauer, Ph. 1911. *Le palais du Latran: Étude historique et archéologique*. Paris: Leroux.

Laurentin, R. 1988. *Le voeu de Louis XIII passé ou avenir de la France, 1638–1988: 350e anniversaire*. Paris: O.E.I.L.

Leber, M. C. 1825. *Des cérémonies du sacre*. Paris and Reims: Baudouin frères–Fréman fils.

Legg, J. W. 1896. *The Sacring of the English Kings*. AJA, LI:28–42.

Le Goff, J. 1990a. "A Coronation Program for the Age of Saint Louis: The Ordo of 1250." In Bak 1990, 46–71.

———. 1990b. "La genèse du miracle royal." In *Marc Bloch aujourd'hui: Histoire comparée et sciences sociale,* Actes du Colloque Marc Bloch, edited by H. Atsma and A. Burguière, 147–56. Paris.

———. 1996. *Saint Louis*. Paris: Gallimard.

Lerch, E. 1964. "Anthropological Aspects of Language: Animal Categories and Verbal Abuse." In *New Directions in the Study of Language,* edited by E. H. Lannenberg, 23–63. Cambridge, Mass.: MIT Press.

Le Roy Ladurie, E. 1979. *Le carnaval de Romans*. Paris: Gallimard.

———. 1982. "Après du roy, la Cour." AESC, XXXVIII:21ff.

Lessius [Leonard Leys]. 1605. *De justitia et jure caeterisque virtutibus cardinalibus libri IV*. Louvain: Masi.

L'Estoile, P. de. 1621. *Journal des choses mémorables advenues durant tout le règne de Henri III*. N.p.

Leti, G. 1669. *Vita di Sisto V, pontefice romano*. Lausanne: G. Gree.

Lettre de consolation à la Reine d'Angleterre sur la mort du Roi son mary et ses derniers paroles. 1649. Paris: G. Sassier.

Lettre du prince de Galles envoyée à la Reyne d'Angleterre: Avec le regrets du mesme Prince sur la mort du Roy de la grand Bretagne, son Seigneur et père: Arrivée d'Amsterdam le 24. Fevrier 1649. 1649. Paris: A. Musnier.

Levi, A. 1889. *L'ingresso di Borso in Reggio nel 1453*. Reggio: n.p.

Levy-Bruhl, L. 1927. *L'âme primitive*. Paris.

Lewis, A. W. 1981. *Royal succession in Capetian France: Studies on Familial Order and the State*. Cambridge, Mass.: Harvard University Press.

Liberati, F. [1658.] *Il perfetto maestro di casa distinto in tre libri*. Rome: M. Hercole.

Liber pontificalis. [1886–92] 1955–57. Edited by L. Duchesne. Paris: Boccard.

Liber regalis seu Ordo consecrandi regem solum; Ordo consecrandi reginam cum rege; Ordo consecrandi reginam solam; Rubrica de regis exequiis. 1870. London: Roxborough Club.

Lison Tolosana, C. 1992. *La imagen del rey (monarquía, realeza y poder ritual en la Casa de los Austrias)*. Madrid: Colección Austral.

Litta, P., ed. 1819–83. *Famiglie celebri italiane*. Milan: Giusti.

Livro Vermelho do Senhor Rey Dom Alfonso o Quimto . . . , in *Collecao de livros ineditos de historia portugueza.* . . . 1793. Edited by J. Corréa da Serra. Lisbon: Academia Real das Sciencias.

Llewellyn, P. 1990. "Le contexte romain du couronnement de Charlemagne: Le temps de l'Avent de l'année 800." *Le Moyen Âge 2*, XCVI:209–25.

Lomazzo, G. P. 1584. *Trattato dell'arte della pittura*. Milan: P. G. Pontio.

L'Orange, H. P. 1935. "Sol Invictus Imperator: Ein Beitrag zur Apotheose." *Symbolae Osloenses* XIV:86–114.

———. 1953. *Studies on the Iconography of Cosmic Kingship in the Ancient World*. Oslo: Aschenhourg.

———. 1955. "The Adventus Ceremony and the Slaying of Pentheus." In *Late Classical and Mediaeval Studies in Honor of A. M. Friend Jr.,* 7–14. Princeton: Princeton University Press.

Lucci, M. L. 1964. "Il porfido nell'antichità." *Archeologia classica* XVI.

Lunadoro, C. G. 1650. *Relatione della Corte di Roma e de' riti da osservarsi in essa.* . . . Bracciano: Fei.

———. 1774. *Lo stato presente o sia Relatione della Corte di Roma [. . .] ora ritoccata, accresciuta ed illustrata da F. Zaccaria.* Rome: Bartolomicchi.

Luzio, A. 1887. *Federico Gonzaga ostaggio alla corte di Giulio II.* Rome: n.p.

Maas, P. 1912. "Metrische Akklamationen der Byzantiner." *Byzantinische Zeitschrift:* 28–51.

Mabillon, J. 1687. *Iter Italicum.* Paris: Martin.

Maccarrone, M. 1950. "La teoria ierocratica e il canto xvi del Purgatorio." *RSCI,* iv:359–98.

———. 1959. "Il sovrano 'vicarius Dei' nell'alto medio evo." In *La regalità sacra,* 581–94.

Macchiori, S. 1984. "Tre lettere di Ferdinando I." In *Studi in onore di GC Argan,* 1:219–26. Rome: Multigrafica.

MacCormack, S. G. 1981. *Art and Ceremony in Late Antiquity.* Berkeley and Los Angeles: University of California Press.

McCormick. 1986. *Eternal Victory: Triumphal Rulership in Late Antiquity, Byzantium, and the Early Medieval West.* Cambridge: Cambridge University Press.

McGovern, J. 1982. *Anatomy of a Lynching: The Lynching of Claud Neal.* Baton Rouge: Louisiana State University Press.

McGowman, M. 1968. "Forms and Themes in Henry II's Entry into Rouen." *Renaissance Drama,* n.s., 1:199–251.

McIlwain, C. H., ed. 1918. *The Political Works of James I.* Cambridge, Mass.: Harvard University Press.

McNeill, J. T., and H. M. Gamer, eds. 1938. *Medieval Handbooks of Penance.* New York: Columbia University Press.

Makin, E. 1921. "The Triumphal Route, with Particular Reference to the Flavian Triumph." JRS, xi:25–36.

Malalas. See Johannes Malalas.

Mâle, E. 1922. *L'art religieux du xiie siècle en France: Étude sur les origines de l'iconographie du moyen âge.* Paris: Colin.

Malinowski, B. 1922. *Argonauts of the Western Pacific: An Account of Native Enterprise and Adventure in the Archipelagoes of Melanesian New Guinea.* London: Routledge.

———. 1989. *Diary in the Strict Sense of the Term.* London: Athlone Press.

Mamone, S. 1987. *Firenze e Parigi: Due capitali dello spettacolo per una regina: Maria de' Medici.* Milan: A. Pizzi.

Manara, G. 1668. *Notti malinconiche.* Bologna: Ferroni.

Mancini, F., ed. 1968. *Feste ed apparati civili e religiosi in Napoli dal Viceregno alla Capitale.* Naples: ESI.

Mandrou, R. 1968. *Magistrats et sorciers en France au xviie siècle: Une analyse de psychologie historique.* Paris: Plon. (Italian trans., Bari: Laterza, 1971.)

Manger et boire au Moyen Âge: Actes du Colloque de Nice (15–17 Octobre 1982). 1984. Paris: Les Belles Lettres.

Marche, Olivier de la. 1883–88. *Mémoires.* Edited by H. Beaune and J. d'Arbaumont. Paris: Renouard.

Marchionne di Coppo Stefani. 1903. *Cronaca fiorentina.* Edited by N. Rodolico. RIS², xxx, 1.

Marillac, M. de. 1937. *Relation exacte de tout ce qui s'est passé à la mort du Mareschal d'Ancre.* In *Nouvelle collection des mémoires pour servir à l'histoire de France,* edited by Michaud and Poujoulat, v, xix. Paris.

Marini, A. 1903. *De pompa ducatus Venetorum.* Edited by A. Segarizzi. Venice: Nodati.

Marion, M. 1923. *Dictionnaire des institutions de la France aux xviie et xviiie siècle.* Paris: Picard.

Marlot, G. 1846. *Histoire de la ville, cité et université de Reims.* Reims: L. Jaquet et Bussart-Binet.

Marot de Caen, J. 1977. *Sur les deux heureux voyages de Gènes et Venise.* Vol. ii, *Le voyage de Venise.* Edited by G. Trisolini. Geneva: Droz.

Marsys, Sieur de. 1649. *Le Procez, l'adiovrnement personel, l'interrogatoire, et l'arrest de mort dv roy d'Angleterre.* Paris: Preuveray.

Martene, E., and U. Durand. 1717. *Voyage littéraire de deux religieux bénédictins de la congrégation de Saint-Maur.* Paris: Delaulne.

Martin, J. R. 1972. *The Decorations for the Pompa Introitus Ferdinandi.* Corpus Rubenianum Ludwig Nurchard, xvi. London: Phaidon.

Martin, Palacios. See Palacios Martin, B.

Martinelli, B. See Biagio da Cesena.

Marvick, E. W. 1975. "Childhood History and Decisions of State: The Case of Louis XIII." In *The New Psychohistory,* edited by L. De Mause. New York.

Masur, L. P. 1989. *Rites of Execution: Capital Punishment and the Transformation of American Culture, 1776–1865.* Oxford: Oxford University Press.

Mathieu d'Escouchy. 1863. *Chronique.* Edited by G. du Fresne de Beaucourt. Paris: Renouard.

Matres matutae dal Museo archeologico di Capua. n.d. Milan: Angelicum-Mundo X.

Matthaeus Parisiensis. [1874] 1964. *Chronica Maiora.* Edited by R. Luard. Vaduz: Craus Reprint.

Maturanzio, F. 1851. "Cronaca della città di Perugia dal 1492 al 1503." Edited by A. Fabretti. ASI, ser. 1, xvi.

Mauss, M. 1965. *Sociologie et anthropologie* (in Italian trans.). Turin: Einaudi. (French original, Paris: PUF, 1950).

Maxwell, H. 1992. *"Uno elefante grandissimo con uno castello di sopra": Il trionfo aragonese del 1423.* ASI, xxx.

———. 1994. "Trionfi terrestri e marittimi nell'Europa medievale." ASI, clii:641–67.

Mayer, H. E. 1967. "Das Pontifikale von Tyrus und die Krönung der lateinischen König von Jerusalem." *Dumbarton Oaks Papers* XXI:141–232.

Mazzoldi, L. 1961. *Mantova: La storia*. Vol. II, *Da Ludovico Secondo marchese a Francesco Secondo duca*. Mantua: Ist. C. d'Arco.

Mejan, M. 1814. *Histoire du procès de Louis XVI*. Paris: Patris.

Mellini, G. L. 1971. *Scultori veronesi del trecento*. Milan: Electa.

Melloni, G. B. 1773–1818. *Atti e Memorie degli uomini illustri in saantità nati o morti in Bologna*. Bologna: Lelio della Volpe.

Les memoires du roy d'Angleterre escrite de sa propre main dans sa prison, traduits fidellement de l'Anglois en nostre langue par le sieur De Marsys. 1649. Paris: F. Preuveray.

Menin, Monsieur. 1723. *Traité historique et cronologique du sacre*. Paris: Dauché.

Messi Sbugo, C. di. 1557. *Libro novo nel qual s'insegna a far d'ogni sorte di vivande*. Vinegia: Heredi di G. Padoano. (Reprint, Bologna: Forni, n.d.)

Millet, G. 1916. *Recherches sur l'iconographie de l'Evangile au XIVe, XVe et XVIe siècles d'après les monuments de Mistra, de la Macédoine et du Mont-Athos*. Paris: Fontemoing.

Millon, Ch. 1931. *Cérémonial du sacre des rois de France.* . . . La Rochelle: Édit. Respella.

Milton, J. 1651. *Johannis Miltoni Angli, Defensio pro Populo Anglicano contra Claudii Anonimi, alias Salmasii, Defensionem regiam*. London: Du Gardianis.

———. 1654. *Defensio secunda Pro populo Anglicano: contra infamem libellum anonymum cujus titulus Regis sanguinis clamor . . . , Accessit Alexandri Mori Fides publica, contra calumnias Ioannis Miltoni scurrae*. The Hague: A. Vlacq. (Bound together with More 1655 in the Vatican copy.)

Missale ad usum Ecclesie Westmonasteriensis. 1893. Edited by J. Wickham Legg. HBS, v.

Mitchell, B. 1979. *Italian Civic Pageantry in the High Renaissance: A Descriptive Bibliography of Triumphal Entries and Selected Festivals for State Occasions*. Florence: Olschki.

———. 1986. *The Majesty of the State: Triumphal Progresses of Foreign Sovereigns in Renaissance Italy (1494–1600)*. Florence: Olschki.

Mitchell, W. M. 1957. *The Rise of the Revolutionary Party in the English House of Commons, 1603–1629*. New York: Columbia University Press.

Monasticum Anglicanum. 1819–30. Edited by Sir W. Dugdale. *Monasticon Anglicanum (1655–73): A History of the abbies and other monasteries, hospitals, frieries and cathedral and collegiate churches . . . in England and Wales*. . . . London: Longman.

Montaigu, H. 1990. *Reims: Le sacre des rois: Mythes et symboles*. Artigues-près-Bourdeux: La Place Royale.

Monti, G. M. 1931–32. *Il trionfo di Alfonso I d'Aragona in una descrizione contemporanea*. Archivio scientifico del R. Ist. Sup. di scienze econ. e comm. di Bari VI.

More, A. 1655. *Supplementum fidei publicae, contra calumnia Ioannis Miltoni*. The Hague: A. Vlacq.

Moreni, D. 1813. *Delle tre sontuose cappelle medicee situate nella basilica di S. Lorenzo*. Florence: Carli.

Moret, A. 1902. *Du caractère religieux de la royauté pharaonique*. Paris: Leroux.

Morgues, Matthieu de. 1643. *Les deux faces de la vie et de la mort de Marie de Médicis, Reine de France, Vefve de Henri IV . . . Discours funèbre*. Antwerp: Plantin.

Moroni, G. 1840–79. *Dizionario di erudizione storico-ecclesiastica*. Venice: Tip. Emiliana.

Morris, D. 1982. *Manwatching: A Field Guide to Human Behaviour* (in Italian trans.). Milan: Mondadori. (English original, Lausanne and London: Elsevier and Jonathan Cape, 1977.)

Moscovici, S. 1981. *L'âge des foules: Un traité de psychologie des masses*. Paris: Fayard.

Mosén Diego de Valera. See Valera, Mosén Diego de.

Mosse, G. L. 1980. *Masses and Man: Nationalist and Fascist Perceptions of Reality*. New York: Howard Fertig.

Mourey, G. 1930. *Le livre des fêtes françaises*. Paris: Librairie de France.

Mousnier, R. 1964. *L'assassinat d'Henri IV*. Paris, Gallimard.

———. 1968. *Problème de stratification social: Actes du Colloque Internationale (1966) publiés par R. Mousnier*. Paris: PUF.

Muddiman, J. C. n.d. *Trial of Charles the First*. Edinburgh.

Muir, E. 1984. "The Cannibals of Renaissance Italy." *Syracuse Scholar* 5:5–14.

———. 1997. *Ritual in Early Modern Europe*. Cambridge: Cambridge University Press.

Muñoz, A. n.d. *S. Pietro in Vaticano*. Rome: Ediz. Roma-Mantegazza.

Muntoni, F. 1972. *Le monete dei papi e degli Stati pontifici*. Vol. I. Rome: P. & P. Santamaria.

Muntz, E. 1897. *La tiare pontificale du VIIe au XVIe siècle*. Mém. de l'Acad. des Inscriptions et Belles Lettres, XXXVI, I. Paris.

Musi, A. 1989. *La rivolta di Masaniello*. Naples: Guida.

NAACP. 1969. *Thirty Years of Lynching in the United States, 1889–1918*. New York: Arno Press.

Nabuco, J., ed. 1966. *Le cérémoniel apostolique avant Innocent VIII: Texte du manuscrit Urbinate Latin 469*. Rome.

Nardi, E. 1980. *L'otre del parricida e le bestie incluse*. Milan: Giuffrè.

Nattier, J. B. 1710. *Pierre Paul Rubens: La Galérie du*

Palais du Luxembourg. Paris: Duchange.

Necipoglu, G. 1991. Architecture, Ceremonial, and Power: The Topkapi in the Fifteenth and Sixteenth Centuries. Cambridge, Mass.: MIT Press.

Nelson, J. L. 1977. "Inauguration Rituals." In Sawyer and Wood 1977, 50–71.

———. 1980. "The Earliest Surviving Royal Ordo: Some Liturgical and Historical Aspects." In Studies on Medieval Law and Government Presented to Walter Ullmann on His Seventieth Birthday, 29–48. Cambridge: Cambridge University Press.

———. 1986. Politics and Ritual in Early Medieval Europe. London: Hambledon Press.

———. 1990. Hincmar of Reims on King-Making: The Evidence of the Annals of St. Bertin, 861–882. In Bak 1990, 16–32.

Nepote, J. 1976. Jean Golin (1325–1403). Thesis, Université de Paris Sorbonne.

Neumann, E. 1981 La grande madre: Fenomenologia delle configurazioni femminili dell'inconscio. Rome: Astrolabio.

Niccoli, O., ed. 1993. Infanzie: Funzioni di un gruppo liminale dal mondo classico all'Età moderna. Laboratorio di storia 6. Florence: Ponte alle Grazie.

———. 1995. Il seme della violenza: Putti, fanciulli e mammoli nell'Italia tra cinque e seicento. Bari: Laterza.

Nicephorus of Constantinople. 1837. Breviarium rerum post Mauricium gestarum. Edited by B. G. Niebuhr. Bonn: Weber.

Nicol, D. M. 1976. "Kaiseralbung: The Unction of Emperors in Late Byzantine Coronation Ritual." Byzantine and Modern Greek Studies 2:37–52.

Nicolini da Sabio, S. n.d. [1550?] Alcune virtuti de gli Agnus Dei benedetti et consecrati da Nostro Signore. Rome: Nicolini.

Nodet, V. 1906. Les tombeaux de Brou. Bourg: Impr. du "Courier de l'Ain."

Nores, P. 1847. Storia della guerra di Paolo IV sommo pontefice contro gli Spagnoli, corredata da documenti. ASI, ser. I, XII.

Notargiacomo, P. 1845. Cronica di Napoli. Edited by Garzilli. Naples.

Novacula. See Bernardi, A.

Nussdorfer, L. 1987. "The Vacant See: Ritual and Protest in Early Modern Rome." SCJ, XVIII, no. 2:173–89.

O'Donoghue, F. M. 1894. Descriptive and Classified Catalogue of Portraits of Queen Elisabeth. London: Quaritch.

Oman, Ch. 1963. Medieval Silver Nefs. Victoria and Albert Museum Monograph 15. London: Her Majesty's Stationery Office.

Oppenheimer, F. 1954. The Legend of the Sainte Ampoulle. London: Faber & Faber.

Ordericus Vitalis. 1969–80. The Ecclesiastical History. Edited by M. Chinball. Oxford: Clarendon.

L'ordine che si tiene nel creare il sommo pontefice, con le cerimonie che si fanno della coronazione in S. Giovanni Laterano. . . . 1555. N.p.

Die Ordines. See Elze, R., ed.

Ordo eligendi romani pontificis et ratio: De ordinatione et consacratione eiusdem. 1556. Tübingen.

Orfino da Lodi. 1869. Poema De regimine et sapientia potestatis. Edited by A. Ceruti. DSP, "Miscell. di storia italiana" VII. Turin.

Orgel, S. 1974. The Illusion of Power: Political Theater in the English Renaissance. Berkeley and Los Angeles: University of California Press.

Origene [Origen]. 1916. In librum Iudicum homilia. In Überlieferung u. Textgeschichte der lateinischen erhaltenen Origenshomilien zum Alten Testament, Texte u. Untersuchungen zur Gesch. der altchristl. Literatur, XLII, 1, ed. W. A. Baerhens. Leipzig: Hinrich.

Orlandis Rovira, J. 1962. El poder real y la sucesión al trono en la monarquía visigoda. Madrid: Cuadernos del Inst. Jurídico Español.

Pachymere, G. 1666. Historia rerum a Michaele Palaeologo ante imperium et in imperio gestarum. Rome: Typis Barberinis.

———. 1669. Andronicus Palaeologus sive Historia rerum ab Andronico seniore in Imperio gestarum usque ad annum eius aetatis undequinquagesimum. Rome: Typis Barberinis.

Pagden, A. 1982. "Cannibalismo e contagio: Sull'importanza dell'antropofagia nell'Europa preindustriale." In I vivi e i morti (Quaderni storici 50), edited by A. Prosperi.

Palacios Martin, B. 1969. "La Bula de Inocencio III y la coronación de los reyes de Aragón." Hispania XXIX:485–504.

———. 1975. La coronación de los reyes de Aragón, 1204–1410: Aportación al estudio de las estructuras políticas medievales. Valencia: Anubar.

———. 1976. "Los símbolos de la soberanía en la Edad Media Española: El simbolismo de la espada." In VII centenario del infante D. Fernando de la Cerda. Ciudad Real: Instituto de Estudios Manchegos.

———. 1979. La práctica del juramento y el desarrollo constitucional aragonés hasta Jaime I. Madrid.

Pandoni, Giannantonio de' [called Porcellius]. 1539. Trium poetarum elegantissimorum, Porcelii, Basinii et Trebani opuscula. . . . Paris: Simonem Colinaeum.

———. 1895. Triumphus Alhonsi regis Aragoniae devicta Neapoli. Edited by V. Nociti. Bassano.

XII panegyrici latini. 1911. Edited by E. and W. A. Baehrens. Leipzig: Teubner.

Panfili, G. 1556. L'origine del consacrare gli Agnus Dei con le virtù che in quelli si contengono. Rome: Blado.

Panofsky, E. 1930. *Hercules am Scheidewege u. andere antike Bildstoffe in der neueren Kunst.* Leipzig: Teubner.

———. 1964. *Tomb Sculpture: Its Changing Aspects from Ancient Egypt to Bernini.* London: Thames & Hudson.

Panvinio, O. 1560. *De baptismate paschali, origine et ritu consecrandi Agnus Dei, liber ex commentariis in historiarum ecclesiasticam excerptus.* Rome: Blado.

Paolo Diacono [Paul the Deacon]. 1988. *Storia dei Longobardi.* Edited by E. Bartolini. Milan: TEA.

Papon, J. 1568. *Recueil d'arrestz notables des courtz souverains de France. . . .* Paris: Macé.

Paravicini Bagliani, A. 1994. *Il corpo del papa.* Turin: Einaudi.

Pardi, G. 1906–7. "Borso d'Este duca di Ferrara." *Studi Storici* XV–XVI.

"Il Parentado fra la principessa Eleonora de' Medici e il principe don Vincenzo Gonzaga e i cimenti a cui fu costretto il detto principe per attestare come egli fosse abile alla generazione." 1887. *Il Giornale di Erudizione* (Florence).

Paris, G., and J. Ulrich, eds. 1886. *Merlin: Roman en prose du XIIIe siècle avec la mise en prose du poème de Merlin de Robert de Boron.* Paris: Firmin Didot.

Parkes, J. W. 1972. *Bereavement: Studies of Grief in Adult Life.* London: Tavistock Publications.

Passero, G. 1786. *Storie in forma di giornali. . . .* Naples: V. Orsino.

Pastor, L. von. [1906–33] 1950–63. *Storia dei papi.* Rome: Desclée.

Paul, J. 1983. "Le manteau couvert d'étoiles de l'empereur Henri II." In *Le soleil* 1983.

Payne, R. 1962. *The Roman Triumph.* London: R. Hall.

Pellini, P. 1664. *Della historia di Perugia.* Venice: Hertz. (Facsimile edition, Perugia, 1970.)

Penni, J. 1513. *Ceremonia delle magnifiche et honorate pompe fatte in Roma per la creatione et incoronatione di papa Leone X.* Rome: M. Silber. (Reprinted in Cancellieri 1802, 23ff., and Cruciani 1983, 390–405.)

Pere III of Catalonia (Pedro IV of Aragon). 1971. *Cronica.* In *Les quatres grans cròniques,* edited by F. Soldevila. Barcelona: Selecta.

———. 1980. *Cronica.* Translated by M. Hillgarth. Toronto: Pontif. Inst. for Mediaeval Studies.

A Perfect Narrative of the whole Proceedings of the High Court of Justice for the Trial of the King in Westminster Hall: Published by authority to prevent false and impertinent relations: Jan. 20–27, 1649. n.d. Licensed by Gilbert Mabbott. (Reprinted in Cobbett 1809–26, 994–1018.)

Pertusi, A. 1965. "'Quedam regalia insignia': Ricerche sulle insegne del potere ducale a Venezia." *Studi veneziani* 7:3–123.

———. 1976. "Insigne del potere sovrano e delegato

a Bisanzio e nei paesi di influenza bizantina." In *Simboli e simbologia nell'alto medioevo,* Settimane di studio del Centro Italiano di Studi sull'Alto Medioevo, XXIII, 3–9 April 1975, II:481–563. Spoleto: Panetto & Petrelli.

Peters, E. 1970. *The Shadow King: Rex Inutilis in Medieval Law and Literature.* New Haven, Conn.: Yale University Press.

Petrie, Sir Ch. 1958. *The Spanish Royal House.* London: G. Bless.

Pfandl, L. 1958. "Philipp II und die Einführung des burgundischen Hofzeremoniells in Spanien." *Historisches Jahrbuch* XXXVIII.

Phelypeaux de Pontchartrain, P. 1837. *Mémoires.* In *Nouvelle collection des mémoires pour servir à l'histoire de France,* V, XIX. Paris.

Picard, Ch. 1957. *Les trophées romains: Contribution à l'histoire et à la religion de l'art triomphal de Rome.* Bibl. des Écoles françaises d'Athènes et de Rome, fasc. 187. Paris.

Piccolomini, Enea Silvio (Pope Pius II). 1984. *I commentarii.* Edited by L. Totaro. Milan: Adelphi.

Pichon, T. J. 1775. *Journal historique du sacre et du couronnement de Louis XVI, rois de France.* Paris: Vente.

Pieraccini, G. [1924–25] 1986. *La stirpe de' Medici di Cafaggiolo.* Florence: Nardini.

Pietrosanti, S. 1990. "I corpi del morto e del vivo principe: I funerali di Cosimo nella Firenze medicea." In Bertelli and Grottanelli 1990, 88–100.

———. 1991. "'Ben vengha Carlo imperatore': Il trionfo senese di Carlo V." ASI, CXLIX:553–83.

Pilon, E. 1887. *Leone Leoni sculpteur de Charles-Quint et Pompeo Leoni sculpteur de Philippe II.* Paris: Plon.

Pinelli, A. 1985. "Feste e trionfi; continuità e metamorfosi di un tema." In Settis 1985, II:279–350.

Pippidi, D. M. 1945. *Le Numen Augusti.* In *Recherches sur le culte impérial,* Inst. roumain d'études latines, Coll. scientifique, 2:9–46. Paris and Bucharest.

Platina, B. [1479] 1568. *De vitis pontificvm romanorvm.* Cologne: Cholin.

———. [1479] 1730. *Le vite dei pontefici.* Edited by O. Panvinio. Venice: Savioni.

———. 1985. *Il piacere onesto e la buona salute.* Edited by E. Faccioli. Turin: Einaudi.

Pliny the Younger. 1975. *Letters and Panegiricus.* Translated by B. Radice. Cambridge, Mass: Harvard University Press.

Plutarco. 1547. *Symposiaca problemata, hoc est conuiuiales sermones.* Commentary by Hadriano Ivnio. Paris: I. Gazellus.

———. 1696. *Quaestiones Romanae.* In *Thesaurus Antiquitatum romanarum,* ed. J. G. Graeve, V:974ff. Leiden: van der Aa-F. Halm.

Poelnitz, S. Freiherr von. 1973. *Die Bamberger Kaisermantel*. Weisshorn: Konrad.

Poliziano, A. 1856. *Congiura de' Pazzi, narrata in latino e volgarizzata con sue note e illustrazioni*. Florence: A. Bonucci.

Polleross, F. 1988. *Das sakrale Identifikationsporträt: Ein höfischer Bildtypus vom 13. bis zum 20. Jahrhundert*. Worms: Wernersche Verlagsgesellschaft.

———. 1998. "From the Exemplum Virtutis to the Apotheosis: Hercules as an Identification Figure in Portraiture: An Example of the Adoption of Classical Forms of Representation." In Ellenius 1998, 37–86.

Pomey, F. 1659. *Libitina seu de Funeribus epitomes. . . .* Lyons: A. Molin.

Potthast, A. 1874–75. *Regesta pontificum romanorum*. Berolini: de Decker.

Poupardin, R. 1905. "L'onction impériale." *Moyen Âge* II, IX:113–26.

The pourtraicture of his sacred Maiestie in his solitudes and sufferings. 1648. London: Royston.

Pozzi, E. 1990. "Il corpo del profeta: Jim Jones." In *Gli occhi di Alessandro: Laboratorio di storia, II*. Florence: Ponte alle Grazie.

———. 1992. *Il carisma malato: Il People's Temple e il suicidio collettivo di Jonestown*. Naples: Liguori.

Précis des opinions prononcées à la tribune de la Convention par le citoyen Bordas, député de la Haute-Vienne. 1793. Paris: Impr. Nat.

Price, S. 1984. *Rituals and Power: The Roman Imperial Cult in Asia Minor*. Cambridge: Cambridge University Press.

Procès de Louis XVI, de Marie-Antoinette, de Marie-Elisabeth et de Philippe d'Orléans: Discussions législatives sur la famille des Bourbons: Recueil de pièces authentiques: Années 1792, 1793 et 1794. 1821. Paris: A. Eymery-Delaunay; Brussels: De Mat.

Profeti, M. G., ed. 1992. *Codici del gusto*. Milan: Franco Angeli.

Przyborowski, C. 1982. *Die Ausstattung der Furstenkapelle an der Basilika San Lorenzo in Florenz: Versuch einer Rekonstruktion*. Berlin: Froelich & Kaufmann.

The Quenes Maiesties Passage through the Citie of London to Westminster the Day before her Coronation (1558). 1960. Facsimile, Northford, Conn.: Elliot's Bks.

Quintana, J. M. 1965. *Agnus Dei de cera y otras noticias relativas a J.M.Q.* Mexico City.

"Racconti di storia napoletana." 1908–9. *Archivio Storico per le Province Napoletane* XXXIII–XXXIV.

Rahner, H. 1943. "Das Schiff aus Holz." *Zeitschrift für katholische Theologie* LXVII.

Rancour-Laferrière, D. 1979. "Some Semiotic Aspects of the Human Penis." *Quaderni di studi semiotici* 24 (September–December): 37–82.

Ranum, O. 1980. "The French Ritual of Tyrannicide in the Late Sixteenth Century." SCJ, XI:63–81.

Raper, A. F. 1969. *The Tragedy of Lynching*. New York: Arno Press.

Rasponi, C. 1656. *De Basilica et patriarcho Lateranensi libri quattuor*. Rome: Lazzeri.

Raynaud, T. 1665. *De Agno cereo a Pontefice consecrato*. Lyons.

Razzi, S. [1641] 1965. *Vita di santa Caterina de' Ricci*. Edited by G. Di Agresti. Florence: Olschki.

Réau, L. 1955. *Iconographie de l'art chrétien*. Paris: PUF.

La reception du roy d'Angleterre a Saint Germaine en Laye et le souhaits des François pour son etablissement dans son Royaume (letter/pamphlet signed "La tres humble et tres obeissante servante, Susanne de Nervese"). 1649. Paris: G. Sassuer.

La regalità sacra. See *Sacral Kingship*.

Reichler, C. 1985. "La jambe du roi (Rigaud, Saint-Simon et Louis XIV)." *Ecriture* XXIV:55ff.

Reinhard, M. 1969. *La chute de la royauté: 10 Août 1792*. Paris: Gallimard.

Reinhard, M., A. Armenguad, and J. Dupaquier. 1968. *Histoire générale de la population mondiale*. Paris: PUF.

Reiwald, P. 1949. *Masses: Traité de psychologie collective*. Neuchâtel: Delachaux et Niestlé.

Relation veritable de la morte barbare et cruelle du Roy d'Angleterre. Arrivée à Londre le huictiesme Feurier mil six cens quarante-neuf. 1649. [Paris]: F. Mvsnier.

Relazione dell'ultima malattia, morte e sepoltura dell'Altezza Ser.ma Reale il Granduca Cosimo III. . . . 1723. Florence: Partini & Franchi.

Relazione di tutto quello che è seguito in Francia al Louvre doppo la morte del marescial d'Ancre, con li ragionamenti e risposte. . . . 1617. Venice.

Remonstrance à tous les roys et sovverains de l'Europe, touchant les motifs qui les doivent obliger à venger la mort violente de Charle I, roy de la Grand' Bretagne, et réstablir Charles II, son fils, et legitime successeur. 1649. The Hague: L. Breeckevelt.

Remotti, F. 1986. "Il potere interrotto: Capitali mobili nell'Africa centrale." In *Etnicità e potere*, ed. P. Chiozzi. Bologna: Cleup.

———. 1993. *Luoghi e corpi: Antropologia dello spazio, del tempo e del potere*. Turin: Bollati Boringhieri.

Ricci, A. de'. 1597. *Istoria delle pietre*. Florence. (Reprint, Florence: SPES, 1979.)

Rice, E. E. 1983. *The Grand Procession of Ptolemy Philadelphus*. Oxford: Oxford University Press.

Richa, G. 1754–62. *Notizie istoriche delle chiese fiorentine*. Florence: Viviani.

Richard of Devizes. 1848. *De rebus gestis Ricardi Primi*. SSRA, *Chronicles of the Crusades*.

Richard of Hexham. 1861. *De gestis regis Stephani et de bello Standardii*. Edited by R. Howlett. SSRA,

Chronicles of the Reigns of Stephen, Henry II., and Richard I., III.

[Richard, J.] *Agneau pascal, ou Explication des ceremonies que les Juifs observoient en la manducation de l'Agneau de Pasque: Appliquées dans un sens spirituel à la manducation de l'Agneau divin dans l'Eucharistie.* 1686. Cologne: B. d'Egmont.

Richer. 1930–37. *Histoire de France (888–995).* Edited by R. Latouche. Paris: Champion.

Richier. 1912. *La vie de saint Remi, poème du XIIIe siècle.* Edited by W. N. Bolderston. London: Frowde.

Rio, A. del. 1988. *Teatro y entrada triunfal en la Zaragoza del Renacimiento.* Saragossa.

Rivière, J. 1924. "Sur l'expression 'Papa-Deus' au Moyen-Âge." In *Miscellanea F. Ehrle,* Studi e testi 38, II:276–89. Rome: BAV.

Roberts, J. 1999. *The King's Head: Charles I, King and Martyr.* London: Royal Collection.

Robinson, J. A. 1918. "The Coronation Order in the Tenth Century." *Journal of Theological Studies* XIX:56–72.

Rodriguez Villa, A. n.d. *Etiquetas de la Casa de Austria.* Madrid.

———. 1904. "El emperador Carlos V y su corte." *Boletin de la Real Academia de la Historia* XLV.

Roger de Wendover. 1886. *The Flowers of History.* Edited by H. G. Hewlett. SSRA, I.

Rohan de Fleury, Ch. 1877. *Le Latran au Moyen Age.* Paris.

Roheim, G. [1930] 1972. *Animism, Magic, and the Divine King.* London: Routledge & Kegan Paul.

Romei, A. 1586. *Discorsi del conte A.R. gentil'huomo ferrarese.* Ferrara: Baldini.

Romoli, D. n.d. [1560?] *La singolar dottrina di M.D.R. sopranominato Panunto, dell'ufficio dello scalco. . . .* Venice: Tramezzino.

Rossetti, W. M., ed. 1869. *Accounts of Early Italian, German, and French Books on Courtesy, Manners, and Cookery.* London: Early English Text Society, Trubner & Co.

Rossiaud, J. 1976. "Fraternités de jeunesse et niveaux de culture dans les villes du Sud-Est de la fin du Moyen Âge." *Cahiers d'histoire* XXI:69ff.

Rothenbuhler, E. W. 1998. *Ritual Communication: From Everyday Conversation to Mediated Ceremony.* Thousands Oaks, Calif.: Sage Publications.

Rotuli Parliamentorum Anglie hactenus inediti. 1935. Edited by H. G. Richardson and G. Sayles. London: Royal Hist. Society.

[Rowland, J.] *Pro Rege et populo Anglicano Apologia contra Johannis Polypragmatici (alias Miltoni Angli) Defensionem destructivam, Regis et Populi Anglicani.* 1652. Antwerp: H. Verdussen.

Ryber, I. 1976. *Panel Reliefs of Marcus Aurelius.* New York: Archaeological Inst. of America.

Ryder, A. 1976. *The Kingdom of Naples Under Alfonso the Magnanimous: The Making of a Modern State.* Oxford: Clarendon.

The Sacral Kingship—La regalità sacra: Studies in the History of Religions: Contributi al tema dell'VIII Congresso int. di storia delle religioni (Rome, April 1955) (supplements to Numen). 1959. Leiden, Brill.

Le sacre des rois: Actes du Colloque internationale d'histoire sur les sacres et couronnement royaux (Reims, 1975). 1985. Paris: Les Belles Lettres.

Sagard, G. 1632. *Le grand voyage du pays des Hurons, situé en Amerique vers la mer douceez dernières confins de a nouvelle France.* Paris: Denys Moreau.

Saint-Simon, L. de Rouvroy, duc de. 1983–88. *Mémoires: Additions au Journal de Dangeau.* Edited by Y. Coirault. Paris: Gallimard.

Salgado, M. J. Rodriguez. 1989. *The Changing Face of Empire: Charles V, Philip II, and Hapsburg Authority.* Cambridge: Cambridge University Press.

Salimbene de Adam. 1966. *La cronaca.* Edited by G. Scalia. Rome-Bari: Laterza.

Saly, A. 1984. "Les oiseaux dans l'alimentation médiéval d'après le Viander d'espèces et la Ménager de Paris." In *Manger et boire* 1984.

Sanday, P. R. 1986. *Divine Hunger: Cannibalism as a Cultural System.* Cambridge: Cambridge University Press.

Sandford, F. 1687. *The History of the Coronation of the Most High, Most Mighty, and Most Excellent Monarc James II, By the Grace of Gode, King of England . . . And of His Royal Consort Queen Mary. . . .* London: Thomas Newcomb.

Sangiorgi, G. 1922. "Le stoffe e le vesti tombali di Cangrande I della Scala I." *Boll. d'arte,* ser. II, I, April.

Sanglots pitoyables de l'affligée Reyne d'Angleterre du trepas de son mary. 1649. Paris: A. Musnier.

Sansovino, F. 1604. *Venetia città nobilissima e singolare.* Venice: Altobello Salice.

Santi, G. 1985. *La vita e le gesta di Federico di Montefeltro.* Studi e testi 305. Edited by L. Michelini Tocci. Vatican City.

Sanudo, M. 1879–1915. *I Diarii.* Venice: Visentin. (Reprint, Bologna: Forni, 1969.)

Saraina, T. 1649. *Le historie e fatti de' Veronesi ne i tempi del popolo e signori scaligeri (1542).* Verona: Rossi.

Saslow, J. M. 1996. *The Medici Wedding of 1589.* New Haven, Conn.: Yale University Press.

Saumaise, C. 1651. *Defensio regia pro Carolo I. Rege Angliae etc.* [1649] *et Joannis Miltoni Defensio pro populo Anglicano. . . .* Paris: M. du Puis.

———. 1660. *. . . ad Johannem Miltonum Responsio, opus posthumum.* London: Roycroft.

Savelli, M. A. 1697. *Patica universale.* Venice: Baglioni.

Savonarola, G. M. 1508. *Libreto delo excellentissimo physico maistro M:s:: de tute le cose che se manzano comunemente e piu che comune e di quelle che beueno per Italia. . . .* Venice: Simone de Luere.

Saward, S. 1982. *The Golden Age of Marie de' Medici.*

Ann Arbor, Mich.: UMI Research Press.

Sawyer, P. H., and I. N. Wood, eds. 1977. *Early Medieval Kingship.* Leeds: School of History, University of Leeds.

Sbriccoli, M. 1974. *Crimen Lesae Majestatis: Il problema del reato politico alle soglie della scienza penalistica moderna.* Milan: Giuffré.

Scarlatini, O. 1683. *L'huomo e le sue parti figurato e simbolico. . . .* Bologna: G. Monti.

Schaefer, D. 1920. "Mittelalterlicher Brauch bei der Überführung im Leichen." *Sitzungsberichte der Preußischen Akademie der Wissenschaften* (Berlin): 478–98.

Scheid, J. 1986. "Le flamine de Jupiter, les Vestales et le général triomphant: Variations romaines sur le thème de la figuration des dieux." *Le temps de la réflexion* VII (*Corps des dieux*): 213–29.

Schimmelpfennig, G. B. 1974. "Die Krönung des Papstes im Mittelalter dargestellt am Beispiel der Krönung Pius II." *Quellen u. Forschungen aus italienischen Archiven u. Bibliotheken* LIV:129–270.

Schneider, A. M. 1936. *Byzanz: Vorarbeiter zur Topographie u. Archaeologie der Stadt.* Berlin.

Schneider, C. 1936. "Studien zum Ursprung liturgischer Einzelheiten oestlicher Liturgien, I: Katapètasma." *Kyrios* I:53–73.

Schneider, F. 1921. "Über Kalendas Januariae und Marie im Mittelalter." *Archiv für Religionswissenschaft* XX:390ff.

Schramm, P. E. 1937. *A History of the English Coronation.* Oxford: Blackwell.

———. 1938. "Ordines-Studien II: Die Krönung bei den Westfranken und den Franzosen." *Archiv für Urkundenforschung* XV:3–55, 279–86.

———. 1955. "Lo stato post-carolingio e i suoi simboli del potere." In *I problemi comuni dell'Europa post-carolingia: Settimane di studio del Centro It. di studi sull'Altomedioevo,* II:14ff. Spoleto.

———. 1960a. *Las insignias de la realeza en la edad media española.* Madrid: It. de estudios politicos.

———. [1929] 1960b. *Der König von Frankreich: Das Wesen der Monarchie vom 9. zum 16. Jahrhundert.* Weimar: Böhlaus.

———. 1963. "Gli imperatori della casa di Sassonia alla luce della simbolistica dello Stato." In *"Renovatio imperii": Atti della giornata int. di studio per il millenario (Ravenna 4–5 Nov. 1961),* 15–40. Faenza: Lega.

———. 1968. *Kaiser, Könige und Päpste.* Stuttgart: Hiersemann.

Scorpione, D. 1702. *Istruzioni corali . . . a chiunque desidera essere vero professore del Canto Piano.* Benevento: n.p.

Scott, K. 1932. *Humor at the Expense of the Imperial Cult.* Classical Philology 27.

Scribonius, C. 1549. *Le triumph d'Anvers, faict en la susception du Prince Philips, Prince d'Espaigne.* Antwerp.

Scrinari, Santa Maria Valnea. 1991. *Il Laterano imperiale.* Vol. I, *Dalle "aedes Laterani" alla "domus Faustae."* Vatican City: Pont: Ist. di Archeologia Cristiana.

Segni, B. 1857. *Istorie fiorentine.* Florence: Barbèra.

Seguin, A. 1829. *Considérations sur la mort de Louis XVI pour servir à la béatification et canonisation de ce saint roi.* Montpellier: Séguin.

Settis, S., ed. 1985. *Memoria dell'antico: I generi e i temi ritrovati.* Turin: Einaudi.

Settis, S., and C. Frugoni. 1973. *Historia Alexandri levati per griphos ad aerem: Originem iconografia e fortuna di un tema.* Ist. Storico It. per il Medio Evo, Studi Storici 80–82. Rome.

Setton, K. 1931. "The Significance of Statues in Precious Metal in Emperor Worship." *Transactions and Proceedings of the American Philological Association* LXII:101–23.

———. 1941. *Christian Attitude Towards the Emperor in the Fourth Century, Especially as Shown in Addresses to the Emperor.* New York: Columbia University Press.

Shay, F. n.d. *Judge Lynch: His First Hundred Years.* New York: Ives Washburn.

Shearman, J. 1975. "The Florentine Entrata of Leo X, 1515." JW, XXXVIII:136–54.

Sherman, C. R. 1969. *The Portraits of Charles V of France, 1338–1380.* College Art Association of America Monographs 20. New York: Archaeological Inst. of America.

———. 1971. "Representations of Charles V of France (1338–1380) as a Wise Ruler." *Medievalia et humanistica,* n.s., 2:83–96.

Sherwood, R. 1977. *The Court of Oliver Cromwell.* London: Croom Helm.

Shorr, D. C. 1954. *The Christ Child in Devotional Images in Italy During the XIV Century.* New York: Wittenborn.

Las Sietes Partidas del rey don Alfonso el Sabio cotejadas con varios codices antiguos por la Real Academia de la Historia. 1807. Madrid.

Sigebertus Gemblacensis (of Gembloux). 1848. *Vita Wicberti et gesta abbatum gemblacensium.* Edited by G. H. Pertz. MGHSS, VIII.

Signorini, R. 1981. "Gonzaga Tombs and Catafalques." In *Splendours of the Gonzaga,* edited by D. Chambers and J. Martireau. Cinisello Balsamo: A. Pizzi.

Simeoni, L. 1929. *Verona.* Rome: Ed. Tiber.

Simon, R. B. 1981. "Bronzino's Cosimo I de' Medici as Orpheus." *Philadelphia Museum of Art, Bulletin* 81, no. 548:16–32.

Simonetta. 1554. *Francesco Sforza.* Vinegia: Bartolomeo l' imperador.

Simson, O. von. 1979. "Politische Symbolik im Werke des Rubens." In *Rubens kunstgeschichtliche Beiträge,* edited by E. Hubala. Konstanz: Lehonardt.

Smith, E. B. 1936. *Architectural Symbolism of Imperial Rome and the Middle Ages.* Princeton: Princeton University Press.

Smith, M. 1971. "Triumphus." In *Dictionary of Antiquities.*

———. 1973. Review of *Triumphus: An Inquiry into the Origin, Development, and Meaning of the Roman Triumph,* by H. S. Versnel. AJA, 1973:244.

Soboul, A., ed. 1973. *Le procès de Louis XVI.* Paris: Gallimard/Julliard.

La sociabilité à table: Commensalité et convivialité à travers les âges: Actes du colloque de Rouen. . . . 1992. Publication de l'Université de Rouen, 178. Rouen.

Le soleil, la lune et les étoiles du Moyen Âge. 1983. Publications du CUERMA, Université de Provence. Aix-en-Provence: Lafitte.

La solenne entrata dello Illustrissimo et Eccel.mo Sig. il Sig. Duca di Fiorenza et Siena fatta a XXVIII d'Ottobre mdlx in Siena. 1560. Florence: Torrentino.

Solmi, A. 1924. "La distruzione del palazzo regio in Pavia nell'anno 1024." *Rendiconti del R.Ist. Lombardo di scienze, lettere e arti* LVII:351–64.

Sommer, C. 1920. *Die Anklage der Idolatrie gegen Papst Bonifaz VIII. und seine Porträtstatuen.* Freiburg im Breisgau: Kuenzer.

Soria, J. M. Nieto. 1993. *Ceremonia de la realeza: Propaganda y legitimación en la Castilla Trastámara.* Madrid.

Sot, M. 1988. "Hérédité royale et pouvoir sacré avant 987." *AESC,* 43:705–33.

Speck, P. 1978. *Kaiser Konstantin VI.: Die Legitimation einer Fremden u. der Versuch einer eigenen Herrschaft.* Munich: Fink.

Sperber, D. 1984. *On Anthropological Knowledge: Three Essays.* Cambridge: Cambridge University Press.

Splendori di pietre dure: L'arte di corte nella Firenze dei granduchi. 1989. Florence: Giunti.

Stallybrass, P., and A. White. 1986. *The Politics and Poetics of Transgression.* Ithaca, N.Y.: Cornell University Press.

Starkey, D., et al. 1987. *The English Court from the Wars of the Roses to the Civil War.* London: Longman.

Starobinski, J. 1986. "Don fastueux et don pervers." *AESC,* 41:7–26.

Stefani, G. 1974. *Musica barocca.* Milan: Bompiani.

Steinberg, L. 1986. *The Sexuality of Christ in Renaissance Art and in Modern Oblivion.* London: Pantheon.

———. 1996. *The Sexuality of Christ in Renaissance Art and in Modern Oblivion.* Rev. ed. London: Pantheon.

Steinke, K. B. 1984. *Die mittelalterlichen Vatikanpaläste und ihre Kapellen.* Vol. V of *Studi e documenti per la storia del palazzo apostolico vaticano.* Vatican City: BAV.

Sternbach, L. 1902. "Eugenios von Palermo."

Byzantinische Zeitschrift XI.

Storie pistoresi. 1907. Edited by S. A. Barbi. RIS², XI, 5.

Straus, R. 1912. *Carriages and Coaches.* London: M. Secker.

Strong, Mrs. A. 1915. *Apotheosis and After Life.* London: Constable.

Strong, R. 1977. *The Cult of Elizabeth.* Berkeley and Los Angeles: University of California Press.

———. 1984. *Art and Power: Renaissance Festivals, 1450–1650.* Woodbridge: Boydell.

Stubbs, W., ed. 1882. *Chronicles of the Reigns of Edward I. and Edward II.* Vol. I, *Annales Londonienses and Annales Paulini.* London: Longman.

———. 1906. *The Constitutional History of England in Its Origin and Development.* Oxford: Clarendon.

Suarez, J. M. [1656] 1671. *De consacratione agnorum cereorum.* Rome: Tinassi.

Suger. 1964. *Vita Ludovici Grossi regis: Vie de Louis VI le Gros.* Edited by H. Waquet. Paris: Les Belles Lettres.

Tableav et emblèmes de la detestable vie et malhevrevse fin dv maistre Coyon (A' Paris, cheze 24 et 25 Avril). n.d. BNP.

Tanara, V. 1665. *L'economia del cittaidno in villa, riveduta ed accresciuta in molti luoghi dal medesimo Auttore, con l'aggiunta delle qualità del Cacciatore.* Venice: G.-P. Brigonci.

Tardits, C. 1980. *Le Royaume Bamoum.* Paris: Colin.

———. 1985. "L'étiquette à la cour royale bamoum (Cameroun)." In *Culture et idéologie dans la genèse de l'état moderne,* 179–98. Rome: École Française de Rome.

Taylor, A. 1820. *The Glory of Regalty: An Historical Treatise on the Anointing and Crowning of the Kings and Queens of England.* London: Payne & Foss.

Taylor, L. Ross. 1931. *The Divinity of the Roman Emperor.* Middletown, Conn.: American Philological Association.

Tegrimi, N. 1742. *Vita Castruccii Antelminelli . . . Una cum etrusca versione Georgii Dati nunc primum vulgata.* Lucca. (Also in RIS, XI:1308–44.)

Tenfelde, K. 1982. "Adventus: Zur historischen Ikonologie des Festzugs." *Hist. Zeitschrift* 235:45–84.

Tertulliano [Tertullian]. 1971. *Adversus Valentinianos.* Edited by A. Marastori. Padua: Gregoriana.

Testini, P. 1966. *Le catacombe e gli antichi cimiteri cristiani in Roma.* Bologna: Cappelli.

Theophanes. 1883. *Chronographia.* Edited by C. De Boor. Leipzig: Teubner.

Thietmar. 1935. *Chronicon.* Edited by R. Holtzmann. MGHSS, n.s., IX.

Thomas Aquinas. 1948. *Summa Theologiae.* Turin: Marietti.

Thomas, K. [1971] 1973. *Religion and the Decline of Magic.* Harmondsworth, Middlesex: Penguin Books.

Three Coronation Orders. 1900. Edited by J. Wickham Legg. HBS, xix.

Thuillier, J., and J. Foucart. 1967. *Le storie di Maria de' Medici di Rubens al Lussemburgo.* Milan: Rizzoli.

Tietze-Conrat, E. 1954. "The Church Program of Michelangelo's Medici Chapel." *Art Bulletin* 36:222–24.

Tixeront, J. 1921. *Mélanges de patrologie et d'histoire des dogmes.* Paris: Lewcoffre.

Tolomeo da Lucca [Bartolomeo Fiadoni, 1236–1327]. 1909. *Determinatio compendiosa de iurisdictione imperii.* Edited by M. Krammer. Fontes iuris germanici antiqui. Hannover-Leipzig.

Le tombeau du marquis d'Ancre. 1617. Paris: Fleury Bourriqueaut.

Tommaso da Chaula da Chiaromonte. 1904. *Gesta per Alphonsum Aragonum et Siciliae regem. . . .* Edited by R. Starabba. Palermo: Tip. Boccone del povero.

Tommaso di Silvestro, Ser. 1922. *Diario orvietano.* Edited by L. Fiumi. RIS², xv, v, 2.

Torraca, L. 1949–50. "A proposito di un recente episodio di antropofagia." *Atti della Accademia pontaniana,* n.s., III:113–25.

Tosti, L. 1846. *Storia di Bonifacio VIII e de' suoi tempi.* Pe' tipi di Montecassino.

Toynbee, A. 1973. *Costantine Porphyrogenitus and His World.* London: Oxford University Press.

Traeger, J. 1970. *Das reitender Papst: Ein Beitrag zur Ikonographie des Papsttums.* Munich: Verl. Schnell & Steiner.

Treitinger, O. 1956. *Die oströmische Kaiser- und Reichidee nach ihrer Gestaltung im höfischen Zeremoniell vom oströmischen Staats- und Reichsgedanken.* Darmstadt: Gentner.

Trevor Roper, H. 1967. *Religion, the Reformation, and Social Change.* London: Macmillan.

Trexler, R. 1974. "Ritual in Florence: Adolescence and Salvation in the Renaissance." In *The Pursuit of Holiness in Late Medieval and Renaissance Religion,* edited by Ch. Trinkaus. Leiden: Brill.

———. 1980. *Public Life in Renaissance Florence.* New York: Academic Press.

Turner, V. 1967. *The Forest of Symbols: Aspects of Ndembu Ritual.* Ithaca, N.Y.: Cornell University Press.

Ubeda, A. Igual. 1950. *Iconografía de Alfonso el Magnánimo.* Valencia: Institución Alfonso el Magnánimo.

Ullmann, W. 1957. "Thomas Becket's Miraculous Oil." *Journal of Theological Studies,* n.s., VIII:129–33.

———. 1961. Introduction to *Liber Regie Capelle: A Manuscript in the Biblioteca Publica, Evora.* HBS, XCII.

———. 1969. *The Carolingian Renaissance and the Idea of Kingship.* London: Methuen.

Ungaro, L. 1995. *I luoghi del consenso imperiale: Il foro di Augusto, il foro di Traiano.* Rome: Enel.

Valensise, M. 1986. "Le sacre du roi: Stratégie symbolique et doctrine politique de la monarchie française." *AESC,* 41:543–77.

Valera, Mosén Diego de. 1927. *Crónica de los Reyes Católicos.* Edited by J. de M. Carriazo. Madrid: Molina.

Valeriano, P. 1621. *Pro sacerdotum barbis.* Lyon: P. Frellon.

Valgona y Diaz-Varela, D. de la. 1958. *Norma y ceremonia de las reinas Casa de Austria.* Madrid.

Valier, A. 1775. *De benedictione agnorum Dei.* Rome.

van Gennep, A. 1909. *Les rites de passage.* Paris: Nourry.

Vanggard, T. 1969. *Phallos: A Symbol and Its History in the Male World.* New York.

Varchi, B. 1858–59. *Storia fiorentina.* In *Opere ora per la prima volta raccolte.* Trieste: Lloyd Austriaco.

Varela, J. 1990. *La muerte del rey: El ceremonial funerario de la monarquía española (1500–1885).* Madrid: Turner.

Vauchez, A. 1977. "'Beata stirps': Sainteté et lignage en Occident aux XIIIe et XIVe siècles." In *Famille et parenté dans l'Occident médiéval,* edited by J. Duby and J. Le Goff, 397–406. Rome: École Française de Rome.

Venard, M. 1977. *Itinéraires de processions dans la ville d'Avignon.* Ethnologie française, n.s., 7.

Vergerio, P. P. 1556. *Historia di papa Giovanni VIII che fu femmina.* N.p.

Vernant, J. P. 1989. "La belle morte et le cadavre outragé." In *L'individu, la mort, l'amour, soi-même et l'autre en Grèce ancienne,* 41–79. Paris: Gallimard.

Vernant, J. P., and P. Vical-Naquet. 1976. *Mythe et tragédie en Grèce ancienne* (in Italian trans.). Turin: Einaudi. (French original, Paris: Maspero, 1972.)

Versnel, H. S. 1970. *Triumphus: An Inquiry into the Origin, Development, and Meaning of the Roman Triumph.* Leiden: Brill.

Les vertus de l'Agnus Dei: Benediction de l'Agnus Dei. 1662. Rome: Chambre Apostolique.

Vespasiano da Bisticci. 1970. *Le vite.* Edited by A. Greco. Florence: Ist. Naz. di Studi sul Rinascimento.

Villani, G. 1823. *Cronica.* Florence: Magheri.

Villari, R. 1976. *La rivolta antispagnola a Napoli: Le origini 1585/1647.* Rome-Bari: Laterza.

Villena, Enrique de. 1965. *Spanish Life in the Late Middle Ages* (English trans. of *Arte Cisoria o tratado del arte de cortar del cuchillo*). Translated by K. R. Scholberg. Chapel Hill: University of North Carolina Press.

Villette, C. 1611. *Les raisons de l'office et cérémonies qui se font en l'Eglise catholique. . . .* Paris: G. de Rues.

Virtutes Agnus Dei benedicti: Legitur in regesto papae quem Leo Papa III. misit Carolo Magno imperatori unum ex suis Agnus benedictis (broadsheet). n.d. N.p.

Vita Aniani episcopi Aurelianensis. 1896. Edited by B. Krusch. MGHSSRMer., III.

Vita Karolis comitis Flandriae. 1856. Edited by R. Kopke. MGHSS, XII.

Vitry, Jacques de. 1960. *Lettres de Jacques de Vitry (1160/1170–240) évêque de St. Jean-d'Acre.* Edited by R. B. C. Huygens. Leiden: Brill.

Vitry, P., and G. Brière. 1908. *L'église abbatiale de Saint-Denis et ses tombeaux: Notices historiques et archéologiques.* Paris: Longuet.

Voltaire. 1947. *Le siècle de Louis XIV.* Paris: Garnier.

Voltmer, E. 1994. *Il carroccio.* Turin: Einaudi.

Vovelle, M. 1982. *Idéologies et mentalités.* Paris: Maspero.

———. 1989. *Histoire figurales: Des monstres médiévaux à Wondewoman.* Florence: Usher.

Wahl und Crönungshandlung: Das ist Kurze und Warhafftige Beschreibung aller furnembsten Sachen, so bey Erivehlung und Cronung des Allerduchleuchtigisten . . . Auch welcher gestalt die Allerdurchleuchtigste, hochgeborne Furstin und Fram, Fram Anrazu Hungern und Boheimb Königin. . . . 1612. Frankfurt am Main: Johann Bringers & Heinrich Kroners.

Wallace-Hadrill, J. M. 1960. *The Graves of Kings.* "Nuovi studi medievali," ser. III, I.

———. 1971. *Early Germanic Kingship in England and on the Continent.* Oxford: Clarendon Press.

———. [1962] 1982. *The Long-Haired Kings.* Toronto: University of Toronto Press.

Walzer, M., ed. [1974] 1989. *Régicide et révolution: Le procès de Louis XVI: Discours et controverses.* Paris: Payot.

Wanscher, O. 1980. *Sella curulis: The Folding Stool: An Ancient Symbol of Dignity.* Copenhagen: Rosenkilde-Bagger.

Waquet, Fr. 1981. *Les fêtes royales sous la Restauration ou l'Ancien Régime retrouvé.* Geneva: Droz.

Warburg, A. 1932. *Gesammelte Schriften.* Leipzig: Teubner.

Ward, P. 1942. "An Early Version of the Anglo-Saxon Coronation Ceremony." *English Historical Review* 57:345–61.

———. 1939. "The Coronation Ceremony in Medieval England." *Speculum* XIV:160–78.

Watson, J., and E. S. Rawski. 1988. *Death Ritual in Late Imperial and Modern China.* Berkeley and Los Angeles: University of California Press.

Weber, W. 1979. "Die Reliquienprozession auf der Elfenbeintafel des Trierer Domschatzes u. das kaiserliche Hofzeremoniell." *Trierer Zeitschrift für Geschichte u. Kunst des Trierer Landes* 42:135–51.

Weinstock, S. 1971. *Divus Julius.* Oxford: Clarendon.

Weisbach, W. 1919. *Trionfi.* Berlin: G. Grotische Verl.

Wells-Barnett, I. 1969. *On Lynching.* New York: Arno Press.

Weston-Lewis, A. 1999. "Orazio Gentileschi's Two Versions of *The Finding of Moses* Reassessed." In Finaldi 1999, 39–52.

Wey, W. 1857. *The itineraries of William W. fellow of Eaton College, to Jerusalem, a.d. 1458 and a.d. 1462; and to Saint James of Compostella, a.d. 1456.* London: Nichols.

Wheaton, B. K. 1983. *Savoring the Past: The French Kitchen and Table from 1300 to 1789.* Philadelphia: University of Pennsylvania Press.

Wicquefort, A. de. 1874. *Histoire des Provinces Unies des Pais Bas.* Amsterdam: F. Mueller.

Wilson, E. C. 1966. *England's Eliza: A Study of the Idealization of Queen Elizabeth in the Poetry of Her Age.* London: Frank Cass.

Wind, E. [1958] 1971. *Misteri pagani nel Rinascimento.* Milan: Adelphi.

Winzinger, F. 1973. *Die Miniaturen zum Triumphzug Kaiser Maximilians I.* Graz: Akademische Druck-u. Verlagsanstalt.

Wipo. 1915. *Gesta Chuonradi.* Edited by Bresslau. MGHSS, 7.

Wirth, J. 1978. "Sainte Anne est une sorcière?" BHR, XL:449–80.

Witckowski. 1892. *Accouchement celèbres: Les accouchements à la cour de France. Anecdotes et curiosités historiques sur les accouchements.* Paris: Steinheil.

Wood, I. N. 1977. "Kings, Kingdoms, and Consent." In Sawyer and Wood 1977, 6–29.

Woodward, J. 1997. *The Theatre of Death: The Ritual Management of Royal Funerals in Renaissance England, 1570–1625.* Woodbridge: Boydell.

Wordsworth, C. 1892. *The Manner of the Coronation of King Charles the First of England.* HBS.

Yates, F. A. [1975] 1978. *Astrea: L'idea di impero nel cinquecento.* Turin: Einaudi.

Yavetz, Z. 1969. *Plebs and Princeps.* Oxford: Clarendon.

Young, K. 1933. *The Drama of the Medieval Church.* 2 vols. Oxford: Clarendon.

Zarri, G. 2000. *Recinti: Donne, clausura e matrimonio nella prima età moderna.* Bologna: Il Mulino.

Zbarski, I., and S. Hutchinson. 1997. *A l'ombre du Mausolée: Une dynastie d'embaumeurs.* N.p.: Solin.

Ziegler, J. 1931. "Die peregrinatio Aetherie u. die Heilige Schrift." *Biblica* 12.

Zobi, A. 1841. *Notizie storiche riguardanti l'Imperiale e Reale Stabilimento dei lavori di commesso in pietre dure di Firenze.* Florence: Le Monnier.

Zonaras, J. 1868–75. *Epitome historiarum.* Edited by L. Dindorf. Leipzig: Teubner.

Zorzi, A. 1993. "Rituali di violenza giovanile nelle società urbane del tardo Medioevo." In Niccoli 1993, 185–209.

Zurita, J. 1970–77. *Anales de la Corona de Aragón (1578–85).* Edited by A. C. Lopez. Saragossa: C.S.I.C.

Index